CPE

Criminal Law
Textbook

9th edition

Michael T Molan
BA, LLM (Lond), Barrister
Head of Law at South Bank University

HLT Publications

HLT PUBLICATIONS
200 Greyhound Road, London W14 9RY

First published 1987
9th edition 1995

© The HLT Group Ltd 1995

ISBN 0 7510 0548 7

British Library Cataloguing-in-Publication.
A CIP Catalogue record for this book is
available from the British Library.

Acknowledgement
The publishers and author would like to
thank the Incorporated Council of Law
Reporting for England and Wales for kind
permission to reproduce extracts from the
Weekly Law Reports.

Printed and bound in Great Britain

Contents

Read c̄ Case book ¬ articles + judgement

Preface

HLT Textbooks are written specifically for students. Whatever their course they will find our books clear and concise, providing comprehensive and up-to-date coverage. Written by specialists in their field, our textbooks are reviewed and updated on an annual basis.

In addition to the usual updating that we undertake each year for this book, we have added a new chapter called 'Recent Cases'. This chapter includes the most significant cases that have occurred in the last year. In order to assist the student extracts from the judgments and commentary, where appropriate, have been included. In many instances these cases highlight new interpretations of particular facets of existing law.

Knowledge of recent cases is extremely important for those studying for their examinations. It demonstrates not only an active interest in the law as it develops, but also the dynamic nature of the law which is constantly adapting to changing social and economic trends.

The *Criminal Law Textbook* is designed for use by any undergraduates who have Criminal Law within their syllabus. It will be equally useful for all CPE students who must study Criminal Law as one of their compulsory subjects.

In addition, those studying for certain professional examinations, such as the Institute of Legal Executives, will find this textbook gives them sufficient information for their appropriate examinations in Criminal Law.

This ninth edition of the *Criminal Law Textbook* reflects the major recent developments in the area, including House of Lords' decisions in *Mandair* (ss18 and 20 Offences Against the Person Act 1861), *Kingston* (intoxication) and *Adomako* (involuntary manslaughter). In addition, the Law Commission's proposals for reform are considered, with relevant extracts from recent reports and consultation papers dealing with intoxication, manslaughter and accessorial liability. References have also been included to the changes resulting from the Criminal Justice and Public Order Act 1994, the relevant provisions of which will have come into effect by the end of April 1995. The law is stated as of 1 January 1995.

Table of Cases

Table of Statutes

1

Introduction to Criminal Law

1.1 Introduction

The purpose of this book is to provide an introduction to the rules of English law governing criminal liability. It is not the author's intention to provide a comprehensive survey of all criminal offences, but the text does cover the mainstream offences with which the vast majority of criminal law students are concerned. Within each of the following chapters the reader will find a discussion of the broad principles relevant to the area under consideration. Ideally this text should be used as a prelude to studying the caselaw on each topic in depth.

Where appropriate, references have been included to the Law Commission's *Draft Criminal Code for England and Wales* (Law Com No 177, 1989), and references to the 'draft code' are references to the draft bill contained in Volume 1 of Law Com No 177. References to the remainder of the report are to Volumes I or II of the 'Code Report' as appropriate. Reference is also made to:

1. The Law Commission Report (Law Com 218), 'Legislating the Criminal Code: Offences against the Person and General Principles' (1993), referred to as 'Law Com No 218'. Reference to clauses of the Draft Criminal Law Bill contained in Law Com No 218 are indicated as references to the 'DCLB'.
2. Subsequent consultation papers: 'Legislating the Criminal Code: Offences against the Person and General Principles' (1992), referred to as 'LCCP 122';

'Intoxication and Criminal Liability' (1993), referred to as 'LCCP 127'; 'Involuntary Manslaughter' (1994) referred to as 'LCCP 135'; and 'Assisting and Encouraging Crime' referred to as 'LCCP 131'.

1.2 The nature of criminal law

Criminal law is what the layman tends to think of when he refers to 'the law'. It is generally seen as a list of prohibitions; behaviour that the State considers to be unacceptable. The search for a 'watertight' definition of crime is likely to be a sleeveless errand. Perhaps the safest route to follow is that which defines as criminal any activity which may result in a prosecution in the criminal courts. Such an approach avoids any attempt at determining a theoretical basis for the definition of crime, concentrating instead on the procedural distinctions between criminal law and civil law.

Crime and morality

To some extent criminal law can be seen as an embodiment of a society's mores. If a particular activity is regarded as morally offensive within a particular society, for example, torturing children, there may be little prospect of individuals indulging in such behaviour, yet the criminal law still prohibits it, and provides punishments for those who transgress the law. For most of society's members such a law will simply be a reaffirmation of their beliefs, they would not indulge in such behaviour even if it was not prohibited at law, but clearly it is there to be invoked if necessary.

In a country such as England, which is at least nominally Christian, it is interesting to consider the extent to which the moral code laid down in the Ten Commandments (Exodus 20:1–17) is actually reflected in its criminal law. Inter alia the Commandments provide:

1. Thou shalt have no other gods before me.
2. Thou shalt not worship graven images.
3. Thou shalt not take the name of the Lord thy God in vain.
4. Remember the sabbath day, to keep it holy.
5. Honour thy father and thy mother.
6. Thou shalt not kill.
7. Thou shalt not commit adultery.
8. Thou shalt not steal.
9. Thou shalt not bear false witness against thy neighbour.
10. Thou shalt not covet thy neighbour's goods.

Of these, it is submitted that only the prohibitions against murder and theft are clearly reflected in criminal law. The laws against blasphemy and Sunday trading do relate to certain aspects of the above, but these are both areas of law currently subject to criticism and calls for reform. Of the remaining Commandments, the absence of any parallel prohibition in criminal law perhaps indicates that such activities are either impossible to police, or ought to be left as matters of individual conscience. Society's views on such matters can be effected through the democratic process. The legislative enactments which liberalised the laws prohibiting abortion (Abortion Act 1967), and the laws relating to homosexual conduct in private between adults over the age of 21 (Sexual Offences Act 1967), were indicative of society's mood at that time, as reflected in the actions of its elected representatives. In more conservative times such laws might be subject to amendment or repeal if a government has a mandate for such action.

Problems inevitably arise where there is a lack of consensus within society as to whether or not a particular matter should be brought within the scope of the criminal law. The issue of decriminalisation has been raised in respect of so called 'victimless crimes' such as publication of obscene material, or the possession of controlled drugs for personal consumption. On the one hand there is the argument that the law must provide a form of moral yardstick by labelling such activities as criminal, on the other hand it is argued that it is the very criminalisation of such activities that makes them a rich source of profit for those who trade in such commodities. Decriminalisation, it is contended, would release significant law enforcement resources, remove the incentives for profiteering, and cause no appreciable harm to society. The American experience during the Prohibition period is instructive in this argument.

Juries are relied upon in criminal trials to determine issues of fact, but not infrequently they are called upon to determine issues which are essentially moral. The question of dishonesty in relation to the offence of theft is a good example. On the basis of *R* v *Ghosh* [1982] 1 QB 1053, a jury should consider whether a defendant's conduct was dishonest by the standard of ordinary decent people (ie themselves), and then consider whether or not the defendant realised that ordinary decent people would regard his actions as dishonest. Similarly, where members of a jury have to consider whether an assault was indecent, they will inevitably have regard to their own standards. It is in ways such as this that the link between law and current morality is maintained.

As Lord Coleridge observed in *R* v *Dudley and Stephens* (1884) 14 QBD 273:

'Though law and morality are not the same, and many things may be immoral which are not necessarily illegal, yet the absolute divorce of law from morality would be of fatal consequence ... We are often compelled to set up standards we cannot reach ourselves, and to lay down rules which we could not ourselves satisfy.'

Criminal law and the law of torts

When an activity is referred to as being unlawful, one has to consider the sense in which that term is being used. An activity can be unlawful in that it involves a tortious act (a civil wrong), or because it is contrary to the criminal law, or both. How is the distinction between the law of torts and criminal law to be drawn?

Existing as it does in the sphere of private law, the law of torts is primarily concerned with resolving disputes between two parties, with a view to one being compensated for the wrongful actions of the other. By contrast, criminal proceedings, even private prosecutions, are instituted with a view to punishing the defendant if convicted. Magistrates do have limited powers to order a defendant to compensate the victim of his crime, but this is not always possible or appropriate. As there is no compulsion upon one who has suffered loss as a result of a tortious act to commence civil proceedings for compensation, there may be many cases where the tortfeasor is never 'punished' for his wrongdoing. Even where damages are awarded, the defendant will frequently be supported by an insurance company, in which case the amount he is personally having to pay out, in the form of costs and increased premiums, bears little or no relation to the level of compensation actually awarded against him.

How culpable must tortious behaviour be before the law steps in to label it as criminal? In *R* v *Bateman* (1925) 19 Cr App 8, Lord Hewart CJ explained that negligence should be regarded as criminal where:

> '... in the opinion of the jury, the negligence of the accused went beyond a mere matter of compensation between subjects and showed such disregard for the life and safety of others as to amount to a crime against the state and conduct deserving of punishment.'

What seems to be suggested here is that the label 'criminal' will be attached to behaviour that is so unacceptable that the State will punish it, regardless of whether those injuriously affected by it choose to pursue the matter or not. Increasingly the trend is to describe such culpability as recklessness, rather than criminal negligence, in order to make the distinction between civil and criminal liability clearer.

Frequently, the distinction between tortious and criminal behaviour rests upon the presence of some aggravating factor. Hence the tort of conversion can become the crime of theft if there is dishonesty and an intention to permanently deprive; trespass within a building can become burglary where it is accompanied by an intent to steal, rape, cause criminal damage, or to do some grievous bodily harm.

1.3 The classification of crime

Prior to the enactment of the Criminal Law Act 1967 crimes were classified as being either treasons, felonies, or misdemeanours. In general terms felonies were the more serious offences, misdemeanours less serious. The distinction between felonies and misdemeanours was effectively abolished by the 1967 Act, which in turn introduced the concepts of the arrestable and non-arrestable offence. Arrestable offences are those falling within the provisions of s24 Police and Criminal Evidence Act 1984, in respect of which a police officer, and possibly a member of the public, can arrest without a warrant.

An alternative to classifying offences by reference to powers of arrest, is to classify them with reference to the procedure by which they are prosecuted. For these purposes offences are described as either being summary, indictable, or triable either way. The basis for this method of classification is to be found in the Magistrates' Court Act 1980.

Summary offences

Summary offences are those which are only triable summarily, ie before a magistrates' court. Such offences tend to be less serious in nature, which is hardly surprising given the limited powers of sentencing possessed by the magistrates' court when compared to the Crown Court. Typical examples of such offences would be drunken driving, indecent exposure, and assault upon a police officer in the execution of his duty. Common assault and battery are made summary only offences by the Criminal Justice Act 1988.

Indictable offences

Indictable offences are the most serious offences in the criminal calendar such as murder, treason, and robbery, which can only be tried on indictment in a Crown Court before a judge and jury.

Offences triable either way

A number of offences can be tried either summarily before a Magistrates' Court or on indictment before a Crown Court. Examples of such offences are handling stolen goods, theft, reckless driving and obtaining property by deception. The defendant will appear before the Magistrates' Court where the question of mode of trial will be considered, involving representations from the prosecution and the defence. A defendant cannot insist on a summary trial if the court considers trial on indictment more suitable, but if the court considers summary trial to be appropriate the defendant can still insist on his right to a trial on indictment, however unwise this may be.

Certain offences only become triable either way where the amount of damage involved exceeds a certain figure, eg criminal damage. Section 46 of the Criminal Justice and Public Order Act 1994 amends s22(1) of the Magistrates' Courts Act 1980 with the effect that magistrates must try summarily any criminal damage case where the value involved does not exceed £5,000 (an increase from £2,000). Similarly the Magistrates' Court has no discretion where an offence triable either way is being prosecuted by the Attorney-General, Director of Public Prosecutions, or Solicitor-General, and any of these officers requests trial on indictment.

1.4 Criminal procedure

Although this book is intended for use by students preparing for examinations in Criminal Law, it is submitted that some background knowledge of the criminal justice system is necessary in order to gain a fuller understanding of the subject.

The decision to prosecute

Although, subject to the activities of various specialised regulatory bodies, the investigation of crime is a function discharged by the police, the decision to prosecute rests primarily with the Crown Prosecution Service established in the wake of the Prosecution of Offences Act 1985.

The new Code for Crown Prosecutors was issued in June 1994 pursuant to s10 of the Prosecution of Offences Act 1985. The purpose of the Code is to help ensure that prosecutors make fair and consistent decisions about prosecutions. The decision to prosecute follows the application of two tests to the given facts. First, the case is subjected to the evidential test whereby the prosecutor has to be satisfied that there is sufficient evidence to provide a realistic prospect of conviction (ie a properly directed bench or jury would be more likely than not to convict). For this first test to be satisfied the evidence would clearly need to be reliable and admissible. If, and only if, the evidential test is satisfied, the case will be subject to the 'public interest' test.

Factors that suggest that a prosecution will be in the public interest include the:

1. likelihood of a substantial sentence being imposed on conviction;
2. use of a weapon or violence during the offence;
3. position of the victim (eg a person serving the public) and/or the position of the defendant (eg a person in a position of trust or authority);
4. evidence that the offence was premeditated, carried out by a group, or that the defendant was a 'ringleader';
5. effect on the victim;
6. likelihood of the offence being repeated;
7. extent to which the offence, even though not serious, is a common occurrence in the area in which it has been committed.

Factors that suggest that a prosecution will not be in the public interest include:

1. the likelihood that only a nominal penalty will be imposed in the event of a conviction;
2. that the offence was the result of a genuine mistake or misunderstanding;
3. the lapse of time between the offence and the proceedings, except where the offence is serious; the delay has been caused by the defendant; the offence has only recently come to light; or the complexity of the offence has necessitated a lengthy inquiry;
4. where the defendant is elderly or was suffering from a form of mental illness at the time of the offence, unless there is a real possibility of the offence being repeated;
5. the defendant having put right the harm or loss caused;
6. the adverse effect of certain information being made public.

As a rider to the above the Code adds that

> '... Crown Prosecutors must always think very carefully about the interests of the victim, which are an important factor, when deciding where the public interest lies.'

In deciding what offence to charge, Crown Prosecutors should select charges that reflect the seriousness of the offence, give the courts adequate sentencing powers and enable the case to be presented in a clear and simple way. As a result, the CPS will not always proceed with the most serious charge technically possible on the facts, nor necessarily all the possible offences to which the facts give rise.

Magistrates' Courts

Despite the unglamorous nature of much of their work, Magistrates' Courts deal with over 90 per cent of all criminal cases. The vast majority of criminal offences are dealt with summarily, with lay or stipendiary magistrates determining questions of fact, law, and sentence. As Magistrates' Courts are not courts of record, ie decisions of such courts have no value in terms of precedent, their deliberations are of little interest to the student of criminal law, but some consideration should be given to cases on appeal from Magistrates' Courts.

Appeal to the Crown Court
A defendant convicted in the Magistrates' Court can appeal to the Crown Court. Such an appeal involves a complete rehearing of the case before a Crown Court judge and two magistrates. The decision of a Crown Court in such a case has little or no value as a precedent.

Appeal by way of case stated to the Divisional Court
A defendant convicted in the Magistrates' Court may wish to challenge a magistrate's ruling on a question of law, even though none of the facts as found are in dispute. In such a case a complete rehearing in the Crown Court is inappropriate, and the normal procedure would be to appeal by way of case stated to the Divisional Court of the High Court, requesting a ruling on the point of law in issue. If the Divisional Court rules in favour of the defendant the conviction will be quashed. It is open to the prosecution to invoke this procedure where it feels that a defendant has been acquitted in the Magistrates' Court following a wrong ruling on a point of law. If the prosecution succeeds with such an appeal the Divisional Court can order the Magistrates' Court to enter a conviction against the defendant and consider the appropriate sentence.

Appeal by way of case stated from the Crown Court to the Divisional Court
A defendant who appeals to the Crown Court against a decision of a Magistrates' Court is still at liberty to appeal further to the Divisional Court using the case stated procedure, if he wishes to challenge a ruling of the Crown Court in relation to a point of law. Again, this right of appeal is open to both prosecution and defence.

Appeal from the Divisional Court to the House of Lords
A decision of the Divisional Court on a point of law may taken on appeal to the House of Lords. Leave of either the Divisional Court or the House of Lords to appeal is required, and the case must be one involving a point of law of general public importance. The right of appeal is open to both prosecution and defence.

Crown Court trial

A defendant charged with an indictable offence must be tried in the Crown Court. He will, however, make his first appearance in a Magistrates' Court where the magistrates, sitting as examining justices, will conduct committal proceedings to assess whether there is a case to go before the Crown Court. It is open to a defendant at committal proceedings to make a submission of 'no case to answer', which if successful would result in proceedings being terminated before they ever reach the Crown Court. A Crown Court trial might also be the procedure followed in respect to some offences triable either way. The Criminal Justice and Public Order Act 1994 contains provisions which, once in force, will replace the current arrangements for committal proceedings with arrangements for the transfer of trial. It is envisaged that these new proceedures will take effect from the summer of 1995.

Appeal from the Crown Court

Appeals from the Crown Court to the Court of Appeal (Criminal Division) are governed by the Criminal Appeal Act 1968.

Appeal on a point of law
A defendant can appeal as of right against a conviction on a pure point of law. In practice such appeals will be rare, as they involve the defendant contending that even if the jury had been correctly seized of all the evidence, it was not open to them to convict because the facts did not disclose an offence known to law, or at least not that with which the defendant was charged. An appeal on a pure point of law could also involve a challenge to the jurisdiction of the English courts on the basis that the offence was committed abroad. In certain cases the trial judge may certify that the case is one appropriate for appeal, in which case there is no need for the defendant to apply for leave.

Appeal against sentence
The vast majority of appeals from the Crown Court to the Court of Appeal are against sentence, not conviction. In 1992 the court dealt with 1,488 appeals against sentence. Leave to appeal is required, and the Court of Appeal can substitute any sentence that would have been available to the Crown Court at the time of trial. Under s36 of the Criminal Justice Act 1988 the Attorney-General has the power to refer unduly lenient sentences to the Court of Appeal, where a defendant has been tried and convicted on indictment. Again, the Court of Appeal will have the power to impose any sentence that was open to the Crown Court.

Appeal on a mixed question of fact or law

An appeal involving mixed questions of fact and law can only be brought with leave of the Court of Appeal. Applications for leave are normally considered by a single judge of the court, but appeal against a refusal of leave can be renewed before a full Court of Appeal hearing.

Grounds of appeal against conviction

Section 2(1) of the Criminal Appeal Act 1968 sets out three grounds of appeal: that the trial judge made a wrong ruling on a point of law; that there was a procedural irregularity during the course of the trial; and that the conviction should be set aside because in all the circumstances of the case it is unsafe or unsatisfactory. A wrong ruling on a point of law might be a judge's decision not to allow a particular defence raised by the defendant to be put before the jury, perhaps even resulting in a change of plea by the defendant. A procedural irregularity would, for example, be the defendant's previous convictions being allowed in evidence, or a confession being allowed in evidence despite the defendant's contention that it was obtained by oppressive means. That the conviction is unsafe and unsatisfactory is clearly the most generalised of the three grounds of appeal. The test to be applied by the judges of the Court of Appeal is whether, having considered the evidence, there is a reasonable suspicion or 'lurking doubt' that the conviction is unsafe or unsatisfactory. If there is, the appeal should be allowed. Such lurking doubts might arise where a conviction rests upon uncorroborated evidence, where there is dubious identification evidence, or where apparently compelling forensic evidence is later shown to be erroneous. An appellant will not succeed on this ground of appeal simply because he feels that the jury came to the wrong decision. He must particularise in which respects he believes his trial to have been defective. In 1992 the court dealt with 669 appeals against conviction

Powers of the Court of Appeal following an appeal

Having considered an appeal against conviction the Court of Appeal has a number of options. It can dismiss the appeal, leaving the sentence of the Crown Court to stand or reduce the sentence. Alternatively the appeal can be allowed and the conviction quashed, or the conviction can be quashed, and a conviction for a lesser included offence substituted, eg reduce a conviction for murder to manslaughter. Success rate on appeal is not high; only 10 per cent of appellants have their convictions quashed. A further option may be to apply the proviso to s2 of the 1968 Act which enables the Court of Appeal to decide an appeal in favour of the appellant, whilst dismissing the appeal against conviction. It states:

> 'Provided that the Court may, notwithstanding that they are of the opinion that the point raised in the appeal might be decided in favour of the appellant, dismiss the appeal if they consider that no miscarriage of justice has actually occurred.'

Such a procedure would be appropriate where an appellant has correctly shown that there was some error in procedure or law at his trial, but it was not such as could have affected its outcome. To apply the proviso the court must be satisfied that no miscarriage of justice has occurred. The proviso is clearly necessary to prevent defendants escaping punishment on purely technical grounds.

Attorney-General's reference

The prosecution has no right of appeal from the acquittal of a defendant in the Crown Court. A defendant may be acquitted because of a wrong ruling on a point of law by a trial judge, or because a particular point of law is shrouded in uncertainty, any such doubt having to be resolved in favour of the defendant. There is the possibility of such a Crown Court decision being perpetuated in subsequent Crown Court cases, resulting in yet more, possibly unjustified, acquittals. The problem can be remedied to some extent by the Attorney-General invoking his powers under s36 of the Criminal Justice Act 1972 to refer a point of law arising in a Crown Court case to the Court of Appeal. The appeal court's decision can have no effect whatsoever on the acquitted defendant, but it does provide a precedent to be followed in subsequent Crown Court cases.

Appeal to the House of Lords

Both prosecution and defence can appeal from a decision of the Court of Appeal to the House of Lords. Leave to appeal will be required, and the case must be one involving a point of law of general public importance.

Use of the civil courts

The Attorney-General can apply to the High Court for a declaration regarding an issue of criminal law, despite the fact that no criminal proceedings have been commenced. In *A-G* v *Able* [1984] QB 795 the Attorney-General sought a declaration as to the legality of a booklet issued by 'EXIT' which detailed various 'efficient' methods of committing suicide. Woolf J indicated that the civil courts should not generally be used for determining issues of criminal law; to do so would be to usurp the functions of the criminal courts. Perhaps a further ground of objection is the difference in the standard of proof in civil as opposed to criminal proceedings.

Proof

In a criminal trial the burden of proving the charge rests with the prosecution. The standard of proof is 'beyond all reasonable doubt'. In some situations a defendant will bear an evidential burden, ie will have to produce evidence upon which the trial judge can direct the jury, for example, where the defence of provocation is raised, evidence that he was provoked to kill the victim. Alternatively there are occasions when a defendant bears a legal burden of proof, such as the burden of proving diminished responsibility. In such cases the standard of proof that the defendant has to satisfy is the civil standard, ie on the balance of probabilities. In affirming the common law position regarding burden and standard of proof, Lord Sankey LC, in *Woolmington* v *DPP* [1935] AC 462, stated:

'If at any period of a trial it was permissible for the judge to rule that the prosecution had established its case and that the onus was shifted on the prisoner to prove that he was not guilty, and that, unless he discharged that onus, the prosecution was entitled to succeed, it would be enabling the judge in such a case to say that the jury must in law find the prisoner guilty and so make the judge decide the case and not the jury, which is not the common law ... it is not till the end of the evidence that a verdict can properly be found and that at the end of the evidence it is not for the prisoner to establish his innocence, but for the prosecution to establish his guilt. Just as there is evidence on behalf of the prosecution so there may be evidence on behalf of the prisoner which may cause a doubt as to his guilt. In either case, he is entitled to the benefit of the doubt. But while the prosecution must prove the guilt of the prisoner, there is no such burden laid on the prisoner to prove his innocence, and it is sufficient for him to raise a doubt as to his guilt; he is not bound to satisfy the jury of his innocence ... Throughout the web of the English criminal law one golden thread is always to be seen – that it is the duty of the prosecution to prove the prisoner's guilt subject to what I have already said as to the defence of insanity and subject also to any statutory exception. If, at the end of and on the whole of the case, there is a reasonable doubt, created by the evidence given by either the prosecution or the prisoner, as to whether the prisoner killed the deceased with a malicious intention, the prosecution has not made out the case and the prisoner is entitled to an acquittal. No matter what the charge or where the trial, the principle that the prosecution must prove the guilt of the prisoner is part of the common law of England and no attempt to whittle it down can be entertained.'

1.5 Preventing miscarriages of justice

One of the primary purposes of any appeals system must be the remedying of miscarriages of justice that have occurred in the lower courts. The English legal system provides for a judicial solution, through the actions of the Court of Appeal, and a political solution, through the intervention of the Home Secretary. In recent years, however, the operation of this system has been called into question.

Home Secretary's reference – Criminal Appeal Act 1968

Section 17(1):

'Where a person has been convicted on indictment ... the Secretary of State may, if he thinks fit, at any time either:
a) refer the case to the Court of Appeal and the case shall be treated for all purposes as an appeal to the Court by that person; or
b) if he desires the assistance of the Court on any point arising in the case, refer that point to the Court for their opinion thereon accordingly.'

This power is of considerable use if the time limits for appealing against a conviction have passed, but fresh evidence has come to light. It may be exercised following public opinion/political pressure being brought to bear. A case may be referred a number of times as more evidence becomes available.

The exercise of discretion under s17 by the Home Secretary, like all incidents of executive power, is in theory reviewable by the courts. In reality, a prisoner will have to produce compelling evidence of irrationality or a wrongful refusal to exercise discretion on the part of the minister if the courts are to be persuaded to intervene. *R* v *Secretary of State for the Home Department, ex parte McCallion* [1993] COD 148 indicates that it is not sufficient that the prisoner brings to the attention of the Home Secretary some arguable point not considered during the judicial process.

Where the appellant has pleaded guilty

It may seem odd that the courts should allow a defendant who has freely admitted his guilt at his trial to then seek to appeal against his inevitable conviction. There are, however, a number of situations where a possible miscarriage of justice can only be avoided by permitting such a course of action.

A defendant may have pleaded guilty as a result of pressure from counsel, or the trial judge, ie plea bargaining. He may have pleaded guilty as a result of a wrong ruling in law by the trial judge, eg a trial judge rules that the only defence he will allow the defendant to put before the jury is that of insanity. The defendant prefers to plead guilty rather than be found not guilty by reason of insanity, then appeals against the judge's ruling.

More generally it may be in the interests of justice to allow such an appeal to proceed. An example is provided by the case of *R* v *Lee* [1984] 1 All ER 1080. The appellant had pleaded guilty to several counts of manslaughter on the grounds of diminished responsibility, and arson. Following conviction it emerged that some of the fires had been started accidentally, and that the appellant may have pleaded guilty because of pressure by the police, confusion, or a desire for notoriety. The results of an investigation carried out by the *Sunday Times* had also been published, which established that the appellant had irrefutable alibis for some of the offences. The appellant applied for leave to appeal out of time, and during the application the court considered the question of whether or not it had jurisdiction to entertain the appeal, concluding that it did. This conclusion was reached despite the fact that the appellant had pleaded guilty when he was fit to plead, and had received expert advice. The question became one of whether or not it was in the interests of justice to consider evidence that had not been put forward at his trial as a consequence of the defendant's decision to plead guilty.

Fresh evidence

The court has to be careful to prevent a situation where the appellant keeps back some evidence at his trial in case he is convicted, only to produce it at the time of his appeal.

The Court of Appeal has a discretion to hear fresh evidence. It is only under a duty to do so, under s23(2) of the 1968 Act, if the evidence is admissible (ie cannot be hearsay), credible (is it consistent with uncontroverted evidence adduced at the trial?), and there is a good explanation as to why it was not adduced at the time of the trial. The court will expect an appellant to have co-operated with his lawyer at the time of the trial to ensure the availability of all relevant evidence, and in some cases to have employed an inquiry agent.

The court can allow the appeal if there is a 'lurking doubt' as to the safety of the conviction following an examination of the fresh evidence, or it can quash the conviction and order a retrial under s7 of the 1968 Act, if it is in the interests of justice to do so. As a successful appeal in the Court of Appeal places the appellant in the same situation as if he had been acquitted by the jury, this has to be seen as a statutory exception to the autrefois acquit rule. Care must be taken to ensure that the same charge is brought, or a lesser included, or an alternative charge on the indictment. The power to order a retrial is rarely used; in 1992 only 12 were ordered.

Free pardon and compensation

A free pardon can be recommended by the Home Secretary, where fresh evidence emerges that the defendant did not commit the offence for which he was convicted, and such a pardon has the effect of relieving the defendant from any penalty in connection with the conviction. Note that this by-passes the Court of Appeal altogether, but does not, however, quash the conviction as this is something only the Court of Appeal can do. The prisoner may also receive an ex gratia payment. Section 133 of the Criminal Justice Act 1988 has placed this power on a statutory basis, and in fact creates a duty to pay compensation where there has been a miscarriage of justice, but it offers no guidelines as to the basis upon which such compensation is to be paid. Unofficial guidelines indicate that about £10,000 per annum plus expenses and legal fees would be the normal level of payment.

1.6 Criticisms of the current system

Why, despite the measures outlined above to prevent miscarriages of justice, do misgivings still remain?

A number of factors need to be considered. First, the reluctance of Court of Appeal to overturn a jury's verdict in the absence of a procedural irregularity or error of law, even where the only evidence against the defendant is an uncorroborated confession. This problem is exacerbated by the unwillingness of the Court of Appeal to act simply because an appellant has been incompetently represented. Secondly, there is the restrictive approach taken by the Court of Appeal to the admission of fresh evidence. Indeed there may be difficulties in even obtaining legal aid to search for fresh evidence following conviction. Thirdly, there is the alleged reluctance of the Home Secretary to refer cases to the Court of Appeal, and the absence of any power vested in the Home Secretary to quash a conviction.

The operation of the criminal appeal system, in particular the role of the Court of Appeal (Criminal Division) has attracted considerable criticism following the revelations in the cases of the 'Guildford Four', see *R* v *Richardson and Others* (1989) The Times 20 October, and the 'Birmingham Six'. On 15 March 1991 the Home Secretary announced the setting up of a Royal Commission, under Lord Runciman, to investigate every aspect of the criminal process, from pre-trial procedures, to the handling of alleged miscarriages of justice by the Court of Appeal. The Commission delivered its report in July 1993.

The Royal Commission on Criminal Justice

The key recommendations of the Royal Commission on Criminal Justice, as regards reforming the machinery for dealing with alleged miscarriages of justice are as follows:

1. Section 2(1) of the Criminal Appeal Act 1968 should be redrafted to remove the degree of overlap that currently exists regarding the various grounds of appeal, and to clarify the application of the proviso. The majority favoured a single broad ground of appeal based on the assertion that the conviction 'is or may be unsafe'.

   Where the court is of the view that an error at the trial may have rendered the conviction unsafe, a retrial should be ordered. The majority also favoured a redrafting of s2(1) which would make it clear that a conviction should be quashed, even where the jury has been properly directed, and no errors of law or procedure have been committed, if nevertheless the court feels that the conviction is, or may be, unsafe.

2. The test for receiving fresh evidence should be whether ir is 'capable of belief'.

3. Where a defendant has been convicted of conspiracy to pervert the course of justice on the grounds that members of the jury were interfered with in a case that led to the acquittal of the defendant, the trial at which the defendant was acquitted should be regarded as a nullity and a second prosecution instituted.

4. The criterion that for a case to be referred to the House of Lords the Court of Appeal should certify that it involves a point of law of general public importance should be abandoned.

5. The Home Secretary's power to refer cases to the Court of Appeal under s17 of the 1968 Act should be abolished, and a new authority, independent of the courts, should be created to consider allegations of miscarriages of justice, supervise the investigations into the allegations, and where there is evidence that a miscarriage of justice might have occurred, refer the case to the Court of Appeal. The Court

of Appeal should then proceed as if dealing with an appeal from the Crown Court. The new authority should be immune from judicial review.

The proposal to create a new investigative authority to deal with alleged miscarriages of justice has not met with universal approval. *The Times* commented:

'... it would combine the role of quango, judge and investigator, effectively adding a new tier to the judicial system and confusing the public's perception of the Court of Appeal. There is also a risk that such a body would too often take its lead from the level of public pressure. Creating new institutions is no sure way of correcting the faults of the courts.'

Despite such criticisms the Home Secretary announced, in March 1994, plans to introduce a Criminal Cases Review Authority, closely modelled on the proposals in the Royal Commission report. The proposal envisages a body with both lay and professional membership, with police officers seconded to carry out investigations. Critics of the proposals have pointed out that the new authority will still be dependent to a large extent on the integrity of officers carrying out investigations on its behalf.

At present it remains unclear as to when the necessary legislative proposals will be put before Parliament for the establishment of the new review body. No specific commitment was given in the Queen's Speech of November 1994; however, the Home Office has confirmed that it intended to introduce a Bill in the 1994/95 session in the expectation that the cross-party support for the measure would ensure its speedy enactment.

1.7 Sources of criminal law

Despite the growing trend towards codification of English criminal law, as evidenced by the number of offences which have now been placed on a statutory basis, such as the Theft Acts 1968 and 1978, the Criminal Damage Act 1971, and the Criminal Attempts Act 1981, significant aspects of the criminal law are still governed by the common law, such as murder, manslaughter, assault, and incitement. The judiciary have considerable powers to influence the development of criminal law either through the 'discovery' of the common law, or through the exercise of their powers of statutory interpretation. The prospect of the judiciary creating new forms of criminal liability at common law is abhorrent to many, indicating a breach of the separation of powers. The judges are aware of such criticisms and not surprisingly exercise this power with extreme caution, but will nevertheless act to supply the omission of the legislature where they see fit.

As Viscount Simonds commented in *Shaw* v *DPP* [1961] 2 All ER 446, when dealing with the question of whether the courts could recognise a new offence of conspiring to corrupt public morals:

'Need I say my Lords, that I am no advocate of the right of judges to create new criminal offences? ... But, in the sphere of criminal law, I entertain no doubt that there remains in the courts of law a residual power to enforce the supreme and fundamental purpose of the law, to conserve not only the safety and order but also the moral welfare of the state, and that it is their duty to guard it against attacks which may be the more insidious because they are novel and unprepared for.'

Lord Reid, dissenting, stated:

'I think, or at least I hope, that it is now established that the courts cannot create new offences by individuals ... when there is sufficient support from public opinion, Parliament does not hesitate to intervene. Where Parliament fears to tread it is not for the courts to rush in.'

As regards the interpretation of criminal legislation, it is obviously the role of the judiciary to give effect to the intention of Parliament as expressed through such legislation. The rules of statutory interpretation relied upon are well known, but one rule, of particular significance here, is that any ambiguity in a statutory provision should be construed in favour of the defendant. Some observers might suggest that this principle is not applied by the judiciary as frequently as it might be.

There are two situations in which the judicial role in statutory interpretation will be of considerable importance. The first is where an older statute, using archaic terminology, has to be interpreted to deal with current day problems. Section 23 of the Offences Against the Person Act 1861, for example, refers to a defendant acting 'maliciously'. It is inconceivable that Parliament would choose such an adverb today, yet judges have to attach some meaning to it which will be intelligible to juries: see *R v Cunningham* [1957] 2 QB 396. The second situation arises where Parliament has simply failed to express itself clearly. Here the judges are left with the choice of construing any ambiguity in favour of the defendant, with the likely consequence of an acquittal, or of straining the wording of the provision to try to achieve the result Parliament originally intended. A clear example of this dilemma is provided by the House of Lords' difficulties in applying s1(1),(2) and (3) of the Criminal Attempts Act 1981, in *Anderton v Ryan* [1985] AC 560, and *R v Shivpuri* [1987] AC 1.

Parliament's intention in enacting the 1981 Act was to amend the law relating to the offence of attempt, so that a defendant could be guilty of attempting to commit a crime even though the facts were such (unknown to him) that the commission of the completed offence was impossible. If successful, the Act would produce some surprising results. The defendant who, intending to kill, fired a gun at a corpse believing it to be a live human being, could be guilty of attempted murder, even though the completed offence was clearly impossible. The language used in the 1981 Act to achieve this goal, particularly s1(3), is somewhat tortuous. In *Anderton v Ryan*, Lord Roskill indicated that, notwithstanding the 'mischief' rule of interpretation, whereby judges were expected to prefer the construction of a statute which enabled them to tackle the mischief Parliament had sought to combat, he could not allow his loyalty to that principle to lead him to a construction of the statute that would produce a result that he regarded as a manifest absurdity. Such an absurdity, in his view, would have been the conviction of Mrs Ryan, for attempting to handle what she believed to be a stolen video recorder, in the absence of proof by the prosecution that the item had been stolen. In short, his Lordship refused to give effect to the legislation as Parliament had intended. In *R v Shivpuri*, the House of Lords found itself faced with the consequences of its previous decision. The defendant had admitted to the police that he was a drugs courier, but examination of the parcel he had been paid to deliver revealed its contents to be a harmless vegetable matter. The defendant was charged with attempting to deal in a proscribed drug, and the House of Lords had the option of either following *Anderton v Ryan*, a course of action which might have been construed as far too lenient given the nature of the activity involved, or of re-interpreting the legislation to cover the defendant's behaviour. Not surprisingly the latter course was adopted, despite the ambiguities of the legislation: see further Chapter 12.

1.8 The work of the Law Commission

The Report and Draft Criminal Code Bill for England and Wales was published by the Law Commission in 1989 (Law Com No 177). The Law Commission described the purpose of its report as being to address '... the question whether it is desirable to replace the existing fluctuating mix of legislation and common law by one codifying statute' (Vol I para 1.4). Volume I comprises recommendations and a Draft Criminal Code Bill and Appendices. Part I of the bill deals with general principles of liability, whilst Part II deals with specific offences. Appendix B provides a series of illustrative examples of how the code might operate in given situations. Volume II provides a commentary on some of the code provisions. Extracts from the commentary have been included where appropriate, with footnotes omitted.

The origins of the Code can be traced back to 1981 when the preparatory work was started by a small group – the 'Code Team'. The team's terms of reference were:

'(1) to consider and make proposals in relation to
(a) the aims and objects of a criminal code for England and Wales
(b) its nature and scope
(c) its content, structure, lay-out and the interrelation of its parts
(d) the method and style of its drafting and
(2) to formulate, in a manner appropriate to such a code,
(a) the general principles which should govern liability under it
(b) a standard terminology to be used in it
(c) the rules which should govern its interpretation.'

The 'Code Team' submitted their report to the Law Commission in November 1984, and it was published in March 1985. The Law Commission's draft code is based upon that produced by the Code Team, but reflects amendments and reforms suggested during 1985–9, and expands Part II of the draft code which deals with specific offences.

The Law Commission's report explains the background to the moves towards codification in the following terms:

'English criminal law is derived from a mixture of common law and statute. Most of the general principles of liability are still to be found in the common law, though some, for example, the law relating to conspiracy and attempts to commit crime have recently been defined in Acts of Parliament. The great majority of crimes are now defined by statute but there are important exceptions. Murder, manslaughter and assault are still offences at common law, though affected in various ways by statute. There is no system in the relative roles of common law and legislation. Thus, incitement to commit crime – though closely related to conspiracy and attempts – is still a common law offence. Whether an offence is defined by statute has almost always been a matter of historical accident rather than systematic organisation. For example, rape is defined in the Sexual Offences (Amendment) Act 1976 because of the outcry which followed the decision in *DPP* v *Morgan* and led to the subsequent Heilbron Report. The legislation in force extends over a very long period of time. It is true that only a very small amount of significant legislation is earlier than the mid-nineteenth century, but that is quite long enough for the language of the criminal law and the style of drafting to have undergone substantial changes.' [Vol I para 1.3]

The Law Commission cited a number of reasons in support of codification. At a fundamental level there are constitutional arguments to be considered. The criminal justice system should reflect the balance of power between the citizen and the state. The citizen should be presented with a rational and just system of laws. If the criminal law is a known and ascertainable body of rules, it promotes key aspects of 'due process', such as fair warning of potential liability. Professor ATH Smith viewed the introduction of a criminal code as significant because it involved the making of:

'... a symbolic statement about the constitutional relationship of Parliament and the courts, it requires a judicial deference to the legislative will greater than that which the courts have often shown to isolated and sporadic pieces of legislation.' [Vol I para 2.2]

Codification was also seen as a means of promoting consistency. As the Commission's report stated, 'Inconsistency both in terminology and substance is a serious problem in English criminal law'. [Vol I para 2.8]

A common definition of fundamental terms such as 'intention' or 'recklessness' can help to ensure that like cases are treated alike.

The Law Commission was well aware of the fact that legislation containing a criminal code would be subject to interpretation by the courts in the same way that any existing criminal legislation is, and that the result could be the emergence of a daunting body of case law; the experience of the Theft Acts 1968 and 1978 provides ample evidence. The Commission's report stated:

'Our objective ... has been to ensure that the Criminal Code Bill has been drafted with sufficient clarity to reduce difficulties of interpretation as far as is reasonably possible.' [Vol I para 2.22]

The Commission's view was that problems of implementation were not to be confused with objections to codification in principle.

During 1992 the Law Commission's Consultation Paper No 122 was published under the title '*Legislating the Criminal Code: Offences Against the Person and General Principles*', followed in November 1993 by the Law Commission's Report of the same name (Law Com No 218). The Commission, perhaps accepting that enactment of the Code in its totality was unlikely given the amount of parliamentary time that would be absorbed, elected to extract what it saw as the key areas for reform. Thus the report puts forward a draft Criminal Law Bill to reform the criminal law in areas such as intent, recklessness, liability for omissions, assaults, duress, necessity, self-defence and intoxication. As will be seen in the relevant chapters, the draft legislation builds on the Code, and the interrelation between the Code and the draft Bill will be adverted to where appropriate. Note that the Commission chose not to deal with homicide in its report, for two reasons. First, the House of Commons select committee (the Nathan Committee) had recently considered murder and voluntary manslaughter, and there was no evidence that government was likely to act on its proposals. Secondly, because the law relating to involuntary manslaughter would be considered in a Law Commission Consultative Paper during 1994.

A key problem in putting the work of the Law Commission into effect is clearly that of securing adequate time for the enactment of the relevant legislation in an already crowded Parliamentary schedule. In its report for 1993, the Commission expressed its grave concern on this matter, going as far as to suggest that its relationship with the House of Commons had all but broken down. Mr Justice Brooke, Chairman of the Commission, singled out in particular the failure to reform substantial parts of existing criminal law as being 'a disgrace'.

2

Actus Reus and Mens Rea

2.1 Introduction

It is common for criminal lawyers to talk of criminal offences having 'elements'. This is usually a shorthand reference to the actus reus and mens rea of an offence. In literal terms actus reus denotes a guilty act, mens rea denotes a guilty mind. The general basis for imposing liability in criminal law is that a defendant must be proved to have committed the guilty act whilst having had the guilty state of mind. As will be seen in the following chapters, criminal law throws up many exceptions to this general proposition, but as a method of approach to problems of criminal liability it has much to recommend itself to the newcomer to the subject.

When attempting to solve problems in criminal law it is logical to first ask whether the defendant has committed the prohibited act, or actus reus. If the answer to this question is in the affirmative, one can then ask whether the defendant possessed the requisite state of mind at the time of the act, in short whether he had mens rea. If the answer to this second question is also affirmative, one can ask a third question. Are there any defences available to the defendant in respect of his actions which might reduce or remove his criminal liability?

2.2 Actus reus: general considerations

Definition

Professor Glanville Williams has suggested the following approach:

> 'All that can truly be said, without exception, is that a crime requires some *external state of affairs* that can be categorised as criminal. What goes on inside a man's head is never enough in itself to constitute a crime, even though it be proved by a confession that it is fully believed to be genuine.' (*Textbook on Criminal Law*, 2nd ed, p146)

It might be wise, therefore, to proceed on the basis that the actus reus of an offence involves all the elements of the offence, with the exception of those that relate to the defendant's state of mind. Terms such as actus reus should be treated with caution however. As Lord Diplock observed in *R* v *Miller* [1983] 1 All ER 978 at 980:

> 'My Lords, it would I think be conducive to clarity of analysis of the ingredients of a crime that is created by statute, as are the great majority of criminal offences today, if we were to avoid bad Latin and instead to think and speak ... about the conduct of the accused and his state of mind at the time of that conduct, instead of speaking of actus reus and mens rea.'

It should not be assumed that 'actus reus' and 'mens rea' are mutually exclusive concepts. Cases such as *R* v *Miller*, considered at 2.3 below, illustrate the interrelationship between them.

In time the 'bad Latin' may come to be replaced by the more prosaic but accurate terminology preferred by the Law Commission in its Draft Code, which uses 'external elements of the offence' for actus reus, and 'fault element' for mens rea.

Types of actus reus

Offences can be classified on the basis of the type of actus reus involved.

Conduct

Some offences do not require proof of any result or consequence. The action of the defendant is all that has to be proved. A typical example is the offence of 'dangerous driving'. The prosecution does not have to prove that any harm was caused by this activity, or that life was endangered by it. Similarly the offence of perjury, under the Perjury Act 1911, requires the defendant only to make a statement that he knows or believes to be untrue whilst under oath. Liability can arise independently of whether the statement affects the outcome of the proceedings.

Circumstances

The actus reus of an offence can consist of elements which are almost entirely external to the physical actions of the defendant. An example is provided by the offence of 'being found drunk in a public place'. It is true that the prosecution must prove that the defendant was drunk at the time, but beyond that the actus reus is based upon the actions of others, namely those who find the defendant drunk in the highway. See *Winzar* v *Chief Constable of Kent* (at 2.4).

Offences based on possession of prohibited articles such as drugs or offensive weapons might also be seen as examples of this type of actus reus.

Result crimes

Offences such as homicide and assault require proof of a result as part of the actus reus. The defendant must be shown to have caused the death of the victim, or to have caused the injury suffered by the victim, as the case may be. Questions of causation can be very complex. It is not sufficient that the defendant's act can be shown to have been a factual cause of the prohibited act. It must be shown that the act is also a cause in law of the result. This matter is dealt with in more detail in Chapter 6, in the context of homicide

An illustration

The statutory offence of theft provides a useful illustration of the various elements of a criminal offence. Section 1 of the Theft Act 1968 states:

> 'A person is guilty of theft if he dishonestly appropriates property belonging to another with the intention of permanently depriving the other of it ...'

If one deletes those expressions that relate to the mental state of the defendant, ie 'dishonesty' and 'intention to permanently deprive', what remains is the actus reus of the offence. The 'appropriation' could be regarded as the conduct of the defendant; the 'property belonging to another' constitutes the circumstances that must exist for the offence to be made out.

Actus reus must be proved

It is something of a truism in criminal law that there must be an actus reus for there to be any criminal liability. This is sometimes expressed by saying that 'actus reus must be proved'.

The case of *R* v *Deller* (1952) 36 Cr App R 184 illustrates the point. The defendant sold a car which he wrongly believed to be the subject of a hire purchase agreement in respect of which payments were still outstanding. In fact the car was free from all encumbrances. He was charged with what is now the offence of obtaining property by deception. He appealed against his conviction on the basis that, as the car was free from all encumbrances, he had been telling the truth when he had told the purchaser this, even though he had thought he was lying. The Court of Appeal quashed his conviction. As the car was free from encumbrances the defendant had not deceived the purchaser, hence the actus reus of deception was absent. The fact that the defendant had thought he was committing an offence, ie he had mens rea, was insufficient on its own for liability.

The decision raises a number of interesting possibilities, such as the acquittal of the defendant who fires a gun at what he believes to be the sleeping figure of his enemy, intending to kill him, only to discover that in fact he was firing at a wax dummy. Again, the defendant has the mens rea, this time for murder, but has not committed the actus reus, indeed cannot, as there is no human being to be the victim.

It should be noted that Parliament has acted to bring such defendants within the scope of the criminal law. Were the same facts to arise today, Deller would almost certainly be guilty of attempting to obtain property by deception contrary to s1 of the Criminal Attempts Act 1981. Similarly, the would-be murderer could now be charged with attempted murder, even though he was only firing at a wax dummy. How such a result is achieved is detailed in Chapter 12.

Reform

Clause 15 of the draft code proposes the following:

'A reference in this Act to an "act" as an element of an offence refers also, where the context permits, to any result of the act, and any circumstance in which the act is done or the result occurs, that is an element of the offence, and references to a person's acting or doing an act shall be construed accordingly.'

In its commentary in Volume II of the Code Report, the Commission stated:

'Clause 15 ... is an interpretation clause. It does not define "act". It simply explains that where the Code refers to "an act" or to a person's "acting" or "doing an act", the reference embraces whatever relevant results and circumstances the context permits. This clarification of the use of the word "act" is not in fact essential; for we believe that no provision of the Code is on a fair reading truly ambiguous in its use of the term. But the clause may prove useful for the avoidance of doubt in those inexperienced in the reading of criminal statutes and as a protection against perverse reading or hopeless argument.' [Vol II para 7.6]

2.3 Actus reus: omissions

Introduction

It is customary to think of an actus reus as being the positive act of the defendant. In murder this might be the defendant's stabbing of the victim. In theft it might be the defendant's taking of money from a wallet. The matter to be considered here is whether a failure to act on the part of a defendant can form the basis of liability.

The general rule

The general rule in English criminal law is that there can be no liability for failing to act, unless at the time of the failure to act the defendant was under a legal duty to take positive action. A moral duty to act will not suffice here. Hence if D sees P, a blind man, walking towards the edge of a cliff from which there is a sheer drop of 300 feet onto jagged rocks below, he is under no legal duty to call out a warning. D is quite at liberty to watch P walk over the edge of the cliff top to his certain death. Similarly if D were to see a child P drowning in a swimming pool, D would be under no legal duty to prevent this. D could calmly stand at the pool side and film the tragedy if he so wished. The legal position rather reflects the saying that 'you are not your brother's keeper'. As will be explained below, the situation in the latter example would be markedly different were the child in the pool to be D's son, or if D was a pool attendant employed to ensure the safety of swimmers.

It should not be assumed that it is always a simple matter to differentiate between an act and an omission. In *R v Speck* (1977) 65 Cr App R 161, the defendant was convicted of an offence under s1 of the Indecency with Children Act 1960. An eight-year-old girl had approached him and placed her hand on his penis. He allowed her hand to remain there for approximately 5 minutes, during which time he had an erection. He appealed against his conviction on the basis that he had not committed any 'act of gross indecency with or towards a child under the age of 14 '. The Court of Appeal held, dismissing the appeal, that the defendant's inactivity in failing to remove the hand of the little girl could amount to an invitation to the child to undertake the act.

As Lord Widgery CJ observed:

> 'Getting to the essential features of this problem, and accepting that for present purposes there was inactivity on the part of the appellant at all material times, we think that such inactivity can nevertheless amount to an invitation to the child to undertake the act. If a fair view of the facts be that the appellant has in any sense invited the child to do what she did, then the mere fact that the appellant himself remained inactive is no defence to it ...
>
> Since in our opinion the element of invitation is important, and that is an element which the jury ultimately would have to consider, the ruling in law should have been that the conduct described by the learned recorder could be an offence if the jury took the view that it amounted to an invitation from the male to the child, either to start, to stop, or to continue this activity.'

Unless it is accepted that the defendant's demeanour towards the child constituted the positive act here, it is difficult to see on what basis his liability for failing to act could have been imposed, given the absence of any of the duties considered below.

Duty arising from statute

Liability for failing to act will be imposed where the defendant can be shown to have been under a statutory duty to take positive action. A leading example of such a provision is provided by the Children and Young Persons Act 1933, which creates the offence of wilfully neglecting a child. Hence by simply failing to provide food for a child, or failing to obtain appropriate medical care, a parent could be held criminally liable for any harm that results. At a more prosaic level, the Road Traffic Acts place motorists under various duties, such as the duty to report road accidents where persons have been injured, or the duty to provide breath test specimens. In these cases it is the failure to act that results in liability.

Duty arising from contract

Where a defendant is under an ascertainable contractual duty to act, his failure to perform the contractual duty in question can form the basis of criminal liability. Hence in the example detailed above, if D is employed as a swimming pool attendant, and he fails to help a child who appears to him to be drowning in the pool with the result that the child dies, D could be held criminally responsible for the death on the basis that he was under a contractual duty to help save the child. The fact that the child is not a party to the contract upon which the duty is based is not a relevant matter here. An authority for imposing liability on this basis is *R v Pittwood* (1902) 19 TLR 37. The defendant was employed as a gate keeper at a railway crossing. One day he went for lunch leaving the gate open so that road traffic could cross the railway line. A hay cart crossing the line was hit by a train. One man was killed, another was seriously injured. Pittwood was convicted of manslaughter based on his failure to carry out his contractual duty to close the gate when a train approached. The case of *R v Benge* (1865) 4 F & F 594 provides a further illustration of such liability.

Duty arising at common law

In the absence of any statutory or contractual duty, the judiciary have seen fit to create a number of common law duties, where it has been felt that not to do so would be to wrongly relieve the defendant of all criminal liability.

Duties owed to family members

The common law recognises a duty that members of a family may owe to each other to care for each other's welfare. The problem with such common law duties is that their exact limits are rather difficult to define, hence it may be difficult to determine when liability is likely to arise. In *R v Gibbens and Proctor* (1918) 82 JP 287, the court recognised the common law duty that a parent owes towards his or her child, with the result that liability for murder can result if a parent deliberately fails to feed a child. Note however that this common law duty has largely been supplanted by the statutory duty under the Children and Young Persons Act 1933 referred to above. Similarly in *R v Instan* [1893] 1 QB 450, where the defendant lived with her aunt, an elderly woman who developed gangrene in her leg and was unable to look after herself. The defendant was the only person who knew of her condition, but failed to provide her aunt with food or medical assistance. After 12 days of suffering the aunt died. The defendant was convicted of manslaughter and appealed, unsuccessfully, to the Court for Crown Cases Reserved. Lord Coleridge CJ expressed the view that English law would be hopelessly deficient if the judges were to be unable to base liability on the common duty of care owed by one relative to another.

Reliance

Partly because of the difficulties in determining the precise scope of a duty of care based on blood relationships, the courts have, in recent years, moved towards recognising the existence of a common law duty of care where there is a relationship of reliance between defendant and victim. In *R v Stone and Dobinson* [1977] 1 QB 354, the defendants were convicted of the manslaughter of Stone's sister Fanny. Stone was an elderly man, having greatly impaired senses of sight, smell, and hearing. Dobinson, his common law wife, was described as 'weak and ineffectual'. It was accepted that both defendants were of low intelligence and not particularly 'worldly' in character. They were visited by Fanny who was a somewhat eccentric woman, described in court as being morbidly anxious about becoming overweight. The defendants took Fanny in and provided her with a bed, but over the following weeks Fanny's condition worsened. She did not eat properly, developed bed sores, and eventually died of blood poisoning as result of her untreated bed sores becoming infected. The defendants had not obtained any medical assistance for Fanny although they had known that she was unwell. In dismissing the appeal, the Court of Appeal held that the defendants had been under a common law duty to care for Fanny, the duty arising from their voluntarily assuming the responsibility for looking after her, and their knowledge that she was relying on them. The defendants' failure to discharge this duty was the cause of the victim's death. Whilst it is submitted that to base liability on reliance freely assumed, rather than blood relationships, is a more sensible approach, the result may be somewhat counter-productive. In the light of the above decision, surely Stone would have been well advised to turn his sister away when she arrived at his door needing somewhere to stay. By doing so he would have avoided any assumption of a duty to care for her.

The duty to limit harm caused by accidental acts

The instances of liability for failure to act considered above may not be a sufficient basis for imposing liability on a defendant who accidentally commits an act that causes harm, realises what has happened, but then does nothing to prevent further harm from occurring. The problem was considered by the House of Lords in *R v Miller* [1983] 2 AC 161. The defendant, a vagrant, had been occupying an empty house. One evening he laid on a mattress and lit a cigarette. He fell asleep and the lighted cigarette set fire to the mattress. The defendant was woken by the flames, but instead of putting the fire out, he got up and went into an adjoining room where he found another mattress, and went back to sleep. As a result, the house was substantially damaged by fire, and the defendant was convicted of criminal damage. He appealed, contending that liability could not be based on his setting fire to the mattress as he had been asleep at the time, and that there could be no liability based on his failure to act (once he became aware of the fire) as he had not been under a legal duty to take any action. As the law then stood the defendant's contentions were soundly based. A defendant will normally be able to plead the defence of automatism in respect of acts committed whilst asleep (see Chapter 13), and he was not under any statutory, contractual, or common law duty to put the fire out once he discovered it.

The Court of Appeal had dismissed his appeal, relying on the earlier Divisional Court decision in *Fagan* v *MPC* [1968] 3 All ER 442. The House of Lords, however, preferred to base liability on a new type of common law 'duty'. Lord Diplock accepted that the defendant's initial setting fire to the mattress may not have been a culpable act in that he was asleep at the time, but his Lordship was of the opinion that once the defendant awoke and realised what had happened, he came under a responsibility to limit the harmful effects of the fire (his Lordship deliberately avoided use of the word 'duty' for fear that it might confuse juries). The defendant's failure to discharge this responsibility provided the basis for the imposition of liability.

Whilst the decision represents an important development of liability for failing to act at common law, there have been very few reported instances of its application since 1983. Indeed, in *R* v *Ahmad* [1986] Crim LR 739, the only decision in which it has subsequently been considered at any length, the court concluded that it could not be relied upon by the prosecution. In that case the defendant was a landlord who had been charged with (inter alia) doing acts calculated to interfere with the peace and comfort of one of his tenants, contrary to s1(3) of the Protection from Eviction Act 1977. He had agreed with a tenant that certain alterations would be carried out at a property, including the installation of a new stairway and bathroom, and the defendant had instructed men to commence the work, which involved the removal of the tenant's old bathroom. Disputes then arose between the defendant and the tenant and work on the property ceased, leaving the tenant without a bathroom. The defendant was convicted under s1(3) but appealed successfully to the Court of Appeal on the basis that, as the Act required 'the doing of acts' by the defendant, he could not incur liability through mere inactivity. When he had removed the old bathroom, he had lacked the mens rea necessary for the offence. He may have intended the cessation of building work to interfere with the tenant's enjoyment of the property, but this was not accompanied by any 'acts' on the part of the defendant as required by the statute. The court felt that the House of Lords' decision in *R* v *Miller* was of no avail were a statute expressly stated that liability could only arise where positive acts were committed.

Reform

The Code Team's draft published in 1985 did attempt to codify the law relating to liability for failing to act. For reasons outlined below, the Law Commission decided not to make any such provision in its 1989 report, restricting itself to codification of the law relating to 'supervening fault'. Clause 16 of the draft code provides:

> 'For the purposes of an offence which consists wholly or in part of an omission, state of affairs or occurrence, references in this Act to an "act" shall, where the context permits, be read as including references to the omission, state of affairs or occurrence by reason of which a person may be guilty of the offence, and references to a person's acting or doing an act shall be construed accordingly.'

The Commission commented upon the purpose of clause 16 as follows:

> 'In effect, it instructs the user of the Code that, when he is concerned with an offence of omission or with a situational offence, he should substitute a reference to the omission or situation in question (or to making that omission or being in that situation) for a Code provision referring to an act (or to acting or doing an act). He should do so, to be more precise, "where the context permits".' [Vol II para.7.7]

Reference should also be made to clause 33(2) of the draft code (considered in Chapter 13) which deals with the liability of a defendant who fails to act due to physical incapacity.

Regarding the absence of any provision expressly creating liability for failing to act, the Commission's commentary on the code provides the following explanation:

> 'Criminal liability for failing to act is exceptional. Parliament sometimes makes it an offence to fail to do something (as with wilful neglect of a child, the failure of a motorist to exchange particulars after an accident or the failure of a company to make an annual return). Most other instances of liability for omissions depend upon judicial construction of statutory language as referring to omissions as well as to acts, or upon common law (that is, judicial) recognition, in limited and rather ill-defined circumstances, of a duty to act to prevent a particular kind of harm (notably certain harms to the person) or to prevent the commission of an offence.' [Vol II para 7.9]

The commentary goes on to point out that previous efforts at law reform, such as that relating to offences against the person, failed to come up with any satisfactory solution to the problem (see: Criminal Law Revision Committee, 'Fourteenth Report: Offences against the Person' (1980), Cmnd 7844, paras 254–255). Rather than specifying those offences that can be committed by omission and those that cannot, the Commission expresses its preference for a scheme under which terms such as 'act' and 'cause' can be construed as carrying with them the possibility of the offence in question being committed by omission. The existence or otherwise of a duty to act remaining a matter to be determined at common law. The Commission explains the consequence of this as follows:

> 'Clause 17(1) [of the draft code bill] makes it clear that, under the Code, results may be "caused" by omission. The draft Bill therefore defines homicide offences in terms of "causing death" rather than of "killing"; and other offences against the person similarly

require the "causing" of relevant harms. It seems to us to be desirable to draft some other offences at least (most obviously, offences of damage to property) in the same way, in order to leave fully open to the courts the possibility of so construing the relevant (statutory) provisions as to impose liability for omissions. For to prefer "cause death" to "kill" while retaining "destroy or damage property" might be taken to imply an intention to exclude all liability for omissions in the latter case.' [Vol II para 7.13]

In LCCP 122 the Law Commission expressed a preference for the approach demonstrated by the CLRC in its 14th Report (above), and this is re-affirmed in Law Com 218. Clause 19(1) of the Draft Criminal Law Bill ('DCLB'), contained in Law Com 218, states:

'An offence to which this section applies may be committed by a person who, with the result specified for the offence, omits to do an act that he is under a duty to do at common law. Where this section applies to an offence a person may commit an offence if, with the result specified for the offence, he omits to do an act that he is under a duty to do at common law; and accordingly references to acts include references to omissions.'

By virtue of clause 19(2) of the DCLB, clause 19(1) would apply to intentional serious injury, torture, unlawful detention, kidnapping, abduction and aggravated abduction. Note that the duty to act would have to be one recognised at common law, although the authors of the report describe this as a 'provisional conclusion' (para 6.13). The question remains as to whether or not breaches of statutory duty which are in themselves criminal offences, eg under the Health and Safety at Work Act 1974, should form the basis for prosecutions for serious physical harm or even homicide.

Despite its reluctance to provide expressly for liability for omissions, the Law Commission took the view that liability for failing to limit the scope of harm accidentally caused (ie the *R* v *Miller* principle) should be dealt with in the draft code, and its restatement and generalisation of the '*Miller*' principle appeared in clause 23. The Commission was of the view that the principle should apply to all 'result crimes', although it conceded that the courts have not been willing to extend its application beyond this category of offences: see *Wings Ltd* v *Ellis* [1984] 1 WLR 731, *R* v *Ahmad* (above), and Vol II paras 8.52, 8.53 of the Code Report. The commentary noted that:

'(i) Nothing in *Miller* limits the principle to a case in which the original act is blameworthy. Although the original act in that case (falling asleep with a lighted cigarette) was no doubt at least careless, the certified question answered in the affirmative by the House of Lords concerned liability for failure to take steps to extinguish, or prevent damage by, a fire started "accidentally" – which must mean (in the terms of clause 23) "[lacking] the fault required [for the offence]". The question was answered without comment upon this aspect.

(ii) For the principle to apply, the actor must become aware of what he has done and of the risk thereby created (paragraph (a)); the act that he then fails to do must be one that might prevent the occurrence or continuance of the result (paragraph (b)); and the result specified for the offence must occur, or (if it has already occurred) must continue, after the failure to act (paragraph (c)).' [Vol II para 8.54]

Law Com No 218, in DCLB clause 31, restates clause 23 of the draft code, with minor modifications in the light of intervening consultation. It provides:

> 'Where it is an offence to be at fault in causing a result, a person who lacks the fault required when he does an act that may cause, or does cause, the result, he nevertheless commits the offence if –
> (a) being aware that he has done the act and that the result may occur or, as the case may be, has occurred and may continue, and
> (b) with the fault required,
> he fails to take reasonable steps to prevent the result occurring or continuing and it does occur or continue.'

2.4 Involuntary acts

If P is standing in front of X holding a penknife, and D approaching P from the rear takes P's elbow and pushes it forward so that the knife being held by P plunges into X's face, it would seem rather harsh to suggest that it was P's action that caused the harm. He may have been holding the knife, but clearly his stabbing of X was not the result of a voluntary act on his part. Criminal law would place liability on D, relying on the doctrine of innocent agency, ie P was merely the innocent agent through whom D achieved the commission of the offence.

Automatism

There may be any number of reasons as to why a defendant's actions were not freely willed. He may have caused harm whilst sleepwalking, or whilst having a fit. There have been a number of tragic incidents where defendants have killed their partners whilst having nightmares, in the belief that they were struggling with monsters, or enemy soldiers during battle. In these situations the defendant may be able to escape liability by relying on the defence of automatism. The defence involves a defendant in providing evidence that at the time of the offence his brain was not controlling his actions. If the defence succeeds it will result in a complete acquittal for the defendant, because he will have shown that the actus reus was not the result of a freely willed act on his part. The defence of automatism is considered in more detail in Chapter 13.

Difficult cases

Although the statement that 'actus reus must be freely willed' is generally correct, there are a small number of cases that are difficult to reconcile with the proposition, because the actus reus involved is 'passive', in that it does not require proof of any action by the defendant.

R *v* Larsonneur

The defendant in *R* v *Larsonneur* (1933) 97 JP 206 was a French national who had entered the United Kingdom lawfully, but was given only limited permission to remain in the country. Her passport stated that she had to leave the United Kingdom on 22 March 1933. On that day the defendant left England, not to return to France, but to travel to the Irish Free State. The Irish authorities made a deportation order against her, and she was forcibly removed from Ireland and returned to the United Kingdom mainland at Holyhead. On arrival at Holyhead the defendant was charged, under the Aliens Order 1920, with 'being found' in the United Kingdom whilst not having permission to enter the country. The defendant was convicted, and appealed on the basis that her return to the United Kingdom had not been of her own free will, in that she had been forcibly taken to Holyhead by the immigration authorities. The Court of Appeal dismissed her appeal on the simple basis that the prosecution had proved the facts necessary for a conviction. On its face the decision does seem somewhat harsh and contrary to the theory that actus reus must be freely willed. The decision could be explained, however, either on the basis that the actus reus consisted of a 'state of affairs' which had to be found to exist, requiring little or no participation by the defendant, or on the basis that although her return to Holyhead was not freely willed, the defendant's travelling to the Irish Free State was, and it was this that lead to her deportation.

Winzar *v* Chief Constable of Kent

The modern counterpart to *Larsonneur* is the decision of the Divisional Court in *Winzar* v *Chief Constable of Kent* (1983) The Times 28 March. The defendant had been admitted to hospital on a stretcher. Upon examination he was found to be drunk and was told to leave. Later he was found in a corridor of the hospital and the police were called to remove him. The police officers took the defendant outside onto the roadway, then placed him in a police car and drove him to the police station where he was charged with 'being found drunk in a public highway'. The defendant was convicted, and appealed on the ground that he had not been on the public road of his own volition. The Divisional Court upheld the conviction holding that all that was required for liability was that the defendant should be perceived to be drunk whilst on a public highway. There was no need for the court to have any regard as to how he came to be there. It is submitted that, as in *Larsonneur*, the voluntary act leading to liability can be found at an earlier stage, in this case the defendant's voluntarily becoming intoxicated.

As Goff LJ observed:

> 'In my judgment, looking at the purpose of this particular offence, it is designed ... to deal with the nuisance which can be caused by persons who are drunk in a public place. This kind of offence is caused quite simply when a person is found drunk in a public place or in a highway ... [A]n example ... illustrates how sensible that conclusion is. Suppose a person was found as being drunk in a restaurant or a place of that kind and was asked to leave. If he was asked to leave, he would walk out of the door of the restaurant and would

be in a public place or in a highway of his own volition. He would be there of his own volition because he had responded to a request. However, if a man in a restaurant made a thorough nuisance of himself, was asked to leave, objected and was ejected, in those circumstances, he would not be in a public place of his own volition because he would have been put there either by a gentleman on the door of the restaurant, or by a police officer, who might have been called to deal with the man in question. It would be nonsense if one were to say that the man who responded to the plea to leave could be said to be found drunk in a public place or in a highway, whereas the man who had been compelled to leave could not.'

2.5 Actus reus alone as the basis for liability

The vast majority of criminal offences require proof of both actus reus and mens rea. There are certain offences however, nearly all of them statutory, where proof of the actus reus alone is sufficient for the imposition of criminal liability. These are generally referred to as offences of strict or 'absolute' liability. One example has already been encountered in this chapter; the offence with which the defendant in *R* v *Larsonneur* was charged did not require proof of any 'guilty mind' on her part, it was sufficient that she was found in the United Kingdom. This matter is dealt with in more detail in Chapter 25.

2.6 The nature of mens rea

As has been outlined above, mens rea is the term used to describe the state of mind that a defendant must be proved to have had at the time he committed the actus reus of an offence.

Why is mens rea necessary?

One might legitimately ask why mens rea should need to be proved. It would be far more straightforward in many ways if all offences were offences of strict liability, with the defendant's state of mind taken into account as a mitigating factor where necessary. If there is a simple answer, it perhaps lies in the fact that the existence of mens rea justifies punishment. With the notable exception of strict liability, the criminal law does not punish a man for his actions alone. The prohibited actions must be accompanied by a culpable state of mind. The mens rea that must be established can be discovered either by looking at past decisions, as in the case of common law offences such as murder, or by looking at the statute which creates the offence, such as the Criminal Damage Act 1971.

Some states of mind are regarded as being more culpable than others. Hence a defendant who deliberately commits a prohibited act should normally be punished more severely than one who recklessly or carelessly commits the same act.

Furthermore, there are some offences for which a defendant can only be punished if his actions can be shown to have been deliberate, recklessness or carelessness not being sufficient (see s18 Offences Against the Person Act 1861). It should be borne in mind that the allocation of a particular type of mens rea to an offence is a matter of judicial and legislative policy, not science. A question to bear in mind, when considering some of the judicial pronouncements on mens rea, is the extent to which the judges have given sufficient weight to the link between mens rea and punishment.

Subjective mens rea/objective mens rea

It is common to find criminal lawyers referring to a type of mens rea as 'objective' or 'subjective'. This jargon can be a little mystifying to the beginner, so a brief explanation is provided here. Subjective mens rea is based on what the defendant himself actually thought. One would ask questions such as: did the defendant foresee a particular consequence? Where subjective mens rea has to be established the jury must, so far as they possibly can, put themselves in the position of the defendant. They are not permitted to come to the conclusion that he had the necessary mens rea because he 'must have known' that something was going to happen. The question is whether he really did know that a particular consequence would occur.

Where the mens rea involved in an offence is objective, the jury can judge the defendant by the standard of the reasonable man. The defendant will be responsible for causing a particular result, such as criminal damage, if the jury members are convinced, beyond all reasonable doubt, that a reasonable person would have foreseen the consequence. In effect, if they themselves would have foreseen it. It should be obvious that it will be far easier for the prosecution to establish an objective type of mens rea than a subjective one. Such an analysis is, of necessity, simplistic. More complex formulations may be possible which are less easy to classify. An intermediate test might be, would a reasonable person, with the characteristics of the defendant, have been aware of the risks created by a particular activity?

Terminology

As has been mentioned above, one of the confusing aspects of any study of mens rea is the profusion of terms used to describe the different states of mind involved. Intention may seem like a straightforward concept, but one has to distinguish between 'purpose' intent and 'foresight' intent, 'direct' intent and 'oblique' intent, 'basic' intent and 'specific' intent. In addition there are states of mind which are not readily explained by the terms used, such as 'wilfully', and 'maliciously'. The various forms of intention and recklessness will be explored in some detail in the remainder of this chapter. Other expressions will be explained as and when they arise in the context of specific offences dealt with in subsequent chapters.

2.7 Intention

Judges are fond of describing intention as a perfectly ordinary English word that needs little in the way of explanation by a trial judge addressing a jury. If this were so, there would be very little case law on the matter. The truth is that the meaning of intention in English criminal law is somewhat unclear at present. One might go so far as to suggest that there is no legal definition of the concept, simply rules as to how juries are to go about the task of divining its existence. What follows is intended as a simple and generalised guide to the issues involved.

'Purpose' type intent

What the layman would readily recognise as intent is frequently referred to by lawyers as 'purpose' type intent. This involves a defendant not only foreseeing that his actions will bring about a particular consequence, but also a desire, or purpose, on his part that this consequence should occur. The typical example is that of the defendant, possibly an assassin, who places a bomb on a plane carrying passengers. He foresees that passengers will be killed and it is his purpose to cause death. There are relatively few offences requiring proof of 'purpose' type intent, possibly because of the heavy evidential burden that it throws onto the prosecution where it has to be established. At common law it was thought that the offence of attempt required this type of intent, but the statutory form of the offence that has supplanted it appears to be made out upon proof of intention based on foresight. See further s1(1) of the Criminal Attempts Act 1981, and *R* v *Walker & Hayles* (1990) 90 Cr App R 226, considered further in Chapter 12.

The House of Lords had an opportunity to consider the meaning of purpose in *Chandler* v *DPP* [1964] AC 763. The appellants, who were demonstrators opposed to nuclear weapons, planned to demonstrate their opposition by occupying an RAF airfield and preventing aircraft from taking off. They were convicted of conspiring to enter a prohibited place for a purpose prejudicial to the interests of the state, contrary to s1 of the Official Secrets Act 1911. The appellants contended that their purpose had not been to prejudice the interests or safety of the state; on the contrary, they believed that the state would be safer without such weapons, and on that basis appealed against the conviction. It was held by the House of Lords, that a distinction had to be drawn between the 'aims' of the appellants and the 'purpose' with which the appellants had acted. The aim of their actions, or the motive behind them, might have been the perfectly laudable one of ridding the country of nuclear weapons, but the Act required evidence of purpose, which their Lordships took to mean 'immediate purpose' not the long term goals of the appellants. It was not disputed that the immediate purpose of the appellants had been to prevent aircraft from taking off; that having been established it was then a matter of evidence, as provided by the government of the day, as to whether such action would have been prejudicial to the interests of the state.

Intention based on proof of foresight

As already noted, to require proof that it was the defendant's purpose to bring about a particular consequence may involve placing a very heavy evidential burden on the prosecution, possibly producing some anomalous results. Take the example of the defendant who insures an aircraft for several million pounds and then plants a time bomb on board, which explodes killing many passengers. It seems sensible enough to say that he intended to kill the passengers, but in what sense is the word 'intended' being used here? If one asks what the defendant's purpose was, the answer must surely be the destruction of the aircraft, in order that he might recover the insurance monies. The defendant might even express the pious hope that he had wanted all the passengers to escape unharmed, as if by some miracle. Again, the response of the layman would be: 'He must have known that passengers were going to be killed', in the sense that the defendant foresaw that passengers would be killed.

Not surprisingly, given the above illustration, criminal law normally only requires proof of 'foresight' intent as opposed to 'purpose' intent. The problem has been in defining foresight, and in establishing the relationship between foresight of consequences and intention. The development of this branch of the law has not been without its complications over the last 30 years. In *DPP* v *Smith* [1961] AC 290, the House of Lords, in considering the meaning of intention, adopted an objective approach to the concept of foresight, holding that a defendant could be presumed to have foreseen the natural and probable consequences of his act. Hence a defendant could be regarded as having intended a consequence if a reasonable person would have foreseen it. Further, in *Hyam* v *DPP* [1975] AC 55, the House of Lords (by a majority), held that foresight on the part of the defendant that his actions were likely, or highly likely, to cause death or grievous bodily harm was sufficient mens rea for murder. Neither decision now accurately reflects the law.

The relationship between foresight and intention

This matter was twice considered by the House of Lords during the 1980s, first in *R* v *Moloney* [1985] 1 All ER 1025, secondly in *R* v *Hancock and Shankland* [1986] 2 WLR 257. It is the latter decision which correctly states the present law. The defendants in *Hancock* were miners taking part in a strike in South Wales. They had taken up position on a bridge over a motorway, knowing that miners who were not willing to come out on strike would be using the road and passing under the bridge. When a taxi carrying a working miner approached, the defendants dropped two large blocks of concrete over the bridge. One of the blocks fell through the windscreen of the car and killed its driver. The defendants were convicted of murdering the taxi driver, the trial judge having given the jury the *Moloney* guidelines on establishing intent. These involved the jury in asking themselves whether death or serious injury was a natural consequence of what the defendants had done, and if it was, whether the defendants had foreseen death or serious harm as a natural consequence. If the answer to both questions was in the affirmative the jury had been directed that it might be entitled to infer from these findings that the defendants intended to kill or cause serious injury, and that they thus had sufficient mens rea for murder. The defendants, who had been willing to plead guilty to manslaughter, appealed on the ground that their intention had been to block the road and frighten other miners into supporting the strike, not to cause death or serious injury. The Court of Appeal quashed the convictions, the Lord Chief Justice expressing considerable doubt as to the correctness of the *Moloney* guidelines. The Crown appealed unsuccessfully to the House of Lords where it was held, Lord Scarman giving the main speech, that the *Moloney* guidelines on the relationship between foresight and intention were unsatisfactory in that they were likely to mislead a jury.

His Lordship expressed the view that in the majority of cases juries should be left to determine for themselves whether a defendant intended a particular consequence, as it was a matter to which they could apply their own common sense. Where, however, a jury requested some guidance from the trial judge, he should explain to them that intention was not to be equated with foresight of consequences, but could be established if there was evidence that the defendant had foreseen a particular consequence. The stronger the evidence that he did foresee a consequence, then the greater the justification for the jury inferring that the defendant therefore intended the consequence. In short, foresight was to be regarded as evidence of intention, not as an alternative form of it, as was suggested in *Hyam* v *DPP* (above). What Lord Scarman deliberately refrains from explaining is just how much foresight is required for a jury to be justified in inferring that the defendant had the necessary intent. Does a defendant intend a consequence where he foresees it as probable, or must he foresee it as highly probable, or almost certain? It does no credit to English criminal law that such a basic concept as the meaning of intention should be shrouded in so much mystery, but in a practical, even cynical, sense, for as long as intention has no fixed meaning in law, there is less likelihood of judges misdirecting juries on the point, and thus creating opportunities for defendants to appeal against their convictions.

In *R* v *Nedrick* (1986) 83 Cr App R 267, the Court of Appeal had an opportunity to consider the effect of the House of Lords' decision in *R* v *Hancock*. The defendant had been convicted of murder following a direction from the trial judge as to the meaning of intention which was based largely on the now discredited decision in *Hyam* v *DPP*. The Court of Appeal quashed the conviction, substituting it with a conviction for manslaughter. The Lord Chief Justice reaffirmed, as he was bound to do, the approach to intention suggested by Lord Scarman in *R* v *Hancock*. His Lordship usefully summarised the position as follows at (p270):

'In *R* v *Hancock* (1986) 82 Cr App R 264, [1986] AC 455, the House decided that the *Moloney* guidelines require a reference to probability. Lord Scarman said at p276 and p473:
"They also require an explanation that the greater the probability of a consequence the more likely it is that the consequence was foreseen and that if that consequence was foreseen the greater the probability is that that consequence was also intended."

When determining whether the defendant had the necessary intent, it may therefore be helpful for a jury to ask themselves two questions:

1. How probable was the consequence which resulted from the defendant's voluntary act?
2. Did he foresee that consequence?

    If he did not appreciate that death or really serious harm was likely to result from his act, he cannot have intended to bring it about. If he did, but thought that the risk to which he was exposing the person killed was only slight, then it may be easy for the jury to conclude that he did not intend to bring about that result. On the other hand, if the jury are satisfied that at the material time the defendant recognised that death or serious harm would be virtually certain (barring some unforeseen intervention) to result from his voluntary act, then that is a fact from which they may find it easy to infer that he intended to kill or do serious bodily harm, even though he may not have had any desire to achieve that result.' [Note the reference to 'virtually certain'.]

Later in the same judgment the Lord Chief Justice returned to the issue (at p271):

'Where the charge is murder and in the rare cases where the simple direction is not enough, the jury should be directed that they are not entitled to infer the necessary intention, unless they feel sure that death or serious bodily harm was a virtual certainty (barring some unforeseen intervention) as a result of the defendant's actions and that the defendant appreciated that such was the case. Where a man realises that it is for all practical purposes inevitable that his actions will result in death or serious harm, the inference may be irresistible that he intended that result, however little he may have desired or wished it to happen. The decision is one for the jury to be reached upon a consideration of all the evidence.'

There seems to be a subtle but significant shift here from the jury being entitled to infer intent from evidence of foresight, to their not being entitled to do so unless the evidence discloses a minimum level of foresight, ie that of virtual certainty. It is submitted that one of the undercurrents in decisions such as *Hancock* was a desire on the part of the House of Lords to leave the concept of intention as a simple matter to be determined by members of a jury applying their common sense to the facts, and not to have it become a matter for complicated and technical judicial directions. The danger in introducing a test such as 'virtual certainty' is that any departure from the precise wording is likely to create uncertainty and possibly further appeals. This is illustrated to some extent in *R v Walker & Hayles* (above). The appellants had been charged with attempted murder, having carried out a violent attack upon a victim, which involved dropping him from a third floor balcony to the ground. The jury were directed that they could convict if they were sure that the appellants intended to kill the victim, in the sense that they were sure that the appellants knew that there was a 'very high degree of probability' that the victim would be killed. In dismissing their appeals, the Court of Appeal rejected the contention that a judge directing a jury on intention to kill had to keep rigidly to the *Nedrick* formula. As Lloyd LJ commented (at p233):

'[W]e are not persuaded that it is only when death is a virtual certainty that the jury can infer intention to kill.

    Providing the dividing line between intention and recklessness is never blurred, and provided it is made clear, as it was here, that it is a question for the jury to infer from the degree of probability in the particular case whether the defendant intended to kill, we would not regard the use of the words "very high degree of probability" as a misdirection.

To avoid any misunderstanding, we repeat that in the great majority of cases of attempted murder, as in murder, the simple direction will suffice, without any reference to foresight. In the rare case where an expanded direction is required in terms of foresight, courts should continue to use virtual certainty as the test, rather than high probability.'

The nature of foresight

It can be seen from the above that evidence of foresight is fundamental to the proof of intention on the part of the defendant. It is therefore crucial that a jury understands how the existence of such foresight is to be ascertained. In *DPP* v *Smith* (above) the House of Lords held that foresight was an objective concept in that a defendant could be presumed to have foreseen a consequence if the reasonable person would have done. This decision was subject to much criticism, but it was not until Parliament enacted s8 of the Criminal Justice Act 1967 that the law was amended. Section 8 provides :

'A court or jury in determining whether a person has committed an offence,
(a) shall not be bound in law to infer that he intended or foresaw a result of his actions by reason only of its being a natural and probable consequence of those actions; but
(b) shall decide whether he did intend or foresee that result by reference to all the evidence, drawing such inferences from the evidence as appear proper in the circumstances.'

Note that the section does not say when foresight is relevant, that is an issue to be determined by looking at the nature of the mens rea required by the specific offence under consideration.

Specific and basic intent

In simple terms, basic intent is the mens rea that relates to the actus reus committed by the defendant. For example, in the 'simple' offence of criminal damage, the actus reus comprises the damage or destruction of another's property; the mens rea need not go beyond an intention to do criminal damage. An offence of specific intent is one where the mens rea goes beyond the actus reus in the sense that the defendant has some ulterior purpose in mind. An example is provided by the offence of 'aggravated' criminal damage. This offence is committed where a defendant causes damage or destruction to property with the intention of thereby endangering life. The actus reus, it will be noted, is almost identical to that of the simple offence, the differentiating factor is the further or specific intent that the defendant must possess, to endanger life. This issue is considered in more depth in the context of intoxication in Chapter 13.

Reform

Clause 18 of the draft code proposed a definition of intent encompassing the situations where the defendant hoped or knew that a circumstance existed or would exist, or where he acted to bring about a result or was aware that it would occur as a result of his actions in the ordinary course of events.

Despite the evidence that the senior judiciary did not favour a settled definition for intention, as indicated by comments in both *R* v *Moloney*, and *R* v *Hancock and Shankland*, the Law Commission, in the Code Report, sought to justify the position taken by asserting:

> 'We remain of the opinion that it is in the interest of clarity and the consistent application of criminal law to define intention; and that justice requires the inclusion of the case where the defendant knows that his act will cause the relevant result, "in the ordinary course of events" ... It is possible that, under the Code, juries will, in a few cases, find intention to be proved where, under the existing law, they might not have done so.' [para 8.16]

The basis provided by clause 18 of the draft code has been exploited by the Law Commission in Law Com No 218, with the result that clause 1(a) of the DCLB provides that a defendant acts 'intentionally' with respect to a result when:

> '(i) it is his purpose to cause it, or
> (ii) although it is not his purpose to cause it, he knows that it would occur in the ordinary course of events if he were to succeed in his purpose of causing some other result ...'

The commentary in Law Com No 218 envisages that the vast majority of cases where intent has to be proved will fall within 1(a)(i), but accepts that it is the formulation of intent in 1(a)(ii) that is likely to attract most academic discussion. The use of the phrase 'in the ordinary course of events' was to ensure that the proposed definition of intention covered the defendant who knows that the achievement of his purpose will *necessarily* involve the causing of some further event in the absence of some wholly unforeseeable supervening event. The preference for the requirement that the defendant should have to know of the risk of the result occurring, rather than merely be aware of the risk, is designed to prevent any possible overlap between recklessness and intent. The definition treats the defendant as intending a consequence if he knows that it is a necessary concomitant of achieving his main purpose if that purpose is to be achieved. For example, the terrorist cannot be sure that his bomb will go off, but he knows that it must if he is to achieve the destruction of the police station where he has planted it. Clause 1(a)(ii) also excludes the possibility of liability where it is the defendant's intention to avoid harm. Law Com No 218 (para 7.13) gives the example of a father throwing his child from a blazing building to avoid certain death, in the knowledge that the child will be injured on hitting the ground. As the commentary explains:

> 'In the example ... the father ... has as his purpose to prevent injury to the child. He acts to achieve that purpose, however difficult or unlikely that may be in the circumstances. If, applying clause 1(a)(ii), he were to succeed in his purpose, injury to the child would, of necessity and by definition, not occur. Clause 1(a)(ii) therefore excludes any suggestion that in a (hypothetical) case [such as in the example given] injuries that in fact occur, though sought to be avoided, were inflicted intentionally.'

2.8 Recklessness

Perhaps the majority of significant offences in criminal law require proof of either intention or recklessness on the part of the defendant. The result is that the prosecution can secure a conviction for an offence without going as far as proving that the defendant intended to commit it, recklessness being sufficient. Central to the concept of recklessness is the fact that the defendant is, in reality, being punished for taking an unjustified risk. Clearly many human activities involve risk of injury to person or property, but a distinction is drawn between those that have some social utility and those that do not. Hence the brain surgeon performing a delicate operation is taking the risk that the patient might not survive the operation, but the risk here would normally be regarded as justifiable on the basis that there is a high degree of social utility associated with it. By contrast, the vandal throwing a brick over a high wall is taking the risk that there may be a person on the other side who may be injured, or some property that may be damaged. His actions would be labelled as reckless in the sense that they have no apparent social utility.

Subjective recklessness

If it is accepted that recklessness is concerned with the taking of unjustifiable risks, the second issue that arises is the basis upon which liability for recklessness is to be imposed. Should a defendant have to be aware of the risk that he is taking, or should it be sufficient that a reasonable man would have realised that the risk involved was obvious?

Until the House of Lords' decision in *Commissioner of the Police for the Metropolis* v *Caldwell* (considered below), recklessness was widely understood to be a subjective concept, based on what the defendant foresaw. The leading modern authority was the decision of the Court of Appeal in *R* v *Cunningham* [1957] 2 QB 396. The defendant had entered the basement of a building and ripped a gas meter from the wall in order to remove the money that it contained. In his efforts the defendant ruptured the gas supply pipes with the result that gas escaped and seeped through the porous basement wall into an adjoining property, which was occupied. He was convicted of maliciously administering a noxious substance, contrary to s23 of the Offences Against the Person Act 1861, following a direction from the trial judge that the jury were to convict if they were satisfied that the defendant's action had been 'wicked'. The Court of Appeal, allowing the defendant's appeal, held that for a defendant to have acted 'maliciously' as was required by this offence, there had to be proof that he had intended to cause the harm in question, or had been reckless as to whether such harm would be caused. In this context recklessness involved the defendant in being aware of the risk that his actions might cause the prohibited consequence.

Objective recklessness

In *Commissioner of the Police for the Metropolis* v *Caldwell* [1982] AC 341 a majority of Law Lords endorsed the introduction of a new form of recklessness into English criminal law – a recklessness based not simply on the defendant's foresight of a risk, but one that encompassed also his failure to consider a risk that would have been obvious to the reasonable man. In *Commissioner of the Police for the Metropolis* v *Caldwell*, the defendant, who had been sacked from his employment at a hotel, became drunk and returned at night to the hotel, setting it on fire. There were ten people resident in the hotel at the time, but the fire was discovered and extinguished before any serious harm could be caused. The defendant pleaded guilty to a charge under s1(1) of the Criminal Damage Act 1971, but pleaded not guilty to the more serious charge under s1(2) of the 1971 Act, which alleged criminal damage with intent to endanger life or recklessness as to whether life would be endangered. His contention was that due to his drunken state it had never crossed his mind that lives might be endangered by his actions, he had simply set fire to the hotel because of his grudge against his former employer. On appeal, one of the questions certified for consideration by the House of Lords was that of whether or not the defendant had been reckless as to whether the life of another would be endangered, within the meaning of s1(2)(b) of the 1971 Act. The House of Lords held, inter alia (Lords Wilberforce and Edmund-Davies dissenting), that a defendant was to be regarded as reckless where he created an obvious risk of a particular type of harm occurring, and either went on to take that risk, or failed to give any thought to its existence.

The House of Lords in this case did not overrule *Cunningham*; far from it – the speeches of the majority re-affirm its existence as a form of recklessness in criminal law. The significance of the decision is the introduction of an alternative form of recklessness based upon the defendant's failure to advert to a risk that would have been obvious to the reasonable person. How did Lord Diplock (who gave the leading speech on behalf of the majority) justify this extension of liability? His Lordship noted that the *Cunningham* definition of recklessness had come about in the course of attempting to define the term 'maliciously' as it appeared in the Offences Against the Person Act 1861. He felt that in that particular context the form of recklessness identified by the courts would of necessity have to be somewhat restricted, requiring some reference to the foresight of consequences on the part of the accused. He further noted, however, that the Criminal Damage Act 1971 had replaced the Malicious Damage Act of 1861, and that Parliament had chosen to use the word 'reckless' to denote the mens rea rather than 'maliciously'. In Lord Diplock's view this lead to the conclusion that *Cunningham* was not an appropriate authority for use in the interpretation of recklessness as used in the context of a modern statute. As he expressed it, the restricted meaning given to recklessness in *Cunningham*:

> '... was not directed to and consequently has no bearing on the meaning of the adjective "reckless" in section 1 of the Criminal Damage Act 1971. To use it for that purpose can, in my view, only be misleading.'

Lord Diplock concluded by summarising his view in the following terms:

'In my opinion, a person charged with an offence under section 1(1) of the Criminal Damage Act 1971 is "reckless as to whether any such property would be destroyed or damaged" if (1) he does an act which in fact creates an obvious risk that property will be destroyed or damaged and (2) when he does the act he either has not given any thought to the possibility of there being any such risk or has recognised that there was some risk involved and has nonetheless gone on to do it. That would be a proper direction to the jury; cases in the Court of Appeal which held otherwise should be regarded as overruled.'

Lord Diplock firmly rejected the use of 'jargon' such as 'objective' or 'subjective' to describe the type of mens rea involved, stating that mens rea must by definition be the state of mind of the accused as opposed to the state of mind of some mythical reasonable man, but subsequent cases have emphasised the objective nature of what has come to be known as *Caldwell* recklessness.

In *R* v *Lawrence* [1981] 2 WLR 524, where the defendant motor cyclist, who had collided with and killed a pedestrian, was charged with causing death by reckless driving contrary to s1 of the Road Traffic Act 1972, Lord Diplock stated that:

'Recklessness on the part of the doer of an act does presuppose that there is something in the circumstances that would have drawn the attention of an ordinary prudent individual to the possibility that his act was capable of causing the kind of serious harmful consequences that the section which creates the offence was intended to prevent ...'

Despite Lord Diplock's protestations to the contrary it is submitted that this points clearly to an objective basis for liability. Once a risk that would have been obvious to a reasonable man is shown to have existed, all that is needed is evidence that the defendant never thought about it. It is almost as if omitting to think has been elevated to the status of mens rea. Such criticisms have not gone unanswered by the House of Lords. In *R* v *Reid* [1992] 3 All ER 673, where their lordships confirmed their support for Lord Diplock's view of recklessness as illustrated in *R* v *Lawrence*, with reference to the debate as to the subjective/objective nature of the mens rea involved, Lord Keith stated (p674 h–j):

'Absence of something from a person's state of mind is as much part of his state of mind as is its presence. Inadvertence to risk is no less a subjective state of mind than is disregard of a recognised risk.'

This decision also gave the House of Lords the opportunity to assess the alleged inconsistency in Lord Diplock's dictum to the effect that inadvertent recklessness required awareness of an obvious and serious risk, whilst advertent recklessness required evidence that the driver had failed to think about 'some' risk. Rejecting the contention that any such anomaly existed, Lord Keith stated (p675 h–j):

'"Any such risk" is not referring to obvious and serious risk but merely to the risk of causing physical injury or substantial damage to property. "Some risk" means some risk of the same thing. There is thus no inconsistency.'

Lord Goff, whilst agreeing with this analysis, went on to add (at p691j):

'... Lord Diplock's requirement that the risk be obvious must logically relate only to his first category of recklessness; it cannot be relevant where the defendant is in fact aware that there is some risk of the relevant kind.'

If one accepts that there is at least some sound public policy basis for punishing a 'thoughtless' defendant, does this extend to punishing a defendant to whom the risk of harm could never have occurred? The question arose for consideration in *Elliot* v *C* [1983] 1 WLR 939. The defendant, an educationally subnormal 14-year-old schoolgirl, had entered a neighbour's garden shed, poured white spirit on the floor and ignited it. The defendant had then fled as the shed burst into flames. The magistrates dismissed a charge under s1(1) of the Criminal Damage Act 1971, on the basis that the defendant would not have been aware of the risk of damage to property even if she had given thought to the matter. The prosecution appealed by way of case stated to the Divisional Court where it was held, allowing the appeal, that there was no room for importing a subjective element into the definition of recklessness propounded by Lord Diplock in *Caldwell* and *Lawrence*. Robert Goff LJ acknowledged the obvious unfairness in judging someone such as the defendant by the standard of the reasonable adult, but felt constrained to follow the House of Lords' decisions. The House of Lords subsequently refused a petition for leave to appeal, and the decision was subsequently confirmed by the Court of Appeal in *R* v *Stephen Malcom R* (1984) 79 Cr App R 334, and more recently in *R* v *Coles* [1994] Crim LR 820 (see chapter 26, section 26.1, for further details). There might still be a case for arguing that an exception could be made in the case of an educationally sub-normal defendant, on the basis of views expressed by Lord Goff in *R* v *Reid* (below), to the effect that a defendant might not be regarded as reckless where his ability to appreciate risk was adversely affected by illness, although it is conceded that in *Coles* there was little evidence to justify such a conclusion.

A middle way?

In Smith and Hogan's *Criminal Law* (6th ed) p66, the authors suggested that a defendant might escape a finding that he was reckless, if he should establish that he considered whether there was a risk of harm and decided either that there was none, or that it was so negligible that the reasonable person would have confidently ignored it. The contention is that such a defendant is not *Cunningham* reckless because he does not think that he is taking a risk, yet neither is he *Caldwell* reckless because, far from having given no thought to the risk, he has given considerable thought to it, albeit coming to the wrong conclusion as to its significance. The argument has been considered on a number of occasions by the courts. In *Chief Constable of Avon and Somerset* v *Shimmen* (1987) 84 Cr App R 7, the defendant had broken a shop window whilst demonstrating his martial arts skills to his friends. He had made as if to kick at the shop window intending to stop with his foot a fraction away from the glass, thus displaying his self-control. Confirming his liability on a charge of criminal damage, the Divisional Court held that, whilst on the facts there was evidence that the defendant had been reckless in that he had been aware of the risk of damage to the window, there was at least scope for the argument that a defendant might not be reckless where he genuinely believed he had taken sufficient precautions to preclude harm from occurring. See further *R* v *Crossman* [1986] Crim LR 406 where the lacuna was not considered but perhaps should have been. The matter has since been addressed by the House of Lords in *R* v *Reid* (above). The appellant was driving a car with a passenger in the front seat. He attempted to overtake another car whilst still in the nearside lane. A taxi drivers' rest hut protruded some 6 feet into the nearside lane. The appellant's car struck this hut whilst he was attempting the overtaking manoeuvre, the collision resulting in the death of his passenger. The appellant was convicted of causing death by reckless driving, contrary to s1 of the Road Traffic Act 1972 (as amended by the Road Traffic Act 1988).

Their Lordships recognised that there were three situations where the exact form of words used by Lord Diplock may require some alteration to take account of the unusual facts of a particular case. First, where the driver acted under some understandable or excusable mistake of fact. Lord Ackner appeared to accept counsel for the Crown's example of such a case where the driver of a left hand drive car overtaking on the brow of a hill is misinformed as to the safety of doing so by his passenger. His Lordship added an example of his own where the driver of a powerful car attempts an apparently safe manoeuvre that becomes dangerous because of a wholly unexpected fuel line blockage. Lord Goff accepted that:

'... if the defendant is addressing his mind to the possibility of risk and suffers from a bona fide mistake as to specific fact which if true would have excluded the risk, he cannot be described as reckless.'

Secondly, where the driver's capacity to appreciate risk had been adversely affected by some condition ('illness or shock' per Lord Goff at p690 h–j) arising otherwise than through the fault of the driver. Thirdly, where the driver acted under duress.

These examples would seem to involve at least some acceptance of the so-called 'lacuna' in the *Caldwell* tests for recklessness.

Cunningham *or* Caldwell *recklessness?*

A situation now exists whereby there are two distinct concepts of recklessness in criminal law: what might be broadly termed subjective, or *Cunningham* recklessness; and (with all due respect to Lord Diplock) what might be termed objective, or *Caldwell* recklessness. Will proof of either justify a conviction wherever the mens rea of a crime is satisfied by proof of recklessness? It is obvious from the above that *Caldwell* recklessness is sufficient in respect of criminal damage and was sufficient for causing death by reckless driving (now replaced with causing death by dangerous driving: Road Traffic Act 1991). In *R* v *Seymour* [1983] 2 AC 493, Lord Roskill expressed the view that *Caldwell* recklessness should be applied by the courts wherever the mens rea of the offence required proof of recklessness, unless Parliament had expressly ordained otherwise, and in the course of that decision *Caldwell* was applied to the common law offence of manslaughter (see Chapter 8). It is submitted, however, that Lord Roskill's obiter statement may constitute a somewhat sweeping generalisation. In *R v Satnam*; *R v Kewal* (1983) 78 Cr App R 149, the Court of Appeal expressly rejected the application of *Caldwell* recklessness to the offence of rape, Bristow J stating that *Caldwell* and *Lawrence* were concerned with recklessness in different contexts under different statutes.

Similarly in *W (A Minor)* v *Dolbey* [1983] Crim LR 681, the Divisional Court held that the recklessness involved in the offence of malicious wounding under s20 of the Offences Against the Person Act 1861, was *Cunningham* recklessness. Robert Goff LJ expressed the view that nothing said by Lord Diplock in *Caldwell* was intended to have any impact on the interpretation of the word 'malicious' under the 1861 Act. This view was endorsed by the House of Lords in *R v Parmenter* [1991] 3 WLR 914, where it was also confirmed that '*Cunningham*' recklessness applied to assault.

It is further submitted that *Caldwell* recklessness would have no application to offences of fraud or deception. Some support for this is provided by the decision of the Divisional Court in *Large* v *Mainprize* [1989] Crim LR 213. The respondent, a fisherman required by statute to furnish details of the size of his catch, had understated the quantity of a catch by some 50 per cent. He claimed that this was the result of an error in the use of his calculator. He was charged with recklessly furnishing false information as to his catch, contrary to reg 3(2) of the Sea Fishing (Enforcement of Community Control Measures) Regulations 1985. The justices dismissed the information against him and the prosecutor appealed unsuccessfully from this decision. The Divisional Court expressed the view that recklessness, in the context of the offence under consideration, required evidence of some conscious indifference to truth or falsity, or foresight of consequences without desire for them, but with either indifference, or willingness to run the risk. The court concluded that the justices had been entitled to find that the defendant had merely been guilty of a simple error, ie he had given no thought to the possibility of his statement being false.

In conclusion, therefore, the scope for the application of *Caldwell* is severely limited. At present it applies to criminal damage and reckless manslaughter only. What of the future? In *R v Reid* the House of Lords was happy to reaffirm Lord Diplock's approach to recklessness in relation to causing death by reckless driving, but it should be borne in mind that this aspect of the case is somewhat academic given that the offence no longer exists. Does the decision supply support for continued application of *Caldwell* in its current form? It is not without significance that Lord Browne-Wilkinson observed (at p694 a–d):

> 'My first comment is that, in the absence of a general statutory definition of the word "reckless", I do not accept that the constituent elements of recklessness must be the same in all statutes. In particular the following factors may lead to the word being given different meanings in different statutes. First, the history of the legislation. Lord Goff has demonstrated the statutory derivation of the phrase "driving recklessly" in the road traffic

legislation. That history is markedly different from that of s1 of the Criminal Damage Act 1971 which was under consideration in *R* v *Caldwell* [1981] 1 All ER 961, [1982] AC 341. Second, the statutory provision (as in s1 of the Criminal Damage Act 1971) may require proof of recklessness as to a special consequence or, as in the present case, the word may be used on its own simply as a description of the prohibited act. It is not apparent to me that these two different uses of the word necessarily postulate the same ingredients in the mens rea of the offence. Third, the single word "recklessness" may be used as in the Road Traffic Act, to describe both the nature of the actus reus – the type of driving – and also the mental state of the defendant in driving in that manner. This is to be contrasted with cases such as those under the Criminal Damage Act 1971, where the word is directed only to the mental state of the accused not to the act itself. Finally, the word 'reckless' may be used in relation to the doing of one or more isolated acts, as in the Criminal Damage Act 1971, or as in the present case in relation to a continuous course of action (driving) which is part of life for nearly everybody and which, although capable of being done safely, is inherently dangerous. For these reasons, I propose to deal with the decision in *R* v *Lawrence* alone and, despite the close link between the two cases, express no view on the decision in *R* v *Caldwell*.'

Reform

Clause 1(b) of the DCLB proposes that a defendant acts recklessly with respect to:

1. a circumstance when he is aware of a risk that it exists or will exist;
2. a result when he is aware of a risk that it will occur;

and it is unreasonable, having regard to the circumstances known to him, to take that risk.

Save for minor modifications this is effectively the definition proposed in the draft code. As the Code Report observed:

'The modern English criminal law tradition tends to require a positive state of mind with respect to the various external elements of an offence of any seriousness ... [A]lthough this "subjectivist" tradition is not without its critics, we are proposing a Code that stays within the mainstream of English criminal law. But in doing so we do not exclude the possibility that Parliament may hereafter wish to create offences constructed upon a different foundation of liability. The group of House of Lords' cases led by *R* v *Caldwell* [above] can, indeed, be interpreted as having placed some serious offences upon such a different foundation. It will, of course, be open to Parliament to pursue the line followed by those cases by rejecting or modifying the fault requirements proposed for particular offences by providing further key terms to supplement [those] ... that we have defined.' [Vol II para 8.20]

Presumably the defendant who considers a risk, but discounts it as unlikely to materialise, such as the driver of the left hand drive car referred to by Lord Ackner in *Reid*, would not be reckless under clause 1(b) on the basis that, having regard to the circumstances known to him, it was not unreasonable to overtake on the brow of the hill.

It is interesting to note that the Code Team's draft of 1985 included a fault element referred to as 'heedlessness' which equated to the objective form of

recklessness expounded in *R* v *Caldwell*. Of its non-appearance in the draft code bill
the Code Report states:

> 'We have not found occasion to use that expression in the definitions of offences in Part II of
> our Bill ... but it remains available if there should prove to be a use for it.' [Vol II para 8.21]

2.9 Negligence

Negligence, in the sense that the defendant falls below the standard to be expected
of the reasonable man, is clearly sufficient to justify liability in civil law. Whether it
should also constitute the fault element for a criminal offence is more questionable.
In a civil matter the defendant may suffer financially, but there is no question of his
being imprisoned, or acquiring a criminal record in respect his negligence. In
criminal proceedings such consequences are possible, and the criticisms levelled at
the imposition of strict liability, to the effect that a criminal conviction should not
be possible in the absence of fault, can to a limited extent be applied to the
imposition of criminal liability on the basis of negligence. Unlike strict liability
offences, however, negligence has been used as the basis for serious offences, such as
manslaughter. Despite the decision in *Kong Cheuk Kwan* v *R* (1985) 82 Cr App R
18, where Lord Roskill, on behalf of the Privy Council expressly approved of the
obiter statement of Watkins LJ (delivering the judgment of the Court of Appeal in
Seymour (1983) 76 Cr App R 211, to the effect that:

> '... [the court is] ... of the view that it is no longer necessary or helpful to make reference
> to compensation and negligence ...'

the Court of Appeal in *R* v *Prentice* [1993] 3 WLR 927, has confirmed that liability
for killing by gross negligence still exists at common law; see further Chapter 8.

2.10 Transferred malice

Under the doctrine of transferred malice, where a defendant fires a gun intending to
kill X, but misses and instead kills Y, he will not be able to escape liability for the
murder of Y simply because it was his intention to kill X. The defendant has still
committed the actus reus that he intended, namely to cause the death of a human
being. It might be said that the malice against X can be transferred to Y. The basis
for this principle is the decision of the Court for Crown Cases Reserved in *R* v
Latimer (1886) 17 QBD 359, in which the defendant struck a blow with his belt at
Horace Chapple which glanced off him, severely injuring an innocent bystander,
Ellen Rolston. The defendant was convicted of maliciously wounding the woman,
and appealed on the ground that it had never been his intention to hurt her. The
court held that the conviction would be affirmed. The defendant had committed the
actus reus of the offence with the necessary mens rea, ie he had acted maliciously.

There was no requirement in the relevant act that his mens rea should relate to a named victim. This is to be compared with the earlier decision of the same court in *R v Pembliton* (1874) LR 2 CCR 119, where the defendant threw a stone at another person during an argument. The stone missed the intended victim, but instead broke a nearby window. He was charged with malicious damage to property, and although the jury found as a special fact that he had not intended to break the window, he was convicted. The court, in quashing the conviction, held that the doctrine of transferred malice was inapplicable where the defendant's intention had not been to cause the type of harm that actually materialised. His intention to assault another person could not be used as the mens rea for the damage that he had caused to the window.

Reform

Clause 32 of the DCLB provides:

'(1) In determining whether a person is guilty of an offence, his intention to cause, or his awareness of a risk that he will cause, a result in relation to a person or thing capable of being the victim or subject-matter of the offence shall be treated as an intention to cause or, as the case may be, an awareness of the risk that he will cause, that result in relation to any other person or thing affected by his conduct.

(2) Any defence on which a person might have relied on a charge of an offence in relation to a person or thing within his contemplation is open to him on a charge of the same offence in relation to a person or thing not within his contemplation.'

Save for the necessary amendment in relation to recklessness, clause 32 effectively replicates the original proposal in clause 24 of the draft code.

The explanation provided in Law Com No 218 for the provision of a general statement on transferred fault states:

'Where a person intends to affect one person or thing (X) and actually affects another (Y), he may be charged with an offence of attempt in relation to X; or it may be possible to satisfy a court or jury that he was reckless with respect to Y. But an attempt charge may be impossible (where it is not known until trial that the defendant claims to have had X and not Y in contemplation); or inappropriate (as not describing the harm done adequately for labelling or sentencing purposes). Moreover, recklessness with respect to Y may be insufficient to establish the offence or incapable of being proved. The rule stated by [clause 32] overcomes these difficulties.' [para 42.1]

2.11 Coincidence of mens rea and actus reus

It is a general principle in criminal law that for liability to be established it must be shown that the defendant possessed the necessary mens rea at the time the actus reus was committed. For example, D sets off in his car to visit P at his house intending to stab him to death and on the way accidentally runs over and kills a pedestrian who steps into the road without looking. D cannot be charged with murder when he subsequently discovers that the pedestrian he has accidentally killed is in fact P. D had the necessary mens rea when he set out on his journey, and committed the actus reus of murder when he ran P over, killing him. There was, however, no coincidence of the two. At the time of the accident D was not driving his car intending to kill another human being.

Whilst the principle is clearly correct, a strict application of it can produce difficulties for the prosecution as illustrated by the Privy Council decision in *Thabo Meli v R* [1954] 1 WLR 228. The defendants had taken their intended victim to a hut and plied him with drink so that he became intoxicated; they then hit the victim around the head, intending to kill him. In fact the defendants only succeeded in knocking him unconscious, but believing the victim to be dead, they threw his body over a cliff. The victim died of exposure some time later. The defendants were convicted of murder, and appealed to the Privy Council on the ground that there had been no coincidence of the mens rea and actus reus of murder, in the sense that when they had acted with the intention of killing the victim by striking him on the head, they had failed to kill him. On the other hand, when they did actually cause his death, by throwing him over the cliff, they lacked the mens rea for murder as they believed he was already dead. The Privy Council held that the correct view of what the defendants had done was to treat the chain of events as a continuing actus reus. The actus reus of causing death started with the victim being struck on the head and continued until he died of exposure. It was sufficient for the prosecution to establish that at some time during that chain of events the defendants had acted with the requisite mens rea for murder. See also on this point *R v Church* [1966] 1 QB 59.

It is perhaps more realistic to regard the 'coincidence' rule as but an aspect of the wider principles of causation. In both *Thabo Meli* and *Church* the courts were in effect expressing the view that nothing done by the defendants broke the chain of causation between the first violent act and the victim's death. As Smith and Hogan point out in *Criminal Law*, 7th ed (1992), p339, the matter would be otherwise if, for example D, having wounded P, visited him in hospital and accidentally infected him with smallpox causing his death. In such a case liability for the death could not be traced back to the original unlawfully inflicted injury.

It would appear that the defendant's actions will be regarded as falling within the same series of events even where there is a considerable gap in time between the original injury and the act causing death. In *R v Le Brun* [1991] 3 WLR 653, the defendant had punched his wife on the chin and later caused her death when attempting to move her body. Lord Lane CJ commented:

'It seems to us that where the unlawful application of force and the eventual act causing death are part of the same sequence of events, the same transaction, the fact that there is an appreciable interval of time between the two does not serve to exonerate the defendant from liability. That is certainly so where the appellant's subsequent actions which caused death, after the initial unlawful blow, are designed to conceal his commission of the original unlawful assault ... [T]he original unlawful blow to the chin was a causa sine qua non of the later actus reus. It was the opening event in a series which was to culminate in death: the first link in the chain of causation, to use another metaphor. It cannot be said that the actions of the appellant in dragging the victim away with the intention of evading liability broke the chain which linked the initial blow with the death.'

3

Criminal Damage

3.1 Introduction

3.2 The basic offence

3.3 Actus reus

3.4 Mens rea

3.5 The 'aggravated' offence

3.6 'Without lawful excuse'

3.1 Introduction

The Criminal Damage Act 1971 was introduced to replace the old complex law relating to damage and destruction of property based on the Malicious Damage Act 1861. The 1971 Act creates two different types of liability for criminal damage; s1(1) creates the 'basic' or 'simple' offence of damaging/destroying property belonging to another, s1(2) creates the aggravated offence of damaging or destroying property with either intention to endanger life, or recklessness as to whether life is endangered. Under s1(3) the offence committed by destroying or damaging property by fire should be charged as arson. The need to maintain a clear distinction between criminal damage caused by fire and criminal damage otherwise caused is signified by s4(1) which provides for a higher penalty in the case of arson: see *R v Cooper (G) and Cooper (Y)* [1991] Crim LR 524.

It should be noted that, to some extent, the offence of criminal damage complements the offence of theft. Indeed some situations may give rise to the possibility of charging a defendant with either theft or criminal damage, eg where D takes P's car and destroys it by driving it into a brick wall.

Section 2 of the 1971 Act creates the offence of making threats to damage or destroy another's property, intending to cause fear thereby, or making threats to damage his own property in a way which he knows is likely to endanger life, again intending to cause fear as a result.

Section 3 makes it an offence for any person, without lawful excuse, to have in his control anything he intends to use to damage another's property, or which he intends to use to damage his own property in a way which he knows is likely to endanger life.

Conviction for offences under the Act carries the possibility of ten years imprisonment, with the exception of ss1(2) and 1(3) where the maximum sentence available is life imprisonment. Section 46 of the Criminal Justice and Public Order Act 1994 amends s22(1) of the Magistrates' Courts Act 1980 with the effect that magistrates can try summarily any criminal damage case where the value involved does not exceed £5,000 (an increase from £2,000).

3.2 The basic offence

Section 1(1) of the Criminal Damage Act 1971 provides:

'A person who without lawful excuse destroys or damages any property belonging to another intending to destroy or damage any such property or being reckless as to whether any such property would be destroyed or damaged shall be guilty of an offence.'

3.3 Actus reus

'Property'

The basic definition of property, for the purposes of this offence, is provided by s10(1) of the Act which states:

'In this Act "property" means property of a tangible nature, whether real or personal, including money and:
a) including wild creatures which have been tamed or are ordinarily kept in captivity, and any other wild creatures or their carcasses if, but only if, they have been reduced into possession which has not been lost or abandoned or are in the course of being reduced into possession; but
b) not including mushrooms growing wild on any land or flowers, fruit or foliage of a plant growing wild on any land.
For the purposes of this subsection "mushroom" includes any fungus and "plant" includes any shrub or tree.'

Similarities with the definition of property provided by s4 of the Theft Act 1968 are evident, except that criminal damage may be committed in relation to land, whilst land cannot be stolen; conversely intangible property can be stolen, but cannot be the subject of a criminal damage charge.

Whilst a computer programme might not be regarded as tangible property, the material on which the programme is stored certainly will be. In *Cox* v *Riley* [1986] Crim LR 460, the Divisional Court held that a defendant who had damaged a plastic circuit card used to operate a computerised saw so that the card would require reprogramming before it could be used, had damaged tangible property within the scope of s10(1).

This decision has been followed by *R* v *Whiteley* (1991) 93 Cr App R 25, a case in which the appellant gained unauthorised access to a computer network, the Joint Academic Network (JANET), and proceeded to create and delete files, change the passwords of authorised users, and delete the user file to remove evidence of his own use of the system. In seeking to have his convictions for criminal damage quashed the appellant had contended that the magnetic disks on which the system's files were stored had not themselves been damaged by his activities, hence the only damage was to the information stored on the disks, and this fell outside the scope of the offence as it was intangible property. The Court of Appeal rejected this argument, holding that the magnetic disks on which files were stored were clearly tangible property, and by deleting files, the appellant had interfered with the configuration of magnetic particles on the disks. Lord Lane CJ pointed out that it was wrong to conclude that, because the offence of criminal damage required interference with tangible property, the damage itself had to be tangible, in the sense that it had to be observable to the naked eye, or perceptible by touch. Any alteration to the physical nature of the property would suffice. It is interesting to note that the jury acquitted the appellant in respect of the prosecution's other allegations of criminal damage, which had been based on the premise that the appellant had damaged the computer system itself as his activities caused it to be shut down for long periods whilst the effects of his interference were rectified.

In its report, *Computer Misuse* (Cm 189), the Law Commission recommended the introduction of a new offence specifically to deal with the problems of computer misuse. The need for such legislation was further emphasised by the prosecution's failure to sustain charges under the Forgery and Counterfeiting Act 1981 against computer hackers: see *R* v *Gold*; *R* v *Schifreen* [1988] AC 1063. The result of this pressure for reform was the Computer Misuse Act 1990 which creates, inter alia, three new offences, namely: 'unauthorised access to computer material (s1)'; 'unauthorised access with intent to commit or facilitate commission of further offences' (s2); and 'unauthorised modification of computer equipment' (s3). In this respect it is interesting to note that s3(6) of the 1990 Act provides that:

> 'For the purposes of the Criminal Damage Act 1971 a modification of the contents of a computer shall not be regarded as damaging any computer or computer storage medium unless its effects on that computer or computer orage medium impairs its physical condition.'

On the basis of this provision, it is submitted that were the circumstances in *Cox* v *Riley* and *R* v *Whiteley* to re-occur, neither defendant would be guilty of criminal damage. The offence under s3 of the 1990 Act carries up to five years imprisonment. For an illustration of the 1990 Act's potential usefulness in providing ancillary offences, see *Attorney-General's Reference (No 1 of 1991)* [1992] 3 WLR 432.

'Belonging to another'

Section 10(2) provides the basic definition of belonging to another. It states:

> 'Property shall be treated for the purposes of this Act as belonging to any person:
> a) having the custody or control of it;
> b) having in it any proprietary right or interest (not being an equitable interest arising only from an agreement to transfer or grant an interest); or
> c) having a charge on it.'

Section 10(3) provides that where property is 'subject to a trust, the persons to whom it belongs will be taken to include any person having a right to enforce the trust'. Section 10(4) provides that the property of a corporation sole shall be treated as belonging to the corporation, notwithstanding a vacancy in the corporation.

Note that the requirement that the property in question should belong to another is not an element of offences under ss1(2), 2(b), or 3(a) of the Act.

'Damages or destroys'

Whilst the offence contemplates total destruction to property, damage will be sufficient. In *Samuel* v *Stubbs* [1972] 4 SASR 200, the court held that criminal damage had been done to a policeman's helmet when it had been jumped upon, causing 'a temporary functional derangement'. It seems clear that spoiling, polluting, rearranging, dismantling or otherwise physically interfering with an individual's property can constitute criminal damage, the decision to prosecute perhaps being determined by the extent to which property has been reduced in value (eg a priceless painting being slashed with a knife), or the cost to the owner of restoring the property to its original state. For example in *R* v *Henderson and Battley* (1984) 29 November (unreported) unauthorised dumping of waste on a building site which cost £2,000 to remove was held to constitute criminal damage.

Some care may need to be taken in the drafting of the information or indictment. In *Morphitis* v *Salmon* [1990] Crim LR 48, the respondent, S, had erected a barrier, consisting of uprights, a scaffolding bar and a clip, across an access road leading to premises used by both himself and M. M had removed the bar and clip and taken them to his garage. The bar was found to have been scratched but it was not proved that M had caused this. M was convicted of criminal damage to the bar and clip. M appealed by way of case stated alleging that the property had not been damaged within the terms of the 1971 Act. The Divisional Court, quashing the conviction, held that even if M had scratched the bar it would not have amounted to criminal damage as it did not interfere with its usefulness. The dismantling of machinery could amount to criminal damage where this interfered with the working of the machine as a whole, but the information in the present case alleged damage to the individual parts of the barrier, hence the prosecution should not have succeeded. It would appear that the appellant may have been successfully prosecuted had he been charged with criminal damage to the barrier as a whole.

In *Hardman and Others* v *The Chief Constable of Avon and Somerset Constabulary* [1986] Crim LR 330, Bristol Crown Court held, on an appeal from justices, that human silhouettes sprayed onto pavements by CND supporters to indicate vaporised human remains following the dropping of an atomic bomb did constitute damage within the Act, even though the figures would be washed away by the next rainfall. The local authority had been put to the expense of cleaning away the figures. The court expressly approved of the approach taken by Walters J in *Samuels* v *Stubbs* (above) where he stated (at p203):

'It seems to me that it is difficult to lay down any very general and, at the same time, precise and absolute rule as to what constitutes "damage". One must be guided in a great degree by the circumstances of each case, the nature of the article, and the mode in which it is affected or treated. Moreover, the meaning of the word "damage" must as I have already said, be controlled by its context. The word may be used in the sense of "mischief done to property".'

Whether graffiti as such will amount to criminal damage is a question of fact and degree in each case. In *Roe* v *Kingerlee* [1986] Crim LR 735 the Divisional Court held that the application of a brown substance to the walls of a cell, which cost £7 to remove, could constitute criminal damage.

The damage or destruction in issue will normally arise from the defendant's freely willed act; it should be remembered however, that a defendant may be held responsible for failing to halt the spread of harm started accidentally. See further *R* v *Miller* [1983] 2 WLR 539.

3.4 Mens rea

Intention

The defendant must be proved not only to have intended the act which causes the damage, but also to have intended that the act should cause the damage. For example, D may intend to light a fire, but will not be held to have intended criminal damage unless he intended that fire to consume property belonging to others.

It is submitted that a defendant will have the necessary intention for criminal damage where he has the damage or destruction of another's property as his purpose, or where he foresees it as an inevitable consequence of his actions.

The defendant's motive, for example, a belief that his additions or alterations to property make it look more attractive, will normally be irrelevant; see *R* v *Fancy* [1980] Crim LR 171.

Recklessness

The prosecution, in securing a conviction for criminal damage, does not have to establish intention; it will suffice if it can be shown that the defendant was reckless.

The meaning of recklessness in the context of criminal damage has as its basis the decision of the House of Lords in *R* v *Caldwell* [1981] 1 All ER 961.

Prior to the *Caldwell* decision, the recklessness involved in criminal damage was understood to be subjective in nature. A defendant would only be regarded as having been reckless if he took an unjustifiable risk, and was aware at the time that the risk (of criminal damage) might materialise. Decisions such as *R* v *Stephenson* [1979] QB 695 are evidence of this approach.

The 'revolution' introduced by *Caldwell* was the addition of an alternative form of recklessness, one based on the defendant having failed to give any thought to an obvious risk that property would be damaged or destroyed. This type of recklessness is frequently referred to as being 'objective' in nature in that it imposes liability upon the defendant for not adverting to a risk which would have been 'obvious' to the reasonable man. Any doubts as to the objective nature of this liability were dispelled by the Divisional Court's decision in *Elliot* v *C* [1983] 2 All ER 1005 wherein it was held that a defendant could still be regarded as reckless, notwithstanding her inability to recognize a risk due to low intelligence, where a reasonable person would nevertheless have perceived the risk of criminal damage as obvious. The new type of reckless applies equally to the 'basic' offence of criminal damage under s1(1) and to 'aggravated' criminal damage under s1(2). See further the Court of Appeal decision in *R* v *Sangha* [1988] Crim LR 371. Recklessness is considered at 2.8.

'Belonging to another'

Mens rea must extend to this element of actus reus for there to be liability under s1(1). Where, as in *R* v *Smith* [1974] QB 354, a defendant damages property in the mistaken belief that it is his, he will not be guilty of an offence provided the mistake is a honest one. The defendant is judged on the facts as he believes them to be, his mistake in civil law relating to the ownership of property amounting to a defence.

3.5 The 'aggravated' offence

Section 1(2) of the 1971 Act provides:

'A person who without lawful excuse destroys or damages any property, whether belonging to himself or another:
a) intending to destroy or damage any property or being reckless as to whether any property would be destroyed or damaged; and
b) intending by the destruction or damage to endanger the life of another or being reckless as to whether the life of another would be thereby endangered;
shall be guilty of an offence.'

The 'aggravating' factor is clearly that supplied by s1(2)(b), of the intention to endanger life, or recklessness as to whether this occurs. Note that no lives actually have to have been endangered in order for there to be liability here; the defendant's state of mind is what is in issue. Whilst intention and recklessness have the meaning considered at 3.4 (above), it should be noted that the words 'by' and 'thereby' are crucial in s1(2), as is illustrated by the House of Lords' decision in *R v Steer* [1987] 3 WLR 205. The defendant fired an automatic rifle at the bedroom window of his business partner's house. The bedroom was occupied at the time. The defendant, who had pleaded guilty to a charge under s1(2)(b), causing criminal damage being reckless as to whether life would be endangered, following a ruling by the trial judge, appealed on the ground that he had not intended that the criminal damage to the window should endanger life, and therefore lacked the mens rea for the aggravated offence. The defendant was successful before the Court of Appeal, and on appeal by the prosecution, the House of Lords answered the certified question by holding that upon the true construction of s1(2)(b) of the 1971 Act the prosecution were required to prove that the danger to life resulted from the destruction of or damage to property; it was not sufficient for the prosecution to prove that it resulted from the act of the defendant which caused the destruction or damage. In other words the prosecution would have had to show that the defendant intended that the damage to the window would endanger life, or at least be reckless to this possibility.

A defendant can still be guilty of the aggravated offence even though the damage actually caused is not as great as he may have foreseen. In *R v Dudley* [1989] Crim LR 57, the appellant had thrown a fire-bomb at a house causing a small fire that was quickly extinguished, the damage caused being relatively slight. In response to the appellant's contention that there was no evidence upon which the jury could find that the actual damage caused was intended to endanger life, the Court of Appeal held that the intention to endanger life, or recklessness as to whether life would be endangered, should be looked at in the light of the harm he intended to cause, and not by reference to that which he actually caused. See further *R v Parker* [1993] Crim LR 856.

3.6 'Without lawful excuse'

Section 5 of the Criminal Damage Act 1971 provides some elaboration of what is meant by the expression 'lawful excuse' within the scope of criminal damage. Section 5 applies to ss1(1), 2(a) and 3(b) only. Section 5(5) makes it clear that these provisions operate without prejudice to any other defence available in criminal law.

Belief in owner's consent

A person is treated as having a lawful excuse under the 1971 Act where, as provided by s5(2)(a):

> 'At the time of the act or acts alleged to constitute the offence he believed that the person or persons whom he believed to be entitled to consent to the destruction of or damage to

the property in question had so consented, or would have so consented to it if he or they had known of the destruction or damage and its circumstances.'

Section 5(3) further provides that '... it is immaterial whether a belief is justified or not if it is honestly held'. In *R* v *Denton* (1982) 74 Cr App R 81 it was held that no offence was committed where an employee destroyed his employer's property after being ordered to do so, even though the defendant believed that his employer intended to make a bogus insurance claim in respect of the property. Note that the defendant's belief in the employer's authority to order such destruction was sufficient. Whether an employer can in law issue such instructions is more questionable. In *R* v *Appleyard* [1985] Crim LR 723 the Court of Appeal held that a managing director, who had set fire to a store belonging to the company for whom he worked, was guilty of criminal damage. The court rejected his argument that he must have been entitled to consent to such damage on behalf of the company under a 'self-authorisation' principle.

'Defence of property'

Section 5(2)(b) provides that a defendant has a lawful excuse for his destruction of property:

'... if he destroyed or damaged or threatened to destroy or damage the property in question or, in the case of a charge of an offence under section 3 intended to use or cause or permit the use of something to destroy or damage it, in order to protect property belonging to himself or another or a right or interest in property which was or which he believed to be vested in himself or another, and at the time of the act or acts alleged to constitute the offence he believed:
i) that the property right or interest was in immediate need of protection; and
ii) that the means of protection adopted or proposed to be adopted were or would be reasonable having regard to all the circumstances.'

This provision almost amounts to a statutory defence of necessity. Note that the defendant must believe his actions to be reasonable in the circumstances; however s5(3) again provides that his belief that his actions are reasonable does not itself have to be reasonable! Further, the defendant's actions must be taken in order to protect property, and it is for the court to determine whether or not this was the case. In *R* v *Hunt* (1977) 66 Cr App R 105, where the warden of a block of flats deliberately set fire to some bedding to illustrate the inadequacies of the fire alarm system, it was held that he had been rightly convicted, as his purpose had not been the protection of any other property. The decision raises a number of interesting issues. The defendant could, in a sense, be described as acting to save property, in that the building would be damaged if there was a fire which was not extinguished promptly due to the defective alarm system, although there would obviously be difficulties in his establishing his belief as to the immediacy of this threat. A defendant destroying property with a view to preserving life cannot invoke s5(2)(b), but may perhaps seek to rely on s5(2)(a), considered above.

The decision in *R v Hunt* has subsequently been relied upon by the Court of Appeal in *R v Ashford and Smith* [1988] Crim LR 682 and *R v Hill; R v Hall* (1989) Cr App R 74. Both cases involved defendants who sought to rely upon the provisions of s5(2)(b) in relation to damage to perimeter fencing at air bases. The basis for invoking the subsection was that by cutting the perimeter fence of the base they might have persuaded those responsible for the armed forces that such sites were no longer secure, leading to the removal of military hardware, with the result that the bases and surrounding properties might cease to be regarded as targets by Soviet forces. In *R v Hill; R v Hall*, the Court of Appeal indicated that the correct approach to the lawful excuse provisions of s5(2) was first to ascertain what the accused had had in mind, secondly to ascertain whether as a matter of law, on the facts as the accused believed them to be, the actions contemplated could amount to steps taken to protect property in immediate danger. The court felt that the trial judge had correctly proceeded on the basis that the cutting of the wire fence would have been too remote from the protection of property to come within the terms of s5(2), and further, on the evidence, there was no ground for believing that the appellants thought that any property was in immediate danger.

R v Blake [1993] Crim LR 586 reaffirms the objective gloss placed on s5(2)(a) and (b) by *Hunt* and *Hall*. The appellant had participated in a demonstration, in the vicinity of the Houses of Parliament, against the involvement of Allied troops in the Gulf War. Following his arrest for writing a biblical quotation on a pillar, he contended that he had a lawful excuse for the criminal damage to the pillar, either because he had the consent of God as the owner of the property (s5(2)(a)), or because he had acted to protect other property (s5(2)(b)). Dismissing his appeal against conviction the court held that belief that God was the person entitled to consent to the damage would not form the basis of a valid defence, no matter how genuine that belief was. Even if the appellant genuinely believed that property in the Gulf states could be protected by his protest, it was for the court, applying an objective test, to determine whether or not his action did, or could, protect property as he had contended. There was no sufficiently immediate threat to the appellant or others to found a more general defence of duress of circumstances. It is submitted that, on a strict application of s5(2)(a) and (b) the test should be should be subjective, but the uncertainty introduced by permitting a defendant to rely on honest belief in divine commands is self-evident. See further *Johnson v DPP* [1994] Crim LR 673 (chapter 26, section 26.2).

The defendant who, ignoring warning signs about the wheel clamping of illegally parked cars, returns to find his vehicle has been immobilised by a clamp cannot rely on the lawful excuse provision if he uses force to remove the wheel clamp and damages it in the process: see *Lloyd v DPP* [1991] Crim LR 904. If, however, he returns to find his car about to be set alight by vandals, and destroys the wheel clamp so as to move his car to safety, s5(2)(b) presumably would provide an escape route, if not s5(2)(a).

Honesty and reasonableness

It has been noted above that s5(3) requires the defendant's belief to be honest, but not necessarily reasonable. Further evidence of this is supplied by the decision of *Jaggard* v *Dickinson* [1981] QB 527, where the defendant, who was very drunk, caused damage when breaking into a house which she wrongly thought to be owned by her friend who had given her permission to enter at any time. The defendant successfully relied on s5(2)(a) in that she honestly believed she had the consent of the owner to enter the house in that way. Section 5(3) does not state that such belief must be honest *and* sober.

4

Non-Fatal Offences Against the Person I

4.1 Assault and battery

4.2 Is there an offence of assault at common law?

4.3 The defence of consent

4.4 Reform

4.5 Assault upon a police officer in the execution of his duty

4.6 Wilful obstruction of a police officer in the execution of his duty

4.1 Assault and battery

Introduction

Assault is both a tort and a crime. In terms of criminal liability there is some dispute as to whether or not there is still an offence of assault contrary to common law (see below), but the term is used to describe elements of more serious statutory offences, such as assault occasioning actual bodily harm (see s47 of the Offences Against the Person Act 1861), and assault upon a police officer in the execution of his duty (see s51(1) of the Police Act 1964).

The narrow concept

When used in the narrow sense, the term common assault involves the defendant causing the victim to apprehend immediate physical violence. No physical contact is required; see comments of Lord Lane CJ in *R* v *Mansfield Justices, ex parte Sharkey* [1985] QB 613, at p627. Hence it can be committed by D shaking his fist in P's face, or thrusting a knife towards him. The emphasis is on the reaction of the victim. Even if D meant his threats as a joke, an assault is nevertheless committed if P is sufficiently frightened: see *Logdon* v *DPP* [1976] Crim LR 121.

The requirement of immediacy in the crime of assault is generally understood to mean that the victim must perceive the threat as one which can be carried out 'there and then' by the defendant. This raises the interesting possibility that D might not be guilty of assault where he waves his fist angrily at P who is on the other side of a counter behind a toughened glass screen, if the evidence is that there is no way that D can actually make contact with P. Of course, if P knows this then he is unlikely to apprehend any physical violence in any event. Similarly if D sits in the public gallery of a court room looking at a jury member in an intimidatory manner, a charge of assault may not be sustainable in the face of the argument that any threat of force involved in this conduct could not have been carried out until the jury member had left the court building. The courts have, however, on occasion, given a more liberal interpretation to the concept of immediacy. In *Smith* v *Superintendent of Woking Police Station* [1983] Crim LR 323, the defendant was convicted of being on enclosed premises for an unlawful purpose, namely assault. He had terrified a woman occupying a ground floor flat by staring in through the window at her. The Divisional Court was satisfied that even though the defendant was outside the building there was evidence to suggest that the victim was terrified by the prospect of some immediate violence. Note also that the court here stated that it was not necessary for the prosecution to establish precisely what the victim feared would happen. A general apprehension of violence was sufficient.

Words as an assault

It is a statement of the obvious to say that a defendant need not physically threaten a victim in order to cause fear. Words alone can cause terror, such as where D tells P that he is about to stab him to death. It seems all the more surprising, therefore, to find that as a matter of criminal law, words alone cannot constitute an assault. The authority for this proposition is the direction given to the jury in *R* v *Meade & Belt* (1823) 1 Lew CC 184 at 185, to the effect that 'no words or singing could ever constitute an assault'. There is, however, evidence to contradict this view of the law; in particular Lord Goddard CJ's obiter statement in *R* v *Wilson* [1955] 1 All ER 744 at 745, where he states that the phrase 'get out knives' when spoken by the defendant, constituted an assault. It is something of an indictment of English criminal law that such a basic point should be the subject of so much controversy. It is anomalous that words cannot constitute an assault, but threatening to kill someone is an offence under s16 of the Offences Against the Person Act 1861. Does this mean that if D threatens to kill P, and P is so frightened that he suffers a heart attack and dies, D can be charged with unlawful act manslaughter, but not where the threat is only to break P's arm; see further Chapter 8.

What is clear is that words will not constitute an assault if they are phrased in such a way that negatives any threat that D is making. Thus in *Tuberville* v *Savage* (1669) 1 Mod Rep 3 there was held to be no assault when the defendant placed his hand on his sword and said to the victim:

> 'If it were not assize time I would not take such language from you.'

The defendant was in fact saying that he was not going to strike the victim. Perhaps more questionable is the assertion that a defendant does not commit an assault where he tells the victim to be quiet or he will be shot. Although the words suggest that the defendant is not going to assault the victim, it is here conditional on the victim's own behaviour, as opposed to some external factor, such as the presence of judges in the town in *Tuberville* v *Savage*. See further on this point, *Blake* v *Barnard* (1840) 9 C & P 626, and *Read* v *Coker* (1853) 13 CB 850.

The broader concept

Instances of a victim being assaulted without there being any physical contact with the defendant are comparatively rare. There is usually some physical contact between victim and defendant which, technically, will constitute a battery.

Battery is defined in *Cole* v *Turner* (1705) 6 Mod Rep 149, as involving the least touching of another person in anger. If D pushes P out of the way so as to get to the front of a queue, D would have committed a battery, but it should be remembered that there is a certain degree of physical contact that everyone is deemed to have consented to as part of everyday life, such as might occur between respectable passengers on a crowded train or bus. Further, there is no need to establish that the victim of a battery apprehended immediate physical contact, even though this is nearly always involved where the offence is committed. Hence where D approaches P from the rear and hits him on the back of the head, D will have committed a battery, but not necessarily an assault.

Despite the foregoing, it would be regarded as archaic, if not odd, for a victim to describe himself as having been battered; hence the modern trend to use the term assault in a broad sense to include both assault and battery. As James J stated in *Fagan* v *MPC* [1969] 1 QB 439 at p444:

> 'Although "assault" is an independent crime and is to be treated as such for practical purposes today "assault" is generally synonymous with the term "battery", and is a term used to mean the actual intended use of unlawful force to another person without his consent.'

Similar comments are made by Lord Lane LJ in *R* v *Williams (Gladstone)* (1983) 78 Cr App R 276 at p279.

Despite the modern usage of the term 'assault', and the rarity of cases where the facts reveal only a 'narrow' assault, the courts have confirmed that assault and battery are to be regarded as distinct concepts, in the sense that any information alleging assault and battery would be bad for duplicity: see *DPP* v *Taylor* [1992] 2 WLR 460. Mann LJ expressed his preference for the use of the phrase 'assault by beating' in indictments alleging assault in the broad sense. It remains to be seen what the impact of this ruling will be on other offences involving an allegation of assault, eg sexual offences, and offences against police officers. Will indictments for indecent assault have to specify whether there was physical contact?

4.2 Is there an offence of assault at common law?

Section 39 of the Criminal Justice Act 1988

That an offence of assault contrary to common law existed until 1861 is not seriously disputed, but in *R* v *Harrow Justices, ex parte Osaseri* [1986] QB 589, May LJ expressed the view that the effect of s47 of the Offences Against the Person Act 1861, had been to place the common law offence on a statutory basis. He based this assertion on the wording of s47, which creates the offence of assault occasioning actual bodily harm, and goes on to provide that:

> '...whosoever shall be convicted upon an indictment for a common assault shall be liable to be imprisoned for any term not exceeding one year.'

Whilst May LJ left open the possibility that there might still be a remaining common law offence of assault by beating, the existence of the 'remnant' of an offence at common law was later denied by Mann LJ in *DPP* v *Taylor* (above). Mann LJ was of the opinion that both common assault and battery had become subsumed in the statutory offence under s47 and went on to hold that the offences (of assault and battery) should now be charged under s39 of the Criminal Justice Act 1988, which provides:

> 'Common assault and battery shall be summary offences and a person guilty of either of them shall be liable ... to imprisonment for a term not exceeding six months.'

The difficulty with this view is that s39 could be seen as a purely procedural provision. It does not create any offences, but merely prescribes the procedure by which they are enforced. This leads inevitably to the same questions being asked as to the effect of s47 of the 1861 Act. Again it can be argued that the provisions of s47 relating to punishment for common assault do not make the offence statutory, but merely indicate the penalty to be applicable following conviction. Statutory provision of punishments for common law offences is not unknown; consider the position relating to murder and life imprisonment.

Mens rea for common assault and battery

The mens rea required for common assault is intention to cause the victim to apprehend immediate physical violence, or recklessness on the part of the defendant as to whether this will occur. Authority for this proposition is to be found in the Court of Appeal's decision in *R* v *Venna* (1975) 61 Cr App R 310, a decision concerned with a charge under s47 of the 1861 Act. It seems clear that in *Venna* the type of recklessness the court had in mind was *Cunningham*, or subjective recklessness. The court referred approvingly to the earlier case of *R* v *Bradshaw* (1878) 14 Cox CC 83, where recklessness in relation to assault and battery had been defined in terms consistent with *Cunningham*. The acceptance by the Divisional

Court in *DPP* v *Khan* (1990) 91 Cr App R 23, that *Caldwell* recklessness applied to offences of assault, was overruled by the Court of Appeal in *R* v *Spratt* (1990) 91 Cr App R 362, where the court expressed its preference for the subjective approach. Nothing said in *R* v *Savage*; *R* v *Parmenter* [1991] 3 WLR 914, casts any doubt upon this. Similarly, in relation to battery, the mens rea would appear to be intention to cause some impact upon the body of another, or at least an awareness on the part of the defendant that he may cause such impact.

4.3 The defence of consent

General defences in criminal law are dealt with in some detail in Chapters 13 to 15 of this book. Consent is dealt with at this stage, however, given that it is more likely to avail a defendant charged with common law assault and battery, than one charged with the more serious assaults. In considering the following it should also be remembered that consent may be a relevant issue in offences other than assaults. The consent of the owner can provide a defendant with a complete defence on charges of theft, or criminal damage. The statutory offence of rape requires proof not only that the woman was not consenting to intercourse, but also that the defendant knew she was not so consenting, or was reckless as to the fact.

On the basis of the Court of Appeal's decision in *R* v *Donovan* [1934] 2 KB 498, the consent of a victim to suffer harm inflicted by the defendant can only provide the defendant with a defence if the harm inflicted does not amount to bodily harm, or worse. For these purposes Swift J took as the meaning of bodily harm, anything that was calculated to interfere with the health or comfort of the victim. There are two notable exceptions to this rule, however. First, the law does permit the consent of a patient to surgery performed by a suitably qualified doctor. Clearly there is social utility in such operations being performed. This exception would extend even to those patients who agree to undergo pioneering operations where there is a very high risk of death. The overall benefits to society justify the risks involved. Secondly, an exception is made in respect of 'manly diversions', which in *Donovan* were held to include such sports as 'cudgels, foils, and wrestling'. The rationale behind this exception is that it is good public policy to encourage individuals to take up sport, as this helps maintain physical fitness. It is generally accepted that this exception now covers organised sports, played according to recognised rules, with appropriate supervision from a referee or umpire.

A footballer who suffers a sprained ankle following a heavy tackle during a game could not, therefore launch a private prosecution for assault against his opponent, because he will be assumed to have consented to suffering the type of harm that can be reasonably foreseen as a consequence of playing the game. An injury inflicted by an opponent deliberately flouting the rules ought, on the other hand, to at least provide the basis for a criminal prosecution. A number of such cases have come before the courts: see *R* v *Billinghurst* [1978] Crim LR 553.

In *Attorney-General's Reference (No 6 of 1980)* [1981] QB 715, the Court of Appeal was asked for its opinion upon the following point of law:

> 'Where two persons fight (otherwise than in the course of sport) in a public place can it be a defence for one of those persons to a charge of assault arising out of the fight that the other consented to the fight?'

It was held that a fight between two persons would be unlawful, whether in public or private, if it involved the infliction of at least actual bodily harm, or if actual bodily harm or worse was intended. This would make most fights between people wishing to 'settle their differences' in this manner unlawful. Nothing in the decision affects the legality of organised sports such as boxing, provided of course that the boxers are using their skill to win the fight, and not delivering blows in anger. The defence may also extend to injuries caused in the course of rough horseplay or practical jokes, provided there is no intention to do harm, a conclusion supported by the decision of the Court of Appeal in *R v Jones (Terence)* (1986) 83 Cr App R 375, cited with approval in *R v Aitken and Others* [1992] 1 WLR 1066. In this latter case, the victim's participation in practical jokes played on companions was accepted as evidence suggesting that he realised that he too could become a victim and consented to this.

On a more general level one might ask whether it is the business of the criminal law to concern itself with situations where individuals agree to have harm inflicted upon themselves. To what extent should the law adopt a paternalistic approach? Ear piercing involves assault, but will not result in criminal charges where an adult requests such treatment; similarly with tattooing. There have been few occasions where the courts have been invited to consider such questions, but a reaffirmation of the paternalistic approach is evidenced by the views of the majority in *R v Brown* [1993] 2 WLR 556. The House of Lords upheld convictions, under s47 and s20 of the Offences Against the Person Act 1861, in respect of appellants who belonged to a sado-masochistic group, members of which inflicted pain on each other for mutual sexual pleasure. Their activities included the nailing of a 'willing victim's' foreskin or scrotum to a board; the insertion of hot wax into a victim's urethra, followed by the burning of his penis with a candle; and the incising of a victim's scrotum with a scalpel, causing loss of blood. Lord Templeman, rejecting the contention that every person has a right to deal with his body as he pleases, observed that:

> 'Although the law is often broken, the criminal law restrains a practice which is regarded as dangerous and injurious to individuals and which if allowed and extended is harmful to society generally ... Society is entitled and bound to protect itself against a cult of violence. Pleasure derived from the infliction of pain is an evil thing.'

Lord Jauncey regarded the matter as one requiring parliamentary intervention if the law was to be liberalised. Lord Lowry appeared to regard the criminal law as having an important role to play in the promotion of activities conducive to the enhancement or enjoyment of family life and welfare of society. His lordship was unable to recognise sado-masochistic homosexual activity as furthering such aims.

Neither was he willing to recognise an exception in respect of such acts on the basis that they constituted a 'manly diversion'.

Lord Mustill (dissenting), explained that for him the guiding principle was that:

'... the state should interfere with the rights of an individual to live his or her life as he or she may choose no more than is necessary to ensure a proper balance between the special interests of the individual and the general interests of the individuals who together comprise the populace at large.'

On this basis he felt unable to conclude that the denial of the defence of consent in the circumstances of the case was justified. Will the court take a different view of violent acts committed in the course of heterosexual intercourse? In *R* v *Boyea* [1992] Crim LR 575 the appellant inserted his fist into the vagina of the complainant and twisted it around, causing her injury. His conviction for indecent assault was upheld on the basis that the harm caused to the complainant exceeded the level of injury to which she could have consented. The court, however, appeared willing to accept that the degree of harm to which a complainant could be said to have validly consented during heterosexual congress may be greater now than was the case at the time *R* v *Donovan* (above) was decided.

The extent to which the restrictions placed upon the defence of consent by the House of Lords are compatible with the European Convention on Human Rights is yet to be resolved, but the European Commission is due to consider the admissibility of cases brought by the defendants in *Brown* against the United Kingdom in early 1995. In its Consultation Paper 'Consent and Offences Against the Person' (No 134) the Law Commission seeks views on whether the current position represents the correct approach, or whether the defence of consent should be extended. The paper also seeks comment upon the option of retaining the current position, but recognising exceptions such as circumcision, ear piercing, religious mortification, and dangerous exhibits.

Mistake as to consent

In *R* v *Kimber* [1983] 1 WLR 1118, the Court of Appeal considered the case of a defendant who had been convicted of indecently assaulting a female patient at a mental hospital contrary to s14 Sexual Offences Act 1956. He appealed on the ground that he had honestly thought she was consenting. It was held that there had been a misdirection to the extent that the trial judge should have explained to the jury that if the defendant had honestly believed that the victim was consenting to his actions he would not have had the mens rea necessary for the offence. His belief in her consent did not have to be reasonable, merely honest. On the facts, however, it was evident that even if the jury had been properly directed, the defendant would still have been convicted, and on that basis the appeal was dismissed.

The decision is authority for the proposition that an honest mistake as to the consent of the victim will afford a defence to the accused, regardless of whether the mistake is one that the reasonable man would have made or not. Obviously, the more unlikely the defendant's mistake, the less likely the jury will be to believe that he honestly made it. The approach of the court in this case has been confirmed by subsequent decisions such as *Beckford* v *R* [1987] 3 All ER 425: see Chapter 15.

4.4 Reform

The DCLB envisages a significant simplification of the law relating to assault. Clause 6 provides:

> '(1) A person is guilty of the offence of assault if –
> (a) he intentionally or recklessly applies force to or causes an impact on the body of another –
> (i) without the consent of the other, or
> (ii) where the act is intended or likely to cause injury, with or without the consent of the other; or
> (b) he intentionally or recklessly, without the consent of the other, causes the other to believe that any such force or impact is imminent.
> (2) No such offence is committed if the force or impact, not being intended or likely to cause injury, is in the circumstances such as is generally acceptable in the ordinary conduct of everyday life and the defendant does not know or believe that it is in fact unacceptable to the other person.'

To a large extent clause 6(1) implements the recommendation of the Criminal Law Revision Committee (Offences Against the Person (1980) Cmnd 7844) that '... there should be a single offence of assault, whether or not there is a battery'. The proposed offence would encompass immediate threats, and would apply to cases of 'indirect assault', such as those caused by the use of traps.

The DCLB mirrors the approach of the common law to the issue of consent, indicating that it can negative assault, but not, subject to the common law exceptions, injury. As to the DCLB definition of injury, see Chapter 5.

4.5 Assault upon a police officer in the execution of his duty

This offence is created by s51(1) of the Police Act 1964 which states:

> 'Any person who assaults a constable in the execution of his duty, or a person assisting a constable in the execution of his duty, shall be guilty of an offence ...'

For the purposes of this offence, assault bears both its narrow and its broad meaning, considered above. Thus, as was stated by James J in *Fagan* v *Metropolitan Police Commissioner*, a constable can be assaulted, even where he does not apprehend immediate physical harm. A police officer is any person who has been lawfully sworn as such.

'In the execution of his duty'

Ascertaining the scope of a constable's duties is a matter which has given the courts some considerable difficulty, yet it is a matter which is crucial to the offence under s51(1), in that if a police officer is not acting within the execution of his duty, an element of the actus reus is absent and there can be no liability.

The offence certainly extends beyond those situations where a police officer is exercising some positive statutory duty. In the majority of situations a police officer will in fact be exercising powers not duties, but it would be nonsense to therefore suggest that he was no longer acting in the execution of his duty. As a very general statement of the law it might be said that provided a police officer can point to some legal authority for his actions, he is acting within the scope of his duties. This reflects the view adopted by the Divisional Court in *Coffin* v *Smith* (1980) 71 Cr App R 221. The defendant assaulted a police officer who had been called to deal with a group of 'gatecrashers' at a youth club disco. It was accepted that no offences had been committed by the defendant up to this point, but he was nevertheless charged with assaulting a police officer in the execution of his duty. The justices upheld a submission of no case to answer on the basis that the police officer had not been under any duty to compel the defendant to leave the scene. Donaldson LJ regarded this approach as totally wrong. In his view a police officer was acting within the execution of his duty where he was taking steps that were necessary to keep the peace, and was not committing any act which was prima facie an unlawful interference with a person's liberty or property. Similarly in *Weight* v *Long* [1986] Crim LR 746, Watkins LJ held that a police officer would be acting within the scope of his duty where he acted to keep the peace, to prevent the commission of an offence, or to investigate offences already committed.

It is submitted, therefore, that a defendant has to produce some evidence that the police officer has in some way exceeded his powers, in order to succeed with a submission that he was not acting in the execution of his duty. This is supported by a number of decisions. In *R* v *Waterfield* [1964] 1 QB 164, the Court of Appeal held that the defendant was not guilty of an offence under s51(1), where he had assaulted a police officer who had detained his car, the officer not having any specific power to do so. In *Lindley* v *Rutter* [1980] Crim LR 729, a police officer had removed some clothing from an inebriated detainee, but only had power to do this if there was evidence that failure to do so might result in harm to the detainee or others. The detainee resisted the officer's attempts to remove the clothing and was charged under s51(1). The Divisional Court held that the officer had not been acting in the execution of her duty as there were no grounds to justify her removal of the detainee's clothing, hence the offence of assault was not made out. Finally, in *Kerr* v *DPP* (1994) The Times 5 August, it was confirmed that a defendant will not be guilty of the offence under s51(1) where he resists force used against him by a constable who wrongly believes that the defendant is under arrest. See chapter 26, section 26.3, for further details. A charge of common assault always remains a possibility in such cases, but presumably the defendant will be able to raise the defence that he was entitled to use reasonable force.

Mens rea

The defendant must have the intention to assault, as to which see 4 above. The difficult issues here are whether the defendant must know that a police officer is acting in the execution of his duty, and further whether he must know that the person he is assaulting is a police officer. As regards the first matter, the venerable case of *R v Forbes and Webb* (1865) 10 Cox CC 362, is still good authority for the proposition that the offence is not assault knowing the police officer to be in the execution of his duty, but assault upon a police officer who is in the execution of his duty. This rather suggests that liability as to this element of the actus reus is strict, but it is a view which has received implicit approval in subsequent cases such as *R v Prince* (1875) LR 2 CCR 154.

The decisions in *McBride v Turnock* [1964] Crim LR 456, and *Albert v Lavin* [1981] 1 All ER 628, both support the view that a defendant cannot rely on the contention that he honestly believed the person he was assaulting was not a police officer, although the latter case admits of the possibility that a defendant might be permitted to rely on an honest and reasonable mistake that the victim was not a police officer. It might now be the case, however, following the decision of the Court of Appeal in *R v Williams* [1987] 3 All ER 411, which was approved by the Privy Council in *Beckford v R* [1987] 3 All ER 425 (see Chapter 15 for details), that the courts would look more favourably on a defendant relying on an honest belief that the victim of his assault was not a police officer. Both of the decisions referred to approve the principle that where a defendant makes an honest, although not necessarily reasonable mistake as to the existence of an attack by an assailant from which he must defend himself, he should be judged on the facts as he honestly believes them to be, thus justifying the use of reasonable force by way of self-defence. Applying these authorities to a situation under s51(1) a defendant, who honestly believed that a plain clothed police officer making an arrest was in reality a robber attacking an innocent victim, would not be guilty under the section if he used reasonable force on the police officer to prevent the perceived attack. There might still be liability under s51(3), considered below, however. To some extent this view would endorse the obiter statements of Widgery LJ in *R v Fennell* [1970] 3 All ER 215, where he suggests that a defendant who honestly believes that his child is being unlawfully detained by a police officer, and who further honestly believes that the child is in imminent danger of injury, would be justified in using reasonable force in order to secure his child's release.

4.6 Wilful obstruction of a police officer in the execution of his duty

Section 51(3) of the Police Act 1964 provides:

> 'Any person who resists or wilfully obstructs a constable in the execution of his duty, or a person assisting a constable in the execution of his duty, shall be guilty of an offence ...'

Obstruction

Essentially obstruction is any act or omission that makes it appreciably more difficult for an officer to execute his duty: see *Rice* v *Connolly* [1966] 2 QB 414, and *Bennett* v *Bale* [1986] Crim LR 404. Hence to warn drivers that there is a police speed trap in operation so that they slow down from unlawful to lawful speeds can constitute obstruction: see *Betts* v *Stevens* [1910] 1 KB 1. Similarly, to deliberately consume alcohol so as to prevent the administration of a valid breathalyser test has been held to amount to obstruction: see *Dibble* v *Ingleton* [1972] 1 QB 480.

Obviously there are limits. In *Rice* v *Connolly* (above), it was held that the defendant was not guilty of obstruction simply on the basis of his refusal to answer questions when stopped by a police officer in the street. Note that in such cases there is no duty to answer police questions. Where a duty does exist, failure to perform that duty could amount to obstruction. Hence in *Lunt* v *DPP* [1993] Crim LR 534, D, who had refused to admit police officers to his home after being traced following a traffic accident, was convicted of wilful obstruction on the basis that, under the Road Traffic Act 1988, he had been under a duty to admit the officers. It would not amount to obstruction to advise a burglar not to burgle a particular house because the owner has had an alarm fitted, whereas it would be an offence to warn a burglar who was in the act of breaking into the house, of the impending arrival of the police. Further, the fact that a defendant intends to obstruct is not sufficient unless there is some evidence that his actions have actually impeded the police: see *Bennett* v *Bale* (above).

'Police constable in the execution of his duty'

See 4.5 above.

Mens rea

In addition to the matters considered at 4.5 above, the prosecution has to establish that the defendant's obstruction of the police officer was wilful. In general terms an obstruction is wilful, if the defendant intends that his action should make the police officer's execution of his duty more difficult. Uncertainties have arisen, however, with the well-meaning member of the public who intervenes to help the police, but who in fact only succeeds in making the situation worse.

In *Willmott* v *Atack* [1977] QB 498, the defendant was present at the scene of an arrest which the police officers concerned were having some difficulty in carrying out. Believing he could help resolve the situation more effectively, the defendant interposed himself between the arresting officers and the suspect. The defendant was convicted under s51(3). The Divisional Court quashed the conviction, holding that a defendant only obstructed wilfully where he acted with some hostility towards the police, and that had not been the situation here, as the defendant had intended to positively assist the police. This decision was not followed, however, in the subsequent Divisional Court decision in *Hills* v *Ellis* [1983] QB 680. The defendant had witnessed a fight outside a football ground. He later saw the innocent party in the fight being arrested by a police officer. He grabbed the policeman's elbow and shouted at him in order to alert the officer to what the defendant feared would be a miscarriage of justice. The policeman told the defendant to desist, but he refused. The defendant was charged and convicted under s51(3), and appealed unsuccessfully to the Divisional Court. The court held that, looking at the matter objectively, the defendant had in fact obstructed the police officer, and had intended to do so. The 'hostility' referred to in *Willmott* v *Atack* as being a necessary element of the mens rea was held to be satisfied here by evidence that the defendant's actions were 'aimed at' the police officers. The court stressed that the defendant's motive in acting as he had was irrelevant. It seems clear that the court viewed it as being contrary to public policy to encourage members of the public to intervene wherever they thought a police officer to be making an error of judgment.

In *Lewis* v *Cox* [1984] Crim LR 756, the Divisional Court seems to have gone even further in extending the meaning of 'wilfully', by removing any requirement that the defendant's act be aimed at the police officers. In that case the defendant, whose friend had been placed under arrest in the back of a police van, opened the back door of the van to enquire which police station the friend was being taken to, and thereby prevented the van from being driven away. The magistrates had dismissed the obstruction charge brought against the defendant on the basis that his action in opening the van doors had not been directed against the police. The Divisional Court allowed the prosecutor's appeal, holding that it was sufficient for a conviction that the defendant had known that his actions would make it more difficult for the police to drive away.

Reform

Clause 7 of the DCLB proposes the following offence:

> '(1) A person is guilty of an offence if he assaults –
> (a) a constable acting in the execution of his duty, or
> (b) anyone assisting a constable so acting,
> knowing that, or being reckless whether, the person assaulted or the person being assisted is a constable.
> (2) It is immaterial whether the person committing the assault is aware that the constable is or may be acting in the execution of his duty.'

Note that the clause requires proof of knowledge or recklessness as to the fact that the person assaulted is a constable, but does not require proof of knowledge that he is acting in the execution of his duty.

5

Non-Fatal Offences Against the Person II

5.1 Section 47 of the Offences Against the Person Act 1861

Section 47 provides:

> 'Whosoever shall be convicted on indictment of any assault occasioning actual bodily harm shall be ... [liable to punishment]'.

Actus reus

The actus reus of the offence requires proof of three elements: an assault; causation; and actual bodily harm.

Assault
The meaning of assault has already been dealt with in some detail in the preceding chapter. It only needs to be reiterated here that the assault upon which liability for s47 is based can be either 'narrow' or 'broad'. Hence the offence would be made out if D were to rush into a room waving a poker threateningly at P, causing P to jump out of the window to escape, with the result that P sustains a twisted ankle in his fall to the ground. More commonly, the offence will involve direct physical contact between D and P, resulting in some minor harm to P.

Occasioning

The word 'occasioning' as used in s47 can be taken to mean 'causing'. The section provides an example of what is sometimes called a 'result crime', in that it must be shown that the defendant's actions have caused the prohibited result. It is first necessary to ascertain whether or not the defendant is the cause in fact of the injury. This can be resolved by applying the so-called 'but for' test; but for the defendant's actions would the victim have suffered the injury? Assuming that causation in fact can be established, it is then necessary to deal with the second matter, namely, was the defendant the cause in law of the victim's injury?

R v *Notman* [1994] Crim LR 518, applying *R* v *Hennigan* (1971) 55 Cr App R 262, confirms that, whilst a trial judge should make it clear to the jury that the defendant's actions have to be more than a *de minimis* cause of the injury in question, the expression 'substantial cause' is suitable for most purposes in describing the test for causation in law that has to be applied. See chapter 26, section 26.3, for further details.

Where more complex issues of remoteness do arise, ie because the defendant contends that there is some *novus actus interveniens* that breaks the chain of causation, the court should invoke the test explained by Stephenson LJ in *R* v *Roberts* (1971) 56 Cr App R 95. Here the defendant had given a lift to the victim, a young woman, and during the journey he made a number of improper suggestions to her, and at one stage touched her breasts. The victim jumped from the car whilst it was moving (the speed was variously stated as being between 20 and 40 miles per hour), and suffered grazing and concussion in her fall. The defendant was convicted under s47, and appealed on the ground that the victim's action in jumping from the car had broken the chain of causation, thus relieving him of liability for the harm. In dismissing the appeal, his Lordship explained that the correct test for causation in law was to ask: Were the actions of the victim the natural result of what the alleged assailant said and did, in the sense that it was something that could reasonably have been foreseen as the consequence of what he was saying or doing? Only if there was some voluntary act on the part of the victim that could be regarded as 'daft' or unexpected, in the sense that no reasonable man could be expected to foresee it, would the chain of causation in law be broken.

On this basis it might be argued that the victim's actions would have broken the chain of causation had she jumped from a car travelling at 70 miles per hour, but this conflicts with the ratio of *R* v *Blaue* [1975] 1 WLR 1411, which holds that a defendant should have to take his victim as he finds him or her. Thus if the victim is 'daft' enough to try and escape from an indecent assault by jumping from a speeding car should not the defendant be responsible for the consequences? This matter is considered at more length in Chapter 6.

Actual bodily harm

Actual bodily harm was defined by Lynskey J, when addressing a jury at Hampshire Assizes in *R* v *Miller* [1954] 2 QB 282. He explained that the expression covered any hurt or injury likely to interfere with the health or comfort of the victim. In *R v Roberts* (above), the actual bodily harm was grazing and concussion. On the facts of *R v Miller* the jury concluded that inducing a nervous hysterical condition in the victim came within the definition, but some doubt may have been cast on this by the more recent decision of the Court of Appeal in *R v Chan Fook* [1994] 1 WLR 689. Hobhouse LJ, whilst confirming that psychiatric injury could come within the scope of actual bodily harm, provided there was medical evidence to show that the harm was more than mere emotional disturbance, rejected the notion that it could encompass conditions such as fear, distress, panic or other hysterical or nervous conditions. See chapter 26, section 26.3, for further details. It is submitted that actual bodily harm would cover injuries such as bruising (see *R v Reigate Justices, ex parte Counsell* (1983) 148 JP 193), sprained joints and, possibly, concussion, nausea and vomiting.

Mens rea

It is notable that s47 does not expressly state any mens rea requirement – yet it has never been contended that the offence is one of absolute or strict liability. The courts have always 'read in' some mens rea requirement, the basis of the modern interpretation being the Court of Appeal's decision in *R v Venna* (1975) 61 Cr App R 310, where it was held that the prosecution would have to establish intention or recklessness on the part of the accused. Despite the views expressed in decisions such as *DPP v Khan* (1990) 91 Cr App R 23, the issue as to the type of recklessness that has to be established under s47 seems now to have been conclusively resolved in favour of *Cunningham*: see *R v Savage*; *R v Parmenter* [1991] 3 WLR 914.

What is the extent of the mens rea?
In *R v Cunningham* (1957) 41 Cr App R 155, Byrne J referred to a concept of recklessness involving the defendant being:

> '... recklessness as to whether such harm should occur or not (ie the accused has foreseen that the particular kind of harm might be done and yet has gone on to take the risk of it).'

Applied to s47, this would require proof that the defendant foresaw the risk of actual bodily harm resulting from his assault yet went on to take that risk, but does the mental element have to extend beyond the causing of the assault? The matter was addressed by the Court of Appeal in two separate cases which, by coincidence, were before different sittings of that court at exactly the same time. In *R v Savage* (1990) 91 Cr App R 317, the appellant was charged with unlawful wounding contrary to s20 of the Offences Against the Person Act 1861, the prosecution having alleged that the appellant had approached the victim and thrown the contents of an almost full pint glass of beer at her, and that she had let go of the glass which broke, with the result that the victim suffered cuts. The appellant admitted that it had been her intention to throw the beer over the victim but denied any intention to cut her with the glass. The appellant appealed successfully against her conviction under s20 because of the trial judge's misdirection as to the mental element for that offence, but the court substituted a conviction for s47, on the basis that the offence did not require proof of recklessness or 'maliciousness' in relation to the 'occasioning' of the actual bodily harm. The appellant had deliberately thrown the beer over the victim, an act which was obviously an assault, and that 'assault' had undoubtedly occasioned the actual bodily harm which occurred. The court effectively relegated the issue of the resulting harm to one of causation, to be assessed objectively. In the second of these cases, *R v Spratt* (above), the appellant had fired an air pistol from the window of his dwelling into a courtyard below. He claimed that he had been aiming at a sign. A pellet from the gun struck a child playing in the yard. The appellant denied any knowledge that children were in the vicinity of the sign. The appellant pleaded guilty to a s47 offence following his counsel's advice that *Caldwell* recklessness now applied to the offence. As has been indicated above, the Court of Appeal held that *Cunningham* should have been applied, but it is notable that in the headnote to the report it is stated that:

> 'A defendant could not be guilty of an offence under s47 ... where he failed to give thought to the possibility that his action might give rise to a risk of causing bodily harm to another person.'

This clearly required a further element of mens rea not specified in *Savage* and the two decisions were clearly irreconcilable as to this issue. The Court of Appeal attempted to resolve the problem in the course of its decision in *R v Parmenter* (1991) 92 Cr App R 68. Having reviewed the two decisions, Mustill LJ stated (at p74):

> 'It seems to us that they are not in conflict as regards a case where the defendant neither intends nor adverts to the possibility that there will be any physical contact at all. (This case is governed by *Spratt* and not by *Savage*). Nor is there any conflict where the defendant does advert to the possibility of harm, albeit not necessarily of the kind which actually happened.
>
> But in the intermediate case we are driven to conclude that there is a conflict, for if the glass slipped from the defendant's hand in *Savage* [above] by mistake, there would not (even under the wide interpretation given by *Mowatt*) have been the mental element as regards the physical harm which is called for by *Spratt* [above]. We are obliged to resolve this conflict in order to decide the present appeal, and after careful consideration must prefer *Spratt* [above] which was founded on a line of authority leading directly to the conclusion there expressed: whereas these authorities are not mentioned in *Savage*, and cannot have been brought to the attention of the court.'

This analysis was, however, firmly rejected by Lord Ackner by the time the appeals in *R v Savage*; *R v Parmenter* (above) were considered by the House of Lords. Lord Ackner noted that s47 did not expressly require any mens rea as regards the causing of actual bodily harm, and felt unable to conclude that any was required by necessary implication. In his Lordship's view, the words 'occasioning actual bodily harm' were descriptive of the word 'assault' by reference to a particular kind of consequence. In support of this conclusion, Lord Ackner cited *R v Roberts* (above), and the finding in that case that the mens rea for s47 was the same as the mens rea required for common assault.

It now seems settled, therefore, that once an assault is established, the only remaining question under s47 is that of whether or not the actual bodily harm was a consequence of that assault. This matter can be resolved by applying an objective test. It will not be necessary to investigate the defendant's degree of awareness of consequences.

5.2 Section 20 of the Offences Against the Person Act 1861

Section 20 of the Offences Against the Person Act 1861 in effect creates two offences: 'malicious wounding'; and 'maliciously inflicting grievous bodily harm'. Both offences carry the possibility of five years imprisonment.

Malicious wounding

Actus reus
A wounding requires there to have been a break in the surface of the victim's skin. A graze may not be sufficient to satisfy this. The dermis and the epidermis must have been broken. Similarly, where the defendant's action causes internal bleeding only, this will not be held to constitute wounding. The authority for these propositions is the decision of the Divisional Court in *JJC (A Minor)* v *Eisenhower* [1984] QB 331, where it was held that broken blood vessels in the victim's eye, caused by pellets fired from an air gun by the defendant, did not amount to a wounding within s20. A defendant in such a case might, however, still be guilty of actual bodily harm, or even grievous bodily harm in extreme cases. As this is a 'result crime' it will be necessary to establish that the defendant's act is a sufficiently proximate cause of the victim's wound. Complications may arise where the defendant's act is the indirect cause of the wound, eg ordering a dog to bite a victim: see *R* v *Dume* (1987) The Times 16 October.

Mens rea
The mens rea required for the offence is denoted by the word 'malicious'. The basis for the modern interpretation of this somewhat archaic expression is the decision of the Court of Appeal in *R* v *Cunningham* (1957) 41 Cr App R 155. The defendant was charged with unlawfully and maliciously causing a person to take a noxious thing, namely coal gas, so as to endanger her life, contrary to s23 of the Offences against the Person Act 1861, an offence which also has the word 'maliciously' to denote the mens rea required. In the course of his judgment, Byrne J referred (at p159) to:

'... the following principle which was propounded by the late Professor C S Kenny in the first edition of his *Outlines of Criminal Law* published in 1902 and repeated at page 186 of the sixteenth edition edited by Mr J W Cecil Turner and published in 1952. "In any statutory definition of a crime, malice must be taken not in the old vague sense of wickedness in general but as requiring either (1) an actual intention to do the particular kind of harm that in fact was done; or (2) recklessness as to whether such harm should occur or not (ie the accused has foreseen that the particular kind of harm might be done and yet has gone on to take the risk of it). It is neither limited to nor does it indeed require any ill will towards the person injured". The same principle is repeated by Mr Turner in his tenth edition of *Russell on Crime* at p1592: "... in our opinion the word 'maliciously' in a statutory crime postulates foresight of consequence."'

Note that for these purposes maliciousness was equated with intention or recklessness, the recklessness being subjective (requiring proof of foresight on the part of the accused), and the consequence the accused must have been proved to have been aware of, was the harm specified in the offence. For the purposes of s20, therefore, the defendant would at least have to be aware of the risk of causing grievous bodily harm or wounding. A gloss was placed upon the definition in *Cunningham* by Diplock LJ in the later case of *R v Mowatt* (1967) 51 Cr App R 402 at 406 where, having referred to the facts of *Cunningham* he stated:

'No doubt upon these facts the jury should be instructed that they must be satisfied before convicting the accused that he was aware that physical harm to some human being was a possible consequence of his unlawful act in wrenching off the gas meter [the act that caused the coal gas to escape]. In the words of the court, "maliciously in a statutory crime postulates foresight of consequence", and upon this proposition we do not wish to cast any doubt. But the court in that case also expressed approval obiter of a more general statement by Professor Kenny [Kenny's *Outlines of Criminal Law*, extracted above] ... [T]his generalisation is not in our view, appropriate to the specific alternative statutory offences described in ss18 and 20 of the Offences against the Person Act 1861. In the offence under s20, and in the alternative verdict which may be given on a charge under s18, for neither of which is any specific intent required, the word "maliciously" does import upon the part of the person who unlawfully inflicts the wound or other grievous bodily harm an awareness that his act may have caused the consequence of causing some physical harm to some other person. That is what is meant by "the particular kind of harm" in the citation from Professor Kenny. It is quite unnecessary that the accused should have foreseen that his unlawful act might cause physical harm of the gravity described in the section, ie, a wound or serious physical injury. It is enough that he should have foreseen that some physical harm to some person, albeit of a minor character, might result.'

Clearly the interpretation offered by Diplock LJ represents a significant 'watering down' of the mens rea requirement for s20. A defendant could now be guilty of the offence if he punches P foreseeing that he might cause bruising, but actually cuts his face with the force of the blow. Despite Diplock LJ's reference to 'should have foreseen', it would appear that, following the enactment of s8 of the Criminal Justice Act 1967, the defendant must at least foresee some physical harm. Foresight that the victim will be frightened is not of itself sufficient. Hence in *R v Sullivan* [1981] Crim LR 46 the defendant, who had swerved his car towards a group of pedestrians intending to scare them, was acquitted of a charge under s20, when he lost control of the vehicle and subsequently collided with the pedestrians causing injury. As he had only foreseen the risk of 'psychic harm' his liability was reduced to s47.

Any remaining doubts as to the validity of the reasoning in *R* v *Mowatt* have since been swept aside by the House of Lords decision in *R* v *Savage*; *R* v *Parmenter* [1991] 3 WLR 914, in which Lord Ackner confirmed that the gloss placed upon *Cunningham* by *Mowatt* was correct. His Lordship rejected the criticism that the mens rea should extend to the actus reus specified. Consistent with his analysis of s47, considered above, he cited *R* v *Roberts* (above) and the offence of murder, where a defendant can be convicted even though he only foresees grievous bodily harm. In short, he rejected that there was any hard and fast principle in criminal law that the mens rea of an offence should necessarily extend to the actus reus. See further *R* v *Rushworth* (1993) 95 Cr App R 252, where Mann LJ suggested that an accurate statement of what was required when directing a jury as to the meaning of the word 'maliciously' would be the following:

'In order to establish an offence under section 20 the prosecution must prove either that the defendant intended to, or that he actually foresaw his act might cause physical harm to some person albeit harm of a minor character.'

There is one issue of principle that remains unresolved by the decision in *R* v *Savage*; *R* v *Parmenter*. Both s47 and s20 carry the same maximum penalty, ie five years imprisonment, yet they are now distinguished to the extent that the former requires no mens rea as to consequences, whilst the latter requires at least an awareness that some physical harm might occur. The distinction can, of course, be reflected in the exercise of judicial discretion when sentencing, but it is submitted that either the maximum punishment for s47 should reflect the lower degree of mens rea required, or alternatively it should be seen as an offence that does require some mens rea as to consequences, thus placing it on the same footing as s20. Lord Ackner was not unaware of these criticisms, but explained the situation as being the result of 'piecemeal legislation'. He cited with approval JC Smith's view that the 1861 Act was:

'... a ragbag of offences brought together from a wide variety of sources with no attempt, as the draftsman frankly acknowledged, to introduce consistency as to substance or as to form'.

Maliciously inflicting grievous bodily harm

Actus reus: grievous bodily harm

Grievous bodily harm was defined by the House of Lords in *DPP* v *Smith* [1961] AC 290 as 'really serious harm'. Following the more recent Court of Appeal decision in *R* v *Saunders* [1985] Crim LR 230, it is sufficient for a trial judge to direct a jury that grievous bodily harm simply means 'serious harm'. A fractured limb will thus satisfy the definition, as would permanent disablement of the victim, a fractured skull, or the rupturing of internal organs.

In *R* v *Gelder* (1994, unreported, but see the news report in *The Times* of 25 May 1994), the defendant was convicted of grievous bodily harm, contrary to s18 of the

Offences Against the Person Act 1861, on the basis of the distress he had caused to a woman to whom he had repeatedly made obscene telephone calls. The trial judge described the victim as having suffered a 'psychological battering'. As a result of the defendant's calls the victim suffered insomnia, diarrhoea and sickness. Although he successfully appealed against conviction on the basis of the trial judge's misdirection on mens rea (see *The Times* 16 December 1994), the issue of whether or not a telephone call could inflict harm amounting to grievous bodily harm was not dealt with.

Actus reus: 'inflicting'

The statute refers to the infliction of grievous bodily harm, and the question arises as to what extent, if at all, this involves proof of something more than mere causation. In *R v Clarence* (1888) 22 QBD 23, the majority of the court were of the opinion that 'inflict' required proof of some direct assault. The decision was to some extent at odds with the earlier case of *R v Martin* (1881) 8 QBD 54, in which the defendant blocked the exit doors of a theatre, put out the lights in a passageway, and shouted 'Fire!' as the theatre-goers were leaving the performance. In the ensuing panic, many were severely injured by being crushed against the locked doors. The defendant was convicted under s20 and appealed. His conviction was confirmed by the Court for Crown Cases Reserved, and it is implicit in the decision that the indirect way in which the defendant's acts had caused the harm presented no bar to liability.

In any event, *R v Clarence* must now be considered as a dubious authority on the point, given the more recent House of Lords' decision in *R v Wilson* [1983] 3 WLR 686. The defendant motorist had been involved in an argument with a pedestrian, which culminated in the defendant punching the pedestrian in the face. The defendant was charged under s20 of the 1861 Act, and the jury found him not guilty under this section, but exercising their powers under s6(3) of the Criminal Law Act 1967, found him guilty of the lesser offence under s47. The defendant appealed on the ground that it had not been open to the jury, acting under s6(3), to return such a verdict, because s47 was not a lesser included offence within s20. The Court of Appeal quashed the conviction, but certified the following point of law for consideration by the House of Lords:

> 'Whether on a charge of inflicting grievous bodily harm contrary to s20 of the Offences Against the Person Act 1861 it is open to a jury to return a verdict of not guilty as charged but guilty of assault occasioning actual bodily harm.'

The House of Lords held that a defendant acquitted under s20 could nevertheless be convicted under s47. A s20 charge did not necessarily have to include an allegation of assault (although almost all would). The House of Lords rejected the narrow approach to the implementation of s6(3), suggested in cases such as *R v Springfield* (1969) 53 Cr App R 608, to the effect that an offence was a lesser included one only if proof of the lesser offence was a precondition to establishing the more serious offence (eg manslaughter and murder). The broad approach was to ask if proof of the greater offence (eg s20) by necessary implication involved proof of the lesser offence (eg s47). It was sufficient for the purposes of s6(3) of the 1967 Act that the more serious charge against a defendant should expressly, or impliedly, amount to, or include, the lesser offence for which he had actually been convicted. This view has subsequently been reaffirmed by Lord Ackner in *R* v *Savage*; *R* v *Parmenter* (above).

In *R* v *Brown* [1993] 2 WLR 556 Lord Jauncey, rejecting the contention that the consent of the victim might be a defence to a charge under s47 but not s20, bases his argument on the fact that complications would arise precisely because s47 is an alternative verdict where D is charged with maliciously inflicting grievous bodily harm.

What of the defendant acquitted of causing grievous bodily harm contrary to s18 of the 1861 Act? Can a jury exercise the discretion granted by s6(3) of the 1967 Act and return a guilty verdict as regards inflicting grievous bodily harm contrary to s20 of the 1861 Act? The question arose, albeit slightly obliquely, in *R* v *Mandair* [1994] 2 WLR 700, where the jury had acquitted the defendant of the s18 offence, but returned a verdict of guilty of 'causing grievous bodily harm' contrary to s20 of the 1861 Act. A majority of their Lordships held that the causing of grievous bodily harm (the defendant had thrown sulphuric acid at his wife causing severe facial burns) had been contrary to s20 in that it had consisted of inflicting grievous bodily harm. The term 'causing' under s18 was wide enough to encompass any manner of 'inflicting' under s20, hence a conviction for inflicting grievous bodily harm contrary to s20 was available as an alternative to causing grievous bodily harm contrary to s18. Given that, read as a whole, it was clear from the jury's verdict that they regarded the defendant as having caused grievous bodily harm, otherwise than by wounding, it was a technicality that the offence on which they had convicted him did not use the word 'causing'. Clearly the issues that gave rise to this appeal could have been circumvented had the prosecution simply added an alternative count to the indictment alleging the infliction of grievous bodily harm contrary to s20. The decision overrules the Court of Appeal's earlier decision in *R* v *Field* [1993] Crim LR 456 (in which it was held that the offence of inflicting grievous bodily harm contrary to s20 of the 1861 Act could not be equated with causing grievous bodily harm). Logic would suggest that, following this decision a charge under s18 also includes an allegation that the defendant has occasioned actual bodily harm contrary to s47 of the 1861 Act. See chapter 26, section 26.3, for further details.

Mens rea
The mens rea requires proof that the defendant acted maliciously, see above.

5.3 Section 18 of the Offences Against the Person Act 1861

Section 18 of the 1861 Act provides (inter alia):

> 'Whosoever shall unlawfully and maliciously ... wound or cause any grievous bodily harm to any person ... with intent to do some grievous bodily harm to any person, ... shall be guilty of an offence ...'

Actus reus

The actus reus of the offence, wounding or causing grievous bodily harm, has been considered at 5.2 above.

Mens rea

The main distinguishing factor separating s18 from s20 is the mens rea required. Again the defendant must be malicious, as to which see 5.2 above, but in addition he must be proved to have had a further specific intent, in that it must have been the defendant's intention to do some grievous bodily harm to the victim. The principal authority on this point is the Court of Appeal's decision in *R* v *Belfon* [1976] 1 WLR 741. The defendant had slashed the victim with a razor causing severe wounds to his face and chest, and was convicted under s18. The trial judge's direction to the jury was that they could convict if they were satisfied that the defendant had foreseen grievous bodily harm as something that would probably result from his actions. The conviction was quashed by the Court of Appeal, Wein J holding that the prosecution had to establish that it was the defendant's purpose to do some grievous bodily harm. Recklessness as to consequences was certainly not sufficient. Since the House of Lords' decision in *R* v *Hancock* [1986] AC 455, it would appear that the existence of the intention to do some grievous bodily harm required under s18 can be inferred by the jury from what the defendant foresaw. Even so, it is submitted that a jury should be warned that evidence that the defendant foresaw grievous bodily harm as a probable consequence of his actions, would not justify them in making that inference: see *R* v *Bryson* [1985] Crim LR 669.

Charging standards

Following the publication, in June 1994, of the revised Code for Crown Prosecutors, the Police and the CPS have co-operated in the development of charging standards on (non-sexual and non-fatal) offences against the person to ensure greater consistency. Key aspects of the charging standards indicate the following:

1. An assault involving a battery that results in harm that technically constitutes actual bodily harm contrary to s47 of the Offences Against the Person Act 1861 should be charged as a common assault contrary to s39 of the 1861 Act where the injury amounts to no more than a graze, scratch, abrasion, bruise (including a 'black eye'), swelling, reddening of the skin or a superficial cut. Where such injuries are the result of an assault upon a constable in the execution of his duty a charge under s51(1) of the Police Act 1964 is to be preferred.

2. The following injuries should normally be charged under s47 of the 1861 Act: loss or breaking of a tooth or teeth; temporary loss of sensory functions; extensive or multiple bruising; displaced broken nose, minor fractures; cuts requiring stitches; and psychiatric injury which goes beyond fear and panic, supported by appropriate expert evidence.

3. Section 20 of the 1861 Act should be reserved for those wounds considered to be serious, ie on a par with grievous bodily harm. Injuries that should be equated with grievous bodily harm include those resulting in: permanent disability or loss of a sensory function; more than minor permanent visible disfigurement; broken or displaced limbs or bones; injuries causing substantial loss of blood (ie necessitating a transfusion); and injury resulting in lengthy treatment or incapacitation.

Reform

The DCLB envisages three new offences replacing the existing offences under ss47, 20 and 18 of the 1861 Act. In place of s18, clause 2(1) provides:

> 'A person is guilty of an offence if he intentionally causes serious injury to another.'

Clause 3(1) proposes a replacement for s20 as follows:

> 'A person is guilty of an offence if he recklessly causes serious injury to another.'

Section 47 would be replaced by clause 4, which states that:

> 'A person is guilty of an offence if he intentionally or recklessly causes injury to another.'

'Injury' would be given the following meaning by clause 18:

> '(a) physical injury, including pain, unconsciousness, or any other impairment of a person's physical condition, or (b) impairment of a person's mental health.'

These proposals should, of course, be read in conjunction with the proposals to rationalise the use of fault elements such as 'intention' and 'recklessness' in criminal law: see Chapter 2.

5.4 Sections 23 and 24 of the Offences Against the Person Act 1861

Section 23 of the 1861 Act creates the offence of 'maliciously administering a noxious substance so as to endanger life, or inflict grievous bodily harm'.

Section 24 also involves the malicious administering of a noxious substance, but requires a further intent, namely that this should 'injure, aggrieve, or annoy' the victim.

Actus reus

Both ss23 and 24 require the administering of a noxious substance.

Noxious substance

In *R v Cato* (1976) 62 Cr App R 41, the Court of Appeal stated that a substance was noxious for the purposes of these offences if it was likely to injure in common use. In *R* v *Marcus* [1981] 1 WLR 774, however, a preferable approach was suggested, where it was held that whether or not a substance was noxious would depend on the circumstances in which it was taken. Such circumstances would involve the quality and quantity of the substance, and the characteristics of the person to whom it was being given.

Administering

The term 'administration' was thought to carrying with it some quasi-medical meaning, with the result that a defendant could not be guilty under s23 where he squirted a noxious substance in the face of his victim: see *R* v *Dones* [1987] Crim LR 682. The correct view is that advanced by the Court of Appeal in *R* v *Gillard* (1988) 87 Cr App R 189, where McNeill J observed that the trial judge had erred in holding that 'administering' and 'taking' were to be treated effectively as synonymous or as conjunctive words. He continued:

> 'The word "takes" postulates some "ingestion" by the victim; "administer" must have some other meaning and there is no difficulty in including in that meaning such conduct as spraying the victim with noxious fluid or vapour, whether from a device such as a gas canister or, for example, hosing down with effluent. There is no necessity when the word "administer" is used to postulate any form of entry into the victim's body, whether through any orifice or by absorption; a court dealing with such a case should not have to determine questions of pathology such as, for example, the manner in which skin irritation results from exposure to CS gas or the manner in which the eye waters when exposed to irritant. The word "ingest" should be reserved to its natural meaning of intake into the digestive system and not permitted to obscure the statutory words.
>
> In the view of this Court, the proper construction of "administer" in section 24 includes conduct which not being the application of direct force to the victim nevertheless brings the noxious thing into contact with his body. While such conduct might in law amount to an assault, this court considers that so to charge it would tend to mislead a jury.'

Mens rea

Both offences require proof of the defendant acting maliciously, as to which see 5.2 above, but note particularly that the defendant in *R* v *Cunningham* [1957] 2 QB 396, was charged under s23.

Section 24 clearly requires proof of a further intent to injure aggrieve or annoy the victim. This means that the defendant's purpose in administering the noxious substance must be examined. In *R* v *Weatherall* [1968] Crim LR 115 the trial judge directed a jury that the necessary mens rea had not been established where the defendant had given his wife sleeping tablets, so that he could look through her handbag for letters revealing details of her adultery whilst she was asleep.

The nature of the 'ulterior intent' was considered by the House of Lords in *R* v *Hill* [1986] Crim LR 815. The defendant, a homosexual man, admitted giving some slimming tablets, which were normally only available on prescription, to a number of small boys. He had hoped that the effect of the tablets would be to lower the boys' inhibitions and make them more susceptible to his advances. The Court of Appeal had quashed his conviction on the ground that the trial judge might have misdirected the jury into assuming that an intention to keep the boys awake amounted to a sufficient ulterior intent for a conviction under s24. The question certified for consideration by their Lordships was:

> 'Whether the offence of administering a noxious substance with intent to injure ... is capable of being committed when a noxious thing is administered to a person without lawful excuse with the intention only of keeping that person awake.'

The House of Lords restored the conviction on the basis that there was overwhelming evidence that the defendant had intended the administration of the tablets to injure the metabolisms of the boys who took them. In answer to the certified question, it was held that (in so far as it could be answered on the facts of this case) the matter had to be approached by looking at the object that the defendant had in mind. To keep a pilot awake by plying him with stimulants so that he could safely land an aircraft would not involve the commission of an offence, whereas to deprive him of sleep for the purposes of interrogation might well do so. Similarly, it was suggested that to keep a child awake in order to greet the arrival of a relative late at night, or view a fireworks display would fall outside s24.

By implication, a man who secretly gives a woman sleeping pills with a view to sexually assaulting her whilst she is asleep would come within s24, but not where he does so in order to ensure that he has an uninterrupted night's sleep when sharing a bed with her.

Consider generally the appropriateness of these two offences for dealing with defendants who knowingly infect other persons with viruses, etc. Should the defendant in *R* v *Clarence* (above) have been charged under either of these sections? Could the offences be used where D causes P to become HIV positive?

A person suffering from AIDS can be detained pursuant to a magistrate's order issued under the Public Health Control of Diseases Act 1984, and the Infectious Diseases Regulations 1985. It would appear that this power could only be used prospectively, where there was a risk to other people, and not retrospectively where deliberate transmission had taken place.

Reform

The DCLB proposes the abolition, without replacement, of s23, and the replacement of s24 with a single offence, detailed in clause 5, which provides:

> '(1) A person is guilty of an offence if, knowing that the other does not consent to what is done, he intentionally or recklessly administers to or causes to be taken by another a substance which he knows to be capable of interfering substantially with the other's bodily functions.
> (2) For the purposes of this section a substance capable of inducing unconsciousness or sleep is capable of interfering substantially with bodily functions.'

5.5 Abortion and child destruction

Sections 58 and 59 of the Offences Against the Person Act 1861

Section 58 of the 1861 Act creates the offence of unlawfully procuring a miscarriage. The offence can be committed by anyone who unlawfully administers any poison or noxious substance, or uses any means to procure a miscarriage. Where the defendant is a woman who has administered such substances to herself, or used such means upon herself, the prosecution must prove that she was actually pregnant at the time. In the case of any other defendant, there can be liability under s58 regardless of whether the woman concerned is pregnant or not.

Note that s58 distinguishes between poison and other noxious substances. It has been held that where the substance administered is not a recognised poison, it must be taken in such quantities that it becomes harmful to health: see *R* v *Marlow* (1964) 49 Cr App R 49.

Where a woman, who wrongly believes herself to be pregnant, persuades another person to commit an offence under the section, she may still be guilty of conspiring to commit the offence or of being an accomplice to the offence, notwithstanding the fact that she herself is not pregnant: see *R* v *Whitchurch* (1890) 24 QBD 420, and *R* v *Sockett* (1908) 72 JP 428.

An important limitation on the scope of the offence is the requirement that the defendant should be proved to have acted unlawfully. In *R* v *Bourne* [1939] 1 KB 687, the defendant doctor performed an abortion upon a 14-year-old girl who had been raped. He performed the operation in a hospital, with the consent of the parents, and did not receive any fee. He had formed the view that if the girl was allowed to give birth she might not survive. The defendant was acquitted by the jury of a charge under s58, following a direction from MacNaghten J, to the effect that such conduct was not to be viewed as unlawful where the defendant acted in good faith, to save the life of the mother. Were the situation to arise today, the doctor might well be protected from a prosecution under s58 by the provisions of the Abortion Act 1967, considered below. The direction in *R* v *Bourne* can also be seen as an indirect recognition of the defence of necessity, although the common law still refuses to permit this as a general defence: see further Chapter 14.

Under s59 of the 1861 Act liability is extended to those who knowingly supply the means for procuring a miscarriage, regardless of whether or not the woman upon whom they are to be used, or to whom they are to be supplied, is pregnant or not.

Infant Life (Preservation) Act 1929

Section 1(1) of this Act provides that any person who intentionally causes the death of a child capable of being born alive shall, following conviction, be liable to life imprisonment. The Act expressly provides that no one who commits such acts in good faith, to preserve the life of the mother, shall be guilty of the offence.

The Act contains a rebuttable presumption in s1(2) that a child is capable of being born alive once 28 weeks of pregnancy has passed. Given that this provision was enacted some 60 years ago, since when the skill of doctors in keeping alive premature babies has increased out of all recognition, there has been considerable pressure for the '28 week rule' to be altered. As stated above it is actually a rebuttable presumption, not a rule, so it is always open to the prosecution to bring a charge under the 1929 Act even though an abortion has been performed on a woman who was less than 28 weeks pregnant, provided it can be proved beyond all reasonable doubt that the baby would have survived had it been born at that stage of the pregnancy. The matter was considered by the Court of Appeal in *C v S* [1987] 2 WLR 1108, where the defendant was a single woman, between 18 and 21 weeks pregnant, who wished to have an abortion. The father applied for an injunction to prevent the abortion, on the ground, inter alia, that if carried out it would constitute an offence under the 1929 Act, since in his view the child was by now a viable foetus, or child capable of being born alive. The court held that whilst a foetus of this age might display rudimentary signs of life, the medical evidence established on a balance of probabilities that such a foetus was not a child capable of being born alive for the purposes of the 1929 Act. The evidence of the foetus' viability was much clearer, however, in *Rance v Mid Downs Health Authority* [1991] 1 All ER 801. The plaintiff sought damages for the alleged failure of the defendant's radiographer to identify a foetus as having spina bifida. The plaintiff's contention was that if the condition had been correctly identified she would have sought an abortion. The court found as a fact that if the abortion had taken place, the foetus would have been 27 weeks old, and thus protected by the terms of the 1929 Act. The '28 week rule' was clearly rebutted by the evidence that if the child had been born after 27 weeks it would have been capable of sustaining an independent existence. In those circumstances the court refused to allow the plaintiff to pursue a cause of action based on the failure of the health authority to carry out an abortion which would in any event have been an offence under the 1929 Act.

Abortion Act 1967

The 1967 Act, as amended by the Human Fertilisation and Embryology Act 1990, provides that doctors carrying out abortions will not incur liability under s58 of the 1861 Act or the Infant Life (Preservation) Act 1929, provided the conditions laid down in s1 of the 1967 Act are complied with.

Such abortion will be lawful if carried out within the first 24 weeks of the pregnancy, where two registered medical practitioners, acting in good faith, are of the opinion that the continuation of the pregnancy would involve risk, greater than if pregnancy were terminated, of injury to the physical or mental health of the pregnant woman or any existing children of her family.

Beyond 24 weeks there are three grounds for permitting a termination. First the doctors must have formed the view that a termination is required to prevent grave permanent injury to the mother's mental or physical health. Secondly, because pregnancy would involve risk to the mother's life greater than if the pregnancy were terminated. Thirdly, because it is necessary due to the substantial risk of the child being born with serious physical or mental handicaps.

Section 5(1) of the 1967 Act, as amended by the 1990 Act, has the further effect of removing the possibility of liability under the Infant Life (Preservation) Act 1929 where an abortion is carried out within the terms of the 1967 Act.

It remains a matter of some doubt as to whether a doctor performing an abortion not permitted by the 1967 Act could nevertheless rely on the decision in *R* v *Bourne* (above) by way of defence.

Reform

The offence of unlawfully procuring a miscarriage set out in s58 of the 1861 Act (with the exception of passages relating to a woman procuring her own miscarriage) would be replaced by clause 66 of the draft code which provides:

> 'A person is guilty of an offence if he intentionally causes the miscarriage of a woman otherwise than in accordance with the provisions of the Abortion Act 1967.'

Self abortion is provided for separately in clause 67, which states that a pregnant woman is guilty of an offence if she intentionally causes her own miscarriage otherwise than in accordance with the provisions of the Abortion Act 1967.

Interestingly, the Code envisages a departure from the usual rules relating to impossibility in that it goes on to provide that a woman who is not pregnant cannot be guilty of an attempt to commit an offence under the draft code. Clause 68 proposes an offence of supplying or procuring an article or substance knowing that it is to be used with the intention of causing the miscarriage of a woman otherwise than in accordance with the provisions of the Abortion Act 1967, whether the woman concerned is pregnant or not. Clause 69 reproduces the effect of s1 of the Infant Life (Preservation) Act 1929 in Code style. Subsection (3) goes on to provide for the situation where a child is killed whilst being born. It states:

> 'A person who is found not guilty of murder or manslaughter (or attempted murder or manslaughter) of a child by reason only of the fact that the jury is uncertain whether the child had been born or whether he had an existence independent of his mother when his death occurred (or, in the case of an attempt, when the act was done) shall be convicted of child destruction (or attempted child destruction).'

5.6 Rape

The statutory basis for the offence of rape is s1(1) of the **Sexual Offences Act 1956**, as amended by s1(2) of the Sexual Offences (Amendment) Act 1976 and s142 of the Criminal Justice and Public Order Act 1994. In its amended form s1 of the 1956 Act now states:

'1(1) It is an offence for a man to rape a woman or another man.

(2) A man commits rape if–

a) he has sexual intercourse with a person (whether vaginal or anal) who at the time of the intercourse does not consent to it; and

b) at the time he knows that the person does not consent to the intercourse or is reckless as to whether that person consents to it.

(3) A man also commits rape if he induces a married woman to have sexual intercourse with him by impersonating her husband.

(4) Subsection (2) applies for the purpose of any enactment.'

Actus reus of rape

The Criminal Justice and Public Order Act 1994, by virtue of s142, has substantially redrawn the offence of rape by introducing the concept of male rape, ie non-consensual buggery committed by one man upon another. The revised offence retains the generic term 'sexual intercourse' to cover both vaginal and anal intercourse, thus creating the possibility that a man could be guilty of raping a woman, even though he has sodomised her, and not had vaginal intercourse. The term 'sexual intercourse' is defined further in s44 of the Sexual Offences Act 1956 which provides:

'Where, on the trial of any offence under this Act, it is necessary to prove sexual intercourse (whether natural or unnatural), it shall not be necessary to prove the completion of the intercourse by the emission of the seed, but the intercourse shall be deemed complete upon proof of penetration only.'

There are still certain forms of violent sexual assault that can be traumatic for the victim that fall outside the scope of rape, eg the penetration of the vagina or anus by means of objects such as bottles or sticks. Similarly, the penetration of other orifices, particularly the mouth in cases of forced oral sex, would have to be charged as indecent assault; see further *R v Kowalski* (1987) 86 Cr App R 339.

Although s1(1) refers to a man committing the offence, it is possible for any male over the age of 10 to be charged with rape, following the enactment of the Sexual Offences Act 1993, which abolishes the presumption that a boy below the age of 14 cannot perform sexual intercourse for the purposes of offences where that is an element. Clearly, it is technically possible for a woman to be charged with rape, but only as an accomplice.

Prior to the reforms effected by s142 of the Criminal Justice and Public Order Act 1994, the prosecution were required to prove that the sexual intercourse in question was 'unlawful'. For centuries this had been taken to mean that the sexual intercourse had to be between parties who were not lawfully man and wife, on the basis that the wife's consent to intercourse was presumed from her having entered into the marriage. As Hale stated (*Pleas of the Crown* Vol 1, p629):

'... by their mutual matrimonial consent and contract the wife hath given up herself in this kind unto her husband which she cannot retract.'

Limits were set upon the rule in relation to married persons no longer living together as man and wife, eg *R* v *Clarke* (1949) 33 Cr App R 216, where it was held that a husband could be guilty of rape upon his wife where a separation order was in force, the wife's consent to intercourse being revoked by the order; and *R* v *Steele* (1976) 65 Cr App R 22, where a husband was convicted of rape having given the court an undertaking that he would not molest his wife from whom he was living apart. See further *R* v *Miller* [1954] 2 QB 282. The House of Lords took the lead in abolishing the common rule against marital rape, however, in *R* v *R* [1991] 3 WLR 767, where Lord Keith noted that:

> 'By the second half of the twentieth century the status of a husband and wife are now for all practical purposes equal partners in marriage and both husband and wife are tutors and curators of their children. A wife is not obliged to obey her husband in all things nor to suffer excessive sexual demands on the part of her husband. She may rely on such demands as evidence of unreasonable behaviour for the purposes of divorce. A live system of law will always have regard to changing circumstances to test the justification for any exception to the application of a general rule. Nowadays it cannot seriously be maintained that by marriage a wife submits herself irrevocably to sexual intercourse in all circumstances. It cannot be affirmed nowadays, whatever the position may have been in earlier centuries, that it is an incident of modern marriage that a wife consents to intercourse in all circumstances, including sexual intercourse obtained only by force. There is no doubt that a wife does not consent to assault upon her person and there is no plausible justification for saying today that she nevertheless is to be taken to consent to intercourse by assault.'

Although their Lordships' ruling was widely applauded as being enlightened and dynamic, the problem remained that the offence of rape, as defined under statute at the time, still required proof that the sexual intercourse was 'unlawful'. At the time Lord Keith dealt with this issue by asserting:

> '... it is clearly unlawful to have sexual intercourse with any woman without her consent, and that the use of the word in the [statute] adds nothing ... it should be treated as being mere surplusage in this enactment ...'

Whilst this reasoning was, with respect, somewhat questionable, the new formulation of the offence of rape provided by s1(1) of the 1956 Act puts the matter beyond doubt by omitting any reference to the intercourse having to be unlawful.

The consent of the victim, to the commission of what would otherwise be an unlawful act, is normally raised as a defence by the defendant. The offence of rape is somewhat unusual in this respect in that the absence of consent on the part of the victim is an element of the crime that has to be positively established by the prosecution. In *R* v *Olugboja* (1981) 73 Cr App R 344 it was held that there should be no need to prove submission on the part of the woman; the simple question for the jury was now one of, did the woman consent? Unfortunately such questions are difficult to answer because in many cases a rape victim only consents to rape because she views herself as having no option, perhaps because the man has a knife at her face, or because he has indicated that he will not continue their relationship unless he can have sexual intercourse with her. The first example is readily identifiable as rape, but the latter is less likely to be so viewed. In both cases it could be claimed that the victim has considered her predicament and decided that she prefers to have intercourse rather than deal with the consequences of not doing so, yet in both cases it could be claimed there is an absence of free and voluntary consent. In reality the matter depends upon the jury's conception of what looks like rape and what does not. As Dunn LJ (in *Olugboja*) expressed the matter:

> 'Although "consent" is [a] common word it covers a wide range of states of mind in the context of intercourse between a man and a woman, ranging from actual desire on the one hand to reluctant acquiescence on the other. We do not think that the issue of consent should be left to a jury without some further direction. What this should be will depend on the circumstances of each case. The jury ... should be directed that consent, or the absence of it, is to be given its ordinary meaning and if need be, by way of example, that there is a difference between consent and submission; every consent involves a submission, but it by no means follows that a mere submission involves consent ... In the less common type of case where intercourse takes place after threats not involving violence or the fear of it ... a jury will have to be ... directed to concentrate on the state of mind of the victim immediately before the act of sexual intercourse, having regard to all the relevant circumstances; and in particular, the events leading up to the act and her reaction to them showing their impact on her mind. Apparent acquiescence after penetration does not necessarily involve consent, which must have occurred before the act takes place ... the dividing line ... between real consent on the one hand and mere submission on the other may not be easy to draw. Where it is to be drawn in a given case is for the jury to decide, applying their combined good sense, experience and knowledge of human nature and modern behaviour to all the relevant facts of that case.'

Although the court in *Olugboja* was concerned with the offence of rape as defined under the pre-1994 law, it is submitted that the general principles stated above in relation to the absence or otherwise of consent on the part of the victim should apply equally whether the victim is male or female.

The consent of the victim may be vitiated by reason of its having been obtained by fraud. A man who induces a married woman to have sexual intercourse with him by impersonating her husband commits rape, by virtue of s1(2) of the 1956 Act, although liability would not extend to a situation where D fraudulently induced P into thinking that they had just been through a marriage ceremony and proceeded to have intercourse with her. If the ceremony was bogus, then P would not be a 'married woman' (*R* v *Papadimitropoulos* (1957) 98 CLR 249) although D might nevertheless be guilty of procurement contrary to s3(1) of the 1956 Act (below).

As regards other types of fraudulent behaviour by which a man might induce a woman to allow him to have sexual intercourse, the law is unclear as to whether such activity amounts to rape. For example, where P agrees to sexual intercourse with D only if he loves her, or where D falsely pretends to be a famous film star and that is the sole reason for P agreeing to intercourse, D may have committed the lesser offence of procuring a woman by false pretences contrary to s3(1) of the 1956 Act, but has he committed rape? In the absence of any clear authority a possible solution might be the adoption of the view that where P is misled by D as to his identity (where this is of importance to P), or as to the nature of what he is going to do, then D should be charged with rape. Hence in *R v Williams* (1923) 17 Cr App R 56, the defendant singing master told his pupil that she needed an operation to improve her singing voice, to which she agreed. The operation consisted of him having sexual intercourse with her. When charged with rape he contended that she had consented to his actions. The court held that there was no consent in this case. What the pupil had thought she was consenting to was something fundamentally different from that which occurred.

Alternatively, where the vitiating factor relates to a non-fundamental matter, it is likely that the consent will be voidable at the option of the victim when he or she discovers the truth.

In *R v Linekar* (1994) The Times 26 October, the appellant had sexual intercourse with the complainant, who had been working as a prostitute. The complainant alleged that prior to sexual intercourse he had promised to pay her £25 for sex, but later refused to do so. On a charge of rape the trial judge directed the jury to the effect that if the complainant's consent to intercourse had been obtained by fraud she could not properly be regarded as having given her consent. Allowing the appeal, Morland J cited with approval the dictum of Willis J in *R v Clarence* (1888) 22 QBD 23 to the effect that the only types of fraud that would destroy the effect of a woman's consent to sexual intercourse were frauds as to the nature of the act being performed or fraud as to the identity of the person performing the act. Further support was drawn from *R v Papdimitropoulos* (1956) 98 CLR 249, where the view was expressed that it was not the fraud producing the mistake that was material but the effect of the mistake itself. On this basis the court in the instant case was satisfied that the appellant's fraud as to payment was not such as could be said to vitiate the complainant's consent. It is perhaps worth noting that the complainant said that she had only consented to intercourse on the basis that the appellant would be wearing a condom, which he did not do. Could it be argued in such cases that she has not consented to intercourse, on the basis that with the obvious danger of AIDS, consent to 'safe' sex is consent to an act that is materially different from unprotected sex? The court noted that the appellant should have been charged with procuring sexual intercourse by false pretences contrary to s3 of the 1956 Act. It is submitted that an alternative would have been to charge him with obtaining services by deception contrary to s1 of the Theft Act 1978.

The mens rea of rape

The defendant must intend to have vaginal or anal intercourse (as defined above), and must know that the person with whom he is having sexual intercourse does not consent to it, or he must at least be reckless as to whether that person consents. Problems arise where, as in *DPP v Morgan* [1975] 2 All ER 347, the defendant claims that he honestly believed that the victim was consenting. The House of Lords held that the mens rea involved is subjective in that regardless of what the reasonable man may have thought or believed, the prosecution must prove that the defendant knew the victim not to be consenting. Section 1(2) of the 1976 Act (as amended by the Criminal Justice and Public Order Act 1994) to some extent states the obvious by providing that:

> '... if at a trial for a rape offence the jury has to consider whether a man believed that a woman or man was consenting to sexual intercourse, the presence or absence of reasonable grounds for such a belief is a matter to which the jury is to have regard, in conjunction with any other relevant matters, in considering whether he so believed.'

Given that recklessness as to consent will suffice, the question arises as to whether the *Cunningham* or *Caldwell* model should apply. The Court of Appeal decision in *R v Satnam and Kewal* (1983) 78 Cr App R 149 indicates that *Caldwell* recklessness should not be relied upon on a charge of rape as it would have the effect of importing an objective element into the mens rea of the crime, where it seemed clear that Parliament had intended this to be subjective. A defendant who failed to advert to an obvious risk that a woman was not consenting to intercourse would not, therefore, be guilty of reckless rape, but one who had intercourse not caring whether the woman consented or not would be guilty. Where the charge is one of attempted rape, D can be convicted provided he intended to have sexual intercourse with another person, in circumstances where that person did not consent, and that he knew that that person was not consenting or was reckless as to whether they were, and had committed some act which was more than merely preparatory to sexual intercourse: see *R v Khan & Others* (1990) 91 Cr App R 29.

Reform

Clause 89 of the draft code, which deals with the definition of rape, has been largely overtaken by the reforms outlined above. To the extent that it addresses the issue of consent, however, it is still worthy of consideration, provided that it is borne in mind that the offence is no longer gender specific. The draft code addresses the difficult problems of distinguishing between consent and submission, and determining the extent to which consent can be vitiated by deception. Clause 89(2) states:

> 'For the purposes of this section a woman shall be treated as not consenting to sexual intercourse if she consents to it –
> (a) because a threat, express or implied, has been made to use force against her or another if she does not consent and she believes that, if she does not consent, the threat will be carried out immediately or before she can free herself from it; or
> (b) because she has been deceived as to –
> (i) the nature of the act; or
> (ii) the identity of the man.'

The Code Report commentary upon this provision states:

> '[S]ubsection (2) makes it clear that a man is guilty of rape where he obtains the woman's consent by a threat to use force against her or another. The [Criminal Law Revision]

Committee thought that "it should not be rape if, taking a reasonable view, the threats were not capable of being carried out immediately." The Committee made no recommendation to require the woman's belief to be based on reasonable grounds. Detention, in itself, would not negative the effect of consent but the Committee thought that it should be rape where a woman is confined by a man for the purpose of sexual intercourse and there is an express or implied threat to use force against her should she try to escape. But, if the woman knows that she can free herself from the effect of the threat and does not do so, her consent to sexual intercourse will negative rape. The effect of the subsection is that consent obtained by other threats – for example, to break off an engagement or to dismiss from employment – will negative rape but the man will be guilty of an offence under clause 90 [procurement of a woman by threats].' [Vol II para 15.13]

As to deception, the commentary goes on to state:

'Subsection (2), again following the Committee, specifies the circumstances in which it will be rape if consent is obtained by deception. There is authority at common law [*R* v *Williams* [1923] 1 KB 34] that it is rape if the woman is deceived as to the nature of the act and the Sexual Offences Act 1956, s1(2), provides that a man who induces a woman to have sexual intercourse with him by impersonating her husband commits rape; but it is by no means clear that intercourse obtained by other deceptions as to identity constitutes rape. The subsection provides that it does. The effect is that consent obtained by any other deception – for example, that the man is not married or that he intends to marry the woman – will negative rape, as under the present law, but the man will be guilty of an offence under clause 91 [procurement of a woman by deception].' [Vol II para 15.15]

5.7 Unlawful sexual intercourse

Intercourse with a girl under thirteen

Section 5 of the 1956 Act states:

'It is [an offence] for a man to have unlawful sexual intercourse with a girl under the age of thirteen.'

The offence is punishable by life imprisonment. Sexual intercourse carries the meaning provided by s44 of the 1956 Act.

The offence would appear to be one of strict liability, hence the defendant will not be able to rely on the defence that he honestly believed the girl in question to be above 13 years of age, no matter how reasonable his belief: see *R* v *Prince* (1875) LR 2 CCR 154.

Intercourse with a girl under sixteen

Section 6 of the 1956 Act states that it is an offence (subject to certain exceptions) for a man to have unlawful sexual intercourse with a girl under the age of 16. Section 6(2) provides for an exception where D, having contracted a marriage which is invalid by virtue of s2 of the Marriage Act 1949, or s1 of the Age of Marriage Act 1929, has intercourse with P whom he honestly and reasonably believes to be his wife in law.

For the purposes of this offence 'sexual intercourse' carries the meaning given at 5.6 above.

Like s5, this offence is one of strict liability, and the decision in *R* v *Prince* applies with full force as regards the woman's age, except in the case of a defendant below the age of 24. Section 6(3) provides that a defendant under 24 will not be guilty of an offence if he has consensual intercourse with a girl under 16 provided he has not previously been charged with the offence, and honestly and reasonably believed her to be older than 16.

5.8 Indecent assault

Section 14(1) of the 1956 Act provides:

'It is an offence ... for a person to make an indecent assault upon a woman.'

Note that since the enactment of this section, the Indecency with Children Act 1960 has been passed with the result that many cases formerly dealt with under the 1956 Act now come within the 1960 Act.

Actus reus

The victim must be female. Section 46 of the 1956 Act extends the meaning of woman to include girl and vice-versa.

The assault required by the offence has been construed so as to include assault in the strict sense, ie causing another to apprehend immediate physical contact, and battery: see *R* v *Rolfe* (1952) 36 Cr App R 4. If there is physical contact it is not necessary to prove the victim's awareness of the contact or the circumstances of indecency. Where there is no such contact, the complainant must be shown to have apprehended the assault and to have been aware of the circumstances giving rise to indecency. Problems may arise where D plays a passive or non-hostile role in the incident, such as where a young girl places her hand on the defendant's penis and he does nothing to avoid or discontinue the contact. Decisions such as *Fairclough* v *Whipp* [1951] 2 All ER 834 suggested that no assault would be committed by the defendant in such cases: similarly *Williams* v *Gibbs* [1958] Crim LR 127, and *DPP* v *Rodgers* (1953) 37 Cr App R 137. More recently in *R* v *M'Cormack* [1969] 2 QB 442 the Court of Appeal held that an indecent act committed upon a 15-year-old girl was an offence notwithstanding that it was done without hostility. In the case of children under 14 many of these incidents would now be dealt with under the 1960 Act mentioned above, where the problem of proving an assault does not arise. Where the woman is over 16, it is submitted that an assault is committed where she apprehends physical contact to which she does not consent. This leaves the problem of victims between the ages of 14 and 16 who by law cannot consent to assault. In such cases the decision in *R* v *M'Cormack* should prevail.

Indecency is not defined by the 1956 Act, but to secure a conviction the prosecution must prove that the assault in question was committed in circumstances of indecency. In *R v Court* [1988] 2 WLR 1071, the House of Lords confirmed the view of the Court of Appeal that indecency involved a contravention of standards of decent behaviour in regard to sexual modesty or privacy. Clearly this is a flexible concept which will vary from case to case. What one jury regards as indecent, another may find amusing and acceptable. Where an assault is objectively incapable of being regarded as indecent, the secret indecent motive subsequently admitted to by the defendant cannot render it indecent. Such was held by the court in *R v George* [1956] Crim LR 52 and affirmed in *R v Court* (above). Alternatively, where an act could be regarded as indecent, the intention of the accused becomes crucial; see below.

The offence can be committed by 'a person'; hence females can be convicted of indecently assaulting other females.

Mens rea

The defendant must know or believe the victim to be a woman. The assault must be committed intentionally or recklessly: see *R v Venna* [1976] QB 421. The recklessness involved is, it is submitted, subjective as in *R v Cunningham* [1957] 2 QB 396. As mentioned above a secret indecent intention on the part of the defendant will not render an overtly innocent act indecent. Where a defendant's actions are capable of being viewed as either innocent or indecent, evidence in the form of statements made by him to the police, could be put before the jury for them to determine the matter. Hence in *R v Court*, above, a majority of their Lordships held that the defendant's statement to the police that he had spanked a 12-year-old girl because of his 'buttock fetish', was admissible as evidence of his indecent intent. Where the defendant's actions are unambiguously indecent, all that is required is proof of his intention to perform such acts. Provided he has an awareness of his actions his purpose appears to be irrelevant. In *R v C* [1992] Crim LR 642, the appellant was found to have inserted his fingers into the vagina of a young girl. In response to a charge of indecent assault he indicated that he had been drinking and could not remember the incident. The trial judge directed the jury that the offence was one of basic intent and the appellant was duly convicted. On appeal, the court rejected the contention that, following *R v Court* (above), the offence required proof of a specific intent. The court expressed the view that the admission of evidence relating to the defendant's purpose in *R v Court* was permissible given the ambiguous nature of the assault. Where, as in the present case, the assault was unequivocally indecent, there was no need to inquire into the appellant's intention or motive. Provided the appellant had not been in a state of automatism (through no fault of his own) the necessary element of liability would have been present. This, perhaps, raises the question of whether the defendant could rely on evidence of self-induced intoxication in a case where the indecent act is ambiguous in nature. If so, it would presumably reduce D's liability to common assault (ie battery). See further *R v Parsons* [1993] Crim LR 792.

A defendant charged under s14(1) may be able to raise the defence that the woman consented to the indecent assault. As in the case of other offences against the person such consent must be genuine and freely given. A woman over 16 can consent to assault (indecent or otherwise) provided it does not constitute actual bodily harm or worse: see *R v Donovan* [1934] 2 KB 498 and *R v Boyea* [1992] Crim LR 574. Where the victim is under 16, s14(2) provides that any consent given by her is of no effect.

What if D wrongly believes P to be consenting to an indecent assault? Where P is over 16, then D can rely on his honest, though mistaken, belief that she is consenting as a defence. Such belief does not have to be reasonable; see *R v Kimber* (above). Where P is under 16, it would appear that D cannot rely on his/her honest belief that she was consenting as such a mental state is rendered irrelevant by s14(2). In short *R v Prince* (1875) LR 2 CCR 154 applies with full force.

A husband who is a party to an invalid marriage does not commit an offence under s14(1) if he honestly and reasonably believed the woman to be his lawful wife at the time of the indecent assault: see s14(3). Section 14(4) provides that a woman who is a defective cannot consent to an indecent assault, but a defendant can only be convicted where he/she is proved to have known or suspected the victim to be a defective.

A husband can be convicted of indecent assault upon his wife, even where the acts complained of are by way of a prelude to sexual intercourse: see *R v Kowalski* (above). Consent to such acts could not be traced back to the woman's marriage vows. Even if a woman has willingly engaged in such activities in the past, her consent could not be assumed, although a defendant who honestly believes his wife to be consenting would still, presumably, escape liability.

5.9 Indecent assault on a man

Section 15 of the 1956 Act creates the offence of indecent assault upon a man by any person. Subject to a few exceptions the offence is very similar to s14 discussed above. In addition it should be noted that where the s15 offence is committed by a man, an offence under s13 of the 1956 Act, indecency between men, may be committed. The offence may be committed on a 'boy' as well as a man: see s46. In relation to assault and indecency, see 5.9 above. The offence can be committed by a man or a woman. Mens rea is as considered above at 5.8.

Reform

Clause 111 provides that:

'A person is guilty of an indecent assault if he assaults another in such a manner, of which he is aware, or in such circumstances, of which he is aware, as are –
(a) indecent, whatever the purpose with which the act is done; or

(b) indecent only if the act is done with an indecent purpose and he acts with such a purpose.'

The clause amalgamates the existing offences dealing with men and women, and also takes account of the House of Lords' decision in *R* v *Court* (above) with its reference to the defendant's purpose.

6

Homicide I

6.1 Introduction

6.2 Who can be a victim?

6.3 Causation

6.4 The mens rea of murder

6.1 Introduction

In English criminal law homicide is a generic term covering a number of offences, such as murder, manslaughter, and causing death by dangerous driving. What all homicides have in common is the unlawful killing of a human being; what distinguishes them is either the state of mind of the defendant who has caused death, or the defences available.

6.2 Who can be a victim?

Homicide is only committed where the defendant is shown to have killed a human being, thus raising questions of when life begins and ends. If the defendant is shown to have killed a newly born child, he can be charged with murder or manslaughter, provided there is evidence that the child had an existence that was independent, in biological terms, from its mother. Such independent existence need only be momentary. There are some old authorities on the point, although they may need to be treated with caution, which suggest that whilst the child's body must have been expelled from the mother's womb, see *R* v *Poulton* (1832) 5 C & P 329, the cord between mother and child does not have to have been cut, see *R* v *Reeves* (1839) 9 C & P 25. In *R* v *Brain* (1834) 6 C & P 349, Parke J directed the jury that a baby could be the victim of homicide, even though it had not started breathing: see further *R* v *Enoch* (1833) 5 C & P 539 and *R* v *Handley* (1874) 13 Cox CC 79. Should there be doubt as to whether a child had become an independent human being at the time of the death, the defendant could always be charged with child destruction under the Infant Life (Preservation) Act 1929, as an alternative, or in addition to murder/manslaughter: see further Chapter 5.5.

At the other extreme, the question arises as to exactly when life ends. Clearly, a defendant cannot be guilty of murdering someone who has already died, although if the defendant honestly believed the victim was still alive he might be guilty of attempted murder (see Chapter 12). Doctors frequently refer to a patient as being 'brain dead', indicating that whilst he can be kept alive on a life support machine, there is no chance of the patient ever recovering consciousness. For the purposes of criminal law such a patient would not be regarded as 'legally dead', in the sense that if a defendant were to enter a hospital ward and deliberately switch off a machine maintaining the vital functions of a 'brain dead' patient, he could be charged with murder or manslaughter: see further on this point *R* v *Malcherek and Steel* (below).

6.3 Causation

Homicide is a 'result crime' in the sense that the defendant must be proved to have caused the victim's death. Two matters have to be considered. Did the defendant in fact cause the victim's death, and if so, can he be held to have caused it in law?

Causation in fact

This can be resolved by the application of the 'but for' test which was considered at 5.1 (above). In the majority of situations proof of causation in fact is almost a formality as it will be self evident; however the case of *R* v *White* [1910] 2 KB 124, illustrates how problems can arise. The defendant placed two grains of potassium cyanide in a glass containing his mother's drink. She drank the contents of the glass, but died of heart failure before the poison could take effect. The defendant was charged with murder, and convicted of attempted murder, a finding against which he appealed unsuccessfully. As regards causation in fact, the defendant's act in placing the poison in his mother's drink did not in any way cause her death. If one were to ask, 'But for the defendant's act would his mother have died?', the answer would obviously have to be in the affirmative; she would have died anyway, thus disproving causation in fact. In such cases the appropriate charge would then be one of attempting to commit the substantive offence, provided the defendant has taken sufficient steps towards its commission (see Chapter 12).

Causation in law

Causation is a mixed question of fact and law. Simply because a chain of causation in fact can be established it cannot be assumed that legal liability will follow. The rules of causation in law exist to prevent a defendant being convicted where his acts are too remote from the death, or where his acts are only a minimal cause of death.

Remoteness may be an issue as regards the interval in time between the defendant's act and the death, or as regards the effect of intervening acts. At common law a defendant will not be guilty of either murder or manslaughter if the victim dies more than 366 days from the date upon which the defendant inflicted harm upon the victim. This results from the operation of the so-called 'year and a day' rule, the origins of which can be traced back to the 12th century. The modern basis for this rule is the Court of Appeal's decision in *R* v *Dyson* [1908] 2 KB 454. The defendant assaulted his own child causing a fractured skull, in November 1906. The child died in March 1908, the medical evidence being that the fractured skull was the main cause of death. The defendant was convicted of manslaughter and appealed successfully, Lord Alverstone CJ confirming that the defendant could not be indicted in respect of a death arising some 17 months after the infliction of harm. It should be noted that the rule has been applied to the findings of Coroners' Courts in relation to suicide: see *R* v *Coroner for Inner West London, ex parte De Luca* [1988] 3 WLR 286, where the Divisional Court also provided that the rule would apply in relation to suicide pacts under s4(1) of the Homicide Act 1957, aiding, abetting, counselling or procuring suicide under s2(1) of the Suicide Act 1961, and infanticide under s1(1) of the Infanticide Act 1938. There remains no authoritative ruling as regards the application of the rule to deaths caused by dangerous driving, contrary to the Road Traffic Act 1991; however, it is submitted that this would be a logical extension of the rule.

Where a victim has been brutally assaulted the prosecution might secure a conviction for grievous bodily harm and, if the victim dies within 366 days of the original attack, the defendant can be charged with either murder or manslaughter, this not being a case of autrefois convict: see *R* v *Golding* (unreported, *The Times* 28 April 1994).

Unsuccessful attempts were made to introduce an amendment to what became the Criminal Justice and Public Order Act 1994 when it was before the House of Commons so as to include a clause abolishing the rule. Proponents of change pointed out that in this respect English law was out of step with that of other comparable countries. The rule had never been part of Scots law, and no longer formed part of the law in any European country other than Cyprus.

It is submitted that the only rationale for the rule's continued existence is that the defendant should not have the threat of a homicide charge hanging over him indefinitely. The argument that the rule is needed because of the evidential difficulty in determining whether D's act caused death, where there is a gap of more than a year between an attack and death, no longer bears close scrutiny. Particularly difficult moral and ethical questions arise where the victim of a criminal attack is in a persistent vegetative state as a result of injuries inflicted by D. Given the technical ability to sustain patients in this condition for many years, is it right that D should escape liability for murder or manslaughter simply because the decision to disconnect a life support system is effected more than 366 days after his unlawful act? The rule can further be criticised on the ground that it presents problems to prosecutors considering manslaughter charges against companies where unsafe working practices have resulted in the deaths of employees some years after being exposed to health dangers in the workplace.

In its Consultation Paper 'The Year and a Day Rule in Homicide' (No 136), the Law Commission recommends the outright abolition of the rule.

Where the passing of time is not an issue, the general test to be applied in order to establish causation in law is that of reasonable foreseeability, an objective test based on what the reasonable person would have foreseen: see Glanville Williams' *Textbook on Criminal Law* (2nd ed p388). Where, for example, D knocks P unconscious and leaves him lying in the middle of the road where he is run over and killed by an innocent motorist, X, one would hold D responsible for causing P's death, on the basis that it was a reasonably foreseeable consequence of what he had done. It could equally be applied to a situation where D strikes P and leaves him unconscious on the sea shore, with the result that P later dies through drowning when the tide comes in. It would be nonsensical to say that D did not cause the death because the water did. An instructive example of the principle's application is provided by the Court of Appeal's decision in *R v Pagett* (1983) 76 Cr App R 279. The defendant had armed himself with a shot-gun and taken a pregnant girl hostage in a block of flats. The police besieged the building, calling on him to come out, which he eventually did, holding the girl in front of him as a human shield. The defendant fired the shot-gun at the police officers who returned fire, striking and killing the girl hostage. The defendant was convicted of her manslaughter, the conviction being upheld by the Court of Appeal which held that the reasonable actions of a third party, by way of self defence, could not be regarded as a novus actus interveniens (ie a new intervening act breaking the chain of causation in law). In this case the police officers had instinctively returned the defendant's fire, the need for them to act in self defence had been caused by the defendant's firing of his own gun, and their actions were reasonable in the circumstances. See further *R v Roberts* (1971) 56 Cr App R 95, considered at 5.1, and *R v Watson* [1989] 1 WLR 684 considered at 8.2.

Medical treatment

In what circumstances can the medical treatment received by a victim, following an attack by the defendant, relieve him of liability for homicide if the victim subsequently dies? Perhaps a logical response would be to contend that whilst it is reasonably foreseeable that the victim of an attack will require medical attention, the chain of causation should be broken if that medical attention is unforeseeably poor or incompetent. Pursuing this line of reasoning prompts the question, how bad does medical treatment have to become in order for the chain of causation to be broken?

In *R v Jordan* (1956) 40 Cr App R 152, the defendant had stabbed the victim who was admitted to hospital where he died some eight days later. The defendant was convicted of murder, but appealed when new evidence came to light that whilst in hospital, the victim had been given a drug to which he was allergic. The Court of Appeal quashed the conviction on the ground that the medical treatment had been 'palpably wrong', with the result that it broke the chain of causation between the stabbing and the death. The evidence was that the original stab wound was well on the way to being healed at the time of death, and thus it could be said to be merely the setting within which another cause of death operated. As Hallett J observed:

> '... we are disposed to accept it as the law that death resulting from any normal treatment employed to deal with a felonious injury may be regarded as caused by the felonious injury, but we do not think it necessary to examine the cases in details or to formulate for the assistance of those who have to deal with such matters in the future the correct test which ought to be laid down with regard to what is necessary to be proved in order to establish causal connection between the death and the felonious injury. Not only one feature, but two separate and independent features, of treatment were, in the opinion of the doctors, palpably wrong and these produced the symptoms discovered at the post-mortem examination which were the direct and immediate cause of death, namely, the pneumonia resulting from the conditions of oedema which was found.'

Jordan, was clearly an extreme case, and in subsequent decisions, the appeal courts have demonstrated their reluctance to allow the defendant to rely on the failings of doctors in order to escape liability. In *R* v *Smith* [1959] 2 QB 35, the defendant had been involved in a barrack room fight with a fellow soldier, during the course of which he had stabbed him several times with a bayonet, resulting in the victim being taken to a medical post where he died approximately one hour later. On being charged with murder the defendant contended that the chain of causation between the stabbing and the death had been broken by the way in which the victim had been treated, in particular the fact that he had been handled roughly whilst being carried to the medical post, and that there had been a delay in providing the victim with treatment because of the number of other cases being dealt with. The defendant was convicted and appealed unsuccessfully to the Court-Martial Appeal Court, where it was held that the defendant's act should be regarded as the cause in law of the victim's death if it could be shown that it was the operating and substantial cause. Only if the original wound could be said to have merely provided the setting in which some other cause of death operated would the courts be likely to view the chain of causation as being broken.

The usefulness of *R* v *Jordan* as an authority has been further limited by the subsequent Court of Appeal decision in *R* v *Malcherek*, *R* v *Steel* (1981) 73 Cr App R 173. Both defendants had, in separate incidents, attacked women, causing injuries that were so severe, that their victims had to be placed on life support machines in hospital. In both cases doctors decided to switch off the machines after determining that the victims were 'brain dead' and that there was no prospect of recovery. Both defendants were convicted of murder. The common ground of appeal in both cases was that the doctors had broken the chain of causation between the defendants' attacks and the deaths of the victims by deliberately switching off the life support machines.

The Court of Appeal held, dismissing the appeals, that in both cases the operating and substantial cause of death had been the original wounds inflicted by the defendants. The effect of the life support machine was merely to hold the effect of those injuries in suspension; as soon as the machine was switched off the original wounds would continue to cause the death of the victim, even if death ensued within seconds of the machine's disconnection. On a broader policy basis, the Lord Chief Justice expressed the view that nothing done by a doctor in the ordinary course of medical treatment could be regarded as a novus actus interveniens, preferring the approach of the court in *R* v *Smith*, to that in *R* v *Jordan*. The latter case was not overruled by the Court of Appeal, but it has been effectively limited to its own facts.

These authorities raise the question of whether anything falling short of palpably wrong medical treatment would be regarded as constituting a novus actus. In *R* v *Cheshire* (1991) 93 Cr App R 251, Beldam LJ noted that even where medical treatment amounts to negligence and can be identified as the immediate cause of death:

> '... the jury should not regard it as excluding the responsibility of the accused unless the negligent treatment was so independent of his acts, and in itself so potent in causing death, that they regard the contribution made by his acts as insignificant.'

In particular, the Court of Appeal rejected the trial judge's direction to the jury that they could regard the medical treatment as a novus actus if they found that the doctors had acted recklessly. This was to confuse the mental element accompanying an act or omission with the effect of the act or omission.

'Escape cases'

A defendant may be guilty of homicide where he causes such fear in the victim, that the victim desperately tries to escape, and is killed in the process of so doing. Early cases on this point establish that such a defendant can be charged with murder or manslaughter, provided the victim's fear was 'well grounded': see *R* v *Pitts* (1842) Car & M 248. More recently, the Court of Appeal, in *R* v *Mackie* (1973) 57 Cr App R 453, upheld the manslaughter conviction of a father whose three-year-old son fell downstairs and died in trying to escape from a beating. The court endorsed the trial judge's direction to the jury which had invited them to consider first whether the boy had been in fear, secondly whether that fear had caused him to try to escape, thirdly whether the fear was well founded, and if so whether it was caused by the unlawful conduct of the accused.

In *DPP* v *Daley* [1980] AC 237, Lord Keith summarised what, in their Lordships' view, the prosecution had to establish in such cases, namely:

> '(1) that the victim immediately before he sustained his injuries was in fear of being hurt physically; (2) that his fear was such that it caused him to try to escape; (3) that whilst he was trying to escape, and because he was trying to escape, he met his death; (4) that his fear of being hurt there and then was reasonable and was caused by the conduct of the defendant; (5) that the defendant's conduct which caused the fear was unlawful; and (6) that his conduct was such as any sober and reasonable person would recognise as likely to subject the victim to at least the risk of some harm resulting from it, albeit not serious harm.'

Despite the detailed nature of these guidelines, it may still be necessary, in some cases, to give a jury further guidance on the issue of causation, particularly where there is a suggestion that the victim's reaction was out of all proportion to the defendant's threat. Note the obiter comments in *R v Roberts* (1971) 56 Cr App R 95 (considered at 5.1 above), to the effect that the chain of causation would be broken by the victim doing something 'daft'. This point was addressed by the Court of Appeal in *R v Williams* [1992] 1 WLR 380, where the deceased had jumped to his death from a moving car in order to escape from a robbery; Stuart-Smith LJ stated:

> '... the nature of the threat is of importance in considering both the foreseeability of harm to the victim from the threat and the question of whether the deceased's conduct was proportionate to the threat; that is to say that it was within the ambit of reasonableness and not so daft as to make his own voluntary act one which amounted to a novus actus interveniens and consequently broke the chain of causation.'

Thin skulls and self-neglect

As in the law of tort, criminal law reflects the view that the defendant should take his victim as he finds him, thus the defendant who stabs the haemophiliac victim who bleeds to death cannot claim that the chain of causation is broken by virtue of the victim's medical condition. The principle as developed in tort related largely to the physical circumstances of the victim; in criminal law, however, it has been extended to encompass the mental state of the victim as well. The effect would appear to be that once a defendant has caused injuries, the victim is under no legal duty to mitigate the effects of the adverse effects. In *R v Holland* (1841) 2 Mood & R 351, the defendant struck the victim's hand with an iron bar causing it to be badly cut. The victim decided not to seek treatment, developed lockjaw, and later died. The court held that the defendant had caused the death; the self-neglect of the victim did not break the chain of causation: see further *R v Wall* (1802) 28 State Tr 51.

The modern authority for the application of the so-called 'thin skull' rule in criminal law is now the decision of the Court of Appeal in *R v Blaue* (1975) 61 Cr App R 271. The defendant had stabbed the victim, who was a Jehovah's Witness, 13 times, and she was rushed to hospital where doctors diagnosed that she would need an immediate blood transfusion if her life was to be saved. The victim refused the necessary transfusion because it was against her religious beliefs and died from her wounds shortly after. The defendant appealed against his conviction for manslaughter on the ground that her refusal of treatment had broken the chain of causation, but the court held that he had to take his victim as he found her, meaning not just her physical condition, but also her religious beliefs.

How far is the 'thin skull' rule to be taken? Suppose that D rapes P, as a result of which she becomes HIV positive and decides to commit suicide rather than die from AIDS. Will D be held to have caused her death? The criminal court may take its lead from civil cases such as *Pigney v Pointers Transport Services* [1957] 2 All ER 807, wherein it was held that the chain of causation was not broken by the plaintiff's suicide which was induced by an anxiety neurosis which he had developed following an accident caused by the defendant's negligence. Caution should be exercised, however, in relying on decisions concerned with claims for compensation, when considering the imposition of criminal liability.

To some extent there appears to be a conflict between the decision in *R v Blaue*, and that in *R v Roberts* (above in 5.1), in that the former states that the defendant must take the victim as he finds him, the latter states that the victim will break the chain of causation by doing something 'daft'. What if the victim does something 'daft' because he is of limited intelligence? Surely *R v Blaue* should apply with the effect that the defendant should have to take his 'daft' victim as he finds him? It is submitted that in such a case *R v Blaue* might be followed on the basis that it is the more recent decision, is based on considerations of public policy (ie that one should not injure people in the first place) and because one is comparing the ratio of *R v Blaue* with an obiter statement in *R v Roberts*.

In *R v Williams* (above) Stuart-Smith LJ adverts to the victim attempting to escape from a perceived threat, and comments that:

> 'It should of course be borne in mind that a victim may in the agony of the moment do the wrong thing ... [T]he jury should bear in mind any particular characteristics of the victim and the fact that in the agony of the moment he may act without thought and deliberation.'

In the light of this, is it ever possible for the victim's actions to break the chain of causation? Two decisions suggest that it might be, the important distinction being drawn between the situation where a victim fails to avail himself of assistance and situations where the victim takes deliberate and positive steps that exacerbate the effects of the defendant's unlawful act. *R v Dalby* [1982] 1 WLR 425, as interpreted in *R v Goodfellow* (1986) 83 Cr App R 23 (see further 8.2), seems to suggest that where a defendant unlawfully supplies a drug which the victim consumes in a quantity and in a manner which proves fatal, the victim's actions will be regarded as a novus actus interveniens. This interpretation of *Dalby* is further supported by *R v Armstrong* [1989] Crim LR 149, a case in which the defendant, a drug addict, supplied the deceased, who had already taken large amounts of alcohol, with heroin and drug-taking paraphernalia. The deceased had died shortly after self-injection. Owen J upheld defence counsel's submissions that either there was, on the facts, no or insufficient evidence that heroin had been a substantial cause of death, or alternatively that if heroin did cause death, the deceased's self-injection was a novus actus interveniens. It is submitted that *Dalby* and *Armstrong* may mark the point at which the defendant is no longer responsible for the actions of the victim.

Reform

The complex issue of causation, which is relevant to all 'result' crimes, is dealt with by clause 17 of the draft code. This is a matter which, to date, has not received consideration by the Criminal Law Revision Committee. The purpose of clause 17 is to restate the principles to be found in the common law. Clause 17(1) provides:

'17(1) Subject to subsections (2) and (3), a person causes a result which is an element of
an offence when –
(a) he does an act which makes a more than negligible contribution to its occurrence; or
(b) he omits to do an act which might prevent its occurrence and which he is under a duty
to do according to the law relating to the offence.

As regards clause 17(1)(a), the Code Report commentary states:

'Under existing law a person's act need not be the sole, or even the major, cause of a
harmful result. It is enough that the act is a "substantial" [*R v Smith*] or "significant"
[*Pagett*] cause of the result, and in this context this means merely that the defendant's
contribution must be outside the de minimis range. Accordingly it is wrong, for example,
to direct a jury that the defendant is not liable if he is less than one-fifth to blame
[*Hennigan* [1971] 3 All ER 133].' [Vol II para 7.15]

The commentary goes on to point out that under the test put forward there may be
more than one cause of a result where two persons are independently liable in
respect of the same harm. The test reflects the existing common law in not taking
account of a victim's peculiar susceptibility to harm.

Clause 17(1)(b) deals with the issue of causation in relation to omissions. The
way in which it would operate is indicated in the example given in Appendix B,
Volume I, example 17(ii):

'E's mistress lives with E and P, E's child by his wife. While E is away P falls seriously ill.
D, wishing P to die, fails to call a doctor. P dies. P's life might have been prolonged by
medical attention. If D was under a duty to obtain medical attention for P she is guilty of
murder. She has caused P's death intending to cause death.'

The possibility of a novus actus interveniens breaking the chain of causation is dealt
with by clause 17(2), which states:

'A person does not cause a result where, after he does such an act or makes such an
omission, an act or event occurs –
(a) which is the immediate and sufficient cause of the result;
(b) which he did not foresee, and
(c) which could not in the circumstances reasonably have been foreseen.

As the commentary upon this sub-section states, this is essentially a restatement of
the common law:

'[The clause] appears to restate satisfactorily for criminal law the principles which
determine whether intervening acts or events are sufficient to break the chain of causation
between the defendant's conduct and the result, as it is sometimes put, whether in the
circumstances the defendant's conduct is a cause in law of the result. According to this
provision a person will still be liable if his intended victim suffers injury in trying to
escape from the threatened attack unless the victim has done something so improbable that
it can properly be said not to have been reasonably foreseeable. Equally, liability for
homicide will be unaffected if the victim refuses medical treatment for a wound caused by
the defendant. Even if the refusal could be said to unforeseeable, it is not sufficient in
itself to cause the victim's death – in such a case, to use the language of the cases, the
original wound is still the "operating and substantial cause" of death.' [Vol II para 7.17]

Clause 17(3) deals with the application of the proposals for causation to accomplices. This will be considered in more detail in Chapter 10.

The Law Commission favours the retention of the common law rule that death must occur within a year and a day of the defendant's act or omission. Clause 53(b) of the draft code provides:

'For the purposes of this Chapter ... a person does not cause death unless the death occurs within a year after the day on which any act causing it was done by that person or on which any fatal injury resulting from such an act was sustained, or (where the fatal injury was done to an unborn child) within a year after the day on which he was born and had an independent existence.'

It is envisaged that the rule would apply to murder, manslaughter, suicide pact killing, complicity in suicide and infanticide.

6.4 The mens rea of murder

Coke's classic definition of murder refers to the defendant having 'malice aforethought'. Whilst this is widely understood by the layman as the mental element required for murder, it is submitted that in modern terms the expression is neither accurate nor helpful, and as such its use should be discouraged. It is likely to mislead in that it suggests some element of planning on the part of the murderer, when in truth murder can be quite spontaneous, and also in that it suggests that the defendant must act with some degree of ill will against the victim, when again no such evidence is required by the law.

Homicide Act 1957

Prior to the enactment of s1 of the Homicide Act 1957, 'constructive malice' was sufficient mens rea for murder. The result was that if a defendant killed in the course of committing a felony, such as burglary, he would be charged with murder because the necessary mens rea would be construed from his having committed the felony. This 'felony murder' rule as it was known, operated in a spectacularly harsh fashion. Where, for example, D burgled P's house wrongly thinking it to be unoccupied, and P on disturbing D in the process of stealing goods died of shock, D could be charged with P's murder, even though he might not have actually had the intention of injuring anyone.

The 1957 Act abolished constructive malice, but did not replace it with a statutory definition of murder. Shortly afterwards in *R v Vickers* [1957] 2 QB 664, the Court of Appeal held that a defendant could be convicted of murder if it was established that he had intended to kill, or had intended grievous bodily harm. The latter was accepted as sufficient mens rea for murder because if a defendant was willing to inflict grievous bodily harm, how was he to know that the victim might not die? An intention to cause grievous bodily harm at least evidenced a willingness to accept a substantial risk that the victim might die.

In *Hyam* v *DPP* [1975] AC 55, a majority of their Lordships extended the mens rea somewhat further by holding that it was sufficient for the defendant to have foreseen that death or grievous bodily harm was a probable, or highly probable consequence of his actions. This 'heretical' confusion of foresight with mens rea was compounded in the subsequent House of Lords' decision in *R* v *Cunningham* [1982] AC 566.

It was not until the House of Lords' decision in *R* v *Moloney* [1985] AC 905, that the law was placed on something resembling a sound footing, in that their Lordships held that foresight of consequences on the part of the defendant was not a form of mens rea, but evidence of it. Even so, the decision was not without its dubious aspects. Lord Bridge suggested that where a jury in a murder trial sought some assistance from the trial judge as to the meaning of intention to kill or intention to do grievous bodily harm, they should be directed to ask themselves whether the death/gbh was the natural consequence of the defendant's act, and further whether the defendant foresaw death/gbh as the natural consequence of his act. If the jury answered both questions in the affirmative they were entitled to infer that the defendant had intended the consequences of his acts. Lord Bridge's obiter statements were subsequently doubted, however, by Lord Scarman, making the main speech in *R* v *Hancock* [1986] AC 455 (see Chapter 2 for facts). In this latter case, which is now the leading authority on the mens rea for murder, the House of Lords reaffirmed that the prosecution has to establish that D intended to kill or do grievous bodily harm; but Lord Scarman emphasised that a defendant cannot be assumed to foresee a consequence simply because it is a natural result of his actions. The jury must consider the evidence of what the defendant actually foresaw, and the more evidence there is that the defendant foresaw death or grievous bodily harm, then the stronger the inference that he intended either of those consequences. In *R* v *Nedrick* [1986] Crim LR 742, the only post-*Hancock* decision so far reported, the Lord Chief Justice went so far as to suggest that a jury would have to be satisfied that a defendant foresaw death or grievous bodily harm as a 'virtual certainty' before they would be entitled to infer that he had intended either consequence, but it is submitted that this may be overstating the case somewhat.

Reform

Clause 54 of the draft code states:

'A person is guilty of murder if he causes the death of another –
(a) intending to cause death; or
(b) intending to cause serious personal harm and being aware that he may cause death [subject to certain defences].'

In the light of the subsequent proposals in the DCLB, the reference to 'serious personal harm' would now presumably be replaced with a reference to 'serious injury'.

Clause 53(a) of the draft code proposes the following codification of the law relating to who can be the victim of homicide:

'... (a) "another" means a person who has been born and has an existence independent of his mother and, unless the context otherwise requires, "death" mean[s] the death of ... such a person.'

The Code Report commentary upon this clause provides:

'The definition of "another" in clause 53(a) effectively defines "the person" against whom the offences in this Chapter ... may be committed. Though, following Coke, the definition of a person "in being" is traditionally discussed only in relation to homicide, it is clear that, in principle, the same definition must apply to offences against the person generally. This is achieved by paragraph (a). That paragraph also makes it clear that a person who intends to cause the death of ... an unborn child does not intend to commit murder and is not, by reason of that intention, guilty of murder if the child is born alive and then dies of the injury. This settles a matter of doubt in the present law in accordance with, as we think, sound principle. A person who intended to kill the mother would be guilty of murder of the child if the injuries he inflicted with that intent caused the child to die after it had been born alive: see ... (transferred fault) [dealt with in Chapter 2].' [Vol II para 14.2]

7

Homicide II: Voluntary Manslaughter

7.1 Introduction

7.2 Provocation

7.3 Diminished responsibility

7.4 Infanticide

7.5 Suicide pact

7.6 Death from excessive force

7.1 Introduction

When a defendant has caused a victim's death, and has been proved to have had the necessary mens rea for murder, he may still be able to avoid a conviction for murder by establishing that he comes within the scope of one of the four defences which are only available to a defendant charged with murder. The four defences are: provocation; diminished responsibility; infanticide; and suicide pact. In each case, if the defendant succeeds with the defence, his liability is reduced from murder to manslaughter, the significance of this being that for murder the punishment is a mandatory life sentence, whereas for manslaughter the sentence is at the discretion of the trial judge. This form of manslaughter is described as 'voluntary' because there will have been evidence that the defendant did intend to kill or cause grievous bodily harm.

7.2 Provocation

Provocation is a common law defence of considerable antiquity. Its existence is a concession to human frailty. The law accepts that even a reasonable even tempered person might be so provoked by certain events, that he or she is driven to kill. It is the closest English law comes to recognising what is sometimes referred to as a 'crime of passion'. Historically, the scope of provocation has always been somewhat limited, the law being reluctant to accept anything as provocation except a serious physical assault or finding one's spouse committing adultery. It was doubted whether words alone could ever constitute provocation.

111

Section 3 of the Homicide Act 1957

Section 3 provides:

> 'Where on a charge of murder there is evidence on which the jury can find that the person charged was provoked (whether by things done or by things said or by both together) to lose his self-control, the question whether the provocation was enough to make a reasonable man do as he did shall be left to be determined by the jury; and in determining that question the jury shall take into account everything both done and said according to the effect which, in their opinion, it would have on a reasonable man.'

It is evident that this does not provide a definition of provocation, but it does provide some indication of what the defence entails, and the way in which the common law has been modified. Since 1957, it has been possible for anything to constitute provocation, including words alone, actions by third parties, and provocation directed at third parties (this latter point was confirmed in *R v Pearson* [1992] Crim LR 193). Hence in *R v Doughty* [1986] Crim LR 625, it was held to be a misdirection for a trial judge to tell a jury that the persistent crying of a 17-day-old baby could not constitute provocation. The jury should have been directed to consider how the reasonable man would have responded. Note that this decision also seems to assume that the provocation can be a lawful act.

If the above is correct, it casts some doubt on the rectitude of the Privy Council's decision in *Edwards v R* [1973] AC 648, where it was held that self-induced provocation (ie where D induces P to provoke him) could not be allowed as a defence, the rationale being that the defendant should not be permitted to escape liability where he has instigated the incident. It is submitted that the better view of self-induced provocation is that expressed by the Court of Appeal in *R v Johnson* [1989] 2 All ER 839, where it was again emphasised that, under s3 of the 1957 Act, anything could amount to provocation including actions provoked by the accused. The appellant in that case had been deprived of the opportunity of having his defence considered properly by the jury, following the trial judge's ruling that he was bound to follow *Edwards v R*.

Section 3 places an evidential burden on the accused. He must raise sufficient evidence of provocation for the judge to leave the defence to the jury. For example, in *R v Cocker* [1989] Crim LR 740 the appellant, whose wife suffered from a long term incurable illness, and who had regularly begged him to kill her, admitted asphyxiating her with a pillow. At his trial for murder, he had originally sought to rely on the defence of provocation, but changed his plea to guilty following the trial judge's ruling that there was no evidence of provocation to put before the jury. In dismissing his appeal, the Court of Appeal expressed the view that the evidence indicated that, far from losing his self-control, the appellant had been aware of his actions, and had killed in cold blood . Of particular significance was the fact that the appellant had paused whilst asphyxiating his wife, only to continue following her entreaties that he should carry on. The judge's role in such cases was described thus by Lord Taylor CJ in *R v Cambridge* [1994] 1 WLR 971:

'The starting point, therefore, is whether there is evidence on which the jury can find the defendant was in fact provoked to lose his self-control. That is a question for the judge. In our judgment, therefore, there must be evidence on the first limb from which a reasonable jury might properly conclude that the defendant was in fact provoked to lose his self-control or may have been so by some words or acts or both together. If the judge decides that there is not such evidence, he ought not to leave provocation to the jury. If, on the other hand, he concludes that there is such evidence on the first limb of the two-stage test, the statute obliges him to leave provocation to the jury, even if he himself believes the circumstances to be such that no reasonable man would have reacted as the defendant did.'

In the event that the trial judge feels uncertain as to whether or not the defendant has discharged the evidential burden, decisions of the Court of Appeal such as that in *R* v *Rossiter* [1994] 2 All ER 752, suggest that the defendant should be given the benefit of the doubt. The appellant killed her husband during a domestic quarrel, the evidence indicating that she had been exposed to physical and verbal abuse by the deceased. She maintained that the killing had been either accidental or had occurred whilst she had been defending herself, and she denied ever having had the intention to kill the deceased or cause grievous bodily harm. Her counsel was thus not able to put the defence of provocation before the jury. Allowing her appeal, the Court of Appeal held that, despite her assertions to the contrary, it was possible to infer from the evidence that the appellant had lost her self control and killed, hence the jury should have been directed to consider the defence of provocation. On the question of provocation, however, Russell LJ observed:

'We take the law to be that whenever there is material which is capable of amounting to provocation, however tenuous it may be, the jury must be given the privilege of ruling upon it.'

Similarly in *R* v *Cambridge* (above), the Court of Appeal held that the trial judge had erred in not leaving the issue of provocation to the jury, even though the appellant's 'defence' had been one of alibi, because witnesses gave evidence at the trial that he had been involved in an altercation with H (the deceased) shortly before H was found dead, hence there was evidence that the appellant might have been provoked (albeit that it would also have meant that his alibi was false!).

The subjective test

The classic definition of provocation is that provided by Devlin J in *R* v *Duffy* [1949] 1 All ER at p932, where he stated:

'Provocation is some act or series of acts, done by the dead man to the accused, which would cause in any reasonable person, and actually causes in the accused, a sudden and temporary loss of self-control, rendering the accused so subject to passion as to make him or her for the moment not master of his mind.'

Obviously certain aspects of this definition would have to be modified in the light of s3 considered above, but two essential elements remain: the subjective condition and the objective condition.

The subjective condition is the requirement that the defendant must have suffered a sudden and temporary loss of self-control. *R* v *Richens* [1993] Crim LR 384 suggests that it would be unwise for a trial judge to embellish this requirement by suggesting to the jury that the appellant should provide evidence of having completely lost his self-control, to the extent that he did not realise what he was doing. Further, the word 'sudden' introduces the issue of 'cooling time', in the sense that where there is a gap in time between the provocation and the killing, the defendant may encounter evidential difficulties in trying to establish the defence. In *R* v *Hayward* (1833) 6 C & P 157, the judge directed the jury to consider whether there had been time between the alleged provocation and killing, 'for the blood to cool, and for reason to resume its seat'. The difficulties that a defendant can encounter were illustrated in *R* v *Ibrams and Gregory* (1981) 74 Cr App R 154. The defendants and a young woman had been terrorised and bullied over a period of time by the deceased, a man called Monk. Believing that police protection would be ineffective, they devised a plan which involved the woman enticing the deceased to her bed, whereupon the defendants would burst into the room and attack him. The plan was carried out as arranged, resulting in the death of Monk. The defendants were convicted of murder following the trial judge's decision to withdraw the defence of provocation from the jury and defendants appealed unsuccessfully to the Court of Appeal. Lawton LJ expressed the view that the gap of seven days between the last act of provocation and the killing refuted any evidence that it had been carried out by defendants suffering from a sudden and temporary loss of self-control as envisaged by Devlin J in *R* v *Duffy* (above).

In *R* v *Brown* [1972] 2 All ER 1328 the Court of Appeal approved a direction to the jury that to find provocation they had to find it in something done on the morning of the killing. By contrast in *R* v *Davies* (1974) Cr App R 253, the same court thought it too generous to the defendant to direct the jury that they could consider the whole of the deceased's conduct throughout the turbulent years preceding the death. It is submitted that the courts should not concern themselves with the creation of time limits within which a defendant must kill in order to come within the defence of provocation, but direct juries to look instead at how a reasonable man or woman would have reacted in the given circumstances.

Cases where the defendant alleges cumulative provocation, ie where the provocation takes the form of a series of small incidents over a period of time, require a careful direction from the trial judge. The case of *R* v *Thornton* [1992] 1 All ER 306 excited much criticism following the Court of Appeal's refusal to quash the appellant's conviction for murdering her husband, where the evidence revealed a history of violent and offensive behaviour by the deceased towards her. Counsel for the appellant had sought to question the trial judge's direction to the effect that provocation required evidence of some sudden and temporary loss of self-control on the part of the accused, on the ground that s3 of the 1957 Act required them to have regard to '... everything both done and said according to the effect which in their opinion it would have on a reasonable man'. The essence of the appeal was that this direction would concentrate the minds of jury members on the final outburst, when they should be concentrating on the events over the years leading up to the killing. In rejecting this contention Beldam LJ stated:

> 'The changes in the law of provocation made by s3 of the 1957 Act and the reasons for them are well known. It has never, so far as we are aware, been suggested that the distinction drawn by Devlin J [in *R v Duffy*] between a person who has time to think and reflect and regain self-control, and a sudden temporary loss of self-control, is no longer of significance. On the contrary, the distinction ... is just as, if not more, important in the kind of case to which Lord Gifford [counsel for Sarah Thornton] referred. It is within the experience of each member of the court that in cases of domestic violence which culminate in the death of a partner there is frequently evidence given of provocative acts committed by the deceased in the past for it is in that context that the jury have to consider the accused's reaction. In every such case the question for the jury is whether at the moment the fatal blow was struck the accused had been deprived for that moment of the self-control which previously he or she had been able to exercise. The epithet "sudden and temporary" is one a jury are well able to understand and to recognise as expressing precisely the distinction drawn by Devlin J.'

It is submitted that some of the criticism engendered by this decision is misplaced. It might be thought generous on the part of the trial judge to have allowed the defence of provocation to go before the jury at all, given the appellant's admission that she had deliberately sharpened the knife with which she stabbed her husband and had commented to the ambulance personnel attempting to save his life that they should let him die. It is the jury that rejected the evidence of provocation, not the trial judge or the Court of Appeal. Criticism is justified, however, where the courts fail to apply the principles illustrated in *R v Thornton* with consistency: see *R v Pearson* [1992] Crim LR 193.

The Court of Appeal decision in *R v Ahluwalia* [1992] 4 All ER 889 possibly represents a more appropriate way of resolving cases where the murder follows in the wake of a history of domestic violence. The appellant had been abused verbally and physically by her husband over a number of years. He had been conducting an adulterous affair about which he taunted her. On the night in question he had argued with her and promised to give her a beating the following morning. After he had fallen asleep, the appellant poured petrol over him and set him alight, causing burns from which he subsequently died. She was convicted of his murder following the trial judge's direction to the jury in accordance with *R v Duffy* (above). The Court of Appeal held that the trial judge had rightly stressed to the jury that provocation was only available to a defendant who killed whilst suffering from a sudden loss of self-control, and that s3 of the Homicide Act 1957 had not been intended by Parliament to affect the operation of the test in *R v Duffy*. Similarly the trial judge had been correct in refusing to direct the jury to apply the test of how the reasonable woman suffering from 'battered woman syndrome' would have responded, as there had been no medical evidence of this condition put before the court. Hence it had not been possible for the court to determine to what extent, if any, the condition satisfied the requirements of 'characteristics' as explained in *R* v *Newell* (1980) 71 Cr App R 331. What the court was willing to accept, however, was that the evidence now available indicated that the appellant may have had an arguable defence on the basis of diminished responsibility, and as such she should be granted a retrial where the defence could be fully ventilated.

Objective test

If the trial judge determines that there is evidence of provocation to put before the jury, they will have to consider how, in the circumstances of the case, a reasonable person would have reacted. In *Mancini* v *DPP* [1942] AC 1 the House of Lords held that, as a matter of law, there had to be a reasonable relationship between the mode of provocation and the acts of the defendant, in the sense that a defendant would be expected to answer words with words, stones with stones, and knives with knives. With the enactment of s3, however, this must now be seen as nothing more that a guideline. The important question is whether the defendant's actions were reasonable, and this is a matter for each jury to determine. The objective test is unobjectionable where the defendant is considered to be very much an 'average' sort of person but, in the past, the test worked unfairly where the defendant laboured under some handicap or abnormality. Hence in *R* v *Lesbini* [1914] 3 KB 1116, the defendant was judged by the standard of the reasonable man despite being of extremely low intelligence. Similarly in *Bedder* v *DPP* [1954] 2 All ER 801, where the defendant, who had killed a prostitute who had made fun of his sexual impotence, was judged by the standard of the reasonable man who was presumed not to be impotent.

The breakthrough in this area was the House of Lords' decision in *DPP* v *Camplin* [1978] AC 705. The defendant, a 15-year-old boy, had been buggered by the deceased and was then taunted by him. The defendant killed the deceased by hitting him over the head with a chappati pan. He was convicted of murder following a direction by the trial judge to the jury that they were to judge him by the standard of the reasonable adult, not a reasonable 15-year-old boy. The Court of Appeal allowed the appeal on the basis that a more subjective test, which took account of the defendant's age, should have been applied, a view that was subsequently endorsed by the House of Lords. Lord Diplock explained that the reasonable man, whilst displaying an even temperament, was to be endowed with those characteristics of the accused that the jury considered would affect the gravity of the provocation as regards him. Hence, whilst the age and sex of the defendant would always be attributed to the reasonable man, other characteristics such as racial origin, or physical peculiarity, would only be considered to the extent that they were relevant. The effect of the decision in *Camplin* can be seen in cases such as *R* v *Raven* [1982] Crim LR 51, where the defendant was aged 22, but had a mental age of nine and had spent the previous three years living in squats. The judge directed the jury to consider the defendant by the standard of the reasonable 22-year-old with a mental age of nine who had lived in the same conditions as the accused. It should not be assumed, of course, that attributing a characteristic such as the age of the accused to the reasonable man, will actually have any affect on the outcome of the case. In *R* v *Ali* [1989] Crim LR 736, the Court of Appeal dismissed the appeal of the 20-year-old appellant, who had appealed on the ground, inter alia, that the trial judge, in directing the jury on the defence of provocation, had failed to focus their attention on his age. The court rejected his contention that a 20-year-old might not be expected to display the self-control of a more mature man, and that thus, following *Camplin*, this characteristic ought to have been attributed to the reasonable man when the trial judge had been directing the jury.

What is a characteristic?

This question was considered by the Court of Appeal in *R* v *Newell* (1980) 71 Cr App R 331. The defendant, a chronic alcoholic, had been in a severely depressed state because his girlfriend had left him. The deceased, who had been a friend of the defendant, made some disparaging remarks about the woman, and the defendant responded by hitting him over the head with a heavy ashtray several times, eventually killing him. Four days before the killing the defendant had taken a drug overdose in an attempted suicide, and he was still suffering from the after effects of this at the time of the killing. At his trial, the defendant sought to have his chronic alcoholism, depression and drug-taking introduced as characteristics with which the reasonable man should be endowed. The trial judge had directed the jury to ignore the defendant's alcoholism, and they found him guilty of murder. The Court of Appeal dismissed the appeal, Lord Lane CJ adopting as an authority on this point the New Zealand case of *R* v *McGregor* [1962] NZLR 1069, in which North J had described a characteristic as:

> '... something definite and of sufficient significance to make the offender a different person from the ordinary run of mankind, and ... also [something having] a sufficient degree of permanence to warrant its being regarded as something constituting part of the individual's character or personality.'

The Court of Appeal went on to hold that for a characteristic to be taken into account it had to be relevant, in the sense that it had to be connected in some fairly obvious way to the provocation. On the facts of the case, Lord Lane CJ expressed the view that the only factor that could remotely be described as a characteristic was Newell's chronic alcoholism, but this was not relevant as the provocation related to the departure of his girlfriend, not his drinking. Further his Lordship refused to accept that such matters as the defendant's grief and the after effects of the failed suicide attempt were sufficiently permanent to be taken into account as characteristics.

Provocation and drunkenness

A defendant cannot claim that he was provoked because he was drunk. Following the decision in *R* v *Wardrope* [1960] Crim LR 770 it is clear that the reasonable man is presumed to be sober; hence evidence of intoxication is irrelevant as far as the objective condition is concerned. This may explain the reluctance of the Court of Appeal in *R* v *Newell* to admit intoxication in the form of chronic alcoholism as a characteristic. In *R* v *Morhall* [1993] Crim LR 957, the Court of Appeal confirmed that the trial judge had been over-generous in his concession to the appellant, in agreeing to direct the jury that the characteristic of glue-sniffing was something that could be attributed to the reasonable man. It is submitted that the fact that the provocation in this case related to the 'characteristic' in question should be irrelevant if as a matter of policy the characteristic is one of which the law takes no cognisance. The wider question of whether or not the law should be willing to take on board a wider range of characteristics when assessing the defence of provocation rests with Parliament or, in an appropriate case, the House of Lords. Given that murder is a specific intent crime, however, a defendant is still at liberty to raise the defence of self-induced intoxication in its own right: see Chapter 13.

Provocation and insanity

As with intoxication, a defendant raising the defence of provocation should not normally be allowed to introduce evidence of insanity, because the reasonable man is presumed to be sane. Again the defendant is at liberty to raise the matter as a defence in its own right, and in relation to a murder charge he is likely to do so in the guise of diminished responsibility: see 7.3 below and *R* v *Ahluwalia* (above).

Provocation and excitability

It is clear from the above that the courts will judge the defendant from the viewpoint of the reasonable person of even temperament. In *Camplin*, Lord Simon stated that the judge should direct the jury that a defendant was not entitled to rely on 'his exceptional excitability (whether idiosyncratic or by cultural environment or ethnic origin) or pugnacity of ill-temper' There will undoubtedly be difficulties in cases where a characteristic upon which the defendant seeks to rely is one having some bearing upon his ability to control his emotions: see, for example, *R* v *Roberts* [1990] Crim LR 122.

Provocation and mistake

It is submitted that a defendant who makes an honest and sober mistake as to the existence of facts which, had they existed, would have provoked a reasonable man to kill, is entitled to be judged on the facts as he believes them to be. There is venerable authority for this proposition in the case of *R* v *Brown* (1776) Leach 148, and it would be consistent with those decisions dealing with the availability of the defence of self-defence where a defendant honestly but mistakenly believes himself to be under attack (see Chapter 15).

Reform

Clause 55 of the draft code envisages a single offence of manslaughter, covering what is at present dealt with at common law under the offences of voluntary and involuntary manslaughter. It provides (inter alia) that a person is guilty of manslaughter if he is not guilty of murder by reason only of the fact that a defence is provided by clause 58 (provocation). The defence of provocation, which would be available to both principals and accessories, is defined in clause 58 as being available to a defendant who:

> '(a) ... acts when provoked (whether by things done or by things said or by both and whether by the deceased person or by another) to lose his self-control; and
> (b) the provocation is, in all the circumstances (including any of his personal characteristics that affect its gravity), sufficient ground for the loss of self-control.'

This provision is largely a restatement of the existing law, with the defendant being judged on the facts as he honestly believes them to be.

7.3 Diminished responsibility

The defence of diminished responsibility was introduced by s2(1) of the Homicide Act 1957, which provides:

> 'Where a person kills or is party to a killing of another, he shall not be convicted of murder if he was suffering from such abnormality of mind (whether arising from a condition of arrested or retarded development of mind or any inherent causes or induced by disease or injury) as substantially impaired his mental responsibility for his acts and omissions in doing or being a party to the killing.'

When the defence was enacted murder was still a capital offence, and for many defendants the only way of avoiding this consequence was to try and raise the defence of insanity. As will be seen from Chapter 13, insanity is a somewhat limited defence of mental abnormality, in that it does not excuse the defendant who knows what he is doing, and who quite possibly knows that it is wrong, but is nevertheless unable to restrain himself. Hence, many defendants charged with murder were unable to avail themselves of an appropriate defence. Since the introduction of diminished responsibility nearly all of those who would formerly have raised the defence of insanity as a defence to murder, now rely on the statutory defence. It is a misdirection, however, for a judge to direct a jury that diminished responsibility amounts to 'borderline insanity': see *R v Seers* [1985] Crim LR 85.

Section 2(2) of the 1957 Act states clearly that the burden of proving the defence rests upon the defendant, there being no duty upon the trial judge to do so on his behalf: see *R v Campbell* [1987] Crim LR 257. Given that the standard of proof which the defendant has to achieve is the balance of probabilities, he will have to obtain cogent medical evidence as to his condition, and trials involving claims of diminished responsibility frequently result in the unedifying spectacle of expert psychiatrists putting forward contradictory views as to the defendant's mental state.

Abnormality of the mind

The meaning of this phrase was considered by the Court of Appeal in *R v Byrne* [1960] 2 QB 396, where the defendant had strangled a young woman, and there was evidence that he was a sexual psychopath, and could exercise but little control over his actions. The defence of diminished responsibility was rejected by the trial judge, and the defendant was convicted of murder. He appealed on the basis that the defence should have been put to the jury. The Court of Appeal allowed the appeal on the basis that the trial judge had been wrong to exclude from the scope of the defence situations where a defendant was simply unable to exercise any self-control over his actions. Lord Parker CJ explained that an abnormality of the mind was simply a state of mind that the reasonable person would find abnormal, and that this was essentially a matter of fact for the jury to determine. The Court of Appeal, in *R v Brown* [1993] Crim LR 961, has confirmed that whilst it is desirable for a trial judge, directing a jury as to the meaning to be given to 'abnormality of the mind', to embellish the provisions of s2(1) of the 1957 Act by adverting to *Byrne*, it would not necessarily amount to a miscarriage of justice if this course of action was not followed. Clearly juries would be influenced by the medical evidence, but they were entitled to come to their own conclusions as to whether an abnormality resulted in a substantial impairment of the defendant's self-control. The danger with this approach, it is submitted, is that it may leave the jury in the position of having to adjudicate between conflicting expert evidence. What of the situation where the expert witnesses are unanimous in finding that the defendant was suffering from diminished responsibility? *R v Sanders* (1991) 93 Cr App R 245 suggests that in such cases the jury should be directed to accept the evidence and return a verdict of guilty of manslaughter. Watkins LJ points out, however, that if there are other circumstances, such as the history of the accused's conduct before and after the killing, the jury should consider the medical evidence in the light of this and may decide to reject it. The fact that the jury reject uncontroverted medical evidence is not of itself a ground of appeal provided they have been directed properly: see *Walton v R* [1978] 1 All ER 542; *R v Matheson* (1958) 42 Cr App R 145; and *R v Kiszko* (1979) 68 Cr App R 62. In *R v Egan* [1992] 4 All ER 470, the Court of Appeal considered the word 'substantial' as used in s2(1) of the 1957 Act, as being descriptive of the degree to which the accused's mental responsibility should be impaired in order for the defence to be made out. The court expressed agreement with the decision in *R v Lloyd* [1967] 1 All ER 107, to the effect that 'substantial' should be approached by the jury in a commonsense way as meaning:

'... more than some trivial degree of impairment which does not make any appreciable difference to a person's ability to control himself, but it means less than total impairment.'

Diminished responsibility and intoxication

The fact that a defendant might have been drunk at the time of committing a murder is largely irrelevant to the issue of diminished responsibility, as it will not constitute an 'inherent cause' within s2. The Court of Appeal in *R v Fenton* (1975) 61 Cr App R 261, acknowledged however, that intoxication could become a relevant factor, where it amounted to chronic alcoholism, in that the defendant's responsibility for his actions became substantially impaired because of his craving for drink. In *R v Gittens* [1984] QB 698, the Court of Appeal suggested that where the jury had to deal with both diminished responsibility and intoxication, they should be directed to consider, first whether the defendant would have killed as he did without having been intoxicated, and if the answer to that was affirmative, the second question would be whether he would have been suffering from diminished responsibility when he did so. This approach has subsequently been approved by the Court of Appeal in *R v Atkinson* [1985] Crim LR 314 and *R v Egan* (above). A distinction must be drawn, however, between a craving for drink which is caused by an abnormality of the mind, and an abnormality of the mind which is caused by a craving for drink. In *R v Tandy* [1989] 1 All ER 267, the Court of Appeal accepted that where a defendant could show that she was suffering from an abnormality of the mind at the time she killed, that it was induced by disease, namely alcoholism, and that it was such as substantially impaired her responsibility for her actions, then the defence of diminished responsibility would be made out. It would fail, however, where the evidence was that the defendant's first drink had been taken voluntarily, in that she had simply not resisted an impulse to drink alcohol and had subsequently ceased to have responsibility for her actions: see further *R v Inseal* [1992] Crim LR 35. The principles developed in *Tandy* in respect of alcoholism and diminished responsibility have been extended to other areas of substance abuse. In *R v Sanderson* (1994) 98 Cr App R 325 the appellant sought to raise the defence of diminished responsibility based on evidence of his long-term use of heroin and cocaine, although there was a conflict of expert medical evidence as to the relevance of the drug taking. For the appellant it was contended that he suffered from an abnormality of the mind, namely paranoid psychosis, that arose from inherent causes, such as the appellant's upbringing, and had been exacerbated by his drug taking. For the Crown it was contended that the appellant did suffer from a form of paranoia that was related to drug use and that he would not suffer from any paranoia if the drug taking ceased. Allowing his appeal and substituting a conviction for manslaughter on the grounds of diminished responsibility, the Court of Appeal held that although, if the jury believed the evidence of the expert witness for the Crown, it would have been open to them to hold that the appellant had not been suffering from diminished responsibility, the trial judge should have directed them that the evidence advanced for the appellant, if correct, did disclose a mental illness that could constitute an abnormality of the mind, which arose from an inherent cause, thus satisfying the requirements of s2(1) of the Homicide Act 1957. In the circumstances the court did not feel that the proviso could be applied. Note that although the matter did not arise directly for consideration, the court appeared to accept the proposition that 'abnormality of the mind' encompassed not only physical or organic disorders, but also mental illness that manifested itself in a functional sense. See chapter 26, section 26.4, for further details.

Reform

As noted above, clause 55 of the draft code provides that a defendant charged with murder and found to be suffering from diminished responsibility should be convicted of manslaughter.

Clause 56 goes on to provide that to bring himself within the terms of the defence, a defendant must be shown to have been suffering from such mental abnormality (at the time of the act causing death) that it amounted to a substantial enough reason to reduce his offence to manslaughter. Mental abnormality is further defined as 'mental illness, arrested or incomplete development of mind, psychopathic disorder, and any other disorder or disability of mind, except intoxication'. The intoxicated defendant wishing to avail himself of the defence will only be permitted to do so where it would have applied even if he were not intoxicated. Whether evidence indicates mental abnormality is to be regarded as a question of law. Mental abnormality is, for the purposes of this clause, to be taken to have the meaning attributed to it in s4 of the Mental Health Act 1959 (now s1(2) of the Act of 1983).

The clause does not attempt to codify the Court of Appeal's decision in *R* v *Tandy* (above) (in which it was held that intoxication may found diminished responsibility if the defendant is suffering from alcoholism, which renders the taking of 'the first drink' involuntary) as this was seen as raising issues which were conceptually over-complex.

7.4 Infanticide

The Infanticide Act 1938 provides that where a woman kills her child before it reaches 12 months in age, and there is evidence to show that at the time of the killing the balance of her mind was disturbed by the effect of giving birth, or the effect of lactation consequent upon giving birth to the child, a jury is entitled to find her not guilty of murder, but guilty instead of infanticide. The defence is clearly designed to cater for women who may be very seriously affected by post-natal depression. Note that it would not afford a defence to a woman suffering from post-natal depression who killed one of her older children, but it is arguable that she would raise diminished responsibility in such circumstances.

Reform

Clause 64 of the draft code provides:

'(1) A woman who, but for this section, would be guilty of murder or manslaughter of her child is not guilty of murder or manslaughter, but is guilty of infanticide, if her act is done when the child is under the age of twelve months and when the balance of her mind is disturbed by reason of the effect of giving birth or of circumstances consequent upon the birth.

(2) A woman who in the circumstances specified in subsection attempts to cause the death of her child is not guilty of attempted murder but is guilty of (1) attempted infanticide.

(3) A woman may be convicted of infanticide (or attempted infanticide) although the jury is uncertain whether the child had been born or whether it had an existence independent of her when its death occurred (or, in the case of an attempt, when the act was done).'

As the commentary upon this clause indicates it incorporates the recommendations of the Criminal Law Revision Committee's Fourteenth Report *Offences Against the Person* (1980) Cmnd 7844, in relation to infanticide. Note in particular the comments concerning the overlap between infanticide and child destruction:

'Subsection (3) provides for the case where the jury is satisfied that the defendant is guilty of either infanticide or child destruction but not satisfied that it was the one rather than the other. If the jury was uncertain, either whether the child had been born, or whether he had an existence independent of the defendant when his death occurred, it would be bound to acquit of murder or manslaughter and it would be impossible to say whether the defendant was guilty of infanticide or of child destruction. Though satisfied that it was either the one offence or the other, the jury would be bound, at least in theory, to acquit of both offences. The Committee [CLRC] thought that there should be provision for cases of this kind. The subsection enables the jury to convict of infanticide. Infanticide is chosen rather than child destruction because, under the Code, infanticide is the less serious offence. We have followed the recommendation of the Committee to reduce the maximum penalty for infanticide to five years but, like the Committee, propose no change in the penalty for child destruction. To do so would inevitably involve reconsideration of the penalty for abortion which would be controversial and could not be undertaken without consultation. If the penalties for the three offences were rationalised, this subsection might require reconsideration.

The subsection provides only for the case where the jury is uncertain. If the jury is satisfied, either that the child had not been born at the material time, or that he did not then have an existence independent of his mother, it would have to acquit of murder, manslaughter and infanticide. The defendant would be guilty of child destruction but it would be wrong to allow conviction of an offence punishable with life imprisonment on a charge of an offence punishable only with a maximum of five years.' [Vol II paras 14.27, 14.28]

7.5 Suicide pact

Section 4 of the Homicide Act 1957 introduces the defence of suicide pact. It would be used in a situation where A and B agree to end their lives by each injecting the other with a massive drug overdose at the same time. The plan is carried out, and A dies, but B is found by C and rushed to hospital, and is saved. B caused the death of A deliberately and is prima facie guilty of murdering him, but B would be able to avail himself of s4, provided that he can show the purpose of the agreement with A was that they should both die, and that when he injected A with the drug, he himself was under a 'settled expectation' of dying. See further *R* v *McShane* (1978) 66 Cr App R 97.

Reform

The draft code contains, in clause 62, proposals for a new offence of 'suicide pact killing', in line with the recommendations of the Criminal Law Revision Committee's Fourteenth Report *Offences Against the Person* (1980) Cmnd 7844. The offence would be punishable with a maximum of seven years' imprisonment. As the Code Report commentary explains:

'It applies to the case of a party to a suicide pact who kills another party to the pact or who procures, assists or encourages a third person to kill a party to the pact. It does not apply to the case of a person who procures the other to take his own life. He is not a person "who, but for this section, would be guilty of murder", because suicide is no longer self-murder, or any offence. He will, however. be guilty of an offence under [clause 63 which deals with complicity in suicide]. Subsection (3) [of clause 62], implementing the Committee's recommendation, provides that it is a defence to a charge of attempted murder that the defendant attempted to kill in pursuance of a suicide pact; but the defendant will be guilty of an attempt to commit the offence.' [Vol II paras 14.23, 14.24]

As indicated above clause 63 provides that a person is guilty of an offence if he, '... procures, assists encourages suicide or attempted suicide committed by another'. The commentary states:

'This clause reproduces the effect of s2 of the Suicide Act 1961 but with the reduced maximum penalty of seven years' imprisonment ... It is made clear that the offence is committed only when the suicide is committed or attempted. A person who attempts to procure the suicide of another will be guilty of an offence under clause 49(1): clause 49(6) does not apply because this is not a case of an attempt to procure the commission of an offence.' [Vol II para 14.25]

7.6 Death from excessive force

In addition to codifying the existing forms of involuntary manslaughter, clause 55 of the draft code seeks to introduce a new head of manslaughter where death results from the use of excessive force by the defendant. The matter is dealt with in more detail by clause 59 which provides:

'A person who, but for this section, would be guilty of murder is not guilty of murder if, at the time of his act, he believes the use of the force which causes death to be necessary and reasonable to effect a purpose referred to in section 44 (use of force in public or private defence), but the force exceeds that which is necessary and reasonable in the circumstances which exist or (where there is a difference) in those which he believes to exist.'

As the commentary notes, this clause implements the recommendations of the Criminal Law Revision Committee's Fourteenth Report *Offences Against the Person* (1980) Cmnd 7844 (paras 95 and 96). The recommendation:

'... adopted a principle then accepted in some parts of the Commonwealth, particularly Australia ... Recently, however, the High Court of Australia, in *DPP* v *Zekelic* (1987) 61 ALJR 375 has overruled its previous decisions on the use of excessive force and followed *Palmer* v *R* [1971] AC 814, bringing Australian law into line with the present law of England: the intentional use of deadly force in self-defence or the prevention of crime is either justified, in which case no crime is committed, or it is not, in which case the killer is guilty of murder. The Australian High Court overruled its previous decisions not because they thought the principle applied was unsound but because of the complexity which had arisen from the courts' attempts to state the law in a form which took account of the burden of proof. The Australian law was changed not because it was thought to be wrong in principle, but because it was too difficult for juries to understand and apply. We do not believe that these difficulties will arise under the Code. Applying clauses 13 (proof) and 44 (use of force in public or private defence), the judge should be able to direct the jury in readily comprehensible terms. *DPP* v *Zekelic* does not, in our opinion, affect the soundness of the Committee's recommendation.' [Vol II para 14.19]

8

Homicide III: Involuntary Manslaughter

8.1 Introduction

8.2 Unlawful act/constructive manslaughter

8.3 Killing by gross negligence

8.4 Reform

8.5 Motor manslaughter

8.1 Introduction

In common with murder and voluntary manslaughter, involuntary manslaughter involves the defendant in causing the death of the victim, but unlike those two forms of homicide the defendant will not have had any intention to kill or do grievous bodily harm; indeed the defendant will probably not have contemplated the death of the victim at all. At present there are three forms of involuntary manslaughter; that which is based on an unlawful act which causes death; that based upon recklessness which causes death; and that based upon killing by gross negligence. As with voluntary manslaughter, if a defendant is convicted of involuntary manslaughter the sentence is at the discretion of the trial judge and can range between life imprisonment and an unconditional discharge.

8.2 Unlawful act/constructive manslaughter

Manslaughter based upon an unlawful act, or constructive manslaughter as it is sometimes known, requires proof that the defendant committed a dangerous criminal act, accompanied by the requisite mens rea, which resulted in the death of the victim. Causation has already been considered in Chapter 6, therefore it is the remaining elements of the offence that are considered here.

Unlawful act

An act can be described as 'unlawful' where it involves a breach of either civil or criminal law. Formerly it was accepted that the unlawful act in unlawful act

126

manslaughter could be something that was merely tortious and not necessarily criminal. For example in *R* v *Fenton* (1830) 1 Lew CC 179, the defendant's liability for manslaughter was based on his tortious act of trespass to property, namely throwing stones down a mine shaft, causing a corf carrying miners to overturn, killing them.

Since the decision in *R* v *Franklin* (1883) 15 Cox CC 163, however, it has been settled law that unlawful act manslaughter must be based on a criminal act. In that case, Field J stated that:

> '... the mere fact of a civil wrong committed by one person against another ought not to be used as an incident which is a necessary step in a criminal case. I have a great abhorrence of constructive crime.'

It follows from the above that if the prosecution cannot establish a criminal act on the part of the defendant, there can be no liability on his part for unlawful act manslaughter. There is more recent authority for this proposition in the Court of Appeal's decision in *R* v *Arobieke* [1988] Crim LR 314, where the defendant had been convicted of manslaughter on the basis that his presence at a railway station had caused the victim, whom he knew to be terrified of him, to attempt an escape by crossing the railway tracks, with the result that he was electrocuted. In quashing the conviction, the Court of Appeal held that there had been no criminal act by the defendant, as the evidence did not show that the defendant had physically threatened or chased the deceased. Similar difficulties resulted in the quashing of the defendant's conviction for manslaughter in *R* v *Evans* [1992] Crim LR 659.

Any criminal act?

As unlawful act manslaughter is a serious offence against the person, must the criminal act upon which it is based also be an offence against the person, or will any criminal offence suffice provided it is the cause of death? Provided the criminal act satisfies the test for 'dangerousness' (as to which see below), it would appear that the courts are willing to adopt a liberal approach to the type of criminal act upon which this form of manslaughter will be based. In *R* v *Cato* [1976] 1 WLR 110, the defendant and the deceased agreed to inject each other with heroin. The deceased (Farmer) had consented to a number of such injections during the course of an evening. The following morning he was found to have died from the effects of the drug-taking. The defendant was convicted of maliciously administering a noxious substance contrary to s23 of the Offences Against the Person Act 1861, and of manslaughter, either on the basis that his unlawful act had caused death, or on the basis that he had recklessly caused Farmer's death. The defendant appealed against his convictions on the grounds, inter alia, that there had been no unlawful act since the deceased had consented to the injection of heroin, and that the consent should have been taken into account in determining whether or not the defendant had acted recklessly. The Court of Appeal held that the defendant had been properly convicted on both counts. Lord Widgery CJ expressed the view of the court that heroin was a noxious substance on the basis that it was likely to injure in common use, and that the defendant had administered it knowing of its noxious qualities. The victim's consent to suffer harm of this nature could never relieve the defendant of his liability, or destroy the unlawfulness of the defendant's act. Even if this was wrong, his Lordship would be willing to base liability for unlawful act manslaughter on the defendant's unlawful possession of heroin at the time he injected the deceased.

The decision has been criticised because, whilst no one would deny the criminality of unlawful possession of heroin, it could not be said that this was an offence that was 'directed at' the victim, any more than the illegal possession of a firearm could be. This point was subsequently considered by the Court of Appeal in *R* v *Dalby* [1982] 1 WLR 425. The defendant had been in lawful possession of a controlled drug which he had supplied to his friend, the deceased. The deceased had consumed a large quantity of the drug in one session, and subsequently injected himself with other substances. The following morning he was found to have died of a drug overdose. The defendant was convicted of unlawful act manslaughter, based on his unlawful supply of the controlled drug, and he appealed on the basis that his supply of the drug was not a dangerous act which had operated as the direct cause of death. He contended that the death was due to the deceased's act in consuming such a large dose of the drug in such a short space of time. The Court of Appeal allowed the appeal, Waller LJ holding that the defendant's act had not in any event been the direct cause of death, but had merely made it possible for the deceased to kill himself. His Lordship went on to state that where manslaughter was based on an unlawful and dangerous act, it had to be an act directed at the victim which was likely to cause immediate injury, albeit slight.

The decision suggested several important limitations upon the scope of unlawful act manslaughter, in that it seemed to exclude the possibility of basing liability on offences against property, or regulatory offences such as those under the Misuse of Drugs Act 1971, and also in that it seemed to introduce an extra element of mens rea into the offence by requiring the defendant to 'direct' his action against the victim. The potential significance of *R* v *Dalby* was greatly reduced, however, following *R* v *Goodfellow* (1986) 83 Cr App R 23. The defendant had deliberately fire bombed his own council house in the hope that he would be rehoused by the council. His wife and children, who had been in the house, were killed in the ensuing blaze. He appealed against his conviction for manslaughter on the ground, inter alia, that his unlawful act (criminal damage) had not been directed at the victims as required by *R* v *Dalby*. The Court of Appeal held that this latter authority should not be construed as requiring proof of an intention on the part of the defendant to harm the victims. It was to be viewed primarily as an authority on causation, in that the prosecution had to establish that there had been no fresh intervening cause between the defendant's act and the death. Clearly that had been an issue in *R* v *Dalby*, but was not an issue on the facts of the present case. The court seems to have been satisfied to accept that any dangerous criminal act causing the death of the victim would provide the basis for an unlawful act manslaughter charge.

In other respects *R* v *Goodfellow* is a decision that has some welcome aspects. For example there is no good reason why an offence such as aggravated criminal damage, given that it involves an intention to endanger life, or recklessness as to whether life is endangered, should not provide the unlawful act in this type of manslaughter. Further, there is clear authority that the defendant's act need not be the direct cause of death. In *R* v *Mitchell* [1983] 2 WLR 938, the Court of Appeal upheld the conviction for manslaughter of a defendant who, having become involved in an altercation whilst queuing in a busy post office, pushed an elderly man, causing him to fall accidentally onto the deceased, an elderly woman, who subsequently died in hospital from her injuries. Staughton J expressed the view of the court that it was sufficient for the jury to be satisfied that the defendant's intentional act had caused the victim's death. The actions of the elderly man in falling on the victim were entirely foreseeable and did not break the chain of causation between the defendant's assault and the victim's death. *R* v *Dalby* was distinguishable on its facts as a case where the victim was not injured as a direct and immediate result of the defendant's act. See further the commentary to *R* v *Ball* [1989] Crim LR 730, at 731–2.

A dangerous criminal act

A point made repeatedly in a number of the authorities cited above is the requirement that the unlawful act upon which constructive manslaughter is based must be dangerous. In *R* v *Larkin* [1943] 1 All ER 217, Humphreys J explained this in terms of the unlawful act being one which was likely to injure another person. In *R* v *Church* [1966] 1 QB 59, Edmund Davies J provided a slightly more elaborate definition of dangerousness where he stated:

> '... the unlawful act must be such as all sober and reasonable people would inevitably recognise must subject the other person to, at least, the risk of some harm resulting therefrom, albeit not serious harm.'

This is clearly an objective test, but it leaves open the question as to the type of harm that has to be reasonably foreseeable. Following the more recent Court of Appeal decision in *R* v *Dawson* (1985) 81 Cr App R 150, it would appear that the jury must be directed to consider the possibility of physical harm as opposed to merely emotional disturbance. Hence if D, dressed as a ghost, jumps out in front of P, who suffers a heart attack and dies, it may be the case that D cannot be convicted of unlawful act manslaughter because the only harm that was reasonably foreseeable as a result of his action was that the victim would be frightened. Compare this with the situation where D loads a sawn-off shot-gun, holds it P's head and crooks his finger around the trigger. If P dies of a heart attack brought on by his fear of dying, D should be guilty of unlawful act manslaughter, on the basis that the reasonable person would not only foresee P being scared, but would have foreseen P being so scared as to suffer physical harm.

The real problem, it is submitted, concerns the victim who has some physical peculiarity, unknown to the defendant, that makes the victim more vulnerable in the event of an attack. On the basis of *R v Blaue* it might be thought that the defendant who frightens a victim, only to find that the victim dies because he has a weak heart, should be required to take his victim as he finds him. Note however that in *R v Dawson*, where the defendants had attacked a petrol filling station attendant who had a weak heart, Watkins LJ, referring to the test for determining whether or not the unlawful act was dangerous, stated:

> '... this test can only be undertaken upon the basis of the knowledge gained by a sober and reasonable man as though he were present at the scene of the crime and watched the unlawful act being performed ... he has the same knowledge as the man attempting to rob and no more.'

This seems to suggest that if the accused makes a reasonable mistake as to the fortitude and strength of the victim, it has to be taken into account in assessing the dangerousness of his unlawful act. Since the decision in *R v Dawson*, the matter has been considered on two occasions by the Court of Appeal. In *R v Watson* [1989] 1 WLR 684, the appellant had burgled a house occupied by an 87-year-old man who suffered from a heart condition. The appellant disturbed the occupant, and abused him verbally, but made off without stealing anything. The police were called shortly afterwards, and a local council workman arrived to repair the windows broken by the appellant in gaining entry. An hour and a half after the burglary the occupant had a heart attack and died. The appellant was convicted of manslaughter but appealed successfully on the ground that his counsel had been denied a sufficient opportunity to address the jury on the issue of whether the excitement caused by the arrival of the police and the council workman could have taken over as the operating and substantial cause of death. As to the nature of the unlawful act however, the court recognised that, following *R v Dawson*, and applying the test established by Watkins LJ, the unlawful act had to be dangerous in the sense that all sober and reasonable persons would foresee that it created a risk of some physical harm occurring to the victim, but added that in applying this test, the reasonable person was to be imbued with all the knowledge that the defendant had gained throughout his burglarious trespass (ie his realisation of the occupant's frailty) and not just the appellant's limited or non-existent knowledge at the moment he first entered the property. On this basis, therefore, the burglary did constitute a dangerous unlawful act, but only because it is assumed by the court that the appellant was aware of the frailty of the victim. Lord Lane CJ stated (at p687) that:

> '... the appellant ... during the course of the unlawful act must have become aware of [the victim's] frailty and approximate age.'

What if the defendant makes an honest but unreasonable mistake as to circumstances? What if Watson had honestly but mistakenly thought that his victim was a much younger and fitter man, even though it would have been obvious to a reasonable man that this was not the case? The Court of Appeal's decision in *R* v *Ball* [1989] Crim LR 730 may go some way towards providing a solution.

The appellant had been involved in a long-running dispute with his neighbour, G, over her parking her vehicle on his land. Eventually the appellant had the vehicle sold whilst it was still parked on his land. G, accompanied by two men, called on the appellant to investigate the disappearance of the vehicle. An altercation developed, which culminated in the appellant grabbing a handful of cartridges, loading his shotgun, and firing at G from approximately 12 yards. G was killed in the attack. The appellant was acquitted of murder, on the basis that he had honestly believed that he had loaded the gun with blank cartridges, and had only intended to frighten G, but was convicted of constructive manslaughter. The appellant appealed on the basis that the trial judge had erred in directing the jury as to how they should have assessed the 'dangerousness' of his unlawful act, in that they had not been told to bear in mind the appellant's mistaken belief that he was firing blanks, when applying the *Dawson* test. In dismissing the appeal, the court held that once it was established that the appellant had intentionally committed an unlawful act, the question of its dangerousness was to be decided by applying the objective test (as in *R* v *Dawson*). The court refused to impute to the reasonable man the appellant's mistake of fact (ie believing the live cartridges to be blanks).

Although the decision in *R* v *Ball* was delivered some three days before that in *R* v *Watson*, the approach taken by the Court of Appeal in the latter case can be relied upon to explain the decision in the former. In *R* v *Watson* the court stressed the need to look at the whole of the defendant's actions in assessing their 'dangerousness', which in that case meant looking at the burglarious trespass in its entirety. In *R* v *Ball*, therefore, the whole of the appellant's actions should be considered, not just his firing of the gun, but also his grabbing a handful of cartridges in order to load them, without checking to see if any were live. It is perhaps to be assumed that the reasonable person would have realised the dangerousness of such behaviour.

The mens rea of unlawful act manslaughter

As mentioned above, the most striking difference between murder and unlawful act manslaughter lies in the mens rea. Whilst the former requires proof that the defendant intended to kill or do grievous bodily harm, the latter does not require any proof that the defendant foresaw death. The House of Lords took the opportunity to reaffirm this point in *DPP* v *Newbury and Jones* [1976] AC 500, wherein the defendants, both teenage boys, had thrown a piece of paving stone from a railway bridge onto a train which had been passing beneath killing the guard who had been sitting in the driver's compartment. The defendants were convicted of manslaughter, and appealed, unsuccessfully, on the ground that they had not foreseen that their actions might cause harm to any other person. Lord Salmon explained that an accused was guilty of manslaughter if it was proved that he intentionally did an act which was unlawful and dangerous and that act caused death, and that it was unnecessary to prove that the defendant had known that the act in question was unlawful or dangerous.

The law can perhaps be summarised by stating that the defendant charged with unlawful act manslaughter must be shown to have had the mens rea appropriate to the unlawful act upon which his liability is based, although it should be noted that one of the more curious aspects of *DPP* v *Newbury and Jones* is the failure by their Lordships to identify exactly what unlawful act was committed by the defendants. One presumes that it was aggravated criminal damage.

Clearly, where the prosecution is unable to establish the mens rea for the unlawful act, the defendant cannot be liable. This statement of the obvious is neatly illustrated by *R* v *Lamb* [1967] 2 QB 981. The defendant, as a joke, pointed a revolver at his friend, the deceased, and pulled the trigger. The defendant had previously checked to ensure that the chamber facing the firing-pin of the gun was empty, and thus did not expect the gun to fire. What the defendant had not known was that his pulling the trigger made the chamber of the gun rotate, so as to present a loaded chamber to the firing-pin. His friend died from his injuries when he was hit by the bullet fired from the gun. The defendant appealed successfully against his conviction for manslaughter, the Court of Appeal ruling that even if it was assumed that the victim had apprehended immediate physical violence, if the defendant thought that it was all a joke, he could not have had the mens rea for the unlawful act of assault, and thus could not be guilty of unlawful act manslaughter.

Similarly, in *R* v *Jennings* [1990] Crim LR 588, the Court of Appeal allowed the appellant's appeal against his conviction for manslaughter, on the basis that the establishing of the unlawful act upon which the prosecution had sought to rely (the offence of carrying an offensive weapon contrary to s1 Prevention of Crimes Act 1953) required evidence of the appellant's intention in relation to the use of the weapon, since it had not been 'made or adapted for use for causing injury to the person'. The issue of intention had not been left to the jury as it should.

8.3 Killing by gross negligence

The origins of the modern law

In addition to manslaughter based on an unlawful and dangerous act that causes death, the common law has traditionally recognised that liability for manslaughter can arise from a grossly negligent act or omission that causes death. Not infrequently juries are invited to consider both types of manslaughter as alternative bases for liability arising out of the same set of facts. Hence in *Cato*, and *Lamb*, considered above, the juries were invited to consider the defendant's liability for manslaughter, either on the basis that he had committed a dangerous unlawful act which had resulted in death, or on the basis that the death had been caused by the defendant's gross negligence.

It is possible to trace the emergence of killing by gross manslaughter to cases where death resulted from medical treatment. The courts took the view that it was unjust and could possibly be counter-productive to hold that liability for manslaughter could flow from mere inadvertence on the part of a medical practitioner, particularly where he found himself having to deal with a pre-existing danger not of his own making. Lord Hewart CJ, in *R v Bateman* [1925] 94 LJKB 791, sought to identify the determinants of liability in such cases. The appellant had operated on a woman who subsequently died. His appeal against his conviction for manslaughter was allowed on the ground that the trial judge had failed to distinguish between the degree of negligence required for civil liability and that required for manslaughter. Lord Hewart CJ held that, to secure a conviction in such cases, the Crown had to prove: (a) that D owed P a duty of care; (b) that D had breached that duty of care; (c) that the breach had caused the death of P; and (d) that D's negligence was gross in that it went beyond a mere matter of compensation between subjects. Whilst *Bateman* was followed in subsequent cases, there emerged a tendency on the part of the courts to conceptualise the fault element required for this head of manslaughter by characterising it as a form of 'recklessness'. Hence in *Andrews v DPP* [1937] AC 576, where the defendant appealed unsuccessfully against his conviction for manslaughter arising out of a 'hit and run' incident, Lord Atkin, observing that a very high degree of negligence is required to secure a conviction, stated:

'... of all the epithets that can be applied "reckless" most nearly covers the case ... but it is probably not all embracing, for "reckless" suggests an indifference to risk, whereas the accused may have appreciated the risk, and intended to avoid it, and yet shown in the means adopted to avoid the risk such a degree of negligence as would justify a conviction.'

Similarly in *R v Stone and Dobinson* [1977] QB 354, Geoffrey Lane CJ, describing the fault element required for killing by gross negligence stated:

'Mere inadvertence is not enough. The defendant must be proved to have been indifferent to a obvious risk of injury to health, or actually to have foreseen the risk but to have determined nevertheless to run it.'

Decisions such as *Andrews* and *Stone and Dobinson* were somewhat problematic in that there was no clear indication of what was meant by indifference. Did it imply that D had never thought about the risk (as in *Caldwell* recklessness where D gives no thought etc), or did it imply that D was aware of the possible outcomes but did not care whether the risk materialised or not?

Killing by gross negligence eclipsed

During the 1980s the tide of judicial opinion turned away from the further development of manslaughter based on killing by gross negligence, and towards the creation of what was arguably a new head of common law manslaughter based on *Caldwell/Lawrence* recklessness. In *R v Seymour* [1983] 2 AC 493 the defendant, in the course of his efforts to move the victim's car out of the way by pushing it with his truck, jammed her body between his truck and her car, as a result of which she sustained fatal injuries. Although he could (at the time) have been charged with causing death by reckless driving contrary to the Road Traffic Act 1972, the prosecution pursued a charge of common law manslaughter (which gave the judge a discretion to impose a higher sentence upon conviction), and the defendant was convicted. The trial judge had directed the jury that they should convict if they were satisfied that the defendant had caused death, and had been reckless in so doing, recklessness here having the meaning attributed to it in *Lawrence*. The House of Lords held that the conviction should stand, Lord Roskill stating that 'objective', or *Caldwell* type, recklessness applied equally to common law manslaughter and the statutory offence of motor manslaughter under the Road Traffic Act 1972. Hence D could be guilty of reckless manslaughter where he, by his conduct, created an obvious and serious risk of physical harm, and either he had given no thought to it or had been aware of it and determined to take it. In *Kong Cheuk Kwan* v *R* (1985) 82 Cr App R 18, the Privy Council (Lord Roskill giving the judgment of the Board) applied the 'new' form of reckless manslaughter to a case involving a collision between two hydrofoils in Hong Kong harbour which had resulted in the deaths of two passengers. Citing Lord Atkin's preference for the epithet 'reckless' to describe the degree of fault required in killing by gross negligence, Lord Roskill promulgated the notion that as *Caldwell/Lawrence* now provided the model definition of recklessness applicable wherever recklessness was involved as a fault element, it should be used as the basis for the trial judge's direction to the jury in cases where formerly an explanation of gross negligence would have been provided. Indeed, Lord Roskill went so far as to expressly endorse the comments of Waller LJ when *Seymour* was before the Court of Appeal, to the effect that, in relation to manslaughter '... it is no longer necessary or helpful to make references to compensation or negligence'.

Killing by gross negligence reinstated

In the wake of the decisions of the House of Lords and Privy Council in *Seymour* and *Kong Cheuk Kwan* respectively, many commentators concluded that killing by gross negligence may have disappeared as a head of manslaughter, although there were clearly some members of the Court of Appeal who did not know this or at least thought otherwise: see *R* v *Ball* [1989] Crim LR 730. The reinstatement of killing by gross negligence arose out of a number of appeals against conviction for manslaughter that were heard together on the basis that they raised identical or sufficiently similar points of law: *R* v *Prentice*; *R* v *Sulman*; *R* v *Adomako*; *R* v *Holloway* [1993] 3 WLR 927. Prentice and Sulman were junior hospital doctors required to carry out a lumbar puncture and other procedures in relation to a patient suffering from leukaemia. The injections were not conducted properly and a drug which should have been administered by injection in the patient's arm was injected into his spine. The patient died despite the efforts of the doctors to rectify the error. Holloway was a qualified electrician who was contracted to fit a central heating programmer in a residential dwelling. The programmer was incorrectly wired by the appellant with the result that, during the operation of certain programmes, the metal parts of the heating system became live. Five months after the installation of the programmer, one of the occupants was killed as a result of electrocution, the death being caused by the incorrect wiring of the programmer. All three appellants were convicted, following directions at first instance in terms of reckless manslaughter, and appealed successfully.

The Court of Appeal held that where death was caused by a breach of duty on the part of the defendant, a prosecution on the basis of reckless manslaughter might be appropriate where the situation was one involving motor manslaughter, as the risk of harm was created by the accused himself. Where, however, the defendant had been under a duty to act in a situation where there was a pre-existing risk of harm to others not of his making, such as a doctor treating a sick patient, it was appropriate to apply a standard of fault that allowed the court to ask questions as to why the defendant might have made errors having fatal consequences. In this regard the Lord Chief Justice observed:

'It might well be unnecessary to ask such questions when the issue is simply as to whether the speed of a person's driving was reckless, but they are central questions when examining the degree of negligence of a skilled man exercising his trade. They are questions which obviously must be asked once the issue is defined as gross negligence, but might well not be asked under the *Lawrence* direction of recklessness.'

It might be observed that the distinction drawn between one who creates a risk, such as a motorist who decides to overtake on the brow of a hill, and one who is presented with a dangerous situation, such as a doctor attending an patient, seems to be sustainable in respect of Prentice and Sulman, but can it really be extended to an electrician contracted to fit a central heating programmer?

In the view of the Court of Appeal, a further distinction between reckless manslaughter and killing by gross negligence related to the assessment of the risk involved. As the Lord Chief Justice explained:

'... the "obvious risk" of Lord Diplock's formulation in *Caldwell* ... meant obvious to "the ordinary prudent individual". Everyone knows what can happen when you strike a match, and practically everyone, whether as a driver or a passenger, knows the risks of the road. But in expert fields where duty is undertaken, be it by a doctor or an electrician, the criteria of what the ordinary prudent individual would appreciate can hardly be applied in the same way.'

The fourth appellant, Adomako, a locum tenens anaesthetist employed at a hospital, was assisting in an operation on a patient for a detached retina. During the operation the tube from the patient's ventilator became detached. By the time the appellant became aware that something had gone wrong the damage caused to the patient had become irreversible and he died. The appellant was convicted of manslaughter following a direction from the trial judge, in terms of gross negligence as the basis for liability rather than recklessness, and his appeal was rejected by the Court of Appeal, which certified the following point of law of general public importance for consideration by House of Lords [1994] 3 WLR 288:

'In cases of manslaughter by gross negligence not involving driving but involving a breach of duty is it a sufficient direction to the jury to adopt the gross negligence test set out by the Court of Appeal in the present case following *R* v *Bateman* (1925) 19 Cr App R 8 and *Andrews* v *DPP* [1937] AC 576 without reference to the test of recklessness as defined in *R* v *Lawrence* 1982 AC 510 or as adapted to the circumstances of the case?': see *R* v *Adomako* [1994] 1 WLR 15.

Dismissing the appeal, and answering the certified question in the affirmative, Lord Mackay LC expressed the view that *Andrews* v *DPP* was a decision of the House of Lords that had not been overruled, and was thus still binding. In his view the ordinary principles of negligence should be invoked, and liability imposed where a grossly negligent breach of duty could be shown to have caused death. He observed:

'The jury will have to consider whether the extent to which the defendant's conduct departed from the proper standard of care incumbent upon him, involving as it must have done a risk of death to the patient, was such that it should be judged criminal. It is true that to a certain extent this involves an element of circularity, but in this branch of the law I do not believe that it is fatal to its being correct as a test of how far conduct must depart from accepted standards to be characterised as criminal.'

In his Lordship's view the variety of fact situations that could give rise to a charge of manslaughter was so great that it was unwise to attempt a more specific direction.

Although in cases of manslaughter cased by breach of duty it was not necessary for the trial judge to refer to *R* v *Lawrence*, it was open to the trial judge to use the word 'reckless' in its ordinary meaning (ie as used in *R* v *Stone, R* v *Dobinson* [1977] QB 354) as part of his exposition of the law if he deemed it appropriate. The Lord Chancellor went on to explain that *Seymour* (above) and *Kong Cheuk Kwan* (above), should no longer be followed as the underlying statutory provisions (ie Road Traffic Act 1972) had been repealed, and because there were problems in distinguishing between cases where death resulted from driving and those where death resulted from the navigation of a craft.

8.4 Reform

The Law Commission's consultation paper No 135 'Criminal Law – Involuntary Manslaughter' details its provisional proposals for reforming this area of liability for homicide. These are:

1. The abolition of unlawful act manslaughter.
2. The introduction of a form of reckless manslaughter where the defendant is reckless (in the subjective sense) as to whether death or serious personal injury

would result from his actions. The offence would still carry the possibility of life imprisonment.

3. a) The abolition of common law 'motor manslaughter', leaving such cases to be dealt with by either the statutory offence of causing death by dangerous driving or the proposed new offence of reckless manslaughter; or

   b) The disapplication of *Caldwell* to the common law form of 'motor manslaughter' established in *Seymour*, so as to amalgamate such offences within the proposed offence of (subjective) reckless manslaughter.

4. The introduction of a new head of involuntary manslaughter, not based on conscious risk-taking. Liability would arise where the accused ought reasonably to have been aware of a significant risk that his conduct could result in death or serious injury, and his conduct fell seriously and significantly below what could reasonably have been expected of him in preventing that risk from occurring or in preventing risk, once in being, from resulting in the prohibited harm. The offence would carry a maximum penalty of ten years' imprisonment.

5. The law relating to involuntary manslaughter should apply equally to corporations as it does to individuals. To this end the Commission favours the application of the new offence of manslaughter based on unconscious risk-taking to corporations. As the Consultation Paper states at para 5.77:

> 'It is in our view much easier to say that a *corporation*, as such, has failed to do something, or has failed to meet a particular standard of conduct than it is to say that a corporation has done a positive act, or has entertained a particular subjective state of mind. The former statements can be made directly, without recourse to the intermediary step of finding a human mind and a decision-making process on the part of an individual within or representing the company; and thus the need for the identification theory, in order to bring the corporation within the subjective requirements of the law, largely falls away.'

The direct question as regards corporate liability for manslaughter would, therefore, be whether the corporation fell within the criteria for liability outlined above in relation to manslaughter based on unconscious risk-taking.

Regarding the need for reform, note the observation of the Lord Taylor CJ when *Prentice* was before the Court of Appeal:

> 'Before parting with [the case], the state of the law of manslaughter prompts us to urge the Law Commission to take the opportunity to examine the subject in all its aspects as a matter of urgency.'

In the House of Lords Lord Mackay, considering the appeal in *Adomako*, declared himself to have derived considerable help from consulting the Law Commission's consultation paper in formulating his view as to the outcome of this appeal.

8.5 Motor manslaughter

Many cases of death resulting from the use of a motor vehicle are classified as 'accidents' and do not result in criminal proceedings as regards the death. Until 1956, if criminal proceedings were brought, drivers who caused death were indicted for manslaughter, but in many cases juries showed themselves reluctant to convict 'fellow motorists' for homicide. As a response to this problem, the Road Traffic Act 1956 introduced the offence of causing death by reckless or dangerous driving, an offence carrying up to five years imprisonment. In 1977 the law was amended by the Criminal Law Act so that the offence became one of causing death by reckless driving alone. In due course the offence of causing death by reckless driving was consolidated in the Road Traffic Act 1988. Difficulties persisted, however, not least in relation to the correct interpretation of recklessness within this particular statutory context: see *R* v *Lawrence* [1982] AC 510, and *R* v *Reid* [1992] 1 WLR 793, considered at Chapter 2. The Road Traffic Law Review Report (1988) (the 'North Committee report') concluded that an entirely objective type of fault was required, and the reformulation of the offence was effected by the Road Traffic Act 1991, amending the Road Traffic Act 1988, so that s1 now provides;

'A person who causes the death of another person by driving a mechanically propelled vehicle dangerously on a road or other public place is guilty of an offence.'

Dangerous driving is further defined in s2(1)(a) as driving that falls below what would be expected of a competent and careful driver, in that it would be obvious to such a person that driving in the manner in question would be dangerous. The danger can relate either to injury to another, or serious damage to property. The new offence carries a maximum penalty of five years imprisonment and/or a fine.

9

Participation I

9.1 Introduction

9.2 Modes of participation

9.3 Mens rea

9.4 Where the principal exceeds the common design

9.5 Transferred malice and accomplices

9.1 Introduction

The commission of a criminal offence will often result from the planning and co-operation of a number of individuals. Provided the individual committing the offence has the requisite mens rea there should be no difficulty in establishing the elements of liability, but problems can arise as regards those who help in the commission of the offence. What sort of activities should be regarded as assistance? How much must the assistant know about the intended offence in order to be convicted as an accomplice? In theory the law does not distinguish between those who commit crimes themselves, and those who help in some way. The basis for this approach is s8 of the Accessories and Abettors Act 1861 (as amended by the Criminal Law Act 1977) which provides:

> 'Whosoever shall aid, abet, counsel, or procure the commission of any indictable offence whether the same be an offence at common law or by virtue of any Act passed or to be passed, shall be liable to be tried, indicted, and punished as a principal offender.'

Similar provision is made in respect of summary trial by the Magistrates' Courts Act 1980. Unless Parliament expressly indicates to the contrary, the common law doctrine of accessorial liability will apply to any statutory offences: see *R* v *Jefferson*; *R* v *Keogh* [1993] Crim LR 880.

Some confusion can arise because of the variety of terms used to describe different types of participation; many cases refer to 'accessories before the fact', 'accessories after the fact', and 'principals in the second degree', etc. For ease of reference, the following terms will be used: '*Principal*', the defendant who has actually committed the offence in question; '*Accomplice*', the defendant who has helped in some way. Accomplices are further subdivided into aiders, abettors, counsellors, and procurers, as detailed below. Reality is never as simple, however, as the theory would suggest and it should be noted that there may be cases where it is not possible to distinguish between principals and accomplices, for example, where there is evidence at a murder trial that the three defendants had each stabbed the victim, but it is not clear which of them actually dealt the fatal blow. In such cases, the defendants can simply be charged as joint principals: see further *Abbott* v *R* [1977] AC 755.

Whilst the principles of accessorial liability are to be found in the common law, it will be noted that a large number of statutes also create specific offences of participation, eg Sexual Offences Act 1956 s28(1) states:

> 'It is an offence for a person to encourage ... the commission of unlawful sexual intercourse with ... a girl under the age of sixteen for whom he is responsible.'

The creation of such offences is largely for the avoidance of doubt, as at common law the activity prohibited by s28 would presumably come within the scope of abetting unlawful sexual intercourse.

9.2 Modes of participation

The broad distinction between counselling and procuring on the one hand, and aiding and abetting on the other, is that the former are thought to occur prior to the commission of the offence, whilst the latter, typically, will occur at the scene of the crime. Whilst this distinction will largely hold true, it should not be regarded as a rule. An accomplice may aid the commission of an offence by supplying the necessary equipment, notwithstanding that he is not at the scene of the crime: see the discussion of this issue in *Gillick* v *West Norfolk and Wisbech Area Health Authority* [1986] AC 112. It might seem logical to assume that each mode of participation requires proof that the accomplice caused the commission of the offence by the principal, and that there must be evidence of a plan or agreement between the parties. As indicated below, the law actually requires these issues to be addressed separately in relation to each mode of participation.

To counsel the commission of an offence involves an accomplice in advising, encouraging, persuading, instructing, pressurising, or even threatening the principal into committing the offence. In *R* v *Calhaem* [1985] 2 WLR 826, Parker LJ described this mode of participation in the following terms:

> 'There is no implication in the word itself that there should be any causal connection between the counselling and the offence ... [but] there must be a connection between the counselling and the [offence committed by the principal]. Equally, the act done must, we think, be done within the scope of the authority or advice ...'

It would suffice, therefore, that the principal offender knew of the advice, threats, encouragement or instructions of the accomplice, and that his actions were within those terms of reference. It would seem that counselling implicitly involves a degree of understanding between the parties, although to describe this as consensus may be inappropriate in those cases where the accomplice orders the principal to commit an offence under duress.

The leading authority as regards the meaning of procuring is *Attorney-General's Reference (No 1 of 1975)* (1975) 61 Cr App R 118. The accused had surreptitiously laced a friend's drinks with double measures of alcohol knowing the friend would shortly afterwards be driving home. The friend was convicted of drunken driving. The accused was charged as an accomplice to this offence, but was acquitted following a successful submission of no case. The trial judge took the view that there had to be evidence of some agreement between the accomplice and the principal for liability to be imposed. The Court of Appeal held that the submission of no case ought not to have been allowed to succeed. Lord Widgery CJ held that to procure meant to produce by endeavour, observing that:

> 'You procure a thing by setting out to see that it happens and taking the appropriate steps to produce that happening.'

The accomplice's acts of procuration must be the cause in fact of the commission of the offence by the principal, ie in this case the amount of alcohol supplied by the accused must be shown to have taken the principal's blood/alcohol level over the legal limit for driving. The court went on to hold that, as regards procuring, there was no requirement to prove any agreement or consensus regarding the commission of the offence.

Aiding involves helping in the commission of an offence. For example if X is committing a burglary, and Y is standing in the grounds of the building keeping a eye out for police officers, Y would be described as aiding in the commission of the burglary by X. Similarly if a man, X, commits the offence of rape upon P, whilst Y, a woman holds P down, Y could be guilty of aiding the rape. Whilst the principal offender may not have committed the offence 'but for' the assistance given by the accomplice, it would perhaps be an over-generalisation to say that the aiding must cause the commission of the offence. There may be instances where the principal would have committed the offence anyway, the involvement of the accomplice simply making it easier, or less risky. In such cases much will depend upon the accomplice's state of mind, ie the extent to which he intended to facilitate the commission of the offence. Further, it should not be assumed that aiding necessarily requires proof of consensus between accomplice and principal. Whilst such cases will frequently involve some pre-planning, an accomplice could incur liability where, for example, he finds the principal about to assault P and, of his own accord, intervenes by holding P down.

Abetting implies encouragement and, as with counselling, it is sufficient that the principal should be aware of the encouragement; there is no need to prove that the principal would not have committed the crime but for being abetted by the accomplice. Equally there is no need to prove any consensus between the parties. Hence in *Wilcox* v *Jeffery* [1951] 1 All ER 464, the defendant, Wilcox, the proprietor of a publication entitled *Jazz Illustrated*, who had written reports of the musician Coleman Hawkins' arrival in the United Kingdom, attended a concert, at which Hawkins delighted the crowd by getting up on stage and playing his instrument, a glowing account of which appeared in *Jazz Illustrated*. Hawkins had been forbidden, under the Aliens Order 1920, from taking any employment in the United Kingdom. The defendant was convicted of aiding and abetting Hawkins in the contravention of the Aliens Order 1920, and appealed unsuccessfully to the Divisional Court, where it was held that, as it had been an illegal act for Hawkins to play, and as the appellant had clearly known that this was illegal, his payment for a ticket and presence at the concert was an encouragement to commit this illegal act. In a memorable passage from his judgment Lord Goddard CJ stated:

> 'The appellant did not get up and protest in the name of the musicians of England that Mr Hawkins ought not to be here competing with them and taking the bread out of their mouths or the wind out of their instruments ... It might have been entirely different ... if he had gone there and protested, saying, "The musicians union do not like you foreigners coming here and playing and you ought to get off the stage." If he had booed it might have been some evidence that he was not aiding and abetting ...'

A duty to prevent crime?

At common law a defendant can only incur liability for failing to act if he is under a legal duty to act in a particular way. The application of this doctrine extends to the imposition of accessorial liability. If A becomes aware that B, a passenger in his car, is in possession of heroin, he does not become an accomplice to the possession offence as such. By contrast, if A sees his wife B torturing their child, his failure to intervene could result in his being charged as an accomplice to her criminal acts. In general, therefore, mere presence at the scene of a crime will not be sufficient to give rise to accessorial liability: see *R v Coney* (1882) 8 QBD 534. In *R v Clarkson* [1971] 1 WLR 1402, the defendants, two soldiers who had been present in a room whilst other soldiers raped a young woman, appealed successfully against their convictions for abetting rape. It was held that the jury should have been directed that there could only be a conviction if (1) the presence of the defendants at the scene of the crime actually encouraged its commission, and (2) the accused had intended their presence to offer such encouragement.

Although the point is not free from difficulty, it would appear that D may escape liability as an accomplice, even where he has full knowledge of the crime the principal intends to commit, if it can be shown that he was under a duty to perform the acts alleged to have assisted in the commission of the offence. In *R v Lomas* (1913) 110 LT 239, the defendant had returned a crowbar to its rightful owner, knowing that it would be used by him to commit further burglaries. The court held that despite the defendant's knowledge, his action could not be regarded as criminal, since if he had deliberately retained the crowbar he could have been liable for the tort of conversion, if not guilty of theft. The principle seems almost perverse. Suppose that X has lent his air rifle to Y, so that Y can scare cats from his garden, and one day, following a furious row with his wife, X rushes into Y's house demanding the return of the gun because he wants to use it to kill his wife. Can Y be absolved of all liability when he calmly hands the gun back to X who proceeds to kill his wife? There is implied support for the *Lomas* approach in obiter comments of Devlin J in *National Coal Board* v *Gamble* (above), and *R* v *Salford Health Authority, ex parte Janaway* [1988] 3 WLR 1350. In the latter case the applicant, a secretary at a doctor's surgery, had refused to type a letter referring a patient to a hospital for an abortion on the ground that, as a Roman Catholic, she did not want to aid the carrying out of an abortion. She sought judicial review of her dismissal by the Area Health Authority, and the Court of Appeal held, inter alia, that as she was carrying out an obligation of her employment she could not be described as counselling or procuring an abortion.

9.3 Mens rea

Strict liability offences

A defendant cannot incur liability as an accomplice unless the prosecution can establish some degree of mens rea. This general proposition applies even where the offence committed by the principal is one of strict or absolute liability. It will obviously not be an excuse for the accomplice to state that he did not know that what the principal was doing was prohibited by the criminal law, but it will negate liability if the accomplice can show that he was unaware of the facts that constituted the offence. The relevant authority is *Johnson* v *Youden* [1950] 1 KB 544. The principal offender in this case was a builder who had been granted a licence to build a house by the local authority, subject to a condition limiting the maximum price at which it could be sold to £1,025. It was an offence of strict liability to sell a house in excess of any such condition. The builder induced another person to buy it from him for £1,275 and instructed the defendant solicitors to act for him in respect of the necessary conveyancing. The court held that of the three solicitors charged with aiding and abetting the builder, two had to be acquitted because they at no time knew what price the house was being sold at. The third would be convicted because he had been aware of the selling price and therefore did know of the facts which constituted the offence: see further *Callow* v *Tillstone* (1900) 83 LT 411. Similarly, in respect of drunken driving offences, it is necessary for the prosecution to prove that the accomplice either knew or was reckless as to whether the driver was unfit to drive through drink: see *Smith* v *Mellors* (1986) The Times 21 November.

Offences requiring proof of fault

If an accomplice can be shown to have had the mens rea required to justify conviction of the principal offender, for example, intention to kill or do grievous bodily harm in the case of murder, there will be little difficulty in imposing accessorial liability. Problems arise, however, in determining whether a lesser degree of fault will suffice, and if so, how it should be defined. Clearly D must be shown to have intended to commit the relevant accessorial acts, but a difficulty arises because he may be unaware of precisely what offence the principal is going to commit. As a matter of public policy it would be unacceptable to acquit an accomplice who supplies equipment in the belief that it will be used in the course of a robbery, when in fact it is used in the course of a burglary, but how are the limits of liability to be designated? The general rule for establishing the mens rea of accomplices who aid and abet the commission of offences is contained in the Court of Appeal's decision in *R* v *Bainbridge* [1959] 3 WLR 356. The defendant had supplied some cutting equipment which was subsequently used to break into the Midland Bank in Stoke Newington. He claimed that he had thought the equipment might be used for some illegal purpose, such as breaking up stolen property, but that he had not known that it was to be used to break into a bank. The defendant appealed unsuccessfully against his conviction for being an accomplice to the break-in. The Court of Appeal endorsed the trial judge's direction to the jury, to the effect that the prosecution was not required to prove that the defendant knew exactly what crime was going to be committed by the principal. As Lord Parker CJ stated:

> '... there must be not merely suspicion but knowledge that a crime of the type in question was intended, and that the equipment was bought with that in view.'

This approach can be summarised by stating that one who aids and abets must have contemplated the type of crime committed by the principal. If this is to be equated with a form of recklessness, it is clear from *Blakely, Sutton* v *DPP* [1991] Crim LR 763 that it is advertent (ie *Cunningham*) recklessness that has to be established, although it is perhaps best to avoid reference to recklessness altogether in this area: see *Chan Wing Siu* v *R* (below).

It is submitted that there is in fact a great deal of confusion and uncertainty as to the fault element that has to be proved in respect of accomplices. As regards one who counsels or procures the commission of an offence, the *Attorney-General's Reference (No 1 of 1975)* (above), appears to support a narrower approach, Lord Widgery commenting that to procure meant setting out to see that the desired consequence happens and taking the appropriate steps to produce that happening. His words are suggestive of more than mere contemplation of a consequence on the part of the procurer, perhaps requiring proof of something closer to intention, a view that receives support from the Divisional Court's ruling in *Blakely, Sutton* v *DPP* (above). In *Gillick* v *West Norfolk and Wisbech Area Health Authority* (above), a majority of their Lordships held, Lord Brandon dissenting, that a doctor, prescribing contraceptives to a girl under the age of 16, would not be guilty of aiding the commission of the offence of unlawful sexual intercourse, provided he was exercising his clinical judgment in good faith. There is, however, some difficulty with this conclusion because the doctor would know of all the facts constituting the offence, and the fact that he acts from the best of motives should have no bearing on his liability. Are the majority of their Lordships suggesting that it must be the doctor's *purpose* that unlawful sexual intercourse takes place before he can incur liability? See further the comment of Devlin J in *National Coal Board* v *Gamble* [1959] QB 11 at 23.

In relation to common or joint unlawful enterprises, particularly murder, the courts have adopted what might be described as a 'broad' approach to the mens rea of accomplices, in that evidence of foresight of consequences falling below that which would be required to support the conviction of a principal offender will suffice to convict the accomplice. The leading authority is the Privy Council's decision in *Chan Wing Siu* v *R* [1985] AC 168, wherein it was held that for an accomplice to be convicted of murder, it was sufficient for the prosecution to establish that he foresaw murder as a possible incident of the 'common design', ie he foresaw that the principal might kill with either the intention to kill or to commit grievous bodily harm. The decision produces what many might regard as a rather grotesque result, in that it appears to be easier for the prosecution to secure the conviction of a defendant as an accomplice to murder, than to secure the conviction of a principal offender. Certainly, it is submitted that 'foresight of a possibility' is a long way removed from 'foresight of death or grievous bodily harm as a virtual certainty' as suggested by the Lord Chief Justice in *R* v *Nedrick* [1986] 1 WLR 1025. Notwithstanding such reservations, the Privy Council's decision has subsequently been approved by the Court of Appeal in *R* v *Jubb and Rigby* [1984] Crim LR 616, *R* v *Ward* [1987] Crim LR 338, and in *R* v *Hyde* [1990] 3 WLR 1115, wherein the Lord Chief Justice attempted to summarise the law thus:

'There are, broadly speaking, two main types of joint enterprise cases where death results to the victim. The first is where the primary object of the participants is to do some kind of physical injury to the victim. The second is where the primary object is not to cause physical injury to any victim but, for example, to commit burglary. The victim is assaulted and killed as a possibly unwelcome incident of the burglary. The latter type of case may pose more complicated questions than the former, but the principle in each is the same. A must be proved to have intended to kill or to do serious bodily harm at the time he killed as was pointed out in *R* v *Slack* [1989] QB 775 at 781. B, to be guilty, must be proved to have lent himself to a criminal enterprise involving the infliction of serious harm or death, or to have had an express or tacit understanding with A that such harm or death should, if necessary, be inflicted.'

His Lordship then referred approvingly to the principles enunciated by Sir Robin Cooke in *Chan Wing-Sui* (at p175):

'The case must depend rather on the wider principle whereby a secondary party is criminally liable for acts by the primary offender of a type which the former foresees but does not necessarily intend. That there is such a principle is not in doubt. It turns on contemplation or, putting the same idea in other words, authorisation, which may be express but is more usually implied. It meets the case of a crime foreseen as a possible incident of the common unlawful enterprise. The criminal culpability lies in participating in the venture with that foresight.'

It is submitted that an accomplice to murder can, at least in cases of so-called joint enterprises, be convicted if it is proved, beyond all reasonable doubt, that he realised that the principal offender might kill or intentionally inflict serious injury, but nevertheless continued to participate in the venture: see also *Hui Chi-Ming* v *R* [1991] 3 WLR 495.

What of the accomplice who contemplates death or grievous bodily harm only to reject it as a possible outcome of the common design? Sir Robin Cooke observed (in *Chan Wing Sui* v *R)* that:

'What has to be brought home to the jury is that occasionally a risk may have occurred to an accused's mind, fleetingly or even causing him some deliberation, but may genuinely have been dismissed by him as altogether negligible. If they think there is a reasonable possibility that the case is in that class, taking the risk should not make that accused a party to such a crime of intention as murder or wounding with intent to cause grievous bodily harm.'

This prompted Lord Taylor CJ, in *R* v *Roberts* (1993) 96 Cr App R 291, to comment:

'... we are doubtful whether the defendant "B" who fleetingly thinks of the risk of "A" using violence with murderous intent in the course of a joint enterprise only to dismiss it from his mind and go on to lend himself to the venture, can truly be said, at the time when he so lends himself, to "foresee" or "realise" that "A" might commit murder. In such a case "B" can hardly have such foresight or realisation at the time he lends himself to the venture because he has banished the risk from his mind. The words "realise" and "realisation" ... aptly describe the test, because to realise something may happen is surely to contemplate it as a real not fanciful possibility. Accordingly, we are inclined to the view that seeking to distinguish between a fleeting but rejected consideration of a risk and a continuing realisation of a real risk will, in most cases, be unnecessary. It would also over-complicate directions to juries and possibly lead to confusion.'

Hopefully, the obiter statements of the Lord Chief Justice will not preclude a defendant from putting forward a genuine case that he stopped to think of whether or not there was a real risk that death or grievous bodily harm might result from the joint enterprise, and wrongly concluded that there was no such risk. There may yet still be scope for some debate as to whether there is any distinction to be drawn between Sir Robin Cooke's reference to the accomplice's contemplation of death or grievous bodily harm as consequences that are possible, and his references to the accomplice foreseeing these events as 'substantial' or 'real' risks. To the extent that they impose a more stringent test for liability, the latter expressions are preferable. Lloyd LJ in *R* v *Rook* [1993] 1 WLR 1005, appeared to endorse this view, and to further reject any contention that the mental element might vary according to the mode of participation:

'... it is not necessary for the prosecution to show that the secondary party intended the victim to be killed, or to suffer serious injury. It is enough that he should have foreseen the event, as a real or substantial risk ... We see no reason why the same reasoning should not apply in the case of a secondary party who lends assistance or encouragement before the commission of the crime ... It follows that it is no defence to a secondary party to say that he did not intend the victim to be killed, or suffer serious harm, if he contemplated or foresaw the event as a real or serious risk.'

There is at present a degree of confusion as to whether the Privy Council's approach to accessorial liability in *Chan Wing-Sui* v *R* can be followed in relation to offences other than murder. In *R* v *Smith* [1988] Crim LR 616, the Court of Appeal quashed the appellant's conviction as an accomplice to an offence contrary to s18 of the Offences Against the Person Act 1861, on the ground that the trial judge had erred in directing the jury to convict if they were sure that the appellant had foreseen a real risk that his co-accused might attack the victim viciously, intending to do him some grievous bodily harm. The Court of Appeal felt that *Chan Wing-Siu* v *R* could not apply where a crime of specific intent was involved, evidence that the appellant had had the necessary intent to do grievous bodily harm being required. It is submitted that the decision is curious in that the court appears to have approached the matter on the basis that an accomplice should be proved to have had the same mens rea as the principal offender, a doctrine difficult to equate with established authorities such as *R* v *Bainbridge* [1959] 3 WLR 356. Further, if the Privy Council's decision in *Chan Wing-Siu* is correctly decided, is there any good reason for its not applying to grievous bodily harm with intent as it does to murder?

What if the accomplice gives the principal a 'blank cheque'?

If, as stated above, the prosecution generally has to prove that the accomplice contemplated the type of crime the principal actually commits, can an accomplice escape liability by claiming that there were so many different crimes the principal might have committed, that he was unable to have any clear idea as to what his liability might have been? On the basis of *DPP for Northern Ireland* v *Maxwell* (1978) 68 Cr App R 128, it would appear that such an accomplice will be a party to all the offences committed by the principal provided they are amongst those contemplated by the him. As Lord Scarman stated:

'An accessory who leaves it to his principal to choose is liable, provided always the choice is made from the range of offences from which the accessory contemplates the choice will be made.'

9.4 Where the principal exceeds the common design

The general rule is that an accomplice will be liable for all the accidental, or unforeseen consequences that flow from the common design being carried out. For example, suppose D1 and D2 agree to rob X, the plan being that D1 will point an imitation gun at X whilst demanding his money, and that D2 will maintain a look-out. D1 points the imitation gun at X, who thinks it is real and dies of a heart attack. D1, as principal, will be charged with unlawful act, or constructive manslaughter. D2 cannot claim that he is not an accomplice to the killing because it was not the type of crime that he contemplated. The plan was to rob X using the imitation gun, which is precisely what D1 did. There were no actions by D1 which involved a deliberate departure from the common design on his part.

Two authorities support this principle. In *R* v *Baldessare* (1930) 22 Cr App R 70, the two defendants took a car to go 'joyriding'. The driver killed another road user and was convicted of manslaughter. Baldessare was convicted as an accomplice to the manslaughter, as it was an unforeseen consequence of the common design (ie driving the car in a reckless manner without headlights), being carried out. In the second case, *R* v *Betts and Ridley* (1930) 22 Cr App R 148, Betts and Ridley agreed that Betts would rob a victim by hitting him to the ground and snatching the bag of money he was carrying, and that Ridley would wait at the wheel of the 'getaway' car. The plan was carried out, but Betts struck the victim with such force that he died from the blow. They were both convicted of murder (under the doctrine of constructive malice, since abolished by the Homicide Act 1957, see Chapter 6), and their convictions were affirmed on appeal. As in the example cited above, Betts had simply carried out the common design as contemplated by Ridley, and Ridley was held responsible for the death resulting from those contemplated unlawful acts, even though the death had not been intended.

Deliberate departure from the common design

It follows from the above, that where the principal deliberately departs from the common design, an accomplice ceases to be a party to his actions. Thus in *Davies* v *DPP* [1954] AC 378, which concerned a gang fight that had taken place on Clapham Common, during which the principal offender had killed an opponent with a knife, the defendant was acquitted of being an accomplice to either murder or manslaughter because the use of a knife during the attack was beyond the scope of what had been contemplated by him. The decision on the part of the principal offender to take a knife involved a deliberate departure from the common design. Had the victim died from blows to the head from the principal's fist or boot, then Davies could have been guilty as an accomplice to manslaughter, because such a mode of attack was contemplated by him, and the death of the victim would have been an unforeseen consequence of its being carried out. Similarly, in *R* v *Anderson and Morris* [1966] 2 QB 110 where the defendants had agreed to 'rough up' a victim named Welch, Anderson, unknown to Morris, took a knife with him, which he used to deliberately stab Welch during the fight, causing his death. Anderson was convicted of murder, but Morris' conviction for manslaughter was quashed on the ground that the cause of the victim's death was an action by Anderson that involved a deliberate departure by him from the common design, ie the use of the knife. Again, if Welch had died from a punch thrown by Anderson, Morris would have been an accomplice to manslaughter.

Whilst it is clearly logical that in situations such as arose in *Davies*, and *Anderson and Morris*, the accomplice should not be guilty of murder, some would question why the accomplice cannot be guilty of manslaughter. The answer lies in the fact that in both cases the unlawful act that causes death, the use of the knife, is not one within the contemplation of the accomplice, unlike, for example, the blow upon the victim's head in *R v Betts and Ridley*. This approach has been reaffirmed by the Court of Appeal in *R v Dunbar* [1988] Crim LR 693. Dunbar was a prostitute who had had a lesbian relationship with the deceased, another prostitute called Christine Offord. They fell out with each other, and Dunbar had expressed a wish to two men, C and P, that Offord might be killed. C and P were in due course convicted of murdering Offord with an iron bar after visiting her in her flat. The iron bar had previously been in Dunbar's flat. Dunbar was charged with counselling the commission of the offence. Her evidence was that she thought the two men might visit Offord in her flat and damage or steal property from her. The trial judge directed the jury that if they were satisfied beyond all reasonable doubt that Dunbar had been a party to an agreement to attack Offord, but had only foreseen slight harm occurring to her, then she should be convicted as an accomplice to manslaughter not murder. The Court of Appeal, somewhat reluctantly, allowed her appeal against her resultant conviction for manslaughter. The court held that in the circumstances there were only two verdicts open to the jury in respect of Dunbar. Either she was an accomplice to murder within *Chan Wing-Siu v R*, or she was not guilty at all because the principals had exceeded the common design.

What constitutes a deliberate departure from the common design?

The evidential difficulties that can arise in attempting to determine whether the actions of the principal were a deliberate or accidental departure from the common design, were considered by the Court of Appeal in *R v Calhaem* (above). The defendant had hired a man named Zajac to carry out a killing, paying him £5,000 in advance. The killing was carried out, but at his trial for murder Zajac testified that after being paid the money by the defendant he had resolved not to carry out the killing, but instead to visit the victim's house, carrying an unloaded shotgun and a hammer, to act out a charade that would give the appearance that he had tried to kill her. He claimed that when he had stepped inside the front door of the victim's house, she had screamed, he had panicked, with the result that he hit her several times with the hammer. On the basis of this evidence, the defendant had contended that she could not be guilty of counselling the victim's murder as the killing had been a direct result of Zajac's panic, not her instructions, which he had in any event decided not to follow. In dismissing her appeal, the court held that liability as a counsellor could be established if it was shown that the offence committed by the principal had been within the scope of the instructions given by the counsellor. It was not necessary to show that the counselling was the substantial cause of the commission of the offence. As Parker LJ explained, if Zajac had been involved in a fight at a football match where he had fatally wounded someone whom it later transpired had been the very person Calhaem had counselled him to kill, he would have been acting outside the scope of his authority and there would have been no liability for counselling on the part of the defendant, even though Zajac would have achieved the result she desired. It is interesting to speculate on how the court would have resolved the matter if Zajac had run the victim over whilst driving up the street on which she lived on his way to murder her.

9.5 Transferred malice and accomplices

Under the doctrine of transferred malice, as will have been seen from chapter 2, a defendant can be held guilty of murdering X , even though when he fired his gun, he was aiming at, and intending to kill, Y: see *R* v *Pembliton*; *R* v *Latimer*, etc. Logically, therefore, one would expect that if D1 supplies D2 with a gun for the express purpose of killing Y, and D2 misses Y but kills X, D2 will be guilty of murder as principal, and D1 will be guilty of procuring murder, given that the principal has committed the type of crime contemplated by the accomplice. As the following authorities illustrate, however, the doctrine of transferred malice does not necessarily apply in full to accomplices.

One of the oldest authorities on this point is *R* v *Saunders and Archer* (1573) 2 Plowd 473. John Saunders wanted to kill his wife so that he could marry his mistress. Alexander Archer provided him with poison in the form of a roasted apple containing arsenic and roseacre. Saunders gave the apple to his wife, but she ate very little of it, handing it instead to their daughter Eleanor, who subsequently died. Saunders was found guilty of the murder of his daughter on the basis of transferred malice. Archer was held not to be a party to the murder because Saunders had wilfully exceeded the common design in allowing the child to eat the apple. In effect the court held that Saunders' inactivity in standing by and allowing the child to consume the poisoned apple amounted to a deliberate departure from the common design, which had been to kill his wife, but it is clear that the court refused to apply the doctrine of transferred malice to Archer.

One wonders what Archer's liability would have been had Saunders been absent from the room when the apple was given to the child. Was Archer not in any event guilty of aiding the attempted murder of Mrs Saunders?

Despite its antiquity, the decision in *R* v *Saunders and Archer* has received implicit support from *R* v *Leahy* [1985] Crim LR 99. In that case a person named Horsman had been in a fight with a man called Pearson and had received some injuries. Horsman told the defendant Leahy of this, and the defendant advised Horsman to 'glass him', meaning Pearson. Horsman then picked up a glass and pushed it into the neck of a man named Gallagher. Horsman was convicted of grievous bodily harm, contrary to s18 Offences Against the Person Act 1861, in respect of this attack, but Leahy, who had been charged with counselling it, succeeded on a submission of no case, the court accepting the argument that the actions of Horsman were a deliberate departure from the common design as contemplated by the defendant, ie an attack on Pearson.

It is submitted that the approach taken by the courts in the above two cases will only be appropriate where the common design is very narrow in its scope, ie the accomplice contemplates a specific named victim being attacked, or specific identified property being stolen or destroyed. Hence, where D1 supplies D2 with a gun and instructs him to prove his skill as an assassin by killing someone, the scope of the common design is very wide, and in theory D1 could be an accomplice to the killing of any victim chosen by D2. Even here, however, there is an argument that D1 might not be guilty if D2 chooses D1's only child as the victim. D1 would presumably contend that he had not contemplated D2 demonstrating his skills on a member of his own family.

10

Participation II

10.1 Withdrawal from the common design

10.2 Problems with liability

10.3 Reform

10.1 Withdrawal from the common design

If D1 supplies D2 with a gun with which he is to kill X on Christmas Day, and on Christmas Eve D1 tells D2 not to carry out the killing, but D2 still does so, can D1 be indicted as an accomplice to the murder of X? The question posed raises the problem of withdrawal from the common design by the accomplice. At what stage must withdrawal take place in order to be effective, and what actions are required on the part of the accomplice?

In *R v Becerra and Cooper* (1975) 62 Cr App R 212, the defendants agreed to burgle a house, and Becarra gave Cooper a knife to use in case there was any trouble. When they were disturbed by the householder, Becarra jumped out of a window and ran off, shouting 'Let's go'. Cooper remained behind and murdered the householder. Becerra was convicted as an accomplice to the murder despite his contention that he had withdrawn from the enterprise. In dismissing his appeal the Court of Appeal held that the withdrawal must effectively let the others know that they are now on their own. What is required will vary with the facts of each case. If the defendant had taken reasonable steps to prevent the commission of further offences by the principal that might have been enough for his actions to have constituted a withdrawal. As Roskill LJ stated:

'... there must be timely communication of the intention to abandon the common purpose from those who wish to dissociate themselves from the contemplated crime to those who desire to continue in it.'

or as Dunn LJ expressed the matter in *R v Whitefield* (1983) 79 Cr App Rep 36:

'If a person has counselled another to commit a crime, he may escape liability by withdrawal before the crime is committed, but it is not sufficient that he should merely repent or change his mind. If his participation is confined to advice or encouragement, he must at least communicate his change of mind to the other, and the communication must be such as will serve "unequivocal notice upon the other party to the common unlawful cause that if he proceeds upon it he does so without the aid and assistance of those who withdraw".'

The emphasis on communication of withdrawal to the other parties was re-affirmed by the Court of Appeal in *R* v *Rook* [1993] 1 WLR 1005, where, citing McDermott J in *Eldredge* v *United States* (1932) 62 F. 2d 449, 451, Lloyd LJ agreed with the view that 'A declared intent to withdraw from a conspiracy to dynamite a building is not enough, if the fuse has been set; D must step on the fuse', save only that his Lordship thought that it would be enough that the defendant should have done his best to step on the fuse.

Hence, in the above example of the murder planned for Christmas Day, it is submitted that, in order to have any hope of persuading the court that he had effectively withdrawn from the plan, D1 would have had to have expressly revoked the authority and support that he had previously given to the scheme: see further *R* v *Grundy* [1977] Crim LR 543 (pulling out two weeks before a burglary probably adequate for withdrawal).

10.2 Problems with liability

No actus reus committed by the principal

If the principal has not committed an actus reus, there will be no unlawful act for the accomplice to be a party to. In *Thornton* v *Mitchell* [1940] 1 All ER 339, the defendant, a bus conductor who had given inadequate hand signals to the driver of his bus (who had been attempting to reverse it), with the result that two pedestrians were hit and injured, one of them fatally, was acquitted of abetting the offence of careless driving. The driver had been acquitted of the offence on the basis that he had not been careless, thus an element of the actus reus in respect of the principal's liability had not been proved (the offence charged was one requiring only proof of an intention to drive). In short, there had been no *careless* driving to abet.

It should be borne in mind, however, that even though a principal offender might not successfully complete the commission of an offence, he may be guilty of an attempt, contrary to the Criminal Attempts Act 1981. Consequently, an accomplice may be charged with aiding and abetting the attempt: see *R* v *Dunnington* [1984] QB 472.

No mens rea on the part of the principal

In a situation where an accomplice causes or assists in the commission of an actus reus by a principal offender, but the principal acts innocently due to his not having mens rea, the accomplice can be charged as if he were the principal offender by virtue of the doctrine of innocent agency. For example, where D hands X a tablet containing a deadly poison, and tells X to place it in P's drink, telling X that it is a headache tablet, with the result that P is killed. Assuming that X has not been reckless (or possibly grossly negligent) in not realising that the tablet was poison, he will not incur any liability for P's death. X would be regarded as the innocent agent of D, and D would in fact be charged as the principal offender: see *R v Michael* (1840) 9 C & P 356.

Difficulties arise, however, where the actus reus of the relevant offence is one that cannot realistically be committed via an innocent agent, in the sense that it requires the personal intervention of the defendant, as is typically the case with offences requiring proof of sexual intercourse, or conduct such as driving.

In *R v Cogan and Leak* (1975) 61 Cr App R 217, Leak persuaded Cogan to have sexual intercourse with Mrs Leak, telling him that she liked being forced to have sex against her will, and that if she struggled it was merely evidence of her enjoyment. Cogan was convicted or raping Mrs Leak, but appealed successfully against his conviction, on the basis that he had honestly thought she was consenting to sexual intercourse. Leak appealed against his conviction for aiding and abetting the rape, on the basis that if the principal had been acquitted, there was no offence to which he could have been an accomplice. In dismissing his appeal, the Court of Appeal held that the actus reus of rape had been committed by Cogan in that Mrs Leak had been forced to submit to sexual intercourse without her consent. Leak had known that she was not consenting, and thus had possessed the necessary mens rea to be an accomplice. Alternatively, the court was willing to view Cogan as an innocent agent through whom Leak had committed the offence of rape (even though as the law then stood a husband could not be guilty of raping his wife), but this is an unsatisfactory analysis for reasons mentioned above.

The problems raised by *Cogan and Leak* stem largely from the fact that English criminal law follows the derivative approach to accessorial liability, in the sense that the accomplice's liability is seen as being dependant upon that of the principal. Looked at independently, Leak intended his wife to be raped and encouraged Cogan to perform the necessary acts. The fact that Cogan believed the victim to be consenting should have been irrelevant. Some indication that the courts are beginning to recognise the limitations created by the derivative approach are provided by decisions such as *R v Millward* [1994] Crim LR 527. The appellant instructed H, his employee, to tow a trailer by means of a tractor on a main road but, because of the defective condition of the hitch mechanism, the trailer became detached and collided with a car, killing a passenger. H was acquitted on a charge of causing death by reckless driving. The appellant contended that, without a conviction of the principal offender, he could not be convicted of procuring the offence, and further, given that the offence was one of recklessness, the acquittal of the principal offender implied that the actus reus had not been committed. The case may be significant in that the Court of Appeal, dismissing the appeal, held that a defendant could be convicted of procuring the actus reus of an offence, in this case taking the vehicle on the road in its defective condition, regardless of the fact that the principal offender had been acquitted due to lack of mens rea. In this respect the case arguably goes further than *Cogan and Leak* (above), although one might query whether Millward had sufficient mens rea to sustain a conviction. He clearly knew of the defective state of the trailer hitch, but did not intend the death of another, or (apparently) foresee such an eventuality. On the one hand it could be argued that, for liability as a procurer to be sustained, D should be shown to have intended to produce the offence by endeavour: see *Attorney-General's Reference (No 1 of 1975)* (above). On the other hand it could be argued that D is liable for all the unforeseen consequences of the common design: see *R v Betts and Ridley* (above). The difficulty with this latter argument, however, is that procuring does not require any evidence of an agreement between the parties involved, merely that the procuring caused the commission of the offence. See further *R v Taylor* [1986] Crim LR 680.

Principal has less mens rea than the accomplice

In the past, problems arose where the principal offender possessed some mens rea but less than the accomplice. In *R v Richards* [1974] 1 QB 776, the Court of Appeal held that unless an accomplice was at the scene of the crime, he (or she as it was in this case), could not be charged with a more serious offence than that brought against the principal offender. Hence in that case, the liability of the defendant, who had hired two men to beat up her husband, was limited to the liability of the principals who carried out the attack for her. The decision has been the subject of considerable academic criticism (see Smith and Hogan's *Criminal Law* (7th ed) p150). If taken to its logical conclusion the decision would produce some grotesque results. Suppose that D1 gives a box containing a time-bomb to D2, telling him that it contains smoke bombs, and asking him to place it in a crowded shop. The liability of D2, in the event of the bomb going off and causing death, would be limited to manslaughter, and as a result D1 could only be charged as an accomplice to the manslaughter. Fortunately the House of Lords' decision in *R v Howe* [1987] AC 417, effectively overrules *R v Richards*, thus opening up the possibility of an accomplice being charged with a more serious offence than the principal.

Principal has a defence not available to the accomplice

The respective liabilities of principals and accomplices may vary where the principal can avail himself of some defence not available to the accomplice. Hence a principal suffering from diminished responsibility may be convicted of manslaughter instead of murder, whilst the accomplice to the killing may still be convicted of murder, provided he is proved to have had the necessary mens rea. This holds true even where the principal succeeds with a defence which results in his being acquitted of all liability, such as mistake, or self-defence. As an example, consider *R v Bourne* (1952) 36 Cr App R 125, wherein the defendant was convicted of aiding and abetting the offence of buggery, having forced his wife to have connection with an alsatian dog. His liability remained unaffected despite the assumption by the court that she would have been acquitted on the grounds of coercion.

Victims as accomplices

On the basis of *R* v *Tyrell* [1894] 1 QB 710, an individual cannot incur liability as an accomplice if the offence in which he or she is alleged to have participated is one created for their protection. Hence, in the above case, the defendant, a girl below the age of 16, was acquitted of aiding and abetting a man to have unlawful sexual intercourse with her. This proposition has been reaffirmed more recently by the Court of Appeal in *R* v *Whitehouse* [1977] QB 868. The defendant had pleaded guilty to the offence of inciting his 15-year-old daughter to commit an act of incest with him. The court took the view that the defendant had in fact pleaded guilty to an offence unknown to law, since although s11 of the Sexual Offences Act 1956 made it an offence for a girl above the age of 16 to commit an act of incest (given that she would be old enough to consent to intercourse), it was not an offence for a girl below that age to permit an act of incest to take place. He could not be guilty of inciting her to aid and abet an act of incest by him upon her since, on the basis of *R* v *Tyrell*, she could not be guilty as an accomplice to an offence created for her protection.

Liability following the commission of an offence

The four modes of participation considered in this and the previous chapter all concern an accomplice's liability before or at the time of the commission of an offence. It should be noted that a defendant can become criminally liable for assisting an offender after the commission of an offence. The relevant statutory provision is s4(1) of the Criminal Law Act 1967 which provides:

> 'Where a person has committed an arrestable offence, any other person who, knowing or believing him to be guilty of the offence or of some other arrestable offence, does without lawful authority or reasonable excuse any act with intent to impede his apprehension or prosecution shall be guilty of an offence.'

Note that on the basis of *R* v *Donald* (1986) The Times 25 February, a defendant can be convicted of this offence before the principal has been convicted of the main offence.

10.3 Reform

Reform of the law relating to accessorial liability has been considered by the Law Commission in Working Papers (Nos 43 and 50), and in the proposed codification of the common law in the DCCB in 1989. Its most recent review of this area of criminal liability is to be found in its consultation paper (No 131) 'Assisting and Encouraging Crime - A Consultation Paper'.

The thrust of the provisional proposals contained in the Commission's paper is that English criminal law should move away from the essentially derivative approach to accessorial lability, whereby the liability of the accomplice is contingent upon that of the principal offender. The paper endorses the view of Professor Sandford Kadish to the effect that any move towards reform had to be based on a recognition that complicity has two basic natures:

'... intentionally influencing the decision of the primary party to commit a crime, and intentionally helping the principal actor commit the crime, where the helping actions themselves constitute no part of the actions prohibited by the definition of the crime'.

The Commission invites comment on two new distinct offences of 'assisting' and 'encouraging' crime. Both offences would be 'inchoate' in the sense that liability would arise as soon as the acts of assistance or encouragement were committed, regardless of whether or not the principal committed the relevant completed crime. The proposed offence of encouragement would encompass activity currently falling within the crime of incitement. Justifying the inchoate nature of the proposed offences the paper notes:

'... under the present law ... the requirement that the principal crime should actually be committed adds nothing to the analysis of accessory liability and does not serve as any sort of principled limitation on that liability. Rather, it serves as an additional condition for liability, that may, however, enable some "assisters" to escape conviction, possibly in a quite erratic and unmeritorious fashion.' [para 4.25]

The provisional definition of the offence of assisting crime provided at para 4.99 provides:

'(1) A person commits the offence of assisting crime if he
(a) knows or believes that another ("the principal") is doing or causing to be done, or will do or cause to be done, acts that do or will involve the commission of an offence by the principal; and
(b) knows or believes that the principal, in so acting, does or will do so with the fault required for the offence in question; and
(c) does any act that he knows or believes assists or will assist the principal in committing that offence.
(2) Assistance includes giving the principal advice as to [how to] commit the offence, or as to how to avoid detection or apprehension before or during the commission of the offence.
(3) A person does not assist the commission of an offence for the purposes of this section if all that he does is to fail to prevent or impede the commission of that offence.
(4) "Offence" in sub-paragraphs (a)–(c) of subsection (1) above means the breach of a specified prohibition laid down by statute or the common law; but, provided the defendant knows or believes sufficient facts to show that such a breach is taking place or will take place, he need not know the time, place or other details of the offence.
(5) A person also commits an offence under this section if he knows or believes that the principal intends to commit one of a number of offences and does any act that he knows or believes will assist the principal in committing whichever of those offences the principal in fact intends.'

The proposed formulation of assisting in crime would go some way towards resolving the problems posed by decisions such as *Bainbridge*, in the sense that the accomplice could only incur liability for assisting crimes committed by the principal if, at the time he gave his assistance, the offence committed by the principal was sufficiently identified by the accomplice as the object of that assistance.

Regarding liability for failing to prevent crime, the paper rejects the approach of the DCCB (ie that liability should arise where the accomplice had a right to prevent the crime, or was under a duty to do so) on the ground that it would extend the proposed offence of assisting too far: see para 4.73.

The paper recognises that some provision would still have to be made for the accomplice who claims to have withdrawn from a common design, but proposes that: '... a defence should only be available if the assister takes all reasonable steps to prevent the commission of the crime towards which he has assisted' (para 4.135).

As indicated above, the proposed offence of encouraging crime is envisaged by the Commission as '... covering the ground that at the moment is addressed not only by the "counselling" element in aiding and abetting but also by the present law of incitement ...'. The rationale for the offence is stated as being that the law should extend to:

> '... all those who give encouragement and moral support to the commission of a crime, whether or not that encouragement has the effect of changing the principal's mind, or is intended to change the principal's mind, in the direction of the commission of that crime'. [para 4.148]

The proposed offence is stated in para 4.163 as follows:

> '1(1) A person commits the offence of encouraging crime if he
> (a) solicits, commands or encourages another ("the principal") to do or cause to be done an act or acts which, if done, will involve the commission of an offence by the principal; and
> (b) intends that that act or those acts should be done by the principal; and
> (c) knows or believes that the principal, in so acting, will do so with the fault required for the offence in question.
> (2) The solicitation, command or encouragement must be brought to the attention of the principal, but it is irrelevant to the person's guilt whether or not the principal reacts to or is influenced by the solicitation, command or encouragement.
> (3) The defendant need not know the identity of the principal, nor have any particular principal or group of principals in mind, provided that he intends his communication to be acted on by any person to whose attention it comes.
> (4) "Offence" in sub-paragraphs (a)-(c) of subsection (1) above means the breach of a specified prohibition laid down by statute or the common law; but for the purposes of this section the defendant may solicit, command or encourage the commission of such an offence without intending that it should be committed at a specific time or place.'

The paper sees no objection in principle to liability for encouraging crime being based on a failure to act, but doubts whether such cases are likely to arise in practice. As with the proposed offence of assisting, the paper envisages an accomplice escaping liability where he has withdrawn from the criminal enterprise if, having encouraged the commission of the crime, he either countermands the encouragement with a view to preventing the commission of the crime, or he takes reasonable steps to prevent its commission.

A number of general issues arising from these proposals were also considered in the paper, and comments invited on the following suggestions:

1. given the inchoate nature of the proposed forms of complicity, impossibility, in the sense that the principal cannot commit the offence encouraged or assisted (or, indeed, unknown to the accomplice, does not have the mens rea for the offence), should be no bar to the accomplice's liability;
2. there should not be liability for assisting or encouraging an inchoate offence;
3. there should not be liability for assisting another to assist or encourage the commission of crime;
4. there should be provision for liability for attempting to assist or encourage crime;
5. there may be a residual role for an offence of procuring where there is no communication between accomplice and principal, and the principal commits the offence without fault. As the paper states:

    '... [such cases] can be met by a provision to the effect that where an offence can be committed without fault on the part of the principal, a person commits the offence of procurement if he does any act with the intent that it should bring about, or being reckless whether that act will bring about, the commission of that offence by another'. [para 4.196];

6: the problems arising in cases such as *Cogan and Leak* (principal acquitted due to lack of mens rea) and *Bourne* (principal has a defence that would result in acquittal) could be addressed by a specific offence of encouragement:

    '... where D solicits etc, acts on P's part which if performed will only fail to involve the commission of an offence by P because either (i) P can adduce a defence of duress based on threats made to him by D; or P is acting under a mistake of fact and that mistake has been intentionally brought about by D'.

11

Inchoate Offences I

11.1 Introduction

Inchoate liability can be imposed upon a defendant who progresses some way towards committing a criminal offence, but does not necessarily succeed in completing the commission of the offence. The earliest stage at which liability can arise is where the defendant commits incitement by suggesting the commission of an offence to another person. This might be followed by conspiracy, where two or more parties agree on a course of conduct which will result in the commission of an offence, and finally a defendant who actually progresses beyond merely preparing to commit an offence may be guilty of attempt. It should be borne in mind that the prosecution is at liberty to charge a defendant with an inchoate form of an offence, even though he appears to have actually committed the completed crime. Frequently this occurs where there is some evidential difficulty with pursuing a prosecution for the full offence. Equally, a defendant cannot be charged with both inchoate and complete offences in respect of the same criminal act, as to do so would amount to 'overloading' the indictment.

11.2 Incitement

Incitement occurs where a defendant suggests the commission of a criminal offence to another person. What follows is an account of incitement at common law, but it should be noted that there are many statutory forms of the offence, such as incitement to racial hatred, or incitement to murder.

Actus reus

The actus reus of incitement is committed where a defendant suggests the commission of an offence to another person. It has to be shown that the suggestion from the incitor has reached the mind of the incitee, but there is no need to provide evidence that the incitee acted on the suggestion. The nature of the actus reus was considered by Lord Denning MR in *Race Relations Board* v *Applin* [1973] QB 815. The defendant had conducted a campaign against a white family's fostering of black children, and he had been charged with inciting the commission of an offence under the Race Relations Act 1968. In concluding that the defendant was guilty of incitement, Lord Denning MR observed:

> '[It was suggested before us] that to "incite" means to urge or spur on by advice, encouragement or persuasion, and not otherwise. I do not think the word is so limited, at any rate in the present context. A person may "incite" another to do an act by threatening or by pressure, as well as by persuasion.'

In theory, therefore, it is possible for a defendant to incite millions of others to commit offences, for example via a television broadcast. In *R* v *Most* (1881) 7 QBD 244 the defendant was convicted of incitement to murder after publishing a newspaper article inciting certain readers to rise up in revolutionary ferment and kill their respective heads of state.

Where the incitement does not actually reach the mind of the incitee, perhaps because he is deaf, out of earshot, or because a letter containing the incitement is never delivered, the incitor can still, in theory be charged with attempted incitement: see *R* v *Ransford* (1874) 13 Cox CC 9, and *R* v *Rowley* (1992) 94 Cr App R 95.

Generally, the incitee must know of the facts that make the conduct incited criminal. Hence a defendant can only be guilty of incitement to handle stolen goods if the incitee knew or believed the goods in question to be stolen. (Again the incitor might still be guilty of attempted incitement here.) In *R* v *Curr* [1968] 2 QB 944, the defendant ran a loan business whereby he would lend money to women with children in return for their handing over their signed family allowance books. He would then use other women to cash the family allowance vouchers. He was convicted of inciting the commission of offences under s9(b) of the Family Allowance Act 1945, which made it an offence for any person to receive any sum by way of family allowance knowing it was not properly payable, but appealed successfully to the Court of Appeal, where it was held that the trial judge had erred in not directing the jury to consider whether those women, who were being incited to use the signed allowance books to collect money on behalf of the defendant, had actually known that what they were being asked to do was unlawful. It would have been more appropriate to have charged the defendant as the principal offender, relying on the doctrine of innocent agency: see Chapter 10.

Inciting incitement

Although such cases will necessarily be rare, an indictment can lie at common law for the doubly inchoate offence of inciting incitement. In *R* v *Sirat* [1986] Crim LR

245, where it was alleged, inter alia, that the appellant had incited a middle man to procure someone who would carry out an attack on the appellant's wife, the Court of Appeal confirmed that liability for inciting incitement could arise, but in so doing recognised the difficulty created by the abolition of liability for inciting conspiracy brought about by s5(7) of the Criminal Law Act 1977. Arguably what the defendant was alleged to have done was to incite the middle man to enter into an agreement which would result in an attack being carried out on the appellant's wife, ie an incitement to conspire. He may thus have been convicted of an offence no longer known to law. This was one of several reasons why the appellant's conviction was quashed by the court. It is submitted that a distinction has to be drawn between the situation where D suggests to X that he arranges with Y for Y to attack P; and the situation where D suggests to X that X pressurises Y into carrying out an attack on P. In the former case there will clearly have to be some agreement between X and Y, and thus D cannot be charged with inciting their conspiracy. In the latter case, however, there need be no agreement as such between X and Y, Y will simply be choosing to respond to what X has said. Here D can be charged with inciting X to incite Y to attack P. Support for this proposition is to be found in the Court of Appeal's decision in *R v Evans* [1986] Crim LR 470.

Mens rea

The mens rea of incitement was considered by the Divisional Court in *Invicta Plastics Ltd v Clare* [1976] RTR 251. The defendants manufactured and advertised for sale a device which would notify drivers that they were entering police speed radar traps. It was not an offence to own one of these devices, but it was an offence to operate one without a licence. In confirming the company's conviction for inciting readers of the advertisements to commit breaches of the Wireless Telegraphy Act 1949, the court held that the mens rea involved not only an intention to incite, but also an intention that the incitee should act upon the incitement. It is submitted further that on the basis of *R v Curr* (above), the defendant should also be proved to have knowledge that the incitee knows that what is being incited is unlawful.

Impossibility

Whilst the law relating to impossibility and statutory conspiracy and attempt is now a matter governed by statute (see below and Chapter 12), impossibility in relation to incitement is still governed by the common law.

In *R v McDonough* (1962) 47 Cr App R 37, the defendant was convicted of inciting a number of butchers to receive stolen meat carcasses. On appeal he had contended that at the time of the incitement the meat carcasses had not been stolen, or possibly had not existed at all, and thus he should have been acquitted. The Court of Appeal held, however, that his conviction should stand, as the essence of the offence lay in the making of the suggestion accompanied by mens rea. Both of these matters could be established quite independently of whether there were actually any stolen meat carcasses in existence.

This decision represented a very straightforward approach to the problem of impossibility, and was to be contrasted with the complexities that were to bedevil impossibility in relation to the other inchoate offences in subsequent years. Indeed when the Law Commission published its report (No 102) on inchoate offences, it recommended changes in the law relating to impossibility as regards conspiracy and attempt, designed to bring those offences into line with the law as expressed in *R* v *McDonough*.

The matter must now be considered, however, in the light of the Court of Appeal's decision in *R* v *Fitzmaurice* [1983] 2 WLR 227. The defendant had been convicted of inciting the commission of a robbery, but appealed against conviction on the ground that what he had incited had in fact been impossible to carry out. The court, in dismissing the appeal, held that in determining the availability of a defence based on impossibility in relation to incitement, a distinction had to be drawn between 'specific' incitements and 'general' incitements. A specific incitement might, for example, involve a suggestion by D to X that X should murder Y. A problem of impossibility would arise if, unknown to D at the time of the incitement, Y had died two days previously. The court suggested that in such cases, following Lord Scarman's speech in *DPP* v *Nock* [1978] AC 979, a defendant should be permitted to rely on the defence of impossibility, since the conduct incited could not be carried out by anyone.

By contrast, where the incitement was general in nature, for example, a suggestion as in *R* v *Fitzmaurice* itself that the incitees should 'rob a woman carrying wages outside a bank in Bow, East London', impossibility would not avail the incitor as a defence. The fact that such a robbery might not have been possible in the situation presently before the court, did not preclude the commission of such an offence at some later stage.

It is submitted that the decision by the Court of Appeal to adhere to the common law doctrine in relation to impossibility, as stated by Lord Scarman in *DPP* v *Nock*, is unhelpful, and arguably perverse. It is unhelpful in that the decision offers little clear guidance as to how one is to distinguish between so-called general and specific incitements. It is arguably perverse in that by the time the case reached the court, the Criminal Attempts Act 1981 had come into force, from which it could clearly be seen that it had been the intention of Parliament to eradicate such arcane distinctions from the inchoate offences of attempt and conspiracy. Further, it ignores the views expressed by the Law Commission in its Report considered above.

Despite these criticisms the decision in *R* v *Fitzmaurice* has subsequently received implicit approval from a differently constituted Court of Appeal in *R* v *Sirat* (above).

Reform

Unlike conspiracy (*Conspiracy and Criminal Law Reform* (1976), Law Com No 76), and attempt (*Attempt, and Impossibility in Relation to Attempt, Conspiracy and*

Incitement (1980), Law Com No 102), the substantive offence of incitement has not been the subject of a Law Commission report in its own right. The major problem with the existing state of the law relating to inchoate offences, or 'preliminary offences' as the draft code terms them, is the inconsistency that exists between them. The aim of the draft code, is stated in the commentary thereon:

'We believe that as far as possible there should be consistency between these offences. They share a common rationale concerned with the prevention of substantive offences and they frequently overlap. When two or more persons engage in conduct preliminary to a substantive offence more than one of these offences may well be involved. It would be illogical and confusing to a court or jury if similar problems were provided with significantly different solutions. Therefore we have regarded the policy concerning those issues in the offence of incitement which arise also in conspiracy and attempt as generally having been settled in the way recently provided by Parliament for conspiracy and attempt. On issues peculiar to incitement we have followed the general principle of restatement of the existing law, having regard also to the comments made to us on consultation on the Code team's draft Bill.' [Vol II para 13.3]

In attempting to codify and rationalise the law relating to incitement, as with other inchoate offences, a number of issues arise. How should the elements of the offence be defined? What should be the relationship between the inchoate offence, other inchoate offences, and participation? How should the issue of impossibility be dealt with? Each of these issues is considered in turn below.

Clause 47(1) of the draft code states:

'A person is guilty of incitement to commit an offence or offences if –
(a) he incites another to do or cause to be done an act or acts which, if done, will involve the commission of the offence or offences by the other; and
(b) he intends or believes that the other, if he acts as incited, shall or will do so with the fault required for the offence or offences.'

'Offence' for the purposes of this provision means any offence triable in England and Wales, ie including incitement to commit summary offences. The retention of such a wide-ranging offence is justified for the following reasons:

'At common law incitement to commit an indictable or a summary offence is itself an offence. [The draft Code] restates the general principle. However, it should be noted that in this respect the draft Bill departs from the principle of consistency among the preliminary offences. There is no liability for attempting to commit a summary offence (Criminal Attempts Act 1981, s1(4)) but there is liability for conspiracy to commit a summary offence (Criminal Law Act 1977, s1). Parliament, in enacting the rule for attempt, rejected our recommendation that an attempt to commit a summary offence should itself be an offence. [Law Com No 102 para 2.105]. The view was taken that there was no need to extend the ambit of attempt to summary offences. Any such extension might, it was felt, result in more time being taken up in magistrates' courts with complicated questions of attempts to commit minor offences than would be justified by any advantage of the extra reach of the law. In the absence of evidence of any need to extend the criminal law on this point we accept the decision. We maintain, nevertheless, that a different rule can be justified for conspiracy and incitement. These offences, which *ex hypothesi* concern more than one person, enable the promoters and organisers of large-scale minor offences to be brought within the reach of the law. Admittedly prosecutions may be appropriate in practice only on rare occasions. It was for this reason that we recommended in our Report on conspiracy that prosecutions for conspiracy to commit summary offences should only be brought with the consent of the Director of Public Prosecutions. We now make a similar recommendation in respect of incitement to commit a summary offence. The requirement of the Director's consent will ensure that the offence is not misused while keeping open the possibility of using such a charge to deal with cases where an element of social danger is involved in the deliberate promotion of offences on a widespread scale.' [Vol II para 13.12]

The elements of the proposed offence

In considering the terminology of the offence of incitement, the Law Commission preferred to retain the term 'incite' to describe the actus reus of the offence, in favour of terms such as 'encourage'. It was persuaded by arguments that the latter word might mislead juries into thinking that there was a need for proof of actual encouragement, and thus missing the point that the incitor may be liable for incitement even though the incitee is not in fact encouraged, indeed may have been quite indifferent to the incitement. As the commentary concludes, the word 'incite':

'... sufficiently conveys, without the need for an explanatory provision, that the person incited need not be influenced by whatever it is that constitutes the incitement.' [Vol II para 13.6]

Note that under subsection (4) of the proposed clause a person may be convicted of incitement to commit an offence although the identity of the person incited is unknown, thus preserving the effect of decisions such as *R* v *Most* (above).

In relation to the mental element, the Code proposes that intention or belief on the part of the defendant that the incitee will commit the offence if he acts as incited, should be sufficient. Whilst it is no surprise to see intention specified as the fault element, the Law Commission felt that some explanation of the inclusion of belief was required:

'It should ... be sufficient if the incitor believes that the person incited, if he acts at all, will do so with the fault required. For example, if D seeks to persuade E to have sexual intercourse with Mrs D, D believing that E knows that Mrs D does not consent to it, there seems to be a clear case of incitement to rape. It should not be necessary to prove that it was D's intention that E should have such knowledge. Whenever the fault required for a substantive offence includes knowledge of or recklessness as to circumstances (such as the absence of consent), it is likely to be more appropriate for the purposes of incitement to refer to the incitor's belief that such knowledge or recklessness exists rather than to his intention that it should.' [Vol II para 13.9]

Note that clause 47 does not restate the common law requirement established in the much criticised case of *R* v *Curr* (above) that the incitee must have known that what was incited was unlawful. The commentary cites with approval the views of the Code Team on this issue:

'... it is not necessary that any offence should be committed or even intended by the person incited, therefore it is irrelevant and confusing to ask whether that person had the mental element for the offence.' [Vol II para 13.11]

Where the incitee is a child, or other 'innocent' person, and he is aware of the incitee's innocence, the incitor may be charged with attempting to commit the relevant offence through an innocent agent. An example is provided in Appendix B to Volume I:

'D tells E, aged nine, to put a certain powder in P's drink "to make him feel ill". D is not guilty of inciting E to administer a substance without consent (cl 73); even if E does this act with the fault required (knowledge that the substance is capable of interfering substantially with the other's bodily functions) he will not commit the offence because he is under ten (cl 32(1)). D may be guilty of attempting to commit the offence by an innocent agent.' [example 47(i)]

Incitement by victims

Subsection (3) incorporates the rule in *R* v *Tyrell* [1894] 1 QB 710, to the effect that a member of a class of persons whom it is the purpose of the enactment creating the offence to protect is exempt from liability for incitement to commit such an offence. For the rationale behind this exemption see the similar limitation on accessorial liability contained in clause 27(7), and the commentary thereon. (Considered elsewhere in Chapter 10).

Incitement and other inchoate offences

Subsection (5)(b) proposes the retention of liability for inciting incitement, and inciting attempt, but interestingly proposes the reintroduction of liability for incitement to conspire. As the commentary explains:

'A number of problems arise concerning the use of preliminary offences in combination. In relation to incitement the present law has reached the point of absurdity. Incitement to conspire was abolished as an offence known to the law by s5(7) of the Criminal Law Act 1977. Recently the Court of Appeal has twice held that incitement to incite is an offence known to the law. It seems, however, that this is so only when the first person incited is to incite, but not to agree with, a second person to commit an offence. If the evidence shows that D incited E to agree with F to wound G, s5(7) of the Criminal Law Act 1977 apparently prevents a charge against D of incitement to conspire or of incitement to incite. But if D incites E to incite F (perhaps by a command, or a letter not requiring an answer) to wound G, D can be charged with incitement to incite. Such an absurd distinction cannot be restated in the Code ... Unlike other provisions of Part I of the Criminal Law Act 1977, s5(7) was not based on a recommendation in our Report, which did not deal with the point. Abolition of incitement to conspire had, however, been recommended by the Working Party. They had argued that to allow an offence of incitement to conspire would be to take the law "further back in the course of conduct to be penalised than is necessary or justifiable". [Working Paper No 50 paras 44,45] The Working Party did not make any express reference to possible charges of incitement to incite, although it may be presumed that logically they would have wished to exclude this possibility also. The Code team's draft Bill followed the Criminal Law Act 1977 in excluding conspiracy from the scope of incitement, but did not exclude incitement itself thereby allowing for the possibility of charges of incitement to incite. The Scrutiny Group on preliminary offences invited us to look again at this problem, indicating that in their view it should be possible to indict for inciting to conspire ... recent Court of Appeal decisions that incitement to incite is an offence known to the law have produced a clear anomaly. It would be illogical, and would bring the law into disrepute, to restate both the effect of these cases and s5(7) of the Criminal Law Act 1977. It would not be right, within the scope of this project, to attempt to overturn the recent decisions. Such a course would require much fuller discussion and consultation. We therefore recommend that neither incitement nor conspiracy should be excluded from the scope of incitement. In this way the anomaly will be eliminated without, we believe, a significant increase in the scope of criminal liability ... [It] is unclear whether an offence of incitement to attempt is known to the law. Virtually all possible instances of incitement are incitements to commit substantive offences, and it is difficult to conceive of a case where a charge of incitement to attempt (to commit an indictable offence) would not be inept. Smith and Hogan, however, suggest one possibility, namely where in the circumstances known to the incitor, but not to the person incited, the completed act will amount only to an attempt. The existence of this, admittedly, rare case, together with the general principle we referred to above of consistency of approach to the preliminary offences, persuade us that it would be preferable not to exclude attempt from the scope of incitement. Accordingly, our draft Bill makes no special provision with regard to incitement to attempt.' [Vol II paras 13.13–13.16]

Incitement and accessorial liability

Subsection (5)(b) proposes that a defendant could be an accomplice to an offence of incitement, but could not incur liability for inciting another to participate in the commission of an offence, as participation per se is not a crime. Consider further the reforms of accessorial liability outlined at 10.3.

Impossibility

As noted above impossibility is an issue that has continued to create confusion and controversy in the area of incitement, and in clause 50, the draft code bill aims to introduce a measure of consistency amongst the inchoate offences. Although the offences of conspiracy and attempt are considered separately later in this chapter and the next, the draft code's proposals relating to impossibility and all three inchoate offences are considered here in the interests of clarity.

The law relating to impossibility and conspiracy, and impossibility and attempt was rationalised by the provisions of the Criminal Attempts Act 1981. In referring to the absence of any provision dealing with incitement and impossibility in the 1981 Act the commentary on clause 50 notes:

'In relation to incitement we had taken the view that legislation was unnecessary. It appeared that the common law, as stated in *McDonough* [above] and *DPP v Nock* [above] was already in accordance with the position recommended for conspiracy and attempt. Subsequently, however, the Court of Appeal held in *Fitzmaurice* [above] that the common law principles relating to impossibility, which it had been our concern to reverse as regards conspiracy and attempt, applied to the offence of incitement. The result, therefore, is that impossibility may in some cases be a defence to incitement but not to conspiracy or attempt ... [W]e agree with the Code team that it would be absurd to perpetuate this distinction. The same principle should apply to all the preliminary offences. This means that the position for incitement must be brought into line with that for conspiracy and attempt. We accept the Code team's view that it is unnecessary to make separate provision for each offence. Only one provision is needed to rule out impossibility as a defence to any of the preliminary offences.' [Vol II paras 13.50–51]

Clause 50, which seeks to achieve this unified approach to impossibility, provides:

'(1) A person may be guilty of incitement, conspiracy or attempt to commit an offence although the commission of the offence is impossible, if it would be possible in the circumstances which he believes or hopes exist or will exist at the relevant time.'

This provision would apply in addition to any other statutory offence of incitement, conspiracy, or attempt.

11.3 Conspiracy: statutory

Until 1977 conspiracy was a common law offence, defined in *R* v *Mulcahy* (1868) LR 3 HL 306 as an agreement between two or more people to do an unlawful act. The difficulty with this definition was that it left open the possibility of a defendant being charged with the criminal offence of conspiring to commit acts which were unlawful merely because they were tortious, eg trespass to land.

The primary purpose of the Criminal Law Act 1977 was to place the offence of conspiracy on a statutory footing, and to limit liability for conspiracy to those situations where there was an agreement to commit a criminal offence, and to this end s5(1) abolishes the common law offence of conspiracy. The Act does, however, expressly preserve two forms of common law conspiracy. Section 5(2) states that conspiracy to defraud is to be retained, and s5(3) states that conspiracy to corrupt public morals is to be preserved. The surviving forms of common law conspiracy are considered at 11.4.

The statutory offence of conspiracy is created by s1(1) of the Criminal Law Act 1977, as amended by s5 of the Criminal Attempts Act 1981, which provides:

'1(1)Subject to the following provision of this part of this Act if a person agrees with any other person or persons that a course of conduct shall be pursued which, if the agreement is carried out in accordance with their intentions, either:
(a) will necessarily amount to or involve the commission of any offence or offences by one or more of the parties to the agreement, or
(b) would do so but for the existence of facts which render the commission of the offence or any of the offences impossible,
he is guilty of conspiracy to commit the offence or offences in question.'

Actus reus

Agreement
The parties to a conspiracy must be proved to have agreed on a course of conduct. Only rarely will the prosecution have direct evidence of an agreement, perhaps in the form of letters or tapes of telephone conversations, most conspirators wishing to avoid any permanent record of their plans coming into existence. In the majority of conspiracy trials it appears that the existence of an agreement is a matter to be inferred

by the jury from the evidence of the parties' conduct. For example, if three men wearing stocking masks and carrying sawn-off shot-guns are arrested by the police whilst sitting in the back of a van parked by a bank, there is an almost irresistible inference that they must have agreed to rob the bank. It can hardly be coincidence that they are all there at the same time with similar clothes and equipment.

The jury should be warned against confusing the term 'agreement' with any notions of contract law. There is no need for the prosecution to prove anything equating to an 'intention to create (il)legal relations' on the part of the conspirators. On the other hand, as stated in a decision on the old common law offence, *R v O'Brien* [1974] 3 All ER 663, conspiracy is not committed simply by talking about the possibility of committing an offence. It seems from this case that the parties must reach a stage where they agree to carry out the commission of the offence so far as it lies within their power to do so. Once agreement is reached it must be communicated between parties to the conspiracy; it cannot be tacit agreement: see *R v Scott* (1979) 68 Cr App R 164.

Form of the conspiracy

In a typical conspiracy involving, say, four parties, it would be normal for them all to have met together and agreed on a plan. It should be noted, however, that it is not necessary for every party to a conspiracy to be aware of the existence of every other party. In 'chain' conspiracies, the sequence of agreements might look as follows:

A agrees with B who agrees with C who agrees with D who agrees with E and so on ...

In such a scheme A might be completely unaware of the involvement of C, D and E, yet they are all parties to the same conspiracy.

An alternative arrangement illustrating the same possibility arises with what are known as 'wheel' conspiracies. Here there may be numerous parties, but each agrees with one central figure, eg:

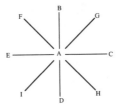

Again, B may be unaware of the existence of C, D, and E, etc, but they can all be charged as parties to the same conspiracy.

Parties

Section 2 of the 1977 Act does place certain restrictions upon those who can become parties to a conspiracy. Section 2(1) provides that a person cannot be charged with conspiracy if he is the intended victim of the crime, and s2(2) provides that a person cannot be charged with conspiracy if the only other party or parties to the conspiracy comprise of, that person's spouse, a person under the age of 10, the intended victim of the conspiracy.

The provision was considered by the Court of Appeal in *R* v *Chrastny* [1991] 1 WLR 1381 where the appellant had been convicted of conspiracy to supply a Class A drug, and sought to challenge her conviction on the ground that the trial judge had erred in law in directing the jury that, although the appellant had only agreed with her husband that the offence should be committed, s2(2)(a) of the Criminal Law Act 1977 provided no protection where she had nevertheless known of the existence of the other conspirators. In dismissing the appeal, Glidewell LJ pointed out that the provision does not enable a wife to escape liability simply by taking care only to agree with her spouse, even though she knows of the existence of other parties to the conspiracy. Only where she remained genuinely ignorant of other parties to such a conspiracy would s2(2)(a) protect her.

'... necessarily amount to ... the commission of any offence'

If these words, which appear in s1(1) of the 1977 Act, were construed strictly, as criminal statutes are supposed to be, it would be extremely difficult to secure any convictions for conspiracy. How is the prosecution to prove beyond all reasonable doubt that the defendants' plan, if carried out, would *necessarily* have resulted in the commission of a particular criminal offence? For example, suppose that D1 and D2 agree to dig a pit so that P will fall into it and be injured when he walks by. Prima facie this appears to be a conspiracy to cause at least actual bodily harm, but can it be shown that P would necessarily have taken the route in question, that he would have failed to notice the pit, or that he would necessarily have suffered actual bodily harm?

Donaldson LJ adverted to these difficulties in *R* v *Reed* [1982] Crim LR 819, where he suggested that a jury should be directed to consider the conspirators' 'plan', and to ask themselves whether an offence would necessarily be committed if the plan is carried out as the conspirators intend. Hence where D1 and D2 agree to rob a bank, provided there are no police officers in the area when they arrive, they should be convicted of conspiracy to rob because that is the offence that they would have committed had events gone as they had wished.

As suggested above, this has to be the sensible approach to the problem because, in a sense, all conspiracies are conditional in as much as the parties agree to commit an offence, provided they can get away with it. Common sense dictates that such conditionality cannot be allowed to defeat a charge of conspiracy.

Mens rea

Essentially, the mens rea of conspiracy requires proof that the defendant intended to agree on the commission of a particular offence, and proof of an intention that the offence should be committed. Even if the completed offence is one in respect of which a defendant can be convicted without knowledge of the facts constituting the offence, he will not be at risk of conspiring to commit such an offence unless he actually knows of the facts or circumstances necessary for its commission; see s1(2) of the 1977 Act. The point is illustrated by the Court of Appeal's decision in *R v Siracusa* (1989) 90 Cr App R 340. The appellants had been convicted of conspiring to import cannabis resin from Kashmir, and heroin from Thailand. In dismissing their appeals, the court held that the mens rea for conspiring to commit an offence was not necessarily to be equated with that required for the completed offence. In the case of murder, intention to kill or do grievous bodily harm was sufficient, whereas for conspiracy to murder an intention to kill had to be established. In the present case, whilst a defendant charged with the completed offence of being knowingly concerned in the prohibited importation of controlled drugs, did not have to be shown to have known what class of controlled drug he was dealing in, a defendant charged with conspiring to commit such an offence had to be shown to have known precisely the class of drugs involved. On the facts the court was satisfied that the judge had made this requirement abundantly clear in his summing up.

Does D have to intend to play an active part in the carrying out of the agreement?
If A agrees with B that B will steal C's car, are A and B guilty of conspiracy to steal? Prima facie the answer would appear to be affirmative, even though A does no more than agree that the crime should take place and desire that it should be committed by B. Such a simple solution has to be considered, however, in the light of the House of Lords' decision in *R v Anderson* [1986] AC 27. The defendant, who had been convicted of conspiring to effect the escape of a prisoner, appealed to the House of Lords contending that he had lacked the mens rea for conspiracy because, although he had received £2,000 as an advance payment for his part in planning the escape and he had admitted intending to acquire some diamond cutting wire that could be used to cut through prison bars, he had never intended the escape plan to be carried into effect and had not believed that it could actually succeed.

In dismissing his appeal the House of Lords held that it was sufficient, on a charge of statutory conspiracy, for the prosecution to establish, by way of mens rea, that the defendant had agreed on a course of conduct which he knew would involve the commission of an offence and, as Lord Bridge stated (at p39):

> '... beyond the mere fact of agreement, the necessary mens rea of the crime is, in my opinion, established if, and only if, it is shown that the accused, when he entered into the agreement, intended to play some part in the agreed course of conduct in furtherance of the criminal purpose which the agreed course of conduct was intended to achieve. Nothing less will suffice; nothing more is required.'

The decision confirms views expressed in earlier cases, such as *R v Allsop* (1976) 64 Cr App R 29, to the effect that a defendant can be convicted of conspiracy regardless of whether he desires the commission of the offence agreed upon. He may be quite indifferent as to whether the object of the conspiracy is achieved, yet it is sufficient that he knows that an offence will be committed if the agreement is carried out in accordance with the wishes of the other parties to the conspiracy. Hence if D1 and D2 agree to kill P, and D3 agrees to supply them with a gun that cannot be traced, with which they can shoot P, D3 can be charged with conspiracy to murder, even though he may be quite disinterested in whether P lives or dies. To paraphrase the words of Lord Bridge (above), D3 will have assented to a course of conduct which he must know will result in the death of P, and he intends to play some part in the furtherance of the criminal purpose which the agreed course of conduct was intended to achieve.

Lord Bridge's words would seem to suggest, however, that in the example of the theft of the car by B, cited above, A could not be guilty of conspiracy to steal because he does not intend to play some part in the commission of the offence. The passage cited has, perhaps not surprisingly, attracted some trenchant criticisms. For example, the authors of Smith and Hogan *Criminal Law* state (7th ed) p273:

> 'It was clear in that case that two or more of the alleged conspirators did intend to carry out the agreement, so [Anderson's] conviction could have been upheld on the ground that he aided and abetted that conspiracy ... [B]ut, if no intention need be proved on the part of one alleged principal offender in conspiracy, it need not be proved on the part of another. A conspiracy which no one intends to carry out is an absurdity, if not an impossibility.'

The Court of Appeal in *R v Siracusa* (above) attempted to clarify Lord Bridge's comments by stating that his speech had to be read as a whole. It was said that his Lordship had not meant that a defendant could only be guilty of conspiracy if it was shown that he intended to play some part in executing the agreement, simply that when the defendant agreed to the course of conduct he knew that it involved the commission of an offence. It would thus appear that a conspirator can now play his part simply by agreeing that others should carry out the commission of an offence. In fact the court goes as far as to state that 'intention to participate in the furtherance of the criminal purpose [can be] established by his failure to stop the unlawful activity'.

One particular problem thrown up by this approach to the mens rea of conspiracy is that of the police officer who is working under cover with a members of a criminal gang in order to collect evidence that can be used to ensure their eventual conviction. He or she will necessarily agree to the commission of various offences, despite having no desire that the agreement should succeed, and may even intend to take some steps short of committing the completed crime. Subject to the discretion to prosecute not being exercised, how can such a person escape liability for conspiracy?

The matter was adverted to by Lord Bridge in *R v Anderson* (above), where he stated that:

> 'The mens rea implicit in the offence of statutory conspiracy must clearly be such as to recognise the innocence of such a person, notwithstanding that he will, in literal terms, be obliged to agree that a course of conduct be pursued involving the commission of an offence.'

Short of recognising a public policy exemption for such a defendant, he or she would be caught by Lord Bridge's assertion, elsewhere in his speech, to the effect that a conspirator could be guilty of the offence even if he was indifferent as to whether the other conspirators actually carried out the agreement.

A more rational approach is demonstrated in the Privy Council's decision in *Yip Chiu-Cheung* v *R* [1994] 3 WLR 514, where the appellant had entered into an agreement with N, an undercover police officer, whereby N would fly from Australia to Hong Kong, collect a consignment of heroin from the appellant, and return with it to Australia. N kept the Australian and Hong Kong authorities fully informed of the agreement, and they undertook to allow him free passage from Hong Kong and into Australia. The purpose of N's mission was to identify not only the suppliers of the drug in Hong Kong, but also the dealers in Australia. N in fact missed his flight to Hong Kong and proceeded no further with the plan to meet the appellant. In due course, however, the appellant was charged with, and convicted of, conspiring to traffic in dangerous drugs. He appealed on the ground that there could be no conspiracy given that his co-conspirator, N, had been acting to promote law enforcement, and that N's purpose had been to expose drug trafficking. Dismissing the appeal, the Privy Council, held that even though N would have been acting courageously and from the best of motives, it had nevertheless been his intention, at the time the agreement was made, to take prohibited drugs from Hong Kong to Australia. If the agreement had been executed he would have committed a serious criminal offence. N, therefore, had possessed the necessary mens rea for the conspiracy, and the appellant's conviction could be sustained.

One assumes that the law enforcement authorities in Hong Kong and Australia had no intention of prosecuting N had he actually imported the heroin into Australia but, as Lord Griffiths indicated, that was not the relevant point in this appeal. The authorities would not have had the power to suspend the relevant laws relating to drug trafficking so as to de-criminalise the activities of N. Hence when N agreed to import the drugs he did have the mens rea for conspiracy. See chapter 26, section 26.6, for further details.

Impossibility

As far as the statutory offence of conspiracy is concerned, impossibility is no longer a bar to liability. The House of Lords' decision in *DPP* v *Nock* (see above), which governs the law in relation to the common law offence, has been overruled, as regards the statutory offence, by s5 of the Criminal Attempts Act 1981 which amends s1(1) of the 1977 Act (see above). Hence D1 and D2 can be indicted for conspiracy, even where the agreement is to assassinate Queen Victoria. The fact that she is already dead appears to be no bar to liability, provided the defendants honestly believe that she is still alive. The effect of the amendment is to judge the defendants on the facts as they honestly believe them to be.

11.4 Conspiracy: common law

As stated above, the 1977 Act did not entirely sweep away all forms of common law conspiracy. Conspiracy to defraud, and conspiracy to corrupt public morals, were preserved largely to act as residual offences, pending reforms of the laws relating to obscenity and fraud. It is tempting to ask, however, to what extent the continued existence of these offences is favoured by the prosecution simply because they can be used where apparent 'loopholes' in the law appear. Certainly, the Law Commission in its *Report on Conspiracy and Criminal Law Reform* (Law Com No 76) felt that the abolition of the common law offence might leave an unacceptable number of gaps in the law.

Conspiracy to defraud

An agreement to commit a substantive criminal offence would normally be charged as a statutory conspiracy contrary to the 1977 Act, a fact that calls into question the reason for the continued existence of this form of the common law offence. The answer, as suggested above, lies in its usefulness as a residual charge. It can be used against defendants who agree upon a course of conduct which, if carried out, might not result in a consequence actually prohibited by the criminal law, but would involve dishonesty adversely affecting the economic interests of another.

In *R v Scott* [1975] AC 819 (a case with facts remarkably similar to those in *R v Lloyd*, considered at 18.2), Viscount Dilhorne offered the following explanation of the offence (at p839):

> '... the words 'fraudulently' and 'defraud' must ordinarily have a very similar meaning. If ... 'fraudulently' means 'dishonestly', then 'to defraud' ordinarily means, in my opinion, to deprive a person dishonestly of something which is his or of something to which he is or would or might but for the perpetration of the fraud be entitled.'

The usefulness of conspiracy to defraud as a residual offence which can be charged in the event of a lacuna in the law is illustrated by *R v Hollinshead* [1985] AC 975. The defendants agreed to supply black boxes (devices which caused electricity meters to under-record the amount of electricity used by a consumer), to a middle man who would then sell them on to customers of various electricity boards. The defendants were charged on two counts: count one alleging a statutory conspiracy to aid, abet, counsel or procure an offence under s2(1)(b) of the Theft Act 1978, and count two which alleged a common law conspiracy to defraud. They were convicted on the second count, and appealed successfully to the Court of Appeal on the ground that there could be no conspiracy to defraud where the dishonest conduct contemplated was to be carried out by a third party (the user of the black box), as opposed to the conspirators. The Crown appealed to the House of Lords, which was asked to consider first, whether such activity could be the subject of a common law conspiracy charge, and secondly, if it could not, whether it could be charged as a statutory conspiracy to participate in the commission of an offence under the Theft Act 1978. It was held that the first question should be answered in the affirmative, because the sole purpose of the agreement was the causing of loss to the electricity boards (the black boxes have no other use). Having answered the first question in this way, their Lordships felt that it was not necessary for them to deal with the second question, but it is perhaps worth noting that the defendants would have to have been charged with conspiring to supply the black boxes to a person who would in turn supply them to the principal offender. It is submitted that it is most unlikely that such a charge could have been sustained.

Note that in this case it could be said that the defendants' 'purpose' had not been to defraud the electricity supplier, but to obtain money for the black boxes. They may have been quite indifferent as to whether the boxes were ever used or not. It would appear from the Court of Appeal's decision in *R* v *Allsop* (1976) 64 Cr App R 29, however, that liability for conspiracy to defraud can arise even though the defendant is not certain that his actions will have an adverse effect upon the victim's economic interests. As Shaw LJ stated (at p31):

> 'Generally the primary objective of fraudsmen is to advantage themselves. The detriment that results to their victims is secondary to that purpose, and incidental. It is "intended" only in the sense that it is a contemplated outcome of the fraud that is perpetrated. If the deceit which is employed imperils the economic interest of the person deceived, this is sufficient to constitute fraud even though in the event no actual loss is suffered and notwithstanding that the deceiver did not desire to bring about an actual loss.'

Despite academic criticism of this decision (see Smith and Hogan, *Criminal Law*, 7th ed, p288) on the ground that it confuses the issue of the mens rea required by possibly blurring the distinction between intention and recklessness, it has subsequently been approved of by the Privy Council in *Wai Yu-Tsang* v *R* [1991] 3 WLR 1006, a case in which the defendant was convicted of conspiring to defraud a bank, of which he was the chief accountant, of US$124 million. The allegation was that he had conspired with the managing director, the general manager and others to dishonestly conceal the dishonouring of certain cheques by not recording them in the bank's account. The defendant contended that he was not guilty as he had been acting on the instructions of the managing director, and had acted in good faith to prevent a run on the bank. The trial judge's direction to the jury, with which the Privy Council agreed, was to the effect that for conspiracy to defraud, no desire to cause loss on the part of the defendant need be shown, it being sufficient that he had imperilled the economic or proprietary interests of another party. As to the nature of the mental element to be established, Lord Goff commented:

> 'Their Lordships are ... reluctant to allow this part of the law to become enmeshed in a distinction, sometimes artificially drawn, between intention and recklessness. The question whether particular facts reveal a conspiracy to defraud depends upon what the conspirators have dishonestly agreed to do, and in particular whether they have agreed to practise a fraud on somebody ... it is enough ... that ... the conspirators have dishonestly agreed to bring about a state of affairs which they realise will or may deceive the victim into so acting, or failing to act, that he will suffer economic loss or his economic interests will be put at risk. It is however important ... to distinguish a conspirator's intention (or immediate purpose) dishonestly to bring about such a state of affairs from his motive (or underlying purpose). The latter may be benign to the extent that he does not wish the victim or potential victim to suffer harm; but the mere fact that it is benign will not of itself prevent the agreement from constituting a conspiracy to defraud.'

Where the intended victim of the conspiracy is a public servant, it is sufficient that the defendants intend to deceive him into contravening that duty. There is no need in such cases to show any 'purpose' of causing economic loss to another: see *R v Moses and Ansbro* [1991] Crim LR 617.

The remaining ingredient of the offence to be proved is that the defendant acted dishonestly. Despite views expressed by the court in *R v McIvor* [1982] 1 WLR 409, the approach to be taken is the same as that applicable to Theft Act offences, which involves adherence to the Court of Appeal's guidelines in *R v Ghosh* [1982] 1 QB 1053 (considered at 18.1).

Can the prosecution choose which form of conspiracy to charge? Prior to the enactment of s12 Criminal Justice Act 1987, prosecutors ran the risk of being wrong-footed if they charged a defendant with common law conspiracy to defraud on facts that revealed conspiracy to commit a substantive criminal offence. In *R v Ayers* [1984] AC 447, the House of Lords held that common law conspiracy to defraud should only be charged where the agreement was one which, if carried out, would not necessarily result in the commission of a substantive criminal offence by any of the conspirators. See also *R v Tonner* [1985] 1 All ER 807. Whilst the House of Lords' decision in *R v Cooke* [1986] AC 909 went some considerable way towards ameliorating the effects of *R v Ayers*, the matter is now governed by s12 of the 1987 Act which provides:

> '12(1) If:
> a) a person agrees with any other person or persons that a course of conduct shall be pursued; and
> b) that course of conduct will necessarily amount to or involve the commission of any offence or offences by one or more of the parties to the agreement if the agreement is carried out in accordance with their intentions,
> the fact that it will do so shall not preclude a charge of conspiracy to defraud being brought against any of them in respect of the agreement.'

The provision effectively reverses the decision in *R v Ayers* and creates a potentially wide overlap between the statutory and common law offences.

Conspiracy to corrupt public morals

A detailed consideration of this offence is outside the scope of this work, but see *Shaw v DPP* [1962] AC 220, and *Knuller v DPP* [1973] AC 435.

11.5 Reform

Clause 48 of the draft code restates the law relating to statutory conspiracy. As explained in the commentary upon the clause, it was not the intention of the Law Commission to tackle the problem of common law conspiracy in the course of preparing the code, as this is currently a matter under review. The Law Commission remains committed, however, to its view that all forms of common law liability should eventually be replaced with statutory provisions. The proposals concerning statutory conspiracy are necessarily complex. In the interests of clarity the external elements (actus reus) and fault elements (mens rea) need to be considered separately.

In relation to the external elements Clause 48 provides:

'(1) A person is guilty of conspiracy to commit an offence or offences if –
(a) he agrees with another or others that an act or acts shall be done which, if done, will involve the commission of the offence or offences by one or more of the parties to the agreement;'

Subsection (5) goes on to state that a conspiracy continues '... until the agreed act or acts is or are done, or until all or all save one of the parties to the agreement have abandoned the intention that such act or acts shall be done'. This reflects the position at common law as established in *DPP* v *Doot* [1973] AC 807. Other subsections, largely for the avoidance of doubt, provide that:

'... a person may become a party to a continuing conspiracy by joining the agreement constituting the offence ... [subsection (6)], and that a person may be convicted of conspiracy even though the other conspirators are unknown, have not been charged, have been acquitted, or cannot be convicted because of the availability of some defence [subsection (8)].'

It is significant that two exceptions to liability currently to be found in s2(2) of the Criminal Law Act 1977, ie that a person cannot be guilty of conspiracy if the only other party is his spouse, or a child under the age of ten, are not reproduced in the draft code. The commentary upon clause 48 explains the reasoning behind this proposed change:

'At common law the offence of conspiracy did not extend to agreements between spouses. The origins of this rule lay in the ancient notion of the unity of husband and wife. Because husband and wife were deemed to be one person they could not form the agreement which is the essence of the offence. It hardly needs to e said that in view of changed attitudes to marriage in modern society this "antique fiction" cannot sustain the rule. In our earlier Report on conspiracy [Law Com No 76 para 1.49], we recommended retention of the exemption for alternative reasons, principally the importance of maintaining the stability of marriage by non-interference with the confidential relationship of husband and wife. We are now persuaded, particularly having regard to subsequent developments in the law, that this argument is insufficient to sustain the rule. First, the exemption is an anomaly. Husbands and wives are capable in law of being accessories to each other's offences. Where, say, a wife agrees that her husband shall commit an offence, that agreement cannot ground liability for conspiracy by either party, but it will ground liability in the wife for aiding and abetting if the husband actually commits the offence. The distinction makes no sense. Secondly, as a result of section 80 of the Police and Criminal Evidence Act 1984, husbands and wives are now competent witnesses for the prosecution against each other in all cases and the privilege against disclosure of marital communications has been abolished. Thirdly the exemption was criticised on consultation. The Scrutiny Group on preliminary offences said that they saw no reasons of social policy for maintaining the rule relating to spouses. In the light of these considerations we recommend that the exemption for agreements with spouses should not be retained ... In our conspiracy Report we proposed that a person agreeing with a child under the age of criminal responsibility to commit an offence should not be liable for conspiracy [ibid paras 1.51 and 1.58]. This reflected the majority view on consultation on our Working Paper No 50 which had expressed the opinion that the law did permit a conviction for conspiracy in such a case. We are inclined to think now that the exemption is unjustified. The justification of conspiracy as a means of enabling early intervention to prevent crime applies as much to this case as to any other. We would now prefer to leave such cases to be dealt with according to general principles of conspiracy in the same way as cases of agreements with mentally disordered persons. That is, if the child understands the nature of the agreement and intends that the offence be committed, his own immunity from prosecution should not affect the liability for conspiracy of the person who is over the age of criminal responsibility. Accordingly, we recommend that the exemption for agreements with children should not be retained.' [Vol II paras 13.30–13.31]

In relation to the mental element in conspiracy, clause 48 provides;

'(1) A person is guilty of conspiracy to commit an offence or offences if –
(a) he agrees (etc, see above); and
(b) he and at least one other party to the agreement intend that the offence or offences shall be committed.
(2) For the purposes of subsection (1) an intention that an offence shall be committed is an intention with respect to all the elements of the offence (other than fault elements), except that recklessness with respect to a circumstance suffices where it suffices for the offence itself.'

In the view of the Law Commission (as expressed in Vol II para 13.22) the purpose of the existing law stating the mental element in statutory conspiracy (s1(1) of the Criminal Law Act 1977) had been to 'express a conception of conspiracy as involving agreement between two or more people both or all of whom intend that the offence shall be committed'. In drafting clause 48, the Commission considered the effect of the House of Lords' decision in *R* v *Anderson* [1986] AC 27, and noted that:

'... [the defendant] was treated by the House of Lords as a principal offender, not simply as an accessory to a conspiracy between the others involved. Their Lordships did not require by way of mens rea for any conspirator more than an intention to play some part in the agreed course of conduct. The implication of this is that there may be a conspiracy although no conspirator actually intends that the offence agreed upon shall be committed. This implication is, in our view, at odds with the plain meaning of the section [ie s1(1) of the 1977 Act]. We think, with respect, that the conviction in *Anderson* is better supported on the ground that the accused was an accessory to a conspiracy between others. He clearly assisted and encouraged the plan, knowing of the circumstances (that the plan was to effect an escape from prison) and of the conspirators' intention to commit that offence. A similar analysis can be applied to the hypothetical case put by Lord Bridge in *Anderson* [at p38]. The proprietor of a car hire firm who agrees to supply a car to a gang for a robbery is equally an accessory to the gang's conspiracy even though he may have no interest in whether the robbery is in fact committed ... A further point arises concerning a dictum in *Anderson* that each conspirator should intend to play some part in furtherance of the agreed course of conduct [at p39]. This contradicts the traditional view of conspiracy that it is necessary, and also sufficient, that each conspirator should intend that the agreed course of conduct be carried out whether by himself or other members of the conspiracy. If A and B agree that B shall murder C, A taking no part in the killing, the law has always taken the view that that is a conspiracy to murder. But, following this dictum, A would not be guilty of conspiracy and therefore B could not be guilty of conspiracy either since no other parties are involved. This seems to us to be contrary to public policy. Our clause does not therefore give effect to the dictum.' [Vol II paras 13.24–13.25]

Note that under subsection (2) recklessness will suffice as the fault element in conspiracy where the same is true of the completed offence. As the commentary illustrates:

'... if A and B agree to have sexual intercourse with C being aware that she may not consent they are guilty of conspiracy to rape. Because their awareness of the risk of her non-consent is sufficient fault in respect of that element of rape it is also sufficient for conspiracy to rape. The rule qualifies the general principle that intention is the characteristic fault requirement of the preliminary offences.' [Vol II para 13.26]

The subsections that follow include provisions broadly similar to those relating to incitement, ie the extension of conspiracy to summary offences (subsection(3)), and the exclusion from liability of those belonging to a class of persons intended to be protected by an enactment creating an offence (subsection (4)). Subsection (7) provides that a person cannot conspire to assist in the commission of an offence, see *R v Hollinshead* [1985] AC 975, but can assist in the commission of a conspiracy, see *R v Anderson* (above). As regards the relationship between conspiracy and the other forms of inchoate liability, subsection(7)(b) expressly preserves the possibility of a charge of conspiring to incite. The commentary explains the reasons for this:

'We commented in our conspiracy Report that conspiracy to incite was a potentially useful offence, [Law Com No 72 para 1.44] and a reminder of its existence was recently given by the Court of Appeal in *Hollinshead* [1985] AC 975 at 987. We do not find it necessary to make any express provision concerning charges of conspiracy to conspire and conspiracy to attempt. We cannot envisage any circumstances in which it would be necessary to bring such charges in preference to charges of conspiracy to commit a substantive offence.' [Vol II para 13.36]

In relation to the Code's proposals for conspiracy and impossibility, see 11.2 (above).

Note that the Code does not attempt to deal with the complex problem of conspiracy to defraud, as the commentary states:

'One important offence of dishonesty is missing from the [Code] ... Conspiracy to defraud, although recently given a maximum penalty by statute [ten years imprisonment, Criminal Justice Act 1987], remains in substance a common law offence. We cannot in the present project either propose its abolition without replacement, or replace it (whether by a new general offence of fraud, or by supplementation and amendment of existing offences, or by a combination of those methods), or attempt a statutory restatement of it. The last of these courses might be thought to be in keeping with the general aim of reducing existing law to consistent statutory form. But (even if it had merit) it would be premature in view of the consultation on conspiracy to defraud on which we have been currently engaged. In December 1987 we published a Working Paper on the subject in which we canvassed all of the above courses as options for consideration [Working Paper No 104, Conspiracy to Defraud (1987)].' [Vol II para 16.2]

12

Inchoate Offences II

12.1 The pre-1981 law

12.2 The Criminal Attempts Act 1981

12.3 Impossibility

12.4 Reform

12.1 The pre-1981 law

Until the enactment of the Criminal Attempts Act 1981, the crime of attempt was a creation of the common law. Despite the fact that the 1981 Act had the effect of abolishing entirely the common law offence of attempt, some knowledge of the pre-1981 law is necessary for a proper understanding of the new law.

Actus reus of common law attempt

One of the difficulties associated with the old law on criminal attempts was the question of how far a defendant would have to progress towards the commission of the completed crime for it to be said that he had committed the actus reus of attempt. A number of tests were propounded by the courts.

In *R* v *Eagleton* (1855) Dears CCR 515, the defendant was convicted of attempting to obtain money by false pretences on the basis that he had committed the 'last act' towards being paid the money. This test was applied more recently in *DPP* v *Stonehouse* [1978] AC 55, where the defendant had faked his suicide, and was subsequently charged with attempting to obtain money (benefits under insurance policies) by deception for another, his wife. The fact that the defendant's wife had taken no steps herself towards claiming the money under the policies was regarded as irrelevant to the question of the defendant's liability. The House of Lords was satisfied that he had committed the last act that lay within his power, towards the commission of the offence.

An alternative test, applied in a number of other authorities, was to ask whether or not the defendant had committed an act which was sufficiently proximate to the commission of the completed crime. On this basis a defendant would be acquitted where his actions were regarded as being no more than merely preparatory to the commission of an offence. Hence in *R* v *Robinson* [1915] 2 KB 342, the defendant, a jeweller who had tied himself up and hidden some of his stock in order to create the impression that he had been robbed, was acquitted of attempting to obtain monies under an insurance policy by false pretences, on the basis that as he had not even made a claim under the policy, he had not gone far enough towards the commission of the completed crime to be convicted of attempt. On the basis of *Comer* v *Bloomfield* (1970) 55 Cr App R 305, a defendant did not incur liability under the common law even where he faked the theft of his motor vehicle and wrote to his insurers to inquire as to whether a claim for theft would be covered by his policy, again the reasoning being that he had done nothing towards the commission of the completed offence that went beyond mere preparation. See further *R* v *Ilyas* (1983) 78 Cr App R 17.

Mens rea of common law attempt

At common law a defendant could only be convicted of attempt if he was shown to have an intent to commit the completed crime. Thus in *R* v *Whybrow* (1951) 35 Cr App R 141, the Court of Appeal held that it had been a misdirection for a trial judge to direct a jury, on a charge of attempted murder, that they should convict if the defendant had intended to kill or do grievous bodily harm. Only an intention to kill would suffice. Similarly in *R* v *Mohan* [1976] QB 1, where the defendant was charged with attempting, by wanton driving, to cause bodily harm to a police officer, the Court of Appeal held that recklessness as to consequences could play no part in the mens rea of attempt; there had to be proof that the defendant intended to bring about the full offence. In short, it had to be the defendant's purpose to commit the completed crime.

12.2 The Criminal Attempts Act 1981

The aim of the 1981 Act was to amend the law relating to criminal attempts. What it in fact achieved was a wholesale replacement of the common law with a new statutory offence of attempt. For the avoidance of doubt, s6(1) of the Act provides:

> 'The offence of attempt at common law and any offence at common law of procuring materials for crime are hereby abolished for all purposes not relating to acts done before the commencement of this Act.'

Section 1(4) also abolishes liability for attempt..ng to aid, abet, counsel or procure the commission of any offence, attempted conspiracy, and attempting to assist an offender contrary to s4(1) of the Criminal Law Act 1967.

The actus reus of statutory attempt

Section 1(1) of the 1981 Act provides:

> 'If, with intent to commit an offence to which this section applies, a person does an act which is more than merely preparatory to the commission of the offence, he is guilty of attempting to commit the offence.'

Under s4(3) of the 1981 Act:

> 'Where, in proceedings against a person for an offence under section 1 above, there is evidence sufficient in law to support a finding that he did an act falling within subsection (1) of that section, the question of whether or not his act fell within that subsection is a question of fact.'

In seeking to produce an acceptable formula for the actus reus of the new statutory offence of attempt, the Law Commission stated in its *Report on Attempt, and Impossibility in Relation to Attempt, Conspiracy and Incitement* (1980 No 102) at para 2.47:

> 'The definition of sufficient proximity must be wide enough to cover two varieties of cases; first, those in which a person has taken all the steps towards the commission of a crime which he believes to be necessary as far as he is concerned for that crime to result, such as firing a gun at another and missing. Normally such cases cause no difficulty. Secondly. however, the definition must cover those instances where a person has to take some further step to complete the crime, assuming that there is evidence of the necessary mental element on his part to commit it; for example, when the defendant has raised the gun to take aim at another but has not yet squeezed the trigger. We have reached the conclusion that, in regard to these cases, it is undesirable to recommend anything more complex than a rationalisation of the present law.'

And continued in para 2.48 it stated:

> 'The literal meaning of "proximate" is "nearest, next before or after (in place, order, time, connection of thought, causation, et cetera)." Thus, were this term part of a statutory description of the actus reus of attempt, it would clearly be capable of being interpreted to exclude all but the "final act"; this would not be in accordance with the policy outlined above.'

Some of the first decisions under the 1981 Act seem to have been decided in ignorance of this policy. For example, in *R* v *Widdowson* (1986) 82 Cr App R 314, the defendant had filled in an application form for credit facilities using a false name and was charged with attempting to obtain services by deception. The Court of Appeal quashed his conviction on the ground, inter alia, that he had not committed any acts more than merely preparatory to the obtaining of the service in question. In the view of the court, the defendant could not incur liability for attempt until he received a favourable response to his request for credit and decided to act upon it. In this respect the court seemed to be applying a type of 'last act' test to determine the defendant's liability which, as noted above, was a feature of the common law offence that the 1981 Act purported to abolish.

The Court of Appeal was swift to correct the error of this interpretation, and the current position is explained in *R* v *Jones* (1990) 91 Cr App R 351. The appellant had bought some guns, shortened the barrel of one of them, and had gone to the place where his intended victim dropped his daughter off for school. As the girl left the car, the appellant jumped in, and took a loaded sawn-off shotgun from a bag, pointing it at the victim from a range of 10–12 inches. The intended victim was able to grab the gun and throw it from the car window before the appellant could fire it.

It is significant that the gun's safety catch had been on throughout the struggle, and the intended victim could not state categorically that the appellant's finger had been on the trigger. In dismissing his appeal against his conviction for attempted murder, Taylor LJ considered how the courts should interpret the new statutory formulation of the actus reus of attempt, and expressed his view that, as the 1981 Act was a codifying statute, seeking to amend and set out completely the law relating to attempt, the correct approach was to 'look first at the natural meaning of the statutory words, not to turn back to earlier case law and seek to fit some previous test to the words of the section' (at p354). His Lordship then cited with approval passages from the judgment of Lord Lane CJ in *R v Gullefer* (1990) 91 Cr App R 356 (Note), wherein he stated:

> 'The first task of the Court is to apply the words of the Act of 1981 to the facts of the case. Was the appellant still in the stage of preparation to commit the substantive offence, or was there a basis of fact which would entitle the jury to say that he had embarked on the theft itself? … So far at least as the present case is concerned, we do not think that it is necessary to examine the authorities which preceded the Act of 1981 save to say that the sections we have already quoted in this judgment seem to be a blend of various decisions, some of which were not easy to reconcile with others … It seems to us that the words of the Act of 1981 seek to steer a midway course. They do not provide, as they might have done, that the *Eagleton* test is to be followed, or that, as Lord Diplock suggested, the defendant must have reached a point from which it was impossible for him to retreat before the actus reus of an attempt is proved. On the other hand the words give perhaps as clear a guidance as is possible in the circumstances on the point of time at which Stephen's "series of acts" begin. It begins when the merely preparatory acts come to an end and the defendant embarks upon the crime proper. When that is will depend of course upon the facts in any particular case.'

Based on the facts before him, Taylor LJ felt that there was evidence from which a reasonable jury, properly directed, could conclude that the appellant had done acts which were more than merely preparatory to murder. The court regarded the appellant's acts in obtaining the gun, in shortening it, in loading it, in putting on his disguise, and in going to the school as merely preparatory to the killing, but his actions in getting into the car, taking out the loaded gun and pointing it at the victim, provided sufficient evidence of acts more than merely preparatory to the killing for the jury to consider.

By contrast, the facts of *R v Gullefer* (above) provide an example of the type of case regarded by the courts as falling short of even the new definition of attempt.

The appellant visited a greyhound race meeting and, during the last race, climbed the fence on to the track in front of the dogs, waving his arms and attempting to distract them. He was unsuccessful, and the stewards decided that it was unnecessary to declare 'no race'. Had they made such a declaration, the bookmakers would have been obliged to repay the appellant's stake money. He was convicted of attempted theft of the stake money and appealed successfully to the Court of Appeal. As the Lord Chief Justice observed (at p358):

> 'Might it properly be said that when he jumped on to the track he was trying to steal £18 from the bookmaker?

'Our view is that it could not properly be said that at that stage he was in the process of committing theft. What he was doing was jumping on to the track in an effort to distract the dogs, which in its turn, he hoped, would have the effect of forcing the stewards to declare "no race", which would in its turn give him the opportunity to go back to the bookmaker and demand the £18 he had staked. In our view there was insufficient evidence for it to be said that he had, when he jumped on to the track, gone beyond mere preparation.'

Given its' ruling on the absence of any attempt it was not necessary for the court to consider whether or not, if the appellant had succeeded and had collected his stake money, he would have committed theft of the £18, although this in itself would have been a vexed question. As stated by Watkins LJ in *R v Campbell* (1991) 93 Cr App R 350, it would now be unwise for any trial judge, directing a jury on a charge of attempt, to embark discursively upon what the law was previously and to provide a jury with elaborate instances of what can and what cannot constitute an attempt.

The Court of Appeal, asked in *Attorney-General's Reference (No 1 of 1992)* (1993) 96 Cr App R 298, to consider the question of 'Whether, on a charge of attempted rape, it is incumbent upon the prosecution, as a matter of law, to prove that the defendant physically attempted to penetrate the woman's vagina with his penis', answered in the negative. As Lord Taylor CJ observed:

'It is not, in our judgment, necessary, in order to raise a prima facie case of attempted rape, to prove that the defendant with the requisite intent had necessarily gone as far as to attempt physical penetration of the vagina. It is sufficient if there is evidence from which the intent can be inferred and there are proved acts which a jury could properly regard as more than merely preparatory to the commission of the offence. For example, and merely as an example, in the present case the evidence of the young woman's distress, of the state of her clothing, and the position in which she was seen, together with the respondent's acts of dragging her up the steps, lowering his trousers and interfering with her private parts, and his answers to the police, left it open to a jury to conclude that the respondent had the necessary intent and had done acts which were more than merely preparatory. In short that he had embarked on committing the offence itself.'

The decision again underlines the point that, provided there is evidence upon which they can act, the issue is one of fact for the jury. It could, for example, be argued that the respondent's act of walking the complainant home was preparatory to the offence. The question of at what point he goes beyond *mere* preparation is one of degree. It is submitted that this can only be resolved by the jury exercising common sense in the light of evidence as to the defendant's intent at the time of the acts alleged: see further *R v Griffin* [1993] Crim LR 515.

The mens rea of statutory attempt

Section 1(1) of the 1981 Act (above) refers to a defendant acting with 'intent' to commit an offence. This rather suggests that far from amending the law in this area, the Act has in fact codified the common law, see 12.1. This view is borne out by the Court of Appeal's decision in *R v Pearman* (1985) 80 Cr App R 259, where the defendant's conviction for attempted grievous bodily harm was quashed, following the trial judge's direction to the jury that it was sufficient for the defendant to have foreseen grievous bodily harm as a probable consequence of his actions. Stuart-Smith J, delivering the judgment of the court, stated that it had not been the purpose of the 1981 Act to alter the law relating to the mens rea of attempt, and that as a result, the court regarded itself as still bound by decisions such as *R* v *Whybrow* (above), and *R* v *Mohan* (above). Consequently, whilst it would be permissible for a judge to direct a jury to consider what the defendant had foreseen as evidence of what he had intended, it was a clear misdirection to equate such foresight with mens rea itself: on the nature of intent (see further Chapter 2).

In *R* v *Walker & Hayles* (1990) 90 Cr App R 226 (discussed at 2.7) the Court of Appeal confirmed that whilst a defendant charged with murder had to be proved to have intended to kill, such intent could be inferred by the jury from evidence of the defendant's foresight that death was a virtually certain consequence of his actions.

The position is now that 'purpose' type intent, involving proof of the defendant's desire to bring about the prohibited consequence, would clearly be sufficient to secure a conviction on a charge of attempt. Indeed, the Court of Appeal in *R* v *Walker & Hayles* (above) expressed the view that a jury, considering a charge of attempted murder, could be directed that 'trying to kill' was synonymous with the defendant having the death of the victim as his purpose. Oblique intent, based on evidence of what the defendant foresaw, would also suffice, provided there was evidence, upon which a jury could act, that the defendant foresaw a consequence as virtually certain. It has been cogently argued (see *R* v *JC Smith* [1990] Crim LR 48), that trying to bring about a result and foreseeing a result as virtually certain will frequently be indistinguishable states of mind.

Where the elements of an offence specify that recklessness will suffice in respect of matters other than the prohibited consequence, the courts will not require proof of intent or knowledge simply because the defendant is charged with attempting to commit such an offence. In *R* v *Khan & Others* (1990) 91 Cr App R 29, the Court of Appeal considered the mens rea for attempted rape and referred to the earlier decision of *R* v *Millard and Vernon* [1987] Crim LR 393, wherein Mustill LJ had raised the matter in the following terms:

> 'Must the prosecution prove not only that the defendant intended the act [ie sexual intercourse], but also that he intended it to be non-consensual? Or should the jury be directed to consider two different states of mind, intent as to the act and recklessness as to the circumstance?'

The court concluded that a defendant could be convicted of attempted rape provided he intended to have sexual intercourse with a woman, in circumstances where the woman did not consent; he knew that she was not consenting or was reckless as to whether she consented, and had committed some act which was more than merely preparatory to sexual intercourse.

The court stressed that the attempt related to the physical activity; the mental state of a defendant charged with attempt was the same as one charged with the completed crime. It did not make sense to talk of a defendant being reckless as to whether he had sexual intercourse, but it did make sense to talk of his recklessness in relation to circumstances, such as the presence or absence of the woman's consent. The words 'with intent to commit an offence' meant, when applied to rape, 'with intent to have sexual intercourse with a woman in circumstances where she does not consent and the defendant knows or could not care less about her absence of consent'.

The rationale of *Khan* has subsequently been applied to attempted aggravated criminal damage, being reckless as to whether life would be endangered thereby, by the Court of Appeal in *Attorney-General's Reference (No 3 of 1992)* [1994] 1 WLR 409. The trial judge directed that the respondents be acquitted on the ground that the endangering of life was a consequence of criminal damage under the aggravated offence, and thus recklessness was not sufficient mens rea where the charge was one of attempt. The Court of Appeal confirmed that reckless as to whether life would thereby be endangered would be sufficient mens rea on a charge of attempt, provided the defendant had taken steps more than merely preparatory to causing criminal damage, with intent to cause criminal damage. In drawing an analogy with *Khan*, Schiemann observed :

'... what was missing [in *Khan*] ... was the act of sexual intercourse, without which the offence was not complete. What was missing in the present case was damage to [the car] without which the offence was not complete. The mental state of the defendant in each case contained everything which was required to render him guilty of the full offence ... The prosecution had to show an intention to damage the [car], and the remaining state of mind required for the aggravated offence of arson.'

See chapter 26, section 26.6, for further details.

12.3 Impossibility

Prior to the enactment of the 1981 Act, a defendant charged with attempt could raise the issue of impossibility to prevent conviction in certain circumstances. The basis for this was the House of Lords' decision in *Haughton v Smith* [1975] AC 476. A lorry-load of stolen meat travelling from Liverpool to London was repossessed by the police, and thereby ceased to be stolen property for the purposes of handling stolen goods under s22 of the Theft Act 1968. The lorry was allowed to continue south, where it was met by the defendants who had intended to unload the meat. The defendants were charged with attempting to handle stolen goods, but the House of Lords held that the defendants could not be guilty of attempting to commit a crime which, in the circumstances, was impossible to carry out.

It was Parliament's intention to reverse the effect of this decision by enacting ss1(2) and 1(3) of the 1981 Act which provide:

'1(2) A person may be guilty of attempting to commit an offence to which this section applies even though the facts are such that the commission of the offence is impossible.
(3) In any case where:
a) apart from this subsection a person's intention would not be regarded as having amounted to an intent to commit an offence; but
b) if the facts of the case had been as he believed them to be, his intention would be so regarded,
then, for the purposes of subsection (1) above, he shall be regarded as having had an intent to commit that offence.'

Initially, the House of Lords was reluctant to interpret these provisions in a manner that would produce the result intended by Parliament. In *Anderton* v *Ryan* [1985] AC 560, the defendant had bought a video recorder for £110, but later confessed to the police that she believed it to have been stolen property when she bought it. The defendant was charged, inter alia, with attempting to handle stolen goods, although the prosecution was unable to prove that the video recorder had in fact been stolen property. The House of Lords (Lord Edmund Davies dissenting) quashed the defendant's conviction on the ground that she could not be guilty of attempting to handle stolen goods unless such property was shown to have existed. A majority of their Lordships refused to accept that the defendant's belief that goods were stolen was sufficient of itself to result in liability. Such a result may have been the aim of the 1981 Act but their Lordships felt that Parliament would have to express its intentions more clearly before the courts would be willing to impose liability solely on the basis of what the defendant had thought she was doing, as opposed to what she was actually doing.

The effect of this decision was short-lived, however. Given the facts of *R* v *Shivpuri* [1986] 2 WLR 988, the House of Lords had little choice but to overrule its own previous decision in *Anderton* v *Ryan*. Shivpuri, whilst in India, was paid £1,000 to act as a drugs courier. He was required to collect a package containing a consignment of drugs which would be delivered to him in England, and distribute its contents according to instructions which would be given to him. On collecting the package, the defendant was arrested by police officers, and he confessed to them that he believed its contents to be either heroin or cannabis. In due course, further analysis revealed the contents of the package not to be drugs, but a harmless vegetable substance. The defendant's appeal to the House of Lords against his conviction for attempting to be knowingly concerned in dealing with and harbouring a controlled drug, namely heroin, was dismissed. It was held that s1 of the 1981 Act was to be interpreted as requiring the defendant to be judged on the facts as he believed them to be. On this basis the defendant had taken steps that he believed to be more than merely preparatory to dealing with a controlled drug.

The decision effectively overrules *Haughton* v *Smith* (above) and gives effect to s1 of the 1981 Act in the manner intended by Parliament. Nevertheless, it does open up a number of interesting, if somewhat hypothetical possibilities, such as the defendant who commits attempted unlawful sexual intercourse by having consensual sexual intercourse with a girl aged 17, believing her to be only 14; similarly the defendant who stabs at a pillow placed under some bedclothes, believing it to be the sleeping figure of his enemy, could now be charged with attempted murder. See further *R* v *Tulloch* [1986] Crim LR 50.

12.4 Reform

Clause 49 of the draft code states:

'(1) A person who, intending to commit an indictable offence, does an act that is more than merely preparatory to the commission of the offence is guilty of attempt to commit the offence.
(2) For the purposes of subsection (1), an intention to commit an offence is an intention with respect to all the elements of the offence other than fault elements, except that recklessness with respect to a circumstance suffices where it suffices for the offence itself.
(3) "Act" in this section includes an omission only where the offence intended is capable of being committed by an omission.
(4) Where there is evidence to support a finding that an act was more than merely preparatory to the commission of the offence intended, the question whether that act was more than merely preparatory is a question of fact.'

The proposed offence of attempt would (with a number of minor exceptions) only relate to indictable offences; see subsection (5). Liability would not extend to a person attempting to procure, assist or encourage as an accessory the commission of an offence by another, but a person could be charged as an accomplice to an attempt; see subsection (6). A charge of attempting to attempt would clearly be otiose, but subsection (6)(b) expressly preserves the possibility of a person being charged with attempting to incite, and attempting to conspire. Beyond these matters the offence proposed in clause 49 largely reflects the current law as stated in the Criminal Attempts Act 1981. Two specific points should be noted, however.

First, the Law Commission's acceptance that recklessness as to circumstances should be sufficient mens rea for attempt where this is sufficient for the completed crime. As the Commission conceded in the commentary upon clause 49:

'[This] represents a change from the policy we formerly recommended of requiring for attempt an intention to bring about each of the constituent elements of the offence attempted. That recommendation was at least partly based on the belief that the decision of the Court of Appeal in *Mohan* [1976] QB 1 to the effect that attempt is a crime of specific intent, applied equally in respect of consequences and circumstances specified in the definition of the offence attempted. However, in *Pigg* [1982] 1 WLR 762, a case on the common law decided after the Criminal Attempts Act 1981 had come into force, the Court of Appeal upheld a conviction for attempted rape on the basis that the accused was reckless whether the woman consented to intercourse ... In their Report the Code team ... sought to clarify the point by providing expressly that the intention required for an attempt was an intention in respect of all the elements of the offence attempted. An illustration was included of the application of the requirement to a case of attempted rape. On consultation the requirement and the illustration were strongly attacked by the

Scrutiny Group on preliminary offences. The Group argued with force that the policy involved was undesirably narrow in relation to circumstantial elements of substantive offences, particularly in cases where intoxication was involved. They recommended that the Code should make clear that the principle of *Pigg* applied to the statutory offence of attempt ... In view of the decision in *Pigg* it is plain that some clarification is required. Section 1(1) of the Criminal Attempts Act 1981 leaves the matter in doubt. We ourselves have no doubt that the criticisms expressed by the Scrutiny Group reflect widely-held social judgments about the need to protect potential victims against certain types of drunken and violent offender. We find the Group's criticisms persuasive and take the view that we should depart from our previous recommendation to the extent provided for in the subsection. A minor complication of the proposed rule is that it erects a distinction between "circumstances" and other elements of the substantive offence attempted. This distinction may occasionally be difficult to apply. We are prepared to tolerate the difficulty because in the mainstream cases where the rule is likely to operate, namely, rape and obtaining property by deception, the rule appears to work well. The distinction between act (sexual intercourse) and circumstance (non-consent) or between result (obtaining) and circumstance (the falsity of the representation) is plain on the face of the definitions of the offences.' [Vol II paras 13.44 & 13.45]

Secondly, the possibility of attempt by omission. As has been noted above, subsection (3) expressly states that '"Act" in this section includes an omission only where the offence intended is capable of being committed by an omission', but the wording of clause 16 (which deals with the meaning to be given to the term 'act' within the Code), envisages offences such as murder and manslaughter being committed by omission. As far as these offences are concerned a charge of attempting to commit such crimes based upon a failure to act could be sustained.

In relation to attempt and impossibility, see comments at Chapter 11.2.

13

Defences I

13.1 Automatism

13.2 Insanity

13.3 Intoxication

13.1 Automatism

It is accepted as a general principle of criminal law that a defendant cannot incur liability without proof of actus reus, and that where the actus reus involves proof of some conduct on his part, such conduct must be shown to have been freely willed, or voluntary. Where a defendant's actions are shown to have been involuntary, he may be able to avoid liability where the involuntariness arises from automatism.

Definition

A defendant is regarded as being in a state of automatism when his actions are 'automatic' or, as Lord Denning stated in *Bratty* v *Attorney-General for Northern Ireland* [1963] AC 386, where something was done by the defendant's muscles without the control of his mind. He considered this definition to include such matters as spasms, reflex actions, sleepwalking, nightmares, fits and so on. Whilst this list is broadly descriptive of conditions that fall within the scope of automatism, care must be taken to identify the causes of such behaviour. In *R* v *Burgess* (1991) 93 Cr App R 41, the defendant claimed to have carried out a violent attack upon the victim whilst sleepwalking. In upholding the trial judge's refusal to allow the defence of automatism to go before the jury, Lord Lane CJ commented:

> 'We accept of course that sleep is a normal condition, but the evidence in the instant case indicates that sleep-walking, and particularly violence in sleep, is not normal.'

Automatism is generally associated with the operation of external factors upon the working of the brain, rather than inherent mental defects. In *R* v *Quick* [1973] QB 910, the defendant, a diabetic, was charged with assaulting a patient. The assault occurred whilst the defendant was in a state of hypoglycaemia (low blood sugar level due to an excess of insulin). Following the trial judge's direction that automatism would not be available as a defence, the defendant changed his plea to one of guilty, and then appealed. It was held that the defendant should have been acquitted on the ground of automatism. His unconscious state had been the result of external factors, the taking of insulin, and was of a transitory nature, therefore it could not properly be described as insanity.

The defence is not one of irresistible impulse, neither is it available where the defendant's mind is functioning, albeit imperfectly. This latter point is illustrated by the decision in *Broome v Perkins* [1987] RTR 321. The defendant, a diabetic, had lapsed into a hypoglycaemic state whilst driving along a familiar stretch of road, despite having taken a 'Mars Bar' to counteract the effect of insulin. Medical evidence was put forward at his trial that it was possible for the defendant to be in a hypoglycaemic state, and yet still be able to exercise some control over his car. He was charged with driving without due care and attention, but the justices dismissed the case against him on the basis that he had been in a state of automatism at the time of the alleged offence. The prosecution appealed successfully to the Divisional Court however, where it was held that the defendant should have been convicted, given that there was evidence that his mind had still been responding to 'gross stimuli', and thus he had been 'driving' at the time of the offence. Once the actus reus was established, the fault element required for this offence, ie carelessness, could be established objectively. Similarly, in *Attorney-General's Reference (No 2 of 1992)* [1993] 3 WLR 982, where the Court of Appeal rejected the appellant's contention that he had been in a state of automatism, referred to as 'driving without awareness', induced by 'repetitive visual stimulus experienced on long journeys on straight flat roads', Lord Taylor CJ, observed:

> 'In our judgment, the "proper evidential foundation" was not laid in this case by … [the] evidence of "driving without awareness". As the authorities … show, the defence of automatism requires that there was a total destruction of voluntary control on the defendant's part. Impaired, reduced or partial control is not enough. Professor Brown [who gave expert evidence for the respondent] accepted that someone "driving without awareness" within his description, retains some control. He would be able to steer the vehicle and usually to react and return to full awareness when confronted by significant stimuli.'

The defendant bears an evidential burden in establishing the defence, which means that he must provide sufficient evidence of automatism for a jury to act upon. Whether or not he has done so is a matter of law for the trial judge, but it is apparent from the decided cases dealing with the defence that the defendant will normally need to produce some expert medical evidence as to his mental and physical state at the time of the offence.

In *R v T* [1990] Crim LR 256 (a decision of Southan J at Snaresbrook Crown Court), the defendant was a woman aged 23, who had been charged with robbery and actual bodily harm. On being arrested, there was evidence that the defendant was passive and indifferent to what was happening. During a subsequent interview, the defendant was only able to recollect some of the events during which the offences were alleged to have been committed. A week after her arrest the defendant was examined by a prison doctor and found to be suffering from a ruptured hymen and injuries posterior to the hymen. The defendant claimed that she had been raped three days prior to her arrest but had not told anyone about it. A psychiatrist subsequently diagnosed her as suffering from Post Traumatic Stress Disorder as a result of the rape, with the consequence that she had been in a Dissociative State at the time of the alleged offences, not acting with a conscious mind or will. On the basis of *Broome* v *Perkins* (above), the prosecution contended that the evidence showed that the defendant had had some awareness of what had happened, and therefore the only 'defence' open to the defendant was 'insane automatism' under the *M'Naghten* Rules. Southan J ruled that a proper foundation had been laid for the matter to go before the jury. It was his view that an incident such as rape could have an appalling effect on a young woman, however stable, and could satisfy the requirement laid down in *R* v *Quick* that there had to be evidence of 'an external factor' causing a malfunctioning of the mind. Post Traumatic Stress, involving as the evidence in the present case suggested, a defendant acting as though in a 'dream', could therefore amount to automatism. It is submitted that the court may have been willing to adopt this lenient approach given the somewhat 'one-off' nature of the circumstances.

Availability of automatism as a defence

It is customary to describe automatism as a general defence in criminal law, meaning that it can be raised by way of defence to any criminal charge. Whilst this is broadly correct, there is some debate as to whether automatism can be raised as a defence to crimes of strict liability. The question arises because it is to some extent unclear whether a defence of automatism merely involves a denial of mens rea or whether it also involves a denial of actus reus. In simple terms the question hinges on the meaning given to the phrase 'voluntariness'. If automatism means that a defendant's actions were not voluntary, in that his mind was not controlling his body, then clearly the defence entails a denial of mens rea – this much is universally accepted. It can be argued, however, that an actus reus is only established where it is shown to have been freely willed, or voluntary, and hence a plea of automatism would involve not only a denial of mens rea, but also a denial of actus reus.

The question acquires a practical significance where the defendant is charged with an offence of strict liability, because if an offence requires proof only of actus reus, a defence which involves only a denial of mens rea will be of little significance; alternatively, if automatism does involve a denial of actus reus, then it is one of the few defences that a defendant can raise in respect of strict liability offences.

There are two points that can be made here. First, as is stated by the authors of Smith and Hogan *Criminal Law* (7th ed) p99, it is somewhat fallacious to assume that offences of strict liability require no proof of mens rea. Many so-called strict liability offences do require some mens rea in respect of some elements of the actus reus, hence even if automatism only amounts to a denial of mens rea, it will still afford a defence to such offences: see further Chapter 25. The preferable view, however, is that automatism does negate the actus reus of an offence, on the basis that actus reus inevitably involves a mental element in the form of voluntariness. Not only does this approach have the virtue of recognising the artificiality of the actus reus/mens rea dichotomy (see Lord Diplock's comments in *R* v *Miller* [1983] 2 WLR 539 and Chapter 2), but it would also result in automatism being a defence to offences of 'absolute' liability, where arguably no mens rea whatsoever need be established on the part of the defendant.

The effect of automatism as a defence

Subject to the above comments concerning strict liability offences, automatism operates as a complete defence, in the sense that if the defendant succeeds in establishing it, he will be acquitted, and the court ceases to have any jurisdiction over him. It is this factor which perhaps explains the reluctance of the courts to recognise the defence of automatism in certain situations.

For example in *R* v *Sandie Smith* [1982] Crim LR 531, the defendant, who had been charged with making threats to kill, sought to raise the defence of automatism based on the effects of her pre-menstrual tension. The Court of Appeal refused to recognise this as the basis for automatism because, if successful, it would result in the defendant being released into society without the courts being able to exercise any effective control over her. The evidence indicated that the defendant needed to have some medical supervision, and the court would only have the power to ensure this if she was convicted.

Where a defence of automatism is raised, the courts will have to consider whether the defendant should in fact be classified as criminally insane. The defence of insanity is considered below, but for present purposes it can be noted that the crude distinctions between insanity and automatism are that the former is associated with some 'internal' mental defect suffered by the defendant which manifests itself in violence and is prone to recur, whereas the latter is associated with some external factor operating on the mind of the defendant in circumstances that indicate that he is not otherwise a danger to society. Hence, a defendant who injures his wife by striking her in bed whilst he is having a nightmare, would normally be expected to succeed with a defence of automatism. If, however, there is evidence that this behaviour occurred because of some inherent defect on the part of the defendant and that it has happened in the past, or is likely to recur in the future, the jury may be directed to consider whether the defendant is criminally insane. Again the significance of the distinction lies in the fact that the courts have extensive powers of disposal over defendants found to be 'not guilty by reason of insanity', and can thus act to protect other members of society.

Self-induced automatism

A defendant may be prevented from raising the defence of automatism, where there is evidence to show that he was in some way at fault in bringing about the state of automatism. Perhaps the most obvious instance of this arises where a defendant voluntarily consumes large amounts of alcohol or other drugs with the result that he ceases to be aware of his actions. Where this is the case, the defendant may be able to rely on the defence of intoxication, which is considered below, at 13.3. Similar problems can arise however, where a defendant becomes increasingly drowsy whilst driving his car, and instead of pulling over to the side of the road, he continues to drive, eventually falling asleep at the wheel, and causing an accident. Clearly he was in a state of automatism at the time of the crash, but equally we might say that it was his fault because he could have avoided the problem by ceasing to drive when he first became drowsy.

The principal authority on this point is the Court of Appeal decision in *R* v *Bailey* (1983) 77 Cr App R 76. The defendant, a diabetic, had felt unwell and had taken a mixture of sugar and water, but had not eaten anything. A short time after this he had struck a man on the head with an iron bar. At his trial the defendant faced charges under both ss18 and 20 of the Offences Against the Person Act 1861. He claimed that he had been unable to control his actions because he had been in a hypoglycaemic state at the time of the attack. The trial judge directed the jury that the defence of automatism was not available where, as in the present case, it was 'self-induced', and the defendant was convicted of the s18 offence. On appeal, the Court of Appeal held that as s18 created a specific intent crime, even self-induced automatism could be relied upon as evidence that the defendant did not have the necessary mens rea for the offence (this is consistent with the availability of self-induced intoxication, considered below at 13.3). In relation to the s20 offence however, the court held that self-induced automatism would not provide a defence, where there was evidence that the defendant had been reckless in failing to eat after taking the insulin. The recklessness here would involve proof that the defendant had known that his failure to eat might make his actions more aggressive or uncontrollable. As Griffiths LJ stated:

> 'The question in each case will be whether the prosecution have proved the necessary element of recklessness.'

Does this mean. therefore, that if the defendant is charged with an offence involving *Caldwell* type recklessness, such as criminal damage, he will not succeed with a defence based on self-induced intoxication where he gave no thought to an obvious and serious risk that he might damage property if he did not take certain steps to avoid entering into a state of automatism?

Reform

The existing common law defence of non-insane automatism is restated by clause 33 of the draft code in the following terms:

> '(1) A person is not guilty of an offence if –
> (a) he acts in a state of automatism, that is, his act –

(i) is a reflex, spasm or convulsion; or

(ii) occurs while he is in a condition (whether of sleep, unconsciousness impaired consciousness or otherwise) depriving him of effective control of the act; and

(b) the act or condition is the result neither of anything done or omitted with the fault required for the offence nor of voluntary intoxication.

(2) A person is not guilty of an offence by virtue of an omission to act if

(a) he is physically incapable of acting in the way required; and

(b) his being so incapable is the result neither of anything done or omitted with the fault required for the offence nor of voluntary intoxication.'

The defence would be available, for example, where D, driving a car, has a sudden 'black-out', as a result of which the car mounts the kerb and comes to rest against a wall. D would not be guilty of driving without due care and attention (Vol I Appendix B example 33(i)). The commentary upon clause 33(1) emphasises, however, the limited scope of the proposed provision:

'The main function of clause 33(1) is to protect a person who acts in a state of automatism from conviction of an offence of strict liability. It is conceded that he does "the act" specified for the offence; but the clause declares him not guilty. One charged with an offence requiring fault in the form of failure to comply with a standard of conduct may also have to rely on the clause. On the other hand, a state of automatism will negative a fault requirement of intention or knowledge or (normally) recklessness; so a person charged with an offence of violence against another, or of criminal damage, committed when he was in a condition of impaired consciousness, does not rely on this clause for his acquittal but on the absence of the fault element of the offence.' [Vol II para 11.2]

References in clause 33(1) to spasms and reflex actions clearly derive from obiter statements of Lord Denning in *Bratty* v *Attorney-General for Northern Ireland* (above). The Law Commission felt, however, that inclusion of references to a 'condition (whether of sleep, unconsciousness, impaired consciousness or otherwise) ...' depriving the defendant of effective control over his actions, was justified:

'... both on principle and by some of the leading cases. The governing principle should be that a person is not guilty of an offence if, without relevant fault on his part, he cannot choose to act otherwise than as he does. The acts of the defendants in several cases have been treated as automatous although it is far from clear, and even unlikely, that they were entirely unconscious when they did the acts and although it cannot confidently be said that they exercised no control. in any sense of that phrase, over their relevant movements [eg *R* v *Kemp* [1957] 1 QB 399; *R* v *Quick* [1973] QB 910].' [Vol II para 11.3]

The Commission was especially critical of decisions such as that in *Broome* v *Perkins* (considered above), commenting that:

'... it seems clear that D's condition was such that he could not choose to behave otherwise than as he did. Cases such as those we have mentioned above appear not to have been referred to. Finding it necessary to choose between the authorities, we propose a formula under which we expect (and indeed hope) that a person in the condition of the defendant in *Broome* v *Perkins* would be acquitted (subject to the question of prior fault).' [Vol II para 11.4]

The doctrine of prior fault, developed at common law in decisions such as *R* v *Bailey* (above), is incorporated in the draft code, as regards offences of strict liability and negligence, at 33(1)(b), and (2)(b).

A defendant charged with an offence involving intention or recklessness who is found to have been in a state of automatism at the time of the offence due to his own prior fault, would be dealt with under clause 22(6) of the draft code: see 13.3 (below).

Clause 33(2) seeks to provide a defence where a person omits to act in a manner required by law because of physical incapacity. For example, D's car passes a red traffic light whilst he is in a state of automatism. D is not guilty of failing to comply with a traffic sign. Similarly, D is involved in a traffic accident which he is under a duty to report to the police within 24 hours. He is seriously injured in the accident and spends more than a day in intensive care. He is not guilty of the offence of failing to report the accident. (Vol I Appendix B examples 33(iv) and 33(v)).

For an explanation of references to voluntary intoxication as that phrase is used in the Code, see clause 22, considered at 13.3, below.

13.2 Insanity

The issue of the defendant's insanity may be relevant at three stages:

1. at the time of the alleged offence;
2. whilst he is being held in detention;
3. when he is asked to plead at the outset of his trial.

For present purposes our concern is primarily with a defendant, in relation to whom the question of fitness to plead has not arisen, who wishes to rely upon his insanity at the time of the alleged offence as a defence. As regards a defendant whose fitness to plead is in issue, however, the provisions of the Criminal Procedure (Insanity and Unfitness to Plead) Act 1991 should be noted.

Prior to the 1991 Act a defendant could be found to be unfit to plead before the issue of liability was investigated. This sometimes resulted in a defendant being detained in a secure hospital simply on the basis of his or her unfitness to plead. The 1991 Act is designed to improve the situation of such defendants by requiring a court, which has found the defendant unfit to plead, to continue with a trial of the facts to the extent of ascertaining whether or not the defendant committed the actus reus of the offence alleged. If the court concludes that he did not, the defendant should be acquitted. Whilst this development is to be welcomed, it should be remembered that the distinction between actus reus and mens rea is somewhat illusory in many cases, and it may be that in practice the court has no option but to investigate both elements.

The special verdict

It is, strictly speaking, inaccurate to describe insanity as a defence. If a defendant succeeds in establishing that he was insane at the time of the offence (something that the defendant has to establish on the balance of probabilities) then under the provisions of s2 of the Trial of Lunatics Act 1883, as amended by the Criminal Procedure (Insanity) Act 1964, the jury will return the special verdict under which the defendant is found to be not guilty by reason of insanity. The real significance of this verdict is that it leaves the defendant under the control of the court. Section 5 of the 1964 Act provides that where a special verdict is returned, the court '... shall make an order that the accused be admitted to such hospital as may be specified by the Secretary of State'. The range of options open to the court in respect of a defendant, provided he has not been charged with an offence to which a mandatory penalty is prescribed, has been increased by the Criminal Procedure (Insanity and Unfitness to Plead) Act 1991. The court can now make a supervision and treatment order, a guardianship order; order the defendant's admission to hospital for a limited or unlimited period, or discharge the defendant completely.

The 1991 Act makes no change to the *M'Naghten's* Rules (*M'Naghten's Case* (1843) 10 C & F 200) as regards the definition of insanity, considered below.

Alternative strategies

Defendants may still find the prospect of the special verdict, with the possibility of hospitalisation, and the stigma of being declared criminally insane, unattractive. Coupled with the narrowness of the actual terms of the defence of insanity, considered below, this perhaps goes some way to explaining why relatively little use is made of the defence in modern day trials.

Where a defendant is charged with murder, which carries a mandatory penalty of life imprisonment, the flexibility introduced by the 1991 Act will not be available to the court dealing with his case. He will almost certainly rely on the defence of diminished responsibility under s2 of the Homicide Act 1957 (see Chapter 7) in preference to a plea of insanity, the principal advantage being the greater discretion left to the trial judge following a finding of diminished responsibility by the jury.

It should be noted, however, that those convicted of manslaughter on the grounds of diminished responsibility will invariably be sentenced to a term of imprisonment, sometimes for life, and in any event, under s6(1)(b) of the Criminal Procedure (Insanity) Act 1964, the prosecution can lead evidence of the defendant's insanity where he has raised the defence of diminished responsibility, although the prosecution must establish this beyond all reasonable doubt.

In relation to any offence, a defendant might regard it as preferable to rely on automatism rather than the defence of insanity but, as considered above at 13.1, the courts cannot permit the defendant to do so where, because of his potentially dangerous and violent nature, he still represents a threat to the safety of other members of society. The common law rule, based on Lord Denning's judgment in

Bratty v *Attorney-General of Northern Ireland* [1963] AC 386, is that wherever the defendant puts his state of mind in issue during a trial, the prosecution can be permitted to adduce evidence of his insanity. Clearly a defendant relying on the defence of automatism is putting his state of mind in issue, but so too, in theory, is the defendant relying on the defence of mistake, or intoxication.

Even if a defendant has not raised the issue of his mental responsibility at all, it appears that the trial judge may, in exceptional circumstances, leave the option of the special verdict to the jury if he thinks fit, see *R* v *Dickie* [1984] 3 All ER 173.

A third option open to a defendant not wishing to be made the subject of a special verdict, is simply to plead guilty to the offence as charged in the hope that he will be sentenced as would a sane defendant, this being perhaps more likely where less serious offences are involved. Again this tactic may prove counter-productive for the defendant, since following conviction the prosecution has a duty to put before the court all relevant evidence for the purposes of sentencing, and this can include evidence as to the defendant's insanity. Although he avoids the stigma of the special verdict, the defendant can still find himself being made the subject of a hospital order.

The definition of insanity

The definition of insanity is based upon the so-called rules laid down in *M'Naghten's Case* (1843) 10 C & F 20, which provide that the defendant must establish that he was suffering from a defect of reason arising from a disease of the mind, having one of two results; either that the defendant was unaware of the nature and quality of his act, or that he did not realise that his actions were wrong.

'Disease of the mind'

The expression 'disease of the mind' has not been interpreted by the courts to mean only a physical defect of the brain. In *R* v *Kemp* [1957] 1 QB 399, the defendant suffered a blackout during which he attacked his wife with a hammer, causing her grievous bodily harm. The evidence showed that he suffered from arterial sclerosis, a condition which restricted the flow of blood to the brain. The trial judge ruled that, for the purposes of the defence of insanity, no distinction was to be drawn between diseases of the mind, and diseases of the body affecting the operation of the mind. Why then, one might ask, was the diabetic defendant in *R* v *Quick* (above), permitted to rely on the defence of automatism, whilst Kemp was not?

The rationale behind the distinction between insane and non-insane automatism may be based on the perceived risk that a defendant presents to society. Whilst a diabetic who suffers from an excess of insulin may experience a hypoglycaemic episode during which he causes injury to others or damages property, such problems might be regarded as 'avoidable' or 'treatable': see *R* v *Bingham* [1991] Crim LR 43.

Where a defendant suffers from a disease of the body which affects the mind in a manner which, to paraphrase Lord Denning in *Bratty* v *Attorney-General for*

Northern Ireland (above), manifests itself in violence and is likely to recur, it will be classified as insanity, thus enabling the courts to order the detention of the defendant in society's interest. The defendant Bratty in fact suffered from psychomotor epilepsy, strictly speaking a disease of the nervous system; yet the House of Lords held that it had not been a misdirection for the trial judge to leave the defence of insanity to the jury rather than automatism.

The House of Lords has subsequently had occasion to reaffirm this approach to the concept of disease of the mind in *R v Sullivan* [1984] AC 156. The defendant had inflicted grievous bodily harm contrary to s20 of the Offences Against the Person Act 1861 whilst suffering from a minor epileptic fit. During the course of the trial the judge had ruled that he would be willing to direct the jury on the defence of insanity, but not that of automatism, whereupon the defendant changed his plea to one of guilty, and appealed on the ground that the trial judge had wrongly denied him the opportunity of raising the defence of automatism. In dismissing the appeal, Lord Diplock, with whom all of their Lordships were in agreement, recognised the natural reluctance that many sensible people would feel in labelling an epileptic as 'criminally insane', but went on to explain that:

> 'If the effect of a disease is to impair [the faculties of reason, memory and understanding] so severely as to have either of the consequences referred to in the later part of the [*M'Naghten*] Rules, it matters not whether the aetiology of the impairment is organic, as in epilepsy, or functional, or whether the impairment itself is permanent or is transient and intermittent, provided that it subsisted at the time of commission of the act. The purpose of the legislation relating to the defence of insanity, ever since its origin in 1800, has been to protect society against recurrence of the dangerous conduct.'

How often the condition must be likely to recur in order for the courts to regard it as constituting a disease of the mind is open to question. As Lord Lane CJ stated in *R v Burgess* (above at 13.1):

> 'It seems to us that if there is a danger of recurrence that may be an added reason for categorising the condition as a disease of the mind. On the other hand, the absence of the danger of recurrence is not a reason for saying that it cannot be a disease of the mind.'

It should be noted that in this case the medical evidence suggested that a recurrence of violence was most unlikely, yet the Court of Appeal still upheld the trial judge's refusal to allow the defence of automatism to be put before the jury.

An alternative rationale for the distinction between insane and non-insane automatism might be that suggested at 13.1; the fact that automatism will generally be caused by the effect of external factors operating upon the body, whilst insanity springs from internal defects. While it is submitted that to pursue such a distinction is likely to lead to a somewhat arbitrary classification of defendants, it would appear to be supported by the decision of the Court of Appeal in *R v Hennessy* [1989] 1 WLR 287. The appellant, a diabetic who failed to take the insulin necessary to stabilise his metabolism, was stopped by police officers whilst driving a stolen car. Medical evidence suggested that the appellant had been in a state of hyperglycaemia (high blood sugar level) at the time the car was taken. The appellant was not permitted to put the defence of automatism before the jury, the trial judge having indicated that he would only be prepared to direct the jury on the defence of insanity. The Court of Appeal, in confirming the correctness of the trial judge's ruling, held that as the appellant's loss of awareness had not resulted from the operation of external factors upon his body, such as the injection of insulin (as in *R v Quick* (above)), but rather had resulted from an inherent physical defect, ie diabetes, the appellant was to be regarded as suffering from a disease of the body which affected the mind for the purposes of the *M'Naghten* Rules. This distinction between hypoglycaemia (too little sugar in the blood caused by treatment with insulin or by inadequate quantities of food) and hyperglycaemia continues to be used as the basis for distinguishing between sane and non-insane automatism: see again *R v Bingham* (above).

'So as not to know the nature and quality of his act'

One of the two grounds upon which insanity can be established is that the defendant's disease of the mind caused him to be unaware of his actions. It has been seen that in *R v Kemp* (above) the defendant was unaware of his actions because of a 'blackout'. Similarly, the defence would be made out where, due to a disease of the mind, the defendant killed a victim believing himself to be chopping down a tree, or where a defendant placed a baby on a fire believing the child to be a log. Were an apparently sane defendant to act in this fashion he would be entitled to rely on the defence of mistake (see Chapter 15), but it should be noted that the more outlandish his mistake, the less likely the jury are to conclude that the defendant honestly believed the facts to be as he claims them to have been. Further, on the basis of *Bratty* (above), such a defence might entitle the prosecution to introduce evidence of insanity.

'Actions were wrong'

The alternative basis upon which the defence can be made out is for the defendant to be shown not to have known that his actions were wrong due to his disease of the mind. 'Wrong' in this context has been interpreted to mean wrong in law, as opposed to simply immoral: see *R v Windle* [1952] 2 QB 826. Hence, the defence of insanity offers one of the very few situations where ignorance of the criminal law can be relied upon to avoid liability.

The limited nature of the defence

The defence of insanity has been the subject of prolonged and cogent academic criticism on a number of grounds, but primarily in relation to its limited scope. It will be apparent from the above that, whilst the defence can cater for the defendant who is unaware of his actions, or their illegality, there is no provision for the defendant who is aware of his actions, and knows them to be unlawful, yet cannot prevent himself from committing offences. Where the defendant kills as a result of such a condition, he can at least avail himself of the defence of diminished responsibility which recognises impairment of responsibility as a partial defence, but in relation to all other offences there exists a serious gap in the provision of defences. This problem is illustrated by the decision in *R v Bell* [1984] Crim LR 685. The defendant had been charged with reckless driving, having used a van as a battering ram to drive through the entrance gates of a Butlins' holiday camp. When interviewed he told the police: 'It was like a secret society in there, I wanted to do my bit against it'. The defendant contended that he had not driven recklessly because, although he knew there was a risk of his causing damage, he felt that he was able to cope with it because he was being instructed to act by God. Following the rejection of his submission of 'no case' on this basis, he changed his plea to one of guilty. The Court of Appeal held, dismissing the appeal, that as the defendant had been aware of his actions he could not have been in a state of automatism, and the fact that he believed himself to be driven by God could not provide an excuse, but merely an explanation for what he had done. In other words he could not rely on the defence of insanity either because the evidence was that he had known what he was doing, or had known that what he was doing was illegal.

Reform

The Butler Committee Report (Cmnd 6244) (1975), recommended the introduction of a new verdict of 'not guilty by reason of mental disorder' which could be returned in two situations:

1. where the defendant was unable to form the requisite mens rea due to mental disorder; or
2. where the defendant was aware of his actions but was at the time suffering from severe mental disorder.

The Report's recommendations have never been implemented and, with the passage of time, their implementation seems increasingly less likely.

The difficulty lies in producing a concept of insanity which is, on the one hand, simple enough for the averagely educated man or woman on a jury to understand, but which on the other hand is sufficiently sophisticated to encompass the varying types of mental abnormality with which other modern courts are likely to have to deal.

The draft code seeks to build upon the foundations laid by the Butler Committee. The commentary on the Code Report states:

'The necessity of incorporating in the projected Criminal Code an appropriate provision to replace the outdated "insanity" defence was one justification given by the [Butler] Committee for its review of the subject. We ourselves are persuaded that implementation of the Committee's proposals would greatly improve this area of the law. We have, however, found it necessary to suggest some important modifications of those proposals. Clauses 34 to 40 therefore aim to give effect to the policy of the Butler Committee as modified by us in ways that will be explained in the following paragraphs.' [Vol II para 11.9]

Clauses 35 and 36 of the draft code detail the circumstances in which the proposed mental disorder verdict would be returned. Clause 35 provides:

'(1) A mental disorder verdict shall be returned if the defendant is proved to have committed an offence but it is proved on the balance of probabilities (whether by the prosecution or by the defendant) that he was at the time suffering from severe mental illness or severe mental handicap.
(2) Subsection (1) does not apply if the court or jury is satisfied beyond reasonable doubt that the offence was not attributable to a severe mental illness or severe mental handicap.
(3) A court or jury shall not, for the purposes of a verdict under subsection (1), find that the defendant was suffering from severe a mental illness or severe mental handicap unless two medical practitioners approved for the purposes of s12 of the Mental Health Act 1983 as having special experience in the diagnosis or treatment of mental disorder have given evidence that he was so suffering.'

This provision would cater for the defendant who currently comes within the second limb of the *M'Naghten* Rules, ie the defendant who commits the actus reus of an offence with mens rea, but who is unaware that his actions are wrong in law.

Clause 36 seeks to provide for the defendant who, through mental disorder, acts without the requisite fault element. It states:

'A mental disorder verdict shall be returned if –
(a) the defendant is acquitted of an offence only because, by reason of evidence of mental disorder or a combination of mental disorder and intoxication, it is found that he acted or may have acted in a state of automatism, or without the fault required for the offence, or believing that an exempting circumstance existed; and
(b) it is proved on the balance of probabilities (whether by the prosecution or by the defendant) that he was suffering from mental disorder at the time of the act.'

As the commentary explains, under clause 36:

'... an acquittal is inevitable because the prosecution has failed to prove that the defendant acted with the required fault (or to disprove his defence of automatism or mistake); but the reason for that failure is evidence of mental disorder, and it is proved that the defendant was indeed suffering from mental disorder at the time of the act. This differs from [clause 35 cases] in casting no burden on the defendant of proving his innocence.' (Vol II para 11.11)

The proposals under the Code envisage either the prosecution adducing evidence of the defendant's mental disorder, or the defendant himself pleading 'not guilty by reason of mental disorder' (clause 37). The prosecution would not be able to adduce such evidence unless the defendant has given or adduced evidence that he acted without the fault required for the offence, or believing that an exempting circumstance existed, or in a state of automatism, or (on a charge of murder) when suffering from mental abnormality as defined in clause 57(2). Whether or not evidence given was to be treated as evidence of mental disorder or automatism would be a question of law for the trial judge.

The definition of 'mental disorder' and associated terms is dealt with by clause 34. Mental disorder is defined as involving:

'... severe mental illness, ... a state of arrested or incomplete development of mind ... a state of automatism (not resulting only from intoxication) which is a feature of a disorder, whether organic or functional and whether continuing or recurring, that may cause a similar state on another occasion ...' The term 'severe mental illness' is itself further explained in clause 34 as involving one or more of the following characteristics:
'(a) lasting impairment of intellectual functions shown by failure of memory, orientation, comprehension and learning capacity;
(b) lasting alteration of mood of such degree as to give rise to delusional appraisal of the defendant's situation, his past or his future, or that of others, or lack of any appraisal;
(c) delusional beliefs, persecutory, jealous or grandiose;
(d) abnormal perceptions associated with delusional misinterpretation of events;
(e) thinking so disordered as to prevent reasonable appraisal of the defendant's situation or reasonable communication with others ...'

For an explanation of references to voluntary intoxication as that phrase is used in the Code, see clause 22, considered at 13.3, below.

13.3 Intoxication

A defendant can become intoxicated, as that term is understood by the criminal law, either through his own voluntary intake of drugs, or through his being forced or tricked into taking drugs. The former is referred to as self-induced intoxication, the latter as involuntary intoxication.

A state of intoxication can arise from the use of any number of stimulants, although those most frequently encountered by the courts are alcohol and hallucinogenics. The defendant seeking to rely on intoxication as a defence will have to produce evidence that he was either incapable of forming the necessary intent, see *DPP* v *Beard* (below) or, even though capable of forming the necessary intent, did not do so because of the intoxication, see *R* v *Pordage* [1975] Crim LR 575 and *R* v *Cole* [1993] Crim LR 300. The fact that a defendant does something whilst drunk that he would not have done when sober, will not, of itself, give rise to the defence of intoxication. A drunken intent is nevertheless an intent: see *R* v *Bowden* [1993] Crim LR 380.

The problem for the criminal law is in developing a defence of intoxication which recognises the defendant's reduced responsibility for his actions, but which also ensures that the defendant is adequately punished, so as not to encourage the irresponsible use of drugs. As will be seen, the solution developed at common law is not without its shortcomings.

The specific intent/basic intent dichotomy

Self-induced intoxication is not a general defence in criminal law. On the basis of two House of Lords decisions, *DPP* v *Beard* [1920] AC 479, and *DPP* v *Majewski*

[1977] AC 142, self-induced intoxication can be raised as a defence where a defendant is charged with a crime of specific intent, but not where the charge involves a crime of basic intent. It is thus essential to be able to distinguish between crimes of specific and basic intent in order to be able to understand the operation of intoxication as a defence.

A basic intent crime is sometimes described as one where the mens rea does not exceed the actus reus. In simple terms this means that the defendant does not have to have foreseen any consequence, or harm, beyond that laid down in the definition of the actus reus. The offence of malicious wounding, contrary to s20 of the Offences Against the Person Act 1861, provides an example. The actus reus of the offence is obviously wounding. The mens rea, denoted by the term 'malicious', was defined by Diplock LJ, in *R* v *Mowatt* [1968] 1 QB 421, as involving proof that the defendant foresaw the possibility of some physical harm occurring to the victim, albeit slight. Thus the defendant charged under s20 can be convicted without proof of his having intended to do anything more than wound the victim. Indeed the defendant can be convicted under s20 even if his mens rea falls some considerable way short of intending to wound, eg foresight of the victim being bruised is sufficient.

A specific intent crime, by contrast, is one where in theory the mens rea goes beyond the actus reus. The offence of wounding with intent to do some grievous bodily harm, contrary to s18 of the Offences Against the Person Act 1861, provides an example of such a crime. As with the s20 offence considered above, the actus reus is 'wounding', but by contrast, the defendant must be shown not only to have had the mens rea for wounding, but also a further or 'specific' mens rea, in the form of an intention to do some grievous bodily harm. Hence the reference to the 'mens rea going beyond the actus reus'.

Unfortunately, one cannot apply the above theory to every criminal offence as a determinant of whether it should be classified as one of basic or specific intent, because the law in this area is as much moulded by public policy as it is by coherent legal theory. The result is that some crimes, which in accordance with the above theory should be classified as specific intent crimes, are in fact classified as basic intent, and vice versa. The offence of murder provides a glaring example of this inconsistent approach. The actus reus of the offence is essentially to cause the death of another human being, yet the mens rea does not 'go beyond' this in any way; in fact it is sufficient for the prosecution to prove that the defendant intended grievous bodily harm, ie the mens rea does not even have to go as far as the actus reus, yet murder is treated as a specific intent crime for the purposes of self-induced intoxication. Conversely, the offence of rape contrary to the Sexual Offences (Amendment) Act 1976, might be thought to be one of specific intent, in that it requires proof not only that the defendant intended to have sexual intercourse, but also that he knew that the woman was not consenting or was at least reckless as to this fact. Given the number of rapists who would raise the issue of self-induced intoxication however, it is not surprising that the courts have dealt with the offence as one of basic intent, see *R* v *Woods* [1982] Crim LR 42.

The present position might be summarised as follows:

Basic intent crimes

1. Common law assault and battery.
2. ss47, 20, and 23 of the Offences Against the Person Act 1861.
3. Manslaughter.
4. Rape.
5. 'Reckless' criminal damage contrary to s1(1) and 1(2) of the Criminal Damage Act 1971.

Specific intent crimes

1. Murder.
2. ss18 and 24 of the Offences Against the Person Act 1861.
3. Criminal damage with intent to endanger life, contrary to s1(2) of the Criminal Damage Act 1971.
4. ss1, 8, 9(1)(a), 15, 16, 21, 22 and 25 of the Theft Act 1968.
5. ss2(1)(b) and 3 of the Theft Act 1978.
6. Inchoate offences.

The above is intended as a general guide only, as it will be realised that in the case of certain offences a degree of subtlety is required to determine the distinction. For example in respect of indecent assault, if the assault is unambiguously indecent, there is no need to prove any mens rea in relation to the indecency, thus the offence would be one of basic intent: see *R* v *C* [1992] Crim LR 642 (D's defence of intoxication disregarded where he had inserted his finger into a child's vagina). Where, however, there is ambiguity regarding the indecent nature of the assault, proof of the defendant's purpose may be relevant; see *R* v *Court* [1989] AC 28. If the defendant's mens rea is sufficiently affected by intoxication his liability should be reduced to that of common assault.

Self-induced intoxication as a defence to crimes of specific intent

Self-induced intoxication will operate as a partial or complete defence to a crime of specific intent, if a defendant can show that he lacked the necessary specific intent due to drink or drugs. The burden rests on the defendant to provide some evidence of intoxication which can be put before the jury; the onus will then be on the Crown to establish beyond all reasonable doubt, that despite such evidence, the defendant still had the necessary mens rea. The effect of a defendant successfully relying on the defence will depend on the nature of the offence with which he is charged.

In the case of murder, the defendant's liability will be reduced to that of the 'lesser included' basic intent crime of manslaughter; similarly wounding with intent reduces to malicious wounding, and s1(2) criminal damage to the s1(1) offence. Where there is no 'lesser included' offence, however, the defendant should be completely acquitted, as would be the case with theft, burglary with intent to steal, and obtaining property by deception.

Self-induced intoxication and basic intent crimes.

Where a defendant commits a basic intent crime and there is evidence that he lacked the necessary mens rea through his voluntary taking of drugs, he will not, subject to possible exceptions considered below, be permitted to rely on the evidence of intoxication as negativing his mens rea. The authority for this proposition is the House of Lords' decision in *DPP* v *Majewski* (above), approving the earlier Court of Appeal decision in *R* v *Lipman* [1970] 1 QB 152.

If a defendant does not have the mens rea required for a basic intent crime, how can the courts justify his conviction and punishment? As Lord Elwyn-Jones LC explained in *DPP* v *Majewski* the 'fault' element is supplied by the defendant's recklessness in becoming intoxicated, this recklessness being substituted for the mens rea that the prosecution would otherwise have to establish.

This approach has had a number of significant consequences. The first is that it is now accepted that where a defendant is charged with a basic intent crime and leads evidence of self-induced intoxication, there is no need for the prosecution to prove that he had mens rea at the time the offence was committed, the defendant's evidence normally being in itself conclusive proof of recklessness. The evidence of self-induced intoxication cannot be relied upon by the defendant to deny intention or foresight because, as a matter of law, it is not relevant evidence within s8 of the Criminal Justice Act 1967 (although see the somewhat exceptional case of *Jaggard* v *Dickinson* [1981] 2 WLR 118).

The second consequence has been the classification of any crime for which 'recklessness' is sufficient mens rea as one of basic intent. The House of Lords' decision in *Commissioner of the Metropolitan Police* v *Caldwell* [1982] AC 341, raised, inter alia, the question of whether self-induced intoxication could be a defence to a charge of causing criminal damage, being reckless as to whether the life of another would be endangered thereby, contrary to s1(2) of the Criminal Damage Act 1971. It was held, by a majority, that whereas self-induced intoxication could be relevant evidence negativing an intention to endanger life by means of criminal damage, it was not relevant where such a charge proceeded on the basis of the defendant's alleged recklessness. It was Lord Diplock's view that the rule in *DPP* v *Majewski* (that the defendant's recklessness in becoming intoxicated supplied the necessary mens rea for the offence in question), applied not only to the recklessness in causing criminal damage, but also the further recklessness as regards the endangering of life. Lord Edmund-Davies, in a powerful dissenting speech, did not seek to detract from the decision in *DPP* v *Majewski*, but saw in it no justification for the extension of its principles to the 'further' intent in crimes such as aggravated criminal damage: see further *R* v *Cullen* [1993] Crim LR 936.

The emphasis in both *Majewski* and *Caldwell*, is on the assumption that the defendant was reckless in voluntarily consuming intoxicants. Such an assumption may be justified in the case of alcohol and other substances which are commonly known to reduce an individual's responsibility for his actions. It would now appear, however, that a distinction should be drawn between such cases, and situations where the defendant has been affected by a substance, voluntarily consumed by him, that would not normally have been expected to have had an adverse effect on his self control. In *R* v *Hardie* [1985] 1 WLR 64, the Court of Appeal quashed the conviction of the defendant, who had been charged with causing aggravated criminal damage whilst under the influence of valium, following the trial judge's direction to the jury that evidence of such self-induced intoxication was irrelevant to a charge involving a basic intent crime. The court held that the trial judge should have distinguished valium, a sedative, from other types of drugs, such as alcohol, which were widely known to have socially unacceptable side effects. Whilst the voluntary consumption of dangerous drugs might be conclusive proof of recklessness, no such presumption was justified in the case of non-dangerous drugs. The jury should have been directed to consider whether the defendant had been reckless in consuming the valium, in the sense that he had been aware of the risks associated with its consumption, although not necessarily aware of the risk that he would actually commit aggravated criminal damage.

'Dutch courage'

On the basis of Lord Denning's speech in *Attorney-General for Northern Ireland* v *Gallagher* [1963] AC 349 at 382, a defendant who deliberately gets himself drunk in order to overcome his nerves or inhibitions in committing a specific intent crime, cannot later rely on his intoxicated state at the time of the offence as evidence negativing his mens rea. As his Lordship stated:

> 'The wickedness of his mind before he got drunk is enough to condemn him, coupled with the act which he intended to do and did do.'

The decision can be criticised on the ground that mens rea requires proof of a present intention to commit an offence, as opposed to an intention to commit an offence at some time in the future. If, due to his intoxicated state, the defendant did not have the necessary mens rea for murder at the time of the killing, he should have been afforded the defence of intoxication. Conversely, if the defendant was still acting with the purpose of killing his victim, the defence of intoxication would not have been made out, and the defendant could have been convicted of murder.

Involuntary intoxication

A defendant may seek to raise the defence of intoxication on the basis of his having been forced to ingest intoxicants, or having been deceived into consuming them. If the result is to reduce the defendant to a state of automatism, he should (assuming no prior fault) be able to raise this as a defence to whatever crimes he is alleged to have committed whilst in this state: see 13.1 (above). Where, despite the involuntary or unwitting consumption of intoxicants, the defendant is still aware of his actions, but does not form the necessary intent, he could, in theory, still rely on the defence of intoxication in respect of specific intent crimes, but this might not absolve him from liability completely where the defence operates only to reduce liability to the lesser included basic intent crime. It might be contended that the decision in *Hardie* (above) provides a possible solution, in the sense that where a defendant's intoxication is involuntary he will not have been reckless in consuming the intoxicant, and will thus not have the necessary degree of prior fault for the application of the *Majewski* rule. Notwithstanding the decision of the Court of Appeal in *R* v *Allen* [1988] Crim LR 698, to the effect that the appellant, who consumed a quantity of wine without realising that it had an exceptionally high alcoholic content, could not contend that his resulting intoxication was involuntary, it is submitted that a defendant who honestly, but mistakenly, believes that he is consuming a low, or non-alcoholic drink, should be able to contend that he did not act recklessly in consuming it.

Subject to these observations, the law has, historically, provided little allowance for the victim of involuntary intoxication charged with a basic intent crime, where the effect of involuntary intoxication has been merely to interfere with the defendant's inhibitions, or perception of circumstances and consequences, but not to prevent him from possessing the necessary mens rea for the offence. The leading authority on this issue is now the House of Lords' decision in *R* v *Kingston* [1994] 3 WLR 519. The respondent, a homosexual paedophile who had committed an indecent assault on a 15-year-old boy, claimed that prior to these acts he had been drugged by his co-defendant, and could not recall the incident. There was a difference of medical opinion as to the extent to which the drugs, believed to have been consumed by the respondent, would have affected his ability to recall the incident. However, there was no evidence to suggest that the drugs would have made the respondent do anything he would not have done under normal circumstances. The trial judge ruled that whilst it was not open to the jury to acquit the respondent if they found that his intent to commit the indecent assault had been induced by the surreptitious administration of drugs by his co-defendant, it was open to them to find that secretly administered drugs could negative the respondent's mens rea. The respondent appealed successfully to the Court of Appeal, where it was held that if there was evidence that his inhibitions had been affected by drugs surreptitiously administered by a third party, with the result that he acted upon an intention to commit an act that he might not have had but for the effect of the drugs, he should not bear criminal responsibility for his actions. Lord Taylor CJ expressed the view that the problem was one that could be addressed by turning to first principles. He observed:

> 'The importance of ensuring, under a system of law, that members of the community are safeguarded in their persons and property is obvious and was firmly stated in *DPP* v *Majewski* ... However, the purpose of the criminal law is to inhibit, by proscription and by penal sanction, antisocial acts which individuals may otherwise commit. Its unspoken premise is that people may have tendencies and impulses to do things which are considered sufficiently objectionable to be forbidden. Having paedophiliac inclinations and desires is not proscribed; putting them into practice is. If the sole reason why the threshold between the two has been crossed is or may have been that the inhibition which the law requires has been removed by the clandestine act of a third party, the purposes of the criminal law are not served by nevertheless holding that the person performing the act is guilty of an offence. A man is not responsible for a condition produced "by stratagem, or the fraud of another". If therefore drink or a drug, surreptitiously administered, causes a person to lose his self-control and for that reason to form an intent that he would not otherwise have formed, it is consistent with the principle that the law should exculpate him because the operative fault is not his. The law permits a finding that the intent formed was not a criminal intent or, in other words, that the involuntary intoxication negatives the mens rea.'

Allowing the appeal by the prosecution, the House of Lords treated the case as effectively being one of disinhibition. The drug did not create a desire that had not previously existed, but enabled an existing desire to be released and acted upon. Lord Mustill, with whom the Law Lords agreed, stated that there was no authority for the Court of Appeal's assertion that mens rea was absent where there was no evidence that the respondent was to blame for his intoxicated condition. In his Lordship's view the epithet *rea* in the expression mens rea referred to the criminality of the respondent's act not its moral blameworthiness. More generally, he felt that there would be difficulties in attempting to reconcile the new defence asserted in the court below with the continued rejection at common law of any defence of irresistible impulse, and expressed fears as to the possibility of spurious defences being raised. In his view justice could be achieved by an appropriate line being taken on sentencing, rather than the creation of a novel defence, although he conceded that difficulties could arise in relation to the mandatory sentence for murder.

The Court of Appeal fell into error by suggesting that an intent induced by the surreptitious administration of narcotics is not mens rea. The Lord Chief Justice regarded the situation as analogous to the defence of duress, ie the defendant does in fact have mens rea, but because of certain circumstances shown to exist should be excused from criminal liability. It is submitted that there should be little surprise that the House of Lords has held back from recognising what would effectively be a new defence (described by Glanville Williams in *Archbold News* 28 May 1993 as a form of exculpatory excuse), given that, as put forward by the respondent, it would be a complete answer to any charge (save perhaps offences of absolute liability), would be subjective in nature, and would require considerable expert evidence as to the effect of the narcotics administered and the psychology of the respondent. See chapter 26.6, for further details. See also *R* v *Leslie Davies* [1983] Crim LR 741.

Reform

The Law Commission's current proposals for reform relating to intoxication are to be found in 'Intoxication and Criminal Liability', Consultation Paper No 127.

Broadly, the paper is critical of the existing law, based upon the House of Lords' decision in *DPP* v *Majewski* [1977] AC 443, on the ground that the examination of the intoxicated defendant's culpability should centre around the issue of whether or not he had mens rea. By contrast, under *Majewski*, the law tries to ensure that the jury does not take into account D's voluntary intoxication when assessing fault for basic intent crimes, despite the fact that most defendants who have taken intoxicants are still capable of performing acts requiring a degree of cognition, usually enough to satisfy the minimum requirements for subjective forms of mens rea. More specific criticisms of the *Majewski* approach were:

1. The decision purports to promote a policy of protecting the innocent citizen against the drunkard, but is patchy in its coverage of offences, because the split between specific and basic intent offences is not based on a coherent policy, and not all specific intent offences have a lesser included offence so as to ensure a conviction of D.
2. The inconsistency in the treatment of offences and defences. It was seen as illogical that a jury should consider intoxication in determining whether or not D had the mens rea for murder, but not in relation to whether or not he thought himself to be acting in self-defence. Similarly, in relation to criminal damage – compare the approach taken by the law to a drunken mistake as to the owner's consent regarding the destruction of the property, and a drunken mistake as to ownership.
3. The impossible task handed to the jury in relation to basic intent crimes if required to assess whether or not D had mens rea disregarding evidence relating to his intoxicated state.

The Consultation Paper reviewed the various options for change and rejected the following:

1. The retention or modified codification of *Majewski*, because of its stated shortcomings and complexities.
2. The suggestion of the CLRC contained in its 14th Report (1980) (Cmnd 7884) that the *Majewski* principle be limited to offences that can be committed recklessly; ie that D should still be convicted if he would have been aware of a given risk had he been sober. Also rejected was the American Model Penal Code approach which is closely linked to the CLRC proposals.

3. The suggestion that the law should be amended so as to prevent the defendant from putting forward any evidence of voluntary intoxication to negative an element of an offence, with or without the provision of a statutory defence.

The two favoured options are:

1. Abolition of the *Majewski* principle without replacement.

   Under this scheme there would be no defence of intoxication, simply an investigation into what mens rea, if any, D had. This is currently the position at common law in Australia and New Zealand. The ordinary rules of mens rea would secure the conviction of all but a very small number of offenders. Underlying this approach is the question: why should the existence of evidence of intoxication be held to reduce the burden on the prosecution of proving all the elements of the offence? Research in Australia conducted subsequent to the adoption of such a rule indicates that there has not been a massive increase in acquittals based on intoxication.

2. A new offence of causing harm whilst deliberately intoxicated that could be brought on its own or as an alternative to an existing offence.

   If D were charged with, for example, unlawful wounding, the jury would (assuming proof of the external elements) consider whether or not D had the mens rea for the offence. If proved, D would be convicted of the substantive offence. If fault was not established the jury could consider an alternative verdict in respect of the proposed 'intoxication' offence.

   Liability for the new offence would require proof that D, whilst deliberately intoxicated, committed an act or omission that constituted or caused a listed type of harm. These harms would include homicide, rape, buggery, criminal damage, indecent assault, causing danger to road users, assaults upon constables and certain public order offences. Inchoate offences such as attempt and offences of dishonesty would be excluded from the list.

   The absence of mens rea in relation to the listed harm would be irrelevant, even if this lack of awareness amounted to automatism.

   The term 'intoxicated' in this context would involve proof that D had taken an intoxicant that caused his awareness, understanding or control to be substantially impaired. The requirement of substantial impairment would operate to rule out the coincidental consumption of intoxicants, eg where D commits an offence having consumed one pint of beer at lunchtime.

   Intoxication would be deliberate where D took the intoxicant of his own will, and was aware that the quantity involved would or might cause him to become intoxicated, provided that D had not taken the intoxicant solely for medicinal, sedative, or soporific purposes.

   A consequence of creating such an offence would be that where D would only be permitted to rely on an intoxicated mistake where, viewed objectively, the mistake was one that would have been made by a reasonable person not in a state of intoxication, but otherwise circumstanced as the defendant was.

The report envisages a defendant convicted of the intoxicated harm offence being subject to a lower maximum sentence than would have been the case had he not been intoxicated. As a rough guide the proposal is that the maximum for the intoxicated harm offence should not exceed two-thirds of what could be imposed for the standard offence, subject to a maximum of ten years' imprisonment.

14

Defences II

14.1 Introduction

14.2 Necessity

14.3 Duress and coercion

14.4 Self-defence and the prevention of crime

14.1 Introduction

The defendant who attempts to plead the defence of necessity is, in reality, asking to be excused for acting criminally on the ground that he had no choice but to commit the offence in question. The law distinguishes however between different types of compulsion. In its strict sense, the defence of necessity arises where a defendant is forced by circumstances to transgress the criminal law. Examples might be the prisoner who flees from a blazing prison in order to save his life, or the motorist who swerves onto the wrong side of the road in order to avoid a rampaging bull that is approaching his car. This form of necessity is to be compared with that which arises where threats are made to a defendant by another person, such as where D1 threatens to kill D2's children unless D2 agrees to help him carry out a bank robbery. If D2 does comply with D1's demands, he will claim that he did so because he 'had no choice'. This form of necessity is referred to as duress, or duress per minas (by menaces). Thirdly, there is the situation where D attacks P with a knife threatening to kill him, and P, in order to save his own life, picks up a broken bottle and plunges it into D's face. As with the first two situations considered above, P will claim that he 'had no choice' but to attack D. In this type of situation P would be relying on the defence of self-defence.

In considering the relationship between the three defences, a simple analysis might be that necessity represents the genus, and duress and self-defence are but species of necessity, yet as will be seen below, it is the latter two defences that are more widely recognised in English criminal law, not the former.

14.2 Necessity

The law relating to the availability of necessity is based upon the decision in *R v Dudley and Stephens* (1884) 14 QBD 273. The defendants, a third man, and a cabin boy, were cast adrift in a boat following a shipwreck. They were some 1,600 miles from land, and had endured over a week without food and water. Dudley and Stephens agreed that as the cabin boy was already weak, and looked likely to die soon, they would kill him and live off his flesh and blood for as long as they could, in the hope that they would be rescued before they themselves died of starvation. Dudley carried out the killing and all three surviving crew members ate the boy's flesh. A few days later they were rescued by a passing ship. On returning to England, the defendants were charged with murder, the jury returning a special verdict to the effect that if the defendants had not eaten the boy they would probably have died; that the boy would have died in any event, and that at the time of the killing the defendants had had no reasonable prospect of being rescued; but that there had been no greater reason to take the life of the cabin boy than that of any other member of the crew. The special verdict was referred for consideration by the judges of the Queen's Bench Division, where it was held that the defendants were guilty of murder in killing the cabin boy.

Lord Coleridge CJ, having referred to Hale's assertion (1 Hale PC 54) that a man was not to be acquitted of theft of food on account of his extreme hunger, doubted that the defence of necessity could ever be extended to a defendant who killed another to save his own life. After referring to the Christian doctrine of actually giving up one's own life to save others, rather than taking another's life to save one's own, he referred to the impossibility of choosing between the value of one person's life as against another's:

> 'Who is to be the judge of this sort of necessity? By what measure is the comparative value of lives to be measured? Is it to be strength, or intellect, or what? It is plain that the principle leaves to him who is to profit by it to determine the necessity which will justify him in deliberately taking another's life to save his own. In [the present case] the weakest, the youngest, the most unresisting life was chosen. Was it more necessary to kill him than one of the grown men? The answer be, No ...'

The defendants were sentenced to death, but this was commuted to six months imprisonment.

The basis for the rejection of the defence of necessity in English law seems to rest on a reluctance by the courts to engage in a choice of lesser evils. Thus, if a motorist driving on a mountain road sees a huge boulder rolling towards his car in which there are four small children, and to avoid the certain death of himself and his passengers he deliberately swerves his car to one side, knowing that he will hit and kill an elderly man standing at the roadside, it will not avail him, when charged with murder, to say that he acted to save five lives at the cost of one.

Whilst English law has set its face against any wholesale recognition of necessity as a defence, it has been permitted to operate, under various guises, on a piecemeal basis, both at common law, and under statute.

Common law exceptions

In *R* v *Bourne* [1939] 1 KB 687, the defendant was a gynaecologist who had performed an abortion on a young girl who had been the victim of a group rape. The operation was performed in a public hospital, with the consent of her parents, and without any fee being paid. The defendant was found not guilty of the offence under s58 of the Offences Against the Person Act 1861 (unlawfully procuring a miscarriage), following a direction from the trial judge to the jury that a defendant did not act 'unlawfully' for the purposes of s58, where he acted in good faith, in the exercise of his clinical judgment. Prima facie this appears to provide an exception to the general rule in *R* v *Dudley and Stephens*, but two points should be noted. First, the case does not provide an authority as such, the jury's verdict having no value as a precedent. Secondly, the case did not actually involve a choice between two living persons, but between the prospective life of the foetus and the actual life of the mother.

More recently the courts have begun to show a willingness to allow the defence of necessity, or duress of circumstances as some judges have described it, at least in relation to motoring offences. In *R* v *Willer* (1986) 83 Cr App Rep 225, the appellant had driven recklessly to escape from a crowd of youths who appeared intent upon causing physical harm to the passengers in his car; in *R* v *Conway* [1988] 3 All ER 1025, the appellant had driven recklessly to protect his passenger from what he had honestly believed was an assassination attempt. In both cases the Court of Appeal ruled that the appellants should have been permitted to put the defence of necessity before the jury, given the apparent threat of death or bodily harm created by the circumstances. In *R* v *Conway* the court appeared to reject the extension of the defence to offences such as causing death by reckless driving, but this perhaps only serves to raise other questions, such as whether a defendant who causes grievous bodily harm as a result of his reckless driving would be allowed to rely on necessity.

In both *R* v *Willer*, and *R* v *Conway*, the threat of death or serious harm arose from the unlawful acts of a third party. Is there scope for suggesting that necessity could be allowed where the threat does not arise from an unlawful act? In *R* v *Martin* (1988) 88 Cr App R 343 the appellant drove whilst disqualified following his wife's threats that she would commit suicide if he did not get their son to work on time. In allowing his appeal against conviction the Court of Appeal, following *R* v *Conway*, recognised that a defence of necessity could exist if the accused was acting reasonably and proportionately in order to avoid a threat of death or serious injury. If the court was satisfied that this was the case, the jury should be directed to determine two questions:

1. was the accused, or may he have been, impelled to act as he did because as a result of what he reasonably believed to be the situation he had good cause to fear that otherwise death or serious physical injury would result? If so;
2. might a sober person of reasonable firmness, sharing the characteristics of the accused, have responded to that situation by acting as the accused acted? If yes, the jury should acquit.

Further, the court was willing to contemplate the defence succeeding where an unqualified, or disqualified, driver took over control of a car to get a person who had suffered a heart attack to hospital.

On the basis of these developments in the common law, could it now be the case that the defence of necessity would be open to a motorist driving on a mountain road, who drives recklessly to avoid a boulder rolling down the mountainside towards his car and its occupants? It is noteworthy that the courts have accepted duress of circumstances as a defence to driving with excess alcohol, where the defendant drove away from pursuers threatening violence: see *DPP* v *Bell* [1992] Crim LR 176.

Exceptions created by statute

There are a number of statutory provisions which, whilst not expressly providing a defendant with the right to plead necessity as a defence, do provide statutory defences which are barely distinguishable from it.

Section 5(2)(b) of the Criminal Damage Act 1971

A defendant is to be treated as having a lawful excuse for damaging and destroying another's property, contrary to s1(1) of the Criminal Damage Act 1971, if he does so in order to protect other property belonging to himself, or that of another, in the belief that such action must be taken immediately, and that it constitutes reasonable steps by way of protection of the property. An obvious example of where such a provision might be invoked is provided by the fire fighters dealing with a blaze spreading along a row of terraced houses. The only way to stop the fire spreading, and thus causing further harm, might be to dynamite one house in the terrace which is as yet untouched by the fire, so as to form a gap which it is hoped the fire will not cross. The fire fighters would be 'excused' under s5(2)(b), on the basis that they had honestly chosen between the lesser of two evils, the very basis upon which the defence of necessity was denied to Dudley and Stephens.

Infant Life (Preservation) Act 1929

The 1929 Act creates the offence of 'child destruction', for the details of which see Chapter 5. The proviso to s1(1) states, however, that:

> 'No person shall be found guilty of an offence under this section unless it is proved that the act which caused the death of the child was not done in good faith for the purpose only of preserving the life of the mother.'

Although the defendant in *R* v *Bourne* (above) was not charged under the 1929 Act, this proviso was referred to the jury as an indication as to how it might deal with the question of whether he had acted unlawfully, and it seems reasonable to assume that a defendant in similar circumstances who was charged under the 1929 Act would also succeed in avoiding liability. Again the defendant's justifiable choice between two evils seems to be the basis of the statutory defence.

Note that s1(4) of the Abortion Act 1967 (also considered in Chapter 5), expressly states that a qualified medical practitioner acting alone can lawfully terminate a pregnancy where:

> '... he is of the opinion, formed in good faith, that the termination is immediately *necessary* to save the life or to prevent grave permanent injury to the physical or mental health of the pregnant woman.'

The pragmatic approach

It might be regarded as preferable for Parliament and the courts to develop specific exceptions to the rule against necessity, which can be based upon a coherent public policy, rather than allow individuals to determine the limits of the law for themselves. As has been said of *R* v *Dudley and Stephens*, to allow the defence of necessity in such a case, would have been to licence the strongest member of the crew to eat his way through the others until rescued!

The practical solution perhaps lies in the way in which the discretion to prosecute is exercised. The defendant who swerves his car to avoid a child who runs into the road in front of him, with the result that he drives over a policeman's foot, might have no defence to a charge of assaulting a police office, but to prosecute him in the first place seems unnecessarily harsh. It is a matter of speculation as to how many cases are not prosecuted because of the element of necessity, but to adopt such a policy would at least have the support of some members of the judiciary. Lord Denning, in *Buckoke* v *GLC* [1971] 1 Ch 655, stated obiter that the driver of an emergency service vehicle who drove through a red traffic signal when responding to an emergency call, whilst he would not be able to rely on the defence of necessity, deserved to be congratulated not prosecuted! Similarly, in *R* v *Howe* [1987] 2 WLR 568 at 591, Lord Griffiths, in considering the hardship that might be caused by not permitting the defence of duress to a defendant forced against his will to participate in a murder, commented:

> 'I am not troubled by some of the extreme examples cited in favour of allowing [duress] to those who are not the killer such as a woman motorist being hijacked and forced to act as a getaway driver, or a pedestrian being forced to give misleading information to the police to protect robbery and murder in a shop. The short, practical answer is that it is inconceivable that such persons would be prosecuted; they would be called as the principal witnesses for the prosecution.'

Reform

The Law Commission's report on Offences Against the Person and General Principles (Law Com 218), contains proposals for reforming and codifying the law relating to duress of circumstances, duress by threats, and the use of force in public or private defence. The DCLB, if enacted, would replace the current common law relevant to these defences. The duress of circumstances defence, illustrated in cases such as *R* v *Martin* (above), is limited to what the defendant reasonably believed the danger to be, and is assessed by reference to what a person of reasonable firmness would have done. The commentary on the DCLB recognises that, notwithstanding the codification of this defence, there might still be a common law concept of necessity that was more widely drawn, for example where a defendant simply has to make a difficult choice between two courses of action. His will to resist is not 'overborne' as is the case with duress by threats, but the issue still arises as to whether he should be punished because of the choice he has made: see Smith and Hogan (7th ed pp245–252). To this end, clause 36(2) of the DCLB provides that the defence of duress, whether by threats or of circumstances, is abrogated, but without prejudice to any distinct defence of necessity. It is the Commission's view that a general defence of necessity could be codified if a more detailed and certain common law definition is developed.

Clause 26 of the DCLB proposes the following defence of duress of circumstances:

'(1) No act of a person constitutes an offence if the act is done under duress of circumstances.

(2) A person does an act under duress of circumstance if –

(a) he does it because he knows or believes that it is immediately necessary to avoid death or serious injury to himself or another, and

(b) the danger that he knows or believes to exist is such that in all the circumstances (including any of his personal characteristics that affect its gravity) he cannot reasonably be expected to act otherwise.

It is for the defendant to show that the reason for his act was such knowledge or belief as is mentioned in paragraph (a).

(3) This section applies in relation to omissions as it applies in relation to acts.

(4) This section does not apply to a person who knowingly and without reasonable excuse exposed himself to the danger known or believed to exist.

If the question arises whether a person knowingly and without reasonable excuse exposed himself to that danger, it is for him to show that he did not.

(5) This section does not apply to –

(a) any act done in the knowledge or belief that a threat has been made to cause death or serious injury to himself or another ... or

(b) the use of force within the meaning of [clause 27 or 28] or an act immediately preparatory to the use of force, for the purposes mentioned in [clause 27 or 28].'

Significantly, the proposal envisages a departure from *R* v *Dudley and Stephens*, a move which is inevitable given the Commission's proposals for reforming the law of duress by threats, considered below. Were the case to come before a court following the enactment of clause 26, it would be for the jury to assess the reasonableness of the defendant's action in the circumstances as they believed them to be.

Note that threats to property would not provide a sufficient basis for the defence.

14.3 Duress and coercion

Whereas necessity is characterised by circumstances that cause D to act under duress, whether it be the need to avoid the falling tree, escape from the rapidly spreading fire, or exceeding the speed limit in order to rush an injured child to hospital, duress per minas is characterised by D feeling compelled to commit a particular offence for fear that death or serious injury will be caused by the threatener if he does not comply. Drawing the dividing line between situations that fall within the scope of necessity as opposed to duress may not always be straightforward, however. In *R v Cole* [1994] Crim LR 582 the appellant was convicted of committing a number of robberies at building societies, having unsuccessfully sought to adduce evidence that he had acted under duress, in the sense that he had owed money to money lenders who had threatened him, his girlfriend, and their child with violence if the money was not repaid. Dismissing his appeal, the Court of Appeal held that the defence of duress per minas was only made out where the threatener nominated the crime to be committed by D. In the present case the threatener had indicated that he wanted the appellant to repay the debt, an action that, if carried out, would not necessarily involve the commission of an offence. For the appellant to have relied on the defence of duress of circumstances, as that defence had been developed in cases such as *Martin* (above), there would have to have been a greater degree of directness and immediacy between the danger to the appellant or others and the offence charged. What was required was evidence that the commission of the offence had been a spontaneous reaction to the prospect of death or serious injury.

What does duress involve?

An immediate threat
A defendant wishing to succeed with the defence of duress must provide evidence that he had no reasonable opportunity to avoid having to comply with the demands made upon him. In this sense it is said that the threat that forms the basis of the alleged duress must be immediate. Hence, the bank manager who is told that his wife will be attacked if he does not provide a team of bank robbers with the details of his bank's security system within the next four days, would be unlikely to succeed with the defence of duress, there being at least prima facie evidence that there was a four-day period in which he could have alerted the police. Failure to avail oneself of such protection will not necessarily be fatal to reliance on duress, however. In *R* v

Hudson and Taylor [1971] 2 QB 202, the defendants were two young women who gave perjured evidence during a criminal trial after threats had been made to them as to the harm they would suffer if they told the truth. The defendants were convicted of perjury following the trial judge's direction to the jury that the defence of duress was not available because the threat was not sufficiently immediate. Allowing the appeals, Lord Widgery LJ stated that although the law would only permit the defence of duress where the threat was effective at the moment the crime was committed, the fact that the women could have gone to the police before giving evidence did not mean that as a matter of law the defence was not available. The matter should have been left to the jury with a direction that, whilst it was always open to the Crown to show that the defendants had not availed themselves of some opportunity to neutralise the threats, and that this might negate the immediacy of the threat, regard had to be had to the age and circumstances of the accused.

Of what?

It would appear that the defence of duress must be based on threats to kill or do serious bodily harm: see *R v Hudson and Taylor* (above). In *DPP for Northern Ireland* v *Lynch* [1975] AC 653, Lord Simon stated obiter, that the law would not regard threats to a person's property as a sufficient basis for the defence. Similarly in *R v Valderrama-Vega* [1985] Crim LR 220, threats to reveal the defendant's homosexuality were rejected as insufficiently compelling.

To whom?

Threats to kill or seriously injure the defendant himself will obviously suffice for these purposes. There is authority suggesting that the defence will be available where the threats are made to the defendant's wife and immediate family: see *R v Hurley and Murray* [1967] VR 526. It is submitted that provided the threat is sufficiently immediate and compelling, it should not matter whether it is made to the defendant, his family and friends, or a complete stranger. To ration the availability of the defence depending on the defendant's family or social connection with the person threatened would not only introduce unjustified uncertainty, but would involve an assumption that some lives are more worthy of protection than others, contrary to the dicta in *R v Dudley and Stephens* (above).

The direction to the jury

The model direction to be given to a jury where the defendant has raised the defence of duress, is that laid down by the Court of Appeal in *R v Graham* (1982) 74 Cr App R 235, as subsequently approved by the House of Lords in *R v Howe* (below).

The jury should first consider whether or not the defendant was compelled to act as he did because, on the basis of the circumstances as he honestly and reasonably believed them to be, he thought his life was in immediate danger. If the jury concludes that this was not the case, then the defence falls at this stage. If, however, they are of the opinion that the defendant has satisfied this first subjective test, they should then consider the second, more objective test; would a sober person of reasonable firmness sharing the defendant's characteristics have responded in the same way to the threats? The jury should be directed to disregard any evidence of the defendant's intoxicated state when assessing whether he acted under duress, although he may be permitted to raise intoxication as a separate defence in its own right.

The extent to which other factors personal to D may amount to 'characteristics' for the purposes of this test has been considered on a number of occasions by the Court of Appeal. In *R v Hegarty* [1994] Crim LR 353, the appellant's conviction for robbery was upheld following the trial judge's refusal to admit evidence from two medical witnesses to the effect that the appellant suffered from a 'grossly elevated neurotic state', was emotionally unstable and thus more likely to accede to threats. Referring to the two-stage test for duress established in *Graham* (above), the Court of Appeal held that the evidence of some serious personality disorder might be relevant to explain why the accused had acceded to the threats, but the evidence in the instant case did not go that far. The court went on to express the view that it was very doubtful whether characteristics such as those advanced by the appellant could be attributed to the 'sober person of reasonable firmness' when assessing the second (objective) stage of the *Graham* test, as there was an inherent contradiction between the assumptions made about the reasonable person and the personality of the accused.

The similarities with the defence of provocation are readily apparent. Where, as regards the test for provocation, the reasonable man is presumed to be even tempered, and hence evidence of irascibility is irrelevant, so with duress per minas (where the reasonable person is of normal fortitude) evidence that D is susceptible to threats is irrelevant. For further confirmation see *R v Horne* [1994] Crim LR 584 (chapter 26, section 26.7). If it were otherwise the objective test would be largely otiose. See further *R v Emery* (1993) 14 Cr App R (S) 394.

Availability of duress

Duress is considered to be a general defence in criminal law, but there are a number of offences in relation to which it cannot be raised as a defence. On the basis of the Privy Council decision in *Abbott v R* [1977] AC 755, duress was not available to a defendant charged with murder as principal, but on the basis of the House of Lords' decision in *DPP for Northern Ireland v Lynch* [1975] AC 653, duress was available to a defendant charged as an accomplice to murder. The matter is now governed by the House of Lords' decision in *R v Howe* [1987] 2 WLR 568, in which it was held (overruling *DPP for Northern Ireland v Lynch*) that duress would not be available to a defendant who committed murder either as principal or accomplice. Lord Hailsham expressed the view, which was shared by his fellow judges, that to permit a defendant to kill an innocent person because of the threats that had been made to his own life, would involve the House in overruling *R v Dudley and Stephens*, which it was not prepared to do.

The removal of the plainly illogical distinction between principals and accomplices to murder as regards the availability of duress is clearly to be welcomed, but the decision does bring within its wake a number of other anomalies. Duress is still available to a defendant charged with grievous bodily harm contrary to s18 of the Offences Against the Person Act 1861. Such a defendant may have acted with sufficient mens rea for murder, yet if he succeeds with the defence of duress he will be completely acquitted. The difference between the victim living or dying could depend on a whole range of arbitrary factors beyond the control of the defendant, such as the speed with which medical assistance can be summoned, or the availability of a particular blood type for transfusion.

The House of Lords appeared unsure as to whether duress would be available on a charge of attempted murder, but the matter has since been considered by the House of Lords in *R v Gotts* [1992] 2 AC 412. In upholding the trial judge's ruling a majority of their Lordships (Lord Keith and Lowry dissenting) held that there was little or no justification for allowing to a defendant charged with attempted murder a defence not available to one charged with the completed crime. The mens rea required for attempted murder was a more culpable state of mind than that required for the completed crime. In most cases, whether the victim lived or died was dependent on arbitrary factors beyond the control of the accused. Despite this ruling, it would appear that duress remains a defence to a defendant charged with wounding with intent contrary to s18 of the 1861 Act, despite the parity of mens rea with the completed offence of murder. By this decision the House of Lords is arguably extending criminal liability in a manner best suited to Parliament: see, in particular, obiter comments by Lord Lowry on this issue (pp439–41).

The decision does not directly address the issue of the availability of duress to a defendant charged with conspiracy to murder, or incitement to commit murder, but the Court of Appeal ([1991] 2 WLR 878) implied that a legitimate distinction could be drawn between the various inchoate forms of liability, in that conspiracy and incitement would be likely to occur at some distance from the completed offence. It is submitted that in such cases, even if the defence of duress is permitted in theory, it may not be established on the facts if there is evidence that the defendant had an opportunity to contact the police and alert them as to the threat that had been made to him.

Criminal association voluntarily joined

In *R v Fitzpatrick* [1977] NI 20, the defendant, who had voluntarily joined the IRA, tried to raise the defence of duress to a charge of robbery. He claimed that he had committed the offence following threats that had been made to him by other IRA members if he did not take part. The appeal court held that the trial judge had been correct in withdrawing the defence of duress from the jury. As a matter of public policy the defence could not be made available to those who voluntarily joined violent criminal associations, and then found themselves forced to commit offences by their fellow criminals. To do so would positively encourage terrorist acts, in that the actual perpetrators could escape liability on the ground of duress, and further, it would result in a situation where the more violent and terrifying the criminal gang the defendant chose to join, the more compelling would be his evidence of the duress under which he had committed the offences charged.

Whilst the above was only a persuasive authority in English law, it has now been endorsed by the Court of Appeal in *R v Sharp* [1987] Crim LR 566, a decision which makes it clear that this is not a principle limited to cases involving terrorist organisations. Where, however, the defendant cannot have been expected to foresee that he would be forced to commit offences by his criminal associates, more recent authority suggests that he may still be permitted to raise the defence of duress: see *R v Shepard* [1987] Crim LR 686.

Superior orders

In English criminal law the absence of any general defence of superior orders means that D cannot rely on the fact that his commission of an offence resulted from his carrying out the instructions of his employer, a police officer, or military officer of higher rank. The authorities may decide not to prosecute in such cases, but that is a matter of administrative justice, rather than substantive law. It is conceivable that one acting under superior orders might be induced to make a genuine mistake of civil law, such as a claim of right, that might negative the mens rea of an offence, but any acquittal would result from the absence of fault, not a substantive defence. In *Yip Chiu-Cheung v R* [1994] 3 WLR 514, Lord Griffith's, denying the existence of a defence based upon superior orders at common law, cited with approval the dictum of Gibbs CJ in the Australian case of *A v Hayden (No 2)* (1984) 156 CLR 552, to the effect that:

> 'It is fundamental to our legal system that the executive has no power to authorise a breach of the law and that it is no excuse for an offender to say that he acted under the orders of a superior officer.'

Lord Griffiths was of the view that this statement was of equal validity as regards the laws of Hong Kong and England. See chapter 26, section 26.6, for further details.

Coercion

At common law a wife was permitted to raise the defence of marital coercion in respect of some crimes committed in the presence of her husband. The presumption was that she had acted under the orders of her husband. Although that presumption was abolished by s47 of the Criminal Justice Act 1925, the defence is still available. On the basis of *R* v *Richman* [1982] Crim LR 507, it would seem that coercion might actually be wider in its scope than duress, in that it encompasses moral pressure as well as threats of physical harm from the husband. Nevertheless, for all practical purposes, it is assumed that duress has effectively replaced coercion as a general defence.

Reform

The proposals contained in the DCLB relating to duress by threats are based upon clause 42 of the draft code, although the matter has been under consideration by the Law Commission since 1974 (Working Paper No 55). The Commission proposes that duress by threats should remain as a 'true' defence, ie not a factor that simply mitigates punishment, should relieve the defendant of all liability (ie not reduce murder to manslaughter), and that the defendant should be required to establish duress on the balance of probabilities. The codified defence would have as its guiding principle 'the reasonable reaction of the defendant in the circumstances as he or she believed them to be'. (Law Com 218 para 29.7). The proposal does not specify to whom the threats must be made, but the closer the connection between the defendant and the person threatened, the greater the evidence of compulsion to act.

Clause 25 of the DCLB provides:

'(1) No act of a person constitutes an offence if the act is done under duress by threats.
(2) A person does an act under duress by threats if he does it because he knows or believes –
(a) that a threat has been made to cause death or serious injury to himself or another if the act is not done, and
(b) that the threat will be carried out immediately if he does not do the act or, if not immediately, before he or that other can obtain official protection; and
(c) that there is no other way of preventing the threat being carried out,
and the threat is one which in all the circumstances (including any of his personal circumstances that affect its gravity) he cannot reasonably be expected to resist.
It is for the defendant to show that the reasons for his act was such knowledge or belief as is mentioned in paragraphs (a) to (c).
(3) This section applied in relation to omissions as it applies in relation to acts.
(4) This section does not apply to a person who knowingly and without reasonable excuse exposed himself to the risk of the threat made or believed to have been made.
If the question arises whether a person knowingly and without reasonable excuse exposed himself to such a risk, it is for him to show that he did not.'

As to the state of mind of a defendant seeking to bring himself within the scope of the restated defence, the Code Report commentary on what was clause 42 of the draft code provides this explanation:

'The emphasis in ... [what is now clause 25(2 of the DCLB] on the actor's knowledge or belief reflects the fact that a defence of duress depends essentially upon a state of mind. In this respect the clause somewhat departs from the prevailing judicial view, according to which a person's belief in the existence of a threat must be "reasonably" held if it is to found the defence. This requirement would, we believe, be inconsistent with the tendency of judicial developments in other contexts [See especially in the context of defences: *Gladstone Williams* (1983) 78 Cr App R 276; *Beckford* v *The Queen* [1988] AC 130]. It would also be at odds with the general policy of the Code, in keeping with those developments, of assigning the reasonableness of a person's asserted belief to the domain of evidence.' [Vol II para 12.15]

The Commission remains convinced that the defence of duress should reflect the subjectivist approach to defences (Law Com No 218 paras. 29.8–29.10).

The Commission has re-affirmed its view that a person's 'firmness', is itself one of his characteristics that may affect the gravity of the threat to him, and remains unconvinced that personal characteristics can be separated in the way that the *Graham* test suggests (Law Com No 218 paras 29.11–29.14).

The most significant departure from the common law signalled by clause 25 is the availability of duress by threats where the defendant is charged with murder. Enactment of the clause would clearly nullify the effect of *Abbott* v *R*, *R* v *Howe*, and *R* v *Gotts*.

The Commission was aware of the cogent arguments against such a change, namely that the State should not sanction deliberate killing, and that the defence might be used in terrorist or organised crime cases, but felt that the counter-arguments out weighed these objections. In particular the Commission felt that:

1. the defendant's failure to attain an heroic level of behaviour should not justify punishment by the state;
2. the simple moral equation derived from *Dudley and Stephens* broke down where the defendant sought to avoid the implementation of threats to a third party, eg where D threatens to kill X unless Z kills Y. In such cases Z is not taking a life in order to preserve his own, but is being forced to chose between the lives of others;
3. fairness to the defendant who kills under duress by threats could not be achieved by executive discretion regarding the decision to prosecute;
4. the defence should not be denied to the innocent simply because terrorists might seek to rely on it.

14.4 Self-defence and the prevention of crime

At common law the defence of self-defence operates in three spheres. First it permits a defendant to use reasonable force to defend himself from an attack. Secondly it permits a defendant to use reasonable force to prevent an attack on another person; for example, *R* v *Rose* (1884) 15 Cox CC 540, where the defendant, who had shot dead his father whilst the latter was launching a murderous attack on the defendant's mother, was acquitted of murder on the grounds of self-defence. See also *R* v *Duffy* [1967] 1 QB 63. Thirdly, a defendant can use reasonable force to defend his property. In *Attorney-General's Reference (No 2 of 1983)* [1984] 2 WLR 465, the Court of Appeal held that the defendant's possession of petrol bombs would not be an offence where it was for a lawful object, and that lawful object could be the defence of his shop from attacks by rioters during civil disturbances.

In addition to the common law defences s3(1) of the Criminal Law Act 1967 provides that:

'A person may use such force as is reasonable in the circumstances in the prevention of crime, or in effecting or assisting in the lawful arrest of offenders or suspected offenders or of persons unlawfully at large.'

It will be seen at once that there is a very large area of overlap between the common law defence of self-defence and the statutory defence under s3(1) of the 1967 Act. A defendant who strikes a would-be assailant over the head with a chair in order to prevent a serious physical attack could contend at common law that he had used reasonable force to defend himself. Equally it would be open to him to claim that the reasonable force was used in order to prevent a serious offence being committed, namely grievous bodily harm upon himself. Similarly, the defendant who beats off a robber who is attacking an elderly woman, or the householder who strikes the graffiti 'artist' about to daub the side of his house. In both cases the defendant may be using reasonable force to defend another, or to defend his property, and in both cases the defendant could contend that he has used reasonable force to prevent the commission of an offence.

The relationship between the common law and statutory defences

To some extent it seems odd that such similar defences should exist under statute and common law, yet Parliament, in enacting the 1967 Act, refrained from abolishing the common law defence of self-defence. Instead s3(2) of the Act provides:

'Subsection (1) ... shall replace the rules of the common law on the question of when force used for a purpose mentioned in the subsection is justified by that purpose.'

The result is that reasonable force can be used under s3(1) to prevent the commission of an offence, in circumstances where it would not have been permissible under the common law, eg to prevent an act of gross indecency, or the supply of a controlled drug. See also *Devlin* v *Armstrong* [1971] NI 13.

In practice it would seem that a defendant can raise the common law defence in parallel with the statutory defence. In *R* v *Cousins* [1982] 2 All ER 115 at 117, Milmo J stated:

'... in criminal proceedings the common law recognises that it is lawful for a person to use reasonable means for self-defence. Consequently it can amount to a lawful excuse for a threat to kill if the threat is made for the prevention of crime or for self-defence, provided it is reasonable in the circumstances to make such a threat. What is reasonable in the circumstances is always a question for the jury, never a "point of law" for the judge.'

Both defences centre around the question of whether or not the defendant's actions were reasonable in the circumstances, and since the passing of the 1967 Act, it seems unlikely that action which is considered reasonable for the purposes of one defence should not also be regarded as reasonable for the other.

The concept of reasonable force

In *Palmer* v *R* [1971] AC 814, Lord Morris described self-defence as a 'straightforward conception' needing only common sense for its understanding. In assessing whether a defendant had used only reasonable force, his Lordship felt that a jury should be directed to look at the particular facts and circumstances of the case. The test to be applied was essentially an objective one, ie whether a reasonable person would have acted as the defendant had. The jury should, however, be directed to take into account the pressure under which the defendant may have acted. As his Lordship stated:

'If there has been an attack so that the defence is reasonably necessary, it will be recognised that a person defending himself cannot weigh to a nicety the exact measure of his necessary defensive action. If a jury thought that in a moment of unexpected anguish a person attacked had only done what he honestly and instinctively thought was necessary that would be most potent evidence that only reasonable defensive action had been taken.'

Whilst this direction has been cited with approval on a number of occasions, reference to the pressure under which the defendant might have acted is only required, where the circumstances of the case warrant it: see *R* v *Whyte* [1987] 3 All ER 416, and *R* v *Ferrari* [1992] Crim LR 747.

Duty to retreat?

It will be very compelling evidence in support of a defence of self-defence that the defendant retreated as far as he possibly could from the source of an attack before taking steps to defend himself, but there is no rule of law that he should have taken all possible evasive action. It is clear that since the passing of the 1967 Act, the question is now simply one of reasonableness. In *R* v *McInnes* (1971) 55 Cr App R 551, Edmund Davies LJ suggested that the reasonableness of a defendant's actions might be looked at in the light of his willingness to 'disengage and temporise', ie calm the situation down, rather than pick a fight with his assailant. It is, therefore, a matter for the jury to decide as to whether the defendant acted reasonably in standing his ground to defend himself, or whether the reasonable man would have taken the opportunity to run away.

Proportionality

As with the so-called duty to retreat, there is no rule of law that a defendant's actions by way of self-defence must be commensurate with the gravity of the danger he faces, but it is clear from the above that the less serious the threat, the less force the jury will consider as having been justifiable by way of self-defence. In the light of this it seems that some older authorities, such as *R* v *Hussey* (1924) 18 Cr App R 160, which suggest that a defendant might be justified in killing a person who sought to unlawfully dispossess him of his property, should now be regarded as too extreme.

In *R* v *Bullerton* ((1992) CA 163/92 unreported), the appellant had received nuisance calls from one F, in which F had made indecent suggestions to the appellant regarding farmyard animals. During one of these calls the appellant activated a 'screech box' which emitted a high pitched tone down the telephone line. F suffered from severe tinnitus as a result, and the appellant was charged under s20 of the 1861 Act. The Court of Appeal took the view that the appellant had not been entitled to use physical force to prevent the psychological harm caused by the obscene calls, on the basis that 'like had to be met with like'. Interestingly, however, the appeal was allowed, on the basis that the appellant's alternative contention, that he acted to defend his property, was not properly put to the jury at his trial. The appellant was a self-employed relief worker, and although the nuisance calls could be stopped if he changed his telephone number, there was a risk that he would suffer a loss of income from so doing. The court was willing to recognise the telephone number as a form of property requiring protection, and it was possible that his actions may have been seen by the jury as reasonable steps to protect it.

It is possible that a defendant might mistakenly believe himself to be threatened, or might mistakenly believe that an offence is being committed by another person. If in fact there is no threat, or no offence, no amount of force used by the defendant would be justifiable. On the basis of *R* v *Williams* (*Gladstone*) (1983) 78 Cr App R 276, and *Beckford* v *R* [1987] 3 WLR 611 (both considered in Chapter 15), it would appear that such a defendant would be entitled to be judged on the facts as he honestly believed them to be, and hence would be permitted to use a degree of force that was reasonable in the context of what he perceived to be happening.

What if the defendant rightly perceives that the use of some force is justified, but is mistaken as to the amount of force needed to deal with the situation? If a strictly objective approach is taken, the defendant's mistake will be irrelevant, he will only be permitted to use such force as was in fact reasonably necessary. The Court of Appeal's decision in *R* v *Scarlett* [1994] 4 All ER 629, however, suggests that some account may be taken of the circumstances as D perceived them to be. The case involved an appellant who had forcibly removed the deceased, a customer, from his public house when he refused to leave after closing time. The appellant pushed him out through the door with the result that the deceased tripped on some steps and suffered fatal head injuries. The jury convicted the appellant of manslaughter following a trial judge's direction to the effect that they could do so if they were satisfied that the appellant had used excessive force in ejecting the deceased. Allowing the appeal, the Court of Appeal held that, since the appellant would have been allowed to rely on an honest but mistaken belief that the use of force was necessary, where for example he mistakenly believed himself to be being attacked, he should also be allowed to rely on an honest mistake as to the amount of force necessary in the circumstances as he believed them to be. It was the view of Beldam J that there was 'no logical basis' for distinguishing between the type of mistake considered in *R* v *Gladstone Williams* and *Beckford* v *R*, and the mistake under consideration in the present case. In his view the jury:

'... ought not to convict ... unless they are satisfied that the degree of force used was plainly more than was called for by the circumstances as [the defendant] believed them to be and, provided he believed that the circumstances called for the degree of force used, he was not to be convicted even if his belief was unreasonable.'

Effect of the defence

Both the common law and statutory defences can be raised in respect of any crime with which the defendant is charged, and if successful, will result in the defendant being completely acquitted. It is thus possible for a defendant to murder his assailant and escape liability, provided his actions were reasonable by way of self-defence. Prima facie this seems at odds with the rationale of *R v Dudley and Stephens* (above), as approved by the House of Lords in *R v Howe* (above), to the effect that the law should not permit one man to value his own life above that of another. The defendant who kills his assailant rather than suffer death himself is clearly choosing to save his own life in preference to that of his assailant, but the vital distinction is that in the necessity and duress situations, the victim is 'innocent', whereas in the self-defence situation the assailant is a 'non-innocent' victim whose death is largely caused by his own wrong-doing.

Note that even where the defence fails, a defendant charged with murder may still be able to rely on the defence of provocation, using the evidence that he acted to defend himself in support of this alternative defence: see *R v McInnes* (above).

Reform

Clause 27 of the DCLB provides:

'(1) The use of force by a person for any of the following purposes, if only such as is reasonable in the circumstances as he believes them to be, does not constitute an offence –
(a) to protect himself or another from injury, assault or detention caused by a criminal act;
(b) to protect himself or (with the authority of that other) another from trespass to the person;
(c) to protect his property from appropriation, destruction or damage caused by a criminal act or from trespass or infringement;
(d) to protect property belonging to another from appropriation, destruction or damage caused by a criminal act or (with the authority of the other) from trespass or infringement; or
(e) to prevent a crime or a breach of the peace.
(2) The expressions "use of force" and "property" in subsection (1) are defined and extended by sections 29 and 30 respectively.
(3) For the purposes of this section, an act involves a "crime" or is "criminal" although the person committing it, if charged with an offence in respect of it, would be acquitted on the ground that –
(a) he was under ten years of age, or
(b) he acted under duress, whether by threats or of circumstances, or
(c) his act was involuntary, or
(d) he was in a state of intoxication, or
(e) he was insane, so as not to be responsible, according to law, for his act.

(4) The references in subsection (1) to protecting a person or property from anything include protecting him or it from its continuing; and the reference to preventing crime or a breach of the peace shall be similarly construed.

(5) For the purposes of this section the question whether the act against which force is used is of a kind mentioned in any of paragraphs (a) to (e) of subsection (1) shall be determined according to the circumstances as the person using the force ("D") believes them to be.

In the following provisions of this section references to unlawful or lawful acts are to acts which are or are not of such a kind

(6) Where an act is lawful by reason only of a belief or suspicion which is mistaken, the defence provided by this section applies as in the case of an unlawful act, unless –

(a) D knows or believes that the force is used against a constable or a person assisting a constable; and

(b) the constable is acting in the execution of his duty,

in which case the defence applies only if D believes the force to be immediately necessary to prevent injury to himself or another.

(7) The defence provided by this section does not apply to a person who causes conduct or a state of affairs with a view to using force to resist or terminate it.

But the defence may apply although the occasion for the use of force arises only because he does something he may lawfully do, knowing that such an occasion may arise.'

In addition clause 28 provides:

'(1) The use of force by a person in effecting or assisting in a lawful arrest, if only such as is reasonable in the circumstances as he believes them to be, does not constitute an offence.

(2) The expression "use of force" in subsection (1) is defined and extended by section 29.

(3) For the purposes of this section the question whether the arrest is lawful shall be determined according to the circumstances as the person using the force believed them to be.'

The use of force is defined by clause 29 which provides:

'(1) For the purposes of sections 27 and 28 –

(a) a person uses force in relation to another person or property not only where he applies force to, but also where he causes an impact on, the body of that person or that property;

(b) a person shall be treated as using force in relation to another person if –

(i) he threatens him with its use, or

(ii) he detains him without actually using it; and

(c) a person shall be treated as using force in relation to property if he threatens a person with its use in relation to property.'

The clause goes on to provide that its provisions apply equally to acts immediately preparatory to the use of force, and states that a threat of force may be reasonable although the actual use of force would not be. The possibility of retreat prior to the use of force is a factor to be taken into account when determining whether the use of force was reasonable. Clause 30 defines property, for the purposes of the defence, in terms similar to those used in s10 of the Criminal Damage Act 1971.

15

Defences III

15.1 Mistake

15.2 Infancy

15.1 Mistake

To talk of mistake in terms of it being a substantive defence in criminal law is somewhat misleading, as a defendant who seeks to rely on a mistake of fact or law by way of defence, is in truth denying that he had the mens rea for the crime with which he is charged. Thus where D fires a gun at P, causing his death, and D claims that he honestly believed he was firing at a wax figure, D might be said to have the defence of mistake, but in reality his 'defence' will simply be a denial of mens rea; he intended to damage a wax figure, not to kill a human being.

Mistake can be raised by a defendant to any charge provided the offence is one requiring some degree of fault on his part. Whilst there is always an evidential burden on the defendant to put evidence before the jury that he did actually make the mistake upon which he relies, the legal burden always rests with the Crown to establish beyond reasonable doubt that the defendant was not mistaken and therefore did have the requisite mens rea for the offence with which he is charged. As is the case in any trial where the prosecution fails to establish mens rea, if the defendant succeeds with his 'defence' of mistake he must be acquitted.

Mistake of law

It might be assumed that, since ignorance of the law is not supposed to provide a defence, there can be no scope for the operation of a defence based on mistake of law. As will be seen below, however, there are a limited number of situations where it can operate to prevent the imposition of criminal liability.

Mistake of criminal law

A defendant who murders a victim is not normally permitted to raise by way of defence the contention that he mistakenly thought homicide to be lawful, but where his ignorance of the law's restraints arises from a disease of the mind that manifests itself in violence and is likely to recur, such a defence could operate so as to relieve him of liability for murder. The defendant would not, however, be regarded as raising the defence of mistake as such, but the defence of insanity: see *M'Naghten's Case* (1843) 10 C & F 200 and Chapter 13.

Similarly a six-year-old child might take sweets from a shop counter in blissful ignorance of the law of theft. His defence to a charge of theft would not be one of mistake, however, but one of infancy: see 15.2 below.

Mistake of civil law

By way of contrast to mistake of criminal law, mistake of civil law can provide a defence to a criminal charge, in that it might lead D to rely on a claim of right. In *R v Smith* [1974] QB 354 the defendant's conviction for criminal damage was quashed by the Court of Appeal, because he had honestly (although as a matter of civil law incorrectly) thought that the fittings he had removed from his rented flat belonged in law to him and not his landlord. As stated above, however, this decision does little more than state the obvious, the defendant did not have the intention to damage property belonging to another, only that which he honestly believed was his. Similarly, under s2(1)(a) of the Theft Act 1968, a defendant is not to be regarded as dishonest for the purposes of theft when he takes property in the honest belief that he has the right in law to do so. The result might be that where D enters into a contract to purchase goods from P under which property in the goods is not to pass to D until two weeks' later, but D, misconstruing the contract, honestly believes he has an immediate right to deal in the goods, D could rely on his honest mistake of contract law as evidence that he honestly believed he had the right in law to treat the goods as his own.

Mistake of fact

The extent to which mistake of fact will be permitted to operate as a denial of mens rea rather depends upon the nature of the offence with which the defendant is charged. If it is an offence of absolute liability, a defence such as mistake, which is simply a denial of mens rea, will not avail the defendant. Where however some mens rea is required, there will normally be some correlation between the type of mens rea that has to be proved and the type of mistake that will successfully negative evidence of mens rea.

Strict liability offences

A statute creating criminal liability may be silent as to the mens rea that must be proved for liability, but the courts will nevertheless presume that some fault must be established on the part of the defendant, unless there is evidence to rebut the assumption (see Chapter 25). Hence there is scope for the operation of a defence of mistake in relation to such offences, although in a somewhat limited form.

In *R v Tolson* (1889) 23 QBD 168, the defendant's husband left her in 1881 and she heard nothing of him for the next five years. In 1887, wrongly believing her husband to have drowned at sea, the defendant remarried. When her husband returned the defendant was charged with bigamy, contrary to s58 of the Offences Against the Person Act 1861 which was silent as to the mens rea that had to be established. On appeal against her conviction, it was held, by a majority, that she should be acquitted. Her honest and reasonable belief that she was a widow provided a good defence, or as it might be expressed, she was permitted to rely on a mistake that a reasonable woman would have made in the circumstances. In the course of submissions made on behalf of the appellants in *DPP* v *Morgan* (below) the House of Lords was invited to reconsider the status of this decision, but the majority felt that it remained unaffected by the outcome of the appeal before them. Lord Hailsham expressed the view that it was something of a special case in that it was, 'a narrow decision based on the construction of a statute'. Lord Fraser adopted the view that the approach of the court in *R* v *Tolson* was one peculiar to statutory offences which were 'absolute' in nature (ie contained no express requirement of mens rea).

It follows, therefore, that a defendant would not be guilty of bigamy, if he honestly and reasonably believed his first marriage to have been void, annulled, or dissolved: see further *R* v *Gould* [1968] 2 QB 65, and Chapter 25.

Offences requiring proof of fault

If a defendant is charged with an offence, the definition of which expressly requires proof of mens rea, then the principles enunciated by the majority in *DPP* v *Morgan* [1976] AC 182 apply to the operation of mistake as a denial of mens rea.

The defendants had been convicted of rape, despite their contentions that they had believed the victim to have been consenting to sexual intercourse. They appealed against the trial judge's direction that a defendant's mistake as to a woman's consent would only provide a defence if it was both honest and reasonable. The Court of Appeal dismissed the appeal, but the House of Lords, by a majority of three to two, held that a defendant was to be judged on the facts as he honestly believed them to be, and thus a mistake of fact would afford a defence no matter how unreasonable it might be, provided it was honestly made. The rationale behind the majority view is illustrated by a passage in the speech of Lord Hailsham where he states:

> 'I believe that "mens rea" means "guilty or criminal mind", and if it be the case, as seems to be accepted here that [the] mental element in rape is ... intent, to insist that a belief [in the consent of the victim] must be reasonable to excuse is to insist that either the accused is to be found guilty of intending to do that which in truth he did not intend to do, or that his state of mind, though innocent of evil intent, can convict him if it be honest but not rational ...'

This does not, of course, give a defendant carte blanche to raise quite spurious defences based on supposed mistakes of fact. An important controlling factor is the part played by the jury. The more unreasonable the mistake a defendant claims to have made, the less likely the jury are to believe that it was honestly made.

Mistake relating to other defences

Whilst the House of Lords in *DPP* v *Morgan* was concerned with the defendant who makes a mistake as to an element of an offence, the question arises as to how the courts should deal with a defendant who makes a mistake about a factor which is external to the definition of the crime, such as the existence of justificatory or exculpatory circumstances. In *R* v *Williams (Gladstone)* (1983) 78 Cr App R 276, a man named Mason had seen a youth trying to rob a woman in the street, and had chased him, eventually knocking him to the ground. The appellant, who had not witnessed the robbery, then came on the scene and was told by Mason that he was a police officer (which was untrue). When Mason failed to produce a warrant card a struggle ensued, the appellant being charged with an offence under s47 of the Offences Against the Person Act 1861. At his trial he claimed that he had mistakenly believed that Mason was unlawfully assaulting the youth and had intervened to prevent any further harm, but was convicted following the trial judge's direction to the jury that his mistake could only afford a defence if it was both honest and reasonable. The Court of Appeal held that *DPP* v *Morgan* should be followed in such cases, and quashed the conviction on the basis that the jury should have been directed to consider the facts as the appellant believed them to be, no matter how unreasonable his belief might have been. One might question the extent to which the Court of Appeal was justified in taking a doctrine developed to deal with mistake as to an element of an offence and applying it without modification to mistakes relating to the availability of defences, but the decision was subsequently approved by the Privy Council in *Beckford* v *R* [1987] 3 WLR 611, where the defendant police officer who had shot dead a suspect, having been told that he was armed and dangerous, was held to be entitled to be judged on the facts as he honestly perceived them to be. Lord Griffiths (having referred to *R* v *Morgan*) observed:

> 'There may be a fear that the abandonment of the objective standard demanded by the existence of reasonable grounds for belief will result in the success of too many spurious claims of self-defence. The English experience has not shown this to be the case. The ... model direction on self-defence which is now widely used by judges when summing up to juries contains the following guidance:
> "Whether the plea is self-defence or defence of another, if the defendant may have been labouring under a mistake as to the facts, he must be judged according to his mistaken belief of the facts: that is so whether the mistake was, on an objective view, a reasonable mistake or not." '

Even though the test for mistaken belief is subjective there must still be adequate evidence of such a belief for the matter to be left before the jury. Where the defendant's explanations are too fanciful to be seriously considered the trial judge may decline to direct the jury on the matter: see *R* v *Oatridge* [1992] Crim LR 205. In extreme cases it may be that the defendant's evidence of mistaken belief indicates the possibility of insanity, an issue that the prosecution would be entitled to raise since the defendant would have put his state of mind in question. The rationale of

Beckford v *R* and *R* v *Williams (Gladstone)*, has since been applied to the defendant who makes a genuine mistake as to the amount of force necessitated by the circumstances: see *R* v *Scarlett* [1994] 4 All ER 629, although note that the court there was concerned with a situation where, judged objectively, *some* force was justified.

In the light of these decisions, it would be logical that a defendant who makes an honest mistake of fact, as a result of which he is provoked to kill, or acts under what he believes to be duress by threats or duress of circumstances, should be permitted to raise those defences.

Drunken mistake

Where a defendant's mistake of fact arises from his self-induced intoxication, it will only provide a (partial) defence to a crime of specific intent, or possibly a defence to a crime of basic intent where the intoxication arises from the consumption of non-dangerous drugs: see Chapter 13. In general, where a defendant is charged with a basic intent crime, the jury will be directed that evidence of self-induced intoxication is irrelevant to the question of what the defendant believed to be happening. Inevitably this results in the jury having to indulge in some rather artificial mental exercises, as the intoxication may be only too relevant to the commission of the offence. In *R* v *Woods* (1981) 74 Cr App Rep 312, the appellant sought unsuccessfully to appeal against his conviction for rape, following the trial judge's direction to the jury to the effect that self-induced intoxication afforded no defence to the allegation that he was reckless as to whether the complainant consented to sexual intercourse. Despite the fact that s1(2) of the Sexual Offences (Amendment) Act 1976 provides that the jury at a trial for rape has to consider all relevant matters in deciding whether a man believed that a woman was consenting to sexual intercourse, the Court of Appeal held that evidence of self-induced intoxication was to be ignored because it was not relevant evidence. Observing that prior to the enactment of the 1976 Act self-induced intoxication had not been recognised as a defence to rape, Griffiths J continued:

'If Parliament had intended to provide in future that a man whose lust was so inflamed by drink that he ravished a woman, should nevertheless be able to pray in aid his drunken state to avoid the consequences we would have expected them to have used the clearest words to excess such a surprising result which we believe would be utterly repugnant to the great majority of people. We are satisfied that Parliament had no such intention and that this is clear from the use of the word "relevant" [which means] ... in this context, legally relevant. The law, as a matter of social policy, has declared that self-induced intoxication is not a legally relevant matter to be taken into account in deciding as to whether or not a woman consents to intercourse. Accordingly, the appellant's drunkenness was not a matter that the jury were entitled to take into consideration in deciding whether or not reasonable grounds existed for the appellant's belief that the woman consented to intercourse.'

The decision prompts the conclusion that the jury must, therefore determine the issue by asking whether or not the defendant would have made the mistake in question even if he had been sober, presumably only acquitting if the prosecution fail to disprove this beyond all reasonable doubt. The *Woods* line of reasoning has since been applied to a defendant who drunkenly mistook a woman for his wife and proceeded to have sexual intercourse with her: see *R* v *Fotheringham* [1988] Crim LR 846.

It would appear that evidence of self-induced intoxication is also irrelevant as regards a defendant's honest belief as to the availability of a common law defence, such as self-defence. In *R* v *O'Grady* [1987] 3 WLR 321, the appellant had spent a day drinking with the deceased prior to their returning to the appellant's flat where they fell asleep. The appellant was later woken by blows to his head being administered by the deceased, and retaliated with what he thought were a few mild blows, after which he fell asleep again. When the appellant woke up again, some time later, he found the body of the deceased who had died from blows to the head. When tried for murder, the appellant claimed that he had been mistaken as to the amount of force that he had needed to use to defend himself because he had been drinking. The trial judge directed the jury that the defendant was entitled to rely on the defence of self-defence, and was to be judged on the facts as he believed them to be, but he was not entitled to go beyond what was reasonable by way of self-defence, and the fact that he might have mistakenly done so due to the effect of drink did not afford him a defence. Rejecting his appeal against conviction for manslaughter, Lord Lane CJ observed:

> '[In] *R* v *Williams (Gladstone)* ... the court was ... considering what the situation might be where the mistake was due to voluntary intoxication by alcohol or some other drug. We have come to the conclusion that where the jury are satisfied that the defendant was mistaken in his belief that any force or the force which he in fact used was necessary to defend himself and are further satisfied that the mistake was caused by voluntarily induced intoxication, the defence must fail. We do not consider that any distinction should be drawn on this aspect of the matter between offences involving what is called specific intent, such as murder, and offences of so called basic intent, such as manslaughter ... Though the problem of violent conduct by intoxicated persons is not new to society, it has been rendered more acute and menacing by the more widespread use of hallucinatory drugs ... in *R* v *Lipman* [1970] 1 QB 152 ... the defence ... was put on the grounds that the defendant, because of the hallucinatory drug which he had taken, had not formed the necessary intent to found a conviction for murder, thus resulting in his conviction for manslaughter. If the appellant's contentions here are correct, Lipman could successfully have escaped conviction altogether by raising the issue that he believed he was defending himself legitimately from an attack by serpents. It is significant that no one seems to have considered that possibility.'

In relation to statutory defences based on the defendant's honest, albeit drunken belief: see *Jaggard* v *Dickinson* [1981] 2 WLR 118, and Chapter 3.

Reform

Clause 21 of the draft code restates the oft cited maxim that ignorance of the law is no excuse, but admits exceptions where the mistake of law negatives the fault element required for an offence. The purpose of the general prohibition upon such a defence is, as the Code Report commentary on this clause indicates:

'... to preclude any attempt to stimulate judicial recognition of exceptions to the general rule by reliance on clause 45(c), under which common law defences can be developed, but only if they are not inconsistent with other Code provisions.' [Vol II para 8.29]

The draft code does not deal directly with mistake of fact as a 'defence' as, given the construction of the Code, it is unnecessary to do so. Clause 14 provides that:

'A court or jury, in determining whether a person had, or may have had, a particular state of mind, shall have regard to all the evidence including, where appropriate, the presence or absence of reasonable grounds for having that state of mind.'

The clause thus states what should be obvious, that mistake of fact relating to an element of an offence is actually a denial of mens rea. The defendant is entitled to be judged on the facts as he believes them to be; thus a defendant who stabs to death a victim in the belief that he was stabbing a wax dummy should be acquitted of murder, but in assessing whether or not the defendant genuinely believed himself to be stabbing a wax dummy, the jury will be entitled to take into account the existence of any reasonable grounds for such belief.

The problem of the defendant who acts in the belief that circumstances justifying his reliance upon a defence exist is dealt with by clause 41 of the draft code, which provides:

'(1) Unless otherwise provided, a person who acts in the belief that a circumstance exists has any defence that he would have if the circumstance existed.
(2) Subsection (1) does not apply in respect of a defence specially provided for a pre-Code offence as defined in section 6 (to which section 2(3) applies).
(3) Any requirement as to proof or disproof of a defence applies to proof or disproof of a belief mentioned in subsection (1).'

The illustrative example provided by Appendix B to Volume 1 cites the following possible application of the provision:

'An offence is created after the Code comes into force of knowingly supplying liquor to a child. An exception is made for liquor in a properly corked and sealed vessel. A supplier has a defence if he believes the liquor to be in a properly corked and sealed vessel. But if it were provided that the offence is not committed if the supplier believes on reasonable grounds that the liquor is in a properly corked and sealed vessel, subsection (1) would not apply.' [Vol I example 41]

The commentary upon clause 41 explains its purpose:

'If knowledge of a particular circumstance is an element of an offence, a belief that that circumstance does not exist means that the offence is not committed. Subsection (1) provides a presumption in favour of a corresponding rule for defences, namely, that a person who acts in the belief that a circumstance exists has any defence that he would have if it existed. The Code thus gives general effect to the *prima facie* principle that a person is to be judged, for purposes of criminal liability, on the facts as he believed them to be. This is the tendency, though not the universal effect, of recent judicial developments in the field of defences. It is desirable that the Code should provide consistently for offences and defences, leaving it to Parliament in particular contexts, if it thinks fit, to exclude the application of this subsection or to limit a defence of belief in the existence of an "exempting circumstance" to a case of a belief based on reasonable grounds. Where a defendant relies on this subsection, the absence of reasonable grounds for the belief he claims to have held is, of course, relevant in determining whether he did hold it ... A defence may have two or more elements, each of which is, in the language of the Code, an "exempting circumstance", and a person's mistaken belief may be as to the existence of one such circumstance. Subsection (1) places him in the position that he would be in if his belief were true. For example, a person may be guilty of manslaughter rather than murder if he kills under provocation – that is, if something done or said causes him to lose his self-control (clauses 55(a) and 58). If he mistakenly believes that just such a thing has been done or said, the supposed provocation is treated as actual provocation, and other elements of this special defence to murder (the alleged loss of self-control and the question whether the provocation was sufficient ground for the loss of self-control) are then considered on that basis.' [Vol II paras 12.6–12.7]

The DCLB, contained in Law Com No 218, reflects the 'subjectivist' approach to mistake giving rise to belief in exempting circumstances, hence the proposals that duress and reasonable force are viewed on the basis of the circumstances the defendant believed to exist: see discussion of reform proposals in Chapter 14.

As indicated in Chapter 13, pending the Law Commission's forthcoming response to LCCP 127, the DCLB simply restates the common law position as regards the defendant who, through voluntary intoxication, believes in the existence of a circumstance that he would not have believed in had he been sober: see clause 23.

15.2 Infancy

Where the defendant is below the age of 10

Under s16 of the Children and Young Persons Act 1963, a child under the age of ten cannot incur criminal responsibility. There is an irrebuttable presumption against mens rea. Where an adult uses such a child in order to commit offences, for example sending a child into a house via a small open window in order to steal, the adult should be charged as the principal offender on the basis of innocent agency.

Where the defendant is between the ages of 10 and 14

Prior to the decision of the Divisional Court in *C (A Minor) v DPP* [1994] 3 WLR 888, the common law rule was that a child between the ages of 10 and 14 could only be criminally liable if he was shown to have had 'mischievous discretion', or to have understood that what he was doing was seriously wrong: see *R v Gorrie* (1919)

83 JP 136. A court was not allowed to assume that the defendant knew that his actions were wrong, simply because the average child of the defendant's age would have: see *IPH* v *Chief Constable of South Wales* [1987] Crim LR 42, *T* v *DPP* [1989] Crim LR 498, and *A* v *DPP* [1992] Crim LR 34. As Robert Goff LJ observed in *JM* v *Runeckles* (1984) 79 Cr App R 255:

> '... the prosecution has to prove that the child knew that what he or she was doing was seriously wrong. The point is that it is not enough that the child realised that what he or she was doing was naughty or mischievous. It must go beyond childish things of that kind. That, as I understand it, is the real point underlying the presumption that a child under the age of 14 has not yet reached the age of discretion, because children under that age may think what they are doing is nothing more than mischievous. It would not be right for a child under that age to be convicted of a crime, even if they had committed the relevant actus reus and had the relevant mens rea specified in the statute, unless they appreciated that what they were doing was seriously wrong and so went beyond childish activity of that kind.'

In *C (A Minor)* v *DPP*, the appellant, a 12-year-old boy, had been convicted by magistrates of interfering with a motor cycle with intent to commit theft, contrary to s9(1) of the Criminal Attempts Act 1981. The court had found that he had done substantial damage to the motor cycle and run away when the police arrived, and inferred from this that the appellant had known that he had done something seriously wrong. On appeal against conviction on the ground that the appellant's actions were merely equivocal, and could simply be evidence that he knew he had been naughty, the Divisional Court, dismissing the appeal, held that rebuttable assumption that a child between the ages of 10 and 14 was incapable of committing a crime should no longer form part of English criminal law. Mann LJ, delivering the judgment of the court expressed the view that, given the impact of universal education, it was no longer necessary for the prosecution to prove that such a defendant had known that his actions were seriously wrong, and this requirement was now out of step with the general principles of criminal liability. In his view the common law could no longer be based on the 'perverse' assumption that a child between the ages of 10 and 14 was presumed to be doli incapax (incapable of committing a crime) unless evidence to the contrary was submitted, as it operated in such a way that it was easier to prove that 'well brought up' children knew the difference between wrong and right, as opposed to 'deprived' children, thus tending to absolve from liability those most likely to commit criminal acts.

The court brushed aside the objection that its ruling would be retro-active, but the point remains that, at the time the 'offence' was committed, the law prima facie prevented the imposition of criminal liability on the appellant. Neither was the court restrained by the submission that in changing the law it was in effect usurping the function of Parliament.

Reform

Clause 32 of the draft code effectively restates the position at common law as it was prior to the decision in *C* v *DPP*, although it contains no conclusive presumption of incapacity as under the existing law.

As regards children between the ages of 10 and 14, the commentary on the Code Report states:

'The phrase "seriously wrong" reflects the most recent judicial statement of what must be proved in order to rebut the traditional presumption that the child was *doli incapax* that he lacked the "mischievous discretion" necessary for criminal liability [see *JM* v *Runeckles* above]. A requirement of knowledge that the act is seriously wrong seems inapt, however, in the case of very minor offences; yet it has never been suggested that a child over ten cannot commit such offences. Knowledge that the act is an offence would seem to suffice.' (Vol II para 10.27)

On the more general issue of whether or not the presumption of doli incapax should be preserved, the Code Report commentary had the following points to make:

'As the Code team pointed out, the *doli incapax* presumption has been said to "[reflect] an outworn mode of thought" and to be "steeped in absurdity" and it has long been recognised as operating capriciously. Its abolition was proposed in 1960 by the Ingleby Committee on Children and Young Persons ... For these reasons the team recommended that it should not survive in the Code. We do not feel able to adopt this suggestion. Parliament did not take the opportunity to implement the Ingleby Committee's proposal in the Children and Young Persons Act 1969 but chose rather to reduce the incidence of criminal proceedings against children and young persons. The recommendation made in 1960 is no longer adequate warrant for a reform on which there has been no recent consultation and which is bound to be controversial. We would add that, while we are alive to the criticisms of the present law, we should in any case be loath to recommend an isolated change in the law that might be interpreted as encouraging greater use of the criminal process as a means of dealing with children.' [Vol II para 10.28]

16 ✳

Introduction to Theft. Property Belonging to Another

16.1 Introduction to theft

16.2 The offence of theft

16.3 What can be stolen?

16.4 Property belonging to another

16.1 Introduction to theft

The Theft Act 1968 is largely the result of preparatory work carried out by the Criminal Law Revision Committee (CLRC) and is based upon the CLRC's Eighth Report (Cmnd 2977). The aim of the Act was to sweep away many of the unnecessarily complex aspects of the existing law, based as it was on the Larceny Act 1916 and common law. In particular the aim of the CLRC was to introduce a new statutory framework, based on concepts, and using language, that ordinary men and women, of average literacy, could comprehend. To some extent this aim has been realised, but two factors should be borne in mind. First, that the criminal law of theft does not exist in a legal vacuum. It rests upon civil law concepts of ownership, property, contract and so on. Not only are such concepts complex in themselves, but they are constantly evolving. Secondly, since the enactment of the Theft Act 1968 a considerable body of caselaw has developed indicating the way in which the courts interpret the provisions of the Act. Not only does the volume of the caselaw increase complexity, but the contradictory nature of some decisions introduces uncertainty and confusion. Further, it rapidly became evident that some provisions of the 1968 Act were unworkable, and that significant loopholes existed, necessitating the enactment of the Theft Act 1978.

Reform

Whereas the draft code encompasses significant reforms of some general principles of criminal liability, it has no major recommendations in respect of the mainstream offences of dishonesty. As the commentary indicates:

'Chapter III of Part II of the Code contains the offences currently to be found in the Theft Act 1968, the Theft Act 1978, Part I of the Forgery and Counterfeiting Act 1981 and s9 of the Criminal Attempts Act 1981 (vehicle interference). It brings together, that is to say, those statutory offences which share (in broad terms) an element of dishonest conduct or intention and which will be conveniently located in the Code. The two Theft Acts obviously belong in this Chapter ... Unlike Chapters I and II, which for the most part implement modern law reform proposals, Chapter III offers no new law. It consists of a restatement of the existing offences, with (in general) only such changes as are required for consistency with the general content and style of the Code. The result, we believe, is that some of the offences are stated a good deal more simply and clearly. Very few amendments with more than merely stylistic significance – and these only minor ones – have been thought to be justifiable. They have been made in order to eliminate manifest error or inconsistency in the existing statutes or to improve clarity without risk of substantive change.' [Vol II paras 16.1 and 16.3]

A consequence of this approach is that the Theft Acts remain largely unreformed by the draft code bill. As the Commission conceded:

'Some will be disappointed by such restraint in the treatment of the Theft Acts. The law penalising dishonest conduct is of central importance and offences under these Acts account for a very large proportion of all the indictable offences with which the courts have to deal. It is a matter for some concern that both the Acts themselves (especially that of 1968) and the substantial case law that they have generated are regarded by some critics as seriously defective. This is not, however, a matter that it would be appropriate to pursue here. Our task at this point is to include in the draft Code the law of criminal dishonesty in its existing statutory condition.' [Vol II para 16.4]

16.2 The offence of theft

Section 1(1) of the Theft Act 1968 creates the offence of theft. It provides:

'A person is guilty of theft if he dishonestly appropriates property belonging to another with the intention of permanently depriving the other of it; and "theft" and "steal" shall be construed accordingly.'

Besides being an offence in its own right, it should be remembered that the elements of theft may need to be established in order to prove liability for other offences, such as robbery (s8), burglary (s9) and, to a lesser extent, going equipped (s25). Whilst s1(1) creates an offence, ss2–6 provide complete or partial definitions of the elements of theft. As s1(3) states:

'The five following sections of this Act shall have effect as regards the interpretation and operation of this section (and, except as otherwise provided by this Act, shall apply only for purposes of this section).'

The maximum punishment that can be imposed where a defendant has been convicted of theft following a trial on indictment, was reduced from ten years to seven by s26 of the Criminal Justice Act 1991.

16.3 What can be stolen?

Section 4(1) provides a general definition of property for the purposes of theft, where it states:

> '"Property" includes money and all other property, real or personal, including things in action and other intangible property.'

This seemingly wide definition is limited however, by the provisions that follow in ss4(2) to 4(4). Before considering those, a number of points need to be considered.

Section 4(1) expressly refers to 'things in action and other intangible property'. Thus the law of theft is extended to protect patents, copyright, shares, and debts. Intangible property may, for example, take the form of a bank account in credit. The balance is owed to the customer by the bank. Where a defendant (D), takes the victim's (P) cheque book and forges P's signature on cheques resulting in a reduction or extinction of P's bank balance, D can be said to have appropriated P's property within s4(1). The Court of Appeal accepted this reasoning in *R v Kohn* (1979) 69 Cr App R 395. Similarly, it is submitted, where P is granted an overdraft facility and D draws on the account using P's cheques, D is 'using up' P's intangible property, namely the right to draw money out up to a certain limit. See further *Chan Man-Sin v R* [1988] Crim LR 319, which provides support for this submission. The phrase 'other intangible property' has been held by the Privy Council to extend to things such as export quotas, which could be traded for value: see *Attorney-General for Hong Kong v Nai-Keung* [1988] Crim LR 125.

Notwithstanding that s4(1) covers intangible property, confidential information has been held to fall outside the definition of property. The Divisional Court in *Oxford v Moss* [1979] Crim LR 119 upheld a decision of the justices that a student, who had obtained a proof of an examination paper he was due to sit, was not guilty of theft on the basis that information could not be stolen. Clearly the paper on which the examination questions were typed was property belonging to the University, but there was no evidence that the defendant intended to permanently deprive the University of it. The implication of the decision is that trade secrets would not be property capable of being stolen either. An agreement to obtain such information might amount, however, to a common law conspiracy to defraud.

Electricity is not property that can be stolen: see *Low v Blease* (1975) 119 Sol Jo 695. The dishonest abstraction of electricity is covered by s13 of the 1968 Act: see 20.4.

At common law a human corpse could not be stolen, on the basis that there was no property in a human corpse: see *R v Sharpe* (1857) Dears & B 160. The situation would appear to be the same under the 1968 Act. It has been suggested, however, that a person might acquire property rights over a human corpse where some skill and effort has been exercised, eg mummification: see *Doodeward v Spence* (1907) 9 SR (NSW) 107. Less doubt surrounds the status of products of the body. In *R v Rothery* [1976] RTR 550 the Court of Appeal held that a human blood sample could be stolen, whilst in *R v Welsh* [1974] RTR 478 the defendant was convicted of stealing a sample of urine that he himself had provided for analysis by the police. It seems reasonable to suggest that human organs donated for transplant operations, and human sperm deposited in sperm banks, would also be regarded as property for the purposes of theft.

Section 4(2) provides:

'A person cannot steal land, or things forming part of land and severed from it by him or by his directions, except in the following cases, that is to say –
a) when he is a trustee or personal representative, or is authorised by power of attorney, or as liquidator of a company, or otherwise, to sell or dispose of land belonging to another, and he appropriates the land or anything forming part of it by dealing with it in breach of the confidence reposed in him; or
b) when he is not in possession of the land and appropriates anything forming part of the land by severing it or causing it to be severed, or after it has been severed; or
c) when, being in possession of the land under a tenancy, he appropriates the whole or part of any fixture or structure let to be used with the land.
For purposes of this subsection "land" does not include incorporated hereditaments; "tenancy" means a tenancy for years or any less period and includes an agreement for such a tenancy, but a person who after the end of a tenancy remains in possession as statutory tenant or otherwise is to be treated as having possession under the tenancy, and "let" shall be construed accordingly.'

It may in some situations be difficult to determine whether property forms part of the land upon which it is sited or not. In *Billing* v *Pill* [1954] 1 QB 70 it was held that an army hut bolted onto a concrete base did not form part of the land, and was therefore a chattel capable of being stolen (under the Larceny Act 1916). Lord Goddard CJ had no doubt that the concrete base itself had become part of the land.

The question of the extent to which plants constitute property for the purposes of theft is provided for by s4(3) which states:

'A person who picks mushrooms growing wild on any land, or who picks flowers, fruit or foliage from a plant growing wild on any land, does not (although not in possession of the land) steal what he picks, unless he does it for reward or for sale or other commercial purpose. For purposes of this subsection "mushroom" includes any fungus, and "plant" includes any shrub or tree.'

Presumably a defendant must intend to sell the produce when he picks it, and would fall outside the section were he to pick mushrooms growing wild and then later decide to sell them. Reference to 'other commercial purpose' suggests that the picking of wild plants should be on an organised basis in order for liability to arise.

As regards animals in the wild, they are referred to in s4(4) which provides:

'Wild creatures, tamed or untamed, shall be regarded as property, but a person cannot steal a wild creature not tamed nor ordinarily kept in captivity, or the carcass of any such creature unless either it has been reduced into possession by or on behalf of another person and possession of it has not since been lost or abandoned, or another person is in course of reducing it into possession.'

Animals in zoos, safari parks, and domestic pets can all be stolen, even if they are appropriated having escaped from captivity. Wild animals are obviously protected by other legislation. Interestingly, the Court of Appeal held in *R* v *Howlett* [1968] Crim LR 222 that mussels in a mussel bed were wild animals 'at large', and could not be stolen.

16.4 Property belonging to another

Section 5(1) of the Theft Act 1968 provides an extended meaning for the phrase 'belonging to another' where it states:

> 'Property shall be regarded as belonging to any person having possession or control of it, or having in it any proprietary right or interest (not being an equitable interest arising only from an agreement to transfer or grant an interest).'

Clearly the section does not require that property should be owned by the person from whom it is appropriated, mere possession is sufficient. Difficult questions may arise where a defendant is charged with theft of property that he himself owns, in which regard the following decisions should be noted.

In *R* v *Turner (No 2)* [1971] 2 All ER 441 the defendant removed his car from outside the garage at which it had been repaired, intending to avoid having to pay for the repair. The Court of Appeal held that the car could be regarded as 'property belonging to another' as against the defendant owner, since it was in the possession and control of the repairer. Were the same facts to present themselves today, a charge of making off without payment contrary to s3 of the Theft Act 1978 would be more appropriate. The repairer might be regarded as having a right to retain goods until the repairs are paid for (a repairer's lien), but the trial judge had directed the jury not to consider the case on this basis.

R v *Meredith* [1973] Crim LR 253 suggests that where the custodian of goods has no right to retain them as against the owner, they will not be regarded as property belonging to another. The defendant here was held by a Crown Court judge to have no case to answer on a charge of theft, where he had removed his car from a police station yard. Further, in *R* v *Bonner* [1970] 1 WLR 838 the Court of Appeal held that a partner could be convicted of theft of partnership property.

Lost and abandoned property

For the purposes of theft the distinction between lost and abandoned property is of significance. Where P loses a £10 note in the street and has no idea of its whereabouts, it still remains property belonging to another as against D who picks it up. On the other hand, where P deliberately leaves his newspaper on a train and it is picked up by D who occupies the seat after him, the newspaper would not be regarded as property belonging to another as against D. The vital distinction between the two situations is that in the latter, P intends to relinquish his rights of ownership (he has *animus revocandi*), and if property is ownerless it cannot be stolen. Caution should be exercised, however, before the conclusion that P has relinquished his rights of ownership is reached. In *R* v *Woodman* [1974] QB 758 the Court of Appeal held that articles on a site, such as pieces of scrap metal, were property belonging to the owner of the site even though he was ignorant of their presence. Similarly in *Hibbert* v *McKiernan* [1948] 2 KB 142, the defendant was convicted of the theft of 'lost' golf balls from a golf course. Where a householder puts refuse out for collection by local authority refuse workers, the Divisional Court in *Williams* v *Phillips* (1957) 41 Cr App R 5 held that such refuse remained property belonging to the householder until collected, whereupon property passed to the local authority. Hence, refuse workers helping themselves to such property could be convicted of theft, on the basis that the property never became ownerless.

Section 5(2)

Section 5(2) provides:

'Where property is subject to a trust, the persons to whom it belongs shall be regarded as including any person having a right to enforce the trust, and an intention to defeat the trust shall be regarded accordingly as an intention to deprive of the property any person having that right.'

Hence, where T holds a stamp collection on trust for P, D will be guilty of theft if he steals the collection from T, and could also be charged with theft from the equitable owner P. Were T to appropriate the collection with mens rea, he too could be guilty of theft from P.

Section 5(3)

Section 5(3), along with s5(4) (below), has the effect of extending the definition of 'belonging to another' to situations in which property would normally pass from P to D. Section 5(3) provides:

'Where a person receives property from or on account of another, and is under an obligation to the other to retain and deal with that property or its proceeds in a particular way, the property or proceeds shall be regarded (as against him) as belonging to the other.'

Where, for example, P enters into a contract with D under which D is to paint P's house and is given an advance of £100 to buy materials, D could be guilty of theft if he subsequently spends that money dishonestly on other items. Section 5(3) would operate so as to prevent property passing, with the result that D would be spending money belonging to P.

The section requires the defendant to be under an obligation to retain the property or its proceeds. *R* v *Gilks* [1972] 3 All ER 280 is authority for the proposition that this obligation must be a legally enforceable one. The obligation is not that any property received should be retained in its original form, but that a separate fund, equal to the value of the property originally received, should be maintained. The court in *R* v *Hayes* (1977) 64 Cr App R 82 proceeded on the basis that the question of whether or not a legal obligation arose for the purposes of s5(3) was one for the jury to determine, whilst in *R v Mainwaring* (1981) 74 Cr App R 99, it was held that the trial judge should direct the jury as to what could give rise to a legal obligation and then leave it to them to determine whether one arose on the facts. Following *R v Dubar* [1994] 1 WLR 1484, it would appear that the latter approach is to be preferred. The Courts-Martial Appeal Court observed that there were irreconcilable differences between the approach of Lawton LJ in *Mainwaring* (above), and the approach of Edmund-Davies LJ in *R v Hall* [1973] QB 126, which had in turn been approved by Lord Widgery CJ in *Hayes* (above). The court held that the judge advocate had correctly expressed the law by directing the court that if it found certain facts to be made out then, *as a matter of law*, an obligation arose to which s5(3) applied. See chapter 26, section 26.7, for further details.

The question is clearly one of civil law, and one has to examine the transaction to determine whether or not the parties intend that there should be legal consequences. In *R v Cullen* ((1974) unreported), the defendant, who was P's mistress, was convicted of theft of £20 that he had given her to buy food, when she dishonestly spent it for her own purposes. The decision has been criticised on the basis that in terms of contract law it may have been a domestic agreement: see *Balfour v Balfour* [1919] 2 KB 571. Where money is given by persons sharing a house to the defendant so that a communal bill can be paid, the argument that there is a legal obligation to deal with the money in that way seems more plausible: see *Davidge v Bunnett* [1984] Crim LR 296.

Whether an obligation exists or not, and if it does, the nature of the obligation, is to be determined by construing the express and implied terms of the contract between the parties. In *R v Hall* (above), the Court of Appeal held that a travel agent who had accepted money for securing airline tickets for customers, was not under an obligation within s5(3). Once the money was paid over to the defendant he was free to use it as he pleased, and was therefore not guilty of theft when he was later unable to provide the tickets required. Similarly in *Lewis v Lethbridge* [1986] QB 491, where the appellant, a competitor in the London Marathon, received £54 in sponsorship money which he did not pass on to the relevant charity. The Divisional Court quashed his conviction for theft on the basis that the requirements of s5(3) were not made out, as the sponsorship arrangements permitted him to do as he pleased with the money, his only obligation being to account in due course for an equivalent sum. As the court observed, the situation might have been otherwise had the appellant been given a collecting tin, as this would have been evidence of a legal duty to deliver the money collected therein. See, further, *R v Rader* [1992] Crim LR 663.

Conversely in *R v Brewster* (1979) 69 Cr App R 375, it was held that an insurance broker could be guilty of theft of insurance premiums collected by him for which he had to account to the insurance company. A determining factor was that the contract between the defendant and the insurance company stated that at all times the premiums were to be the property of the company. In *Attorney-General's Reference*

(No 1 of 1985) [1986] Crim LR 476, the Court of Appeal held that a publican who, contrary to his agreement with a brewery, sold his own beer over the counter of the tied public house of which he was the manager, could not be guilty of theft of the proceeds by keeping them. He was not under an obligation to hand over the proceeds to the brewery within s5(3) (thus they did not become property belonging to another), because he did not receive the proceeds on account of the brewery. See *Lee Cheung Wing* v *R* [1992] Crim LR 440 for possible alternative charges under s17 of the 1968 Act.

In the absence of any formal contractual relationship between the parties, proof of the type of legal obligation required for the purposes of s5(3) is likely to be fraught with difficulty. In *DPP* v *Huskinson* [1988] Crim LR 620, the respondent was charged with theft of the proceeds of a cheque for housing benefit which he had, in part, spent on himself. The Divisional Court held that the only possible basis for the legal obligation required under s5(3) was the legislation under which the benefit had been paid, the Social Security and Housing Benefit Act 1982, and the court was unable to determine any express or implied obligation in those provisions to the effect that the respondent was compelled, as a matter of law, to use the housing benefit to pay off his arrears of rent.

In addition to establishing the legally binding nature of the obligation, the prosecution must establish that the defendant knew that he was under a legal obligation to deal with the property in a particular way. This was the basis for the appellant's successful appeal in *R* v *Wills* (1991) 92 Cr App R 297 where Farquharson LJ commented that:

> 'Whether a person is under an obligation to deal with property in a particular way can only be established by proving that he had knowledge of that obligation. Proof that the property was not dealt with in conformity with the obligation is not sufficient in itself.'

In this particular case it is tempting to ask whether or not the appellant could have denied that he was dishonest in dealing with the proceeds of the cheques. If he was unaware of the transactions creating the obligation he would have believed that the money belonged to his firm to be used as he thought fit. As explained at 18.1, s2(1)(a) of the 1968 Act provides that a defendant is not to be regarded as dishonest if he honestly believes he has the right in law to appropriate property.

Section 5(4)

Section 5(4) deals with the complex problems that arise where a defendant receives property by mistake; it states:

> 'Where a person gets property by another's mistake, and is under an obligation to make restoration (in whole or in part) of the property or its proceeds or of the value thereof, then to the extent of that obligation the property or proceeds shall be regarded (as against him) as belonging to the person entitled to restoration, and an intention not to make restoration shall be regarded accordingly as an intention to deprive that person of the property or proceeds.'

An initial difficulty is the subsection's reliance on the concept of mistake. The purpose of the provision is clearly to stop property passing to the defendant where it otherwise would do at common law, but in what circumstances can property pass where a transaction is vitiated by mistake? The subsection can have no relevance in those situations where the mistake is fundamental, because no property can pass under a void transaction (assuming that one accepts that the effect of a fundamental mistake is to render a transaction void). The property in question would remain, as against the defendant, property belonging to another by virtue of s5(1). The subsection can, therefore, only sensibly apply where the transaction is vitiated by a non-fundamental mistake which renders it voidable. If this analysis is correct, one would then have to ask which situations will involve a *legal* obligation to restore the property received by mistake, since, as with s5(3), the defendant must be under such an obligation, to make restoration of the property, its proceeds, or the value thereof: see *R v Gilks* (above).

Arguably, where P by mistake gives D ten loaves of bread instead of nine, D is not under any obligation to return the extra loaf of bread to P even though he is aware of the mistake. It could be contended that no obligation to return the extra loaf arises until P 'avoids' the transaction by pointing out the error to D (see *Car and Universal Finance Co Ltd v Caldwell* [1965] 1 QB 525), at which point the property in the extra loaf would re-vest in P and by definition would be 'property belonging to another' as against D, quite independently of s5(4).

It would appear that in suggesting a provision in the nature of s5(4), the CLRC intended to bring within the scope of theft behaviour such as that of the defendant in *Moynes v Cooper* [1956] 1 QB 439, where an employee received a wage packet containing money which should have been deducted to take account of advance payments that had already been made to him during the previous week. The overpayment was discovered by the defendant employee some time later when he was at home, and he proceeded to spend the money. As the law then stood he had to be acquitted of theft. It is envisaged that he would now be within the scope of s5(4), as where there is an overpayment of money, D will be under a quasi-contractual obligation to repay the sum. In civil law it could be recovered by way of an action for money had and received. This would be sufficient to create the legal obligation required by the subsection. Hence the provision could be relied upon where D receives too much change in a shop or from a bank clerk.

Following the decision in *Chase Manhattan Bank NA v Israel-British Bank London Ltd* [1981] Ch 105, to the effect that a party transferring money by mistake retains an equitable interest in it where an action will lie to recover sums paid under a mistake of fact, and thus it can be regarded a property belonging to another as against the transferor within s5(1), s5(4) could be regarded as redundant. The courts have extended its operation, however, to encompass bank giro credits made in error, and cheques erroneously drawn in favour of payees.

In *Attorney-General's Reference (No 1 of 1983)* [1985] QB 182, the defendant had been overpaid, the amount being credited directly to her current account. The evidence suggested that having discovered the overpayment, the defendant simply allowed the money to remain in the account, but she was acquitted on a charge of theft of the overpayment. The Court of Appeal offered guidance by suggesting that the defendant had 'got' a chose in action by mistake and was under an obligation to restore 'the value' of the overpayment to her employer. The nature of the obligation was not discussed at length, but Lord Lane CJ suggested it was based on the employer's right to restitution. He further suggested that s5(4) only started to operate from the moment the defendant became aware of the overpayment, implying that, as with s5(3), D will not incur liability unless aware of the obligation to make restoration. Does this mean that the defendant who receives too much money by way of change in a shop, and honestly believes that he does not have to return it unless asked, could escape liability on the basis of his ignorance regarding the obligation? It is submitted that knowledge of the overpayment and knowledge of the obligation to restore are quite different issues.

Note that the subsection extends to proceeds of property and its value. If D receives £5 too much in change from a shopkeeper, buys a book with the £5, and then realises what has happened, the book becomes property belonging to the shopkeeper as against D. Should D resolve to keep it, he could be guilty of theft; see further *R v Stalham* [1993] Crim LR 310.

Chase Manhattan Bank NA v Israel-British Bank London Ltd was applied in *R v Shadrokh-Cigari* [1988] Crim LR 465, where the appellant, who was the guardian of a child to whose bank account $286,000 had been credited in error instead of $286, persuaded the child to sign authorities instructing the bank to issue banker's drafts, in favour of the appellant. The appellant subsequently credited a number of his own accounts with the sums indicated on the drafts, and was convicted of theft of the drafts on the basis that they remained property belonging to another, namely the issuing bank. The Court of Appeal expressed the view that the conviction for theft was sustainable on two grounds. One view was that as the appellant had obtained the drafts as a result of a fundamental mistake of fact on the part of the bank, he was under an obligation to restore them to the bank, and this gave rise to the bank having an equitable interest in the drafts. Under s5(1) of the Theft Act 1968, therefore, the drafts could still be regarded as property belonging to the bank. Alternatively, the situation could be regarded as one falling within s5(4) of the 1968 Act, in that the appellant had obtained the drafts as a result of the bank's mistake, and was under an obligation to restore the property or its proceeds. There may be a difficulty in asserting that the appellant was under an obligation to restore the intangible property represented by the drafts to the bank, as the bank had never had the right to enforce the drafts (as they had never been made out in favour of the bank or assigned to them), but the appellant clearly had obtained the drafts, as documents, and these had been owned by the bank before being transferred to him by mistake. The problem of cheques made out by mistake was also considered by a differently constituted Court of Appeal in *R v Davis* [1988] Crim LR 762, where the appellant, who had been in receipt of housing benefit, was sent duplicate cheques in respect of the benefit, as a result of a computer error, and continued to receive some cheques after he had ceased to be eligible for benefit. In relation to two of the six counts of theft upon which the appellant had been convicted (where there was evidence that he had endorsed cheques in favour of his landlord in order to pay his rent) the Court of Appeal allowed his appeal as there was no evidence that the appellant had received cash in return for the cheques. The court upheld the convictions on the remaining counts however, expressing the view that although the appellant could not be guilty of stealing the intangible property represented by the cheques (ie the right to payment) as this was not, and never had been, a type of property belonging to another as against the appellant, he could be guilty of stealing the proceeds of the cheques obtained by mistake, namely the cash received in return for the endorsing of the cheques. The court further expressed the view that the prosecution did not have to indicate which of the cheques the appellant had been entitled to receive and which he had obtained by mistake. Section 5(4) referred to the obligation to restore the whole or part of property got by another's mistake. Liability for theft attached to the 'surplus', ie the extent to which property that the appellant had obtained by mistake exceeded property to which the appellant had been entitled.

17

Appropriation

17.1 Introduction

17.2 Can a defendant appropriate property when it is not in his possession?

17.3 Can a defendant appropriate property where he comes by it innocently?

17.4 Can a defendant appropriate property even though the owner consents to his actions?

17.1 Introduction

The concept of appropriation lies at the heart of theft. It replaces the more complex notions such as 'trespassory taking' and 'carrying away' that were features of the former law. Appropriation may be a word that is readily understandable by literate men and women, but it has, nevertheless, given rise to considerable debate as to its precise meaning, as will be seen below. Section 3(1) provides:

> 'Any assumption by a person of the rights of an owner amounts to an appropriation, and this includes, where he has come by the property (innocently or not) without stealing it, any later assumption of a right to it by keeping or dealing with it as owner.'

The House of Lords' decision in *R v Morris* [1983] 3 All ER 288 makes it plain that an assumption of any right will suffice.

Appropriation is considered in isolation here to aid clarity, but it should be borne in mind that in practice appropriation, for the purposes of theft, is of no consequence unless accompanied by dishonest intent, dealt with in Chapter 18.

17.2 Can a defendant appropriate property when it is not in his possession?

This problem may arise where D purports to sell property belonging to P, to X. In *R v Bloxham* (1943) 29 Cr App R 37 the defendant purported to sell a refrigerator belonging to the local authority. The defendant was acquitted of attempted theft, but JC Smith contends (*The Law of Theft* 7th ed para 29) that such behaviour could now be theft under the 1968 Act. The refrigerator was property belonging to another, the defendant dishonestly appropriated it by assuming the right of the owner to sell it, and it may be argued that he had intention to permanently deprive

252

within s6(1) by virtue of his treating the property as his own to dispose of. In any event, it is submitted that where the putative purchaser of the goods is unaware of the defendant's dishonesty the appropriate charge would be obtaining by deception contrary to s15. In *R* v *Pitham and Hehl* (1976) 65 Cr App R 45 the Court of Appeal held that a defendant can appropriate another's goods where he purports to sell them even though he is not in possession of the goods at that time. Further, the appropriation (hence, the theft) is complete as soon as the offer to sell is made; a defendant who dishonestly agrees to buy can, therefore, be convicted of arranging to handle stolen goods. The decision has been criticised on the basis that unlike *R* v *Bloxham* (above) the purchaser here knew that the goods did not belong to the seller, and that the situation really involved an agreement to steal the victim's property.

Unauthorised use of cheques and cheque guarantee cards

Where the defendant draws cheques upon his own account.

As is clear from the decision in *R* v *Kohn* (1979) 69 Cr App R 395 (considered in Chapter 16), a person who has a bank account in credit, or an account in relation to which an overdraft facility has been granted, has the right to issue cheques drawn on that account to the extent of its balance, or the extent of the overdraft facility. What of the person whose account is overdrawn without any overdraft having been agreed? On the basis of *MPC* v *Charles* [1977] AC 177, such an individual has no authority to issue cheques drawn on his account, and he may well incur liability in relation to various deception offences if he does, see further 21.1. Could such a person also be committing theft in relation to the issuing bank? The question arose in *R* v *Navvabi* (1986) 83 Cr App R 271, where the defendant had drawn cheques on his account, supported by his cheque guarantee card, when there were insufficient funds in his account to meet the cheques. The appellant's conviction for theft had been based on the ruling that the appropriation of the bank's funds (as represented by the cheques) took place when the cheques were made out.

In allowing his appeal against conviction, Lord Lane CJ expressed the view that the use of the cheque card and delivery of the cheque did no more than give the payee a contractual right to payment as against the bank, and as such there was no usurpation of the bank's rights in relation to its funds either at the time the cheque was made out, or at the time the funds were transferred to the payee. It would appear that the payment of the money by the bank to the payee could only be regarded as an appropriation by the appellant if the bank was in some way acting as his agent. Clearly the bank was transferring the funds to the payee because of the contractual obligations arising from the use of the cheque card, and not because it wished to respond to the appellant's instructions.

Where a defendant draws cheques on the account of another.

A defendant who takes another's cheque book and draws cheques on that account by forging the signature of the drawer is likely to incur liability under the Forgery and

Counterfeiting Act 1981, and also liability for various deception offences. As to whether such actions give rise to liability for theft, the contents of an account (or the overdraft facility available) will clearly be property belonging to another as against the defendant (see *R* v *Kohn*), but is the act of making out the cheque and signing in the name of the account holder to be regarded as an appropriation? An argument might be put forward that, following the decision of the House of Lords in *Tai Hing Cotton Mill Ltd* v *Liu Chong Hing Bank Ltd* [1986] AC 80, the debiting of an account, which occurs as a consequence of a forged cheque having been honoured, is a nullity since the bank only has authority to pay out against valid orders. The account holder has the right in law to have the balance of his account restored by the bank. Since the account holder loses nothing, it might be contended that there is no 'adverse interference' with his rights. The Privy Council was presented with the opportunity to consider such a submission in *Chan Man-Sin* v *R* [1988] 1 WLR 196, wherein it was held that the drawing, presenting, or negotiating of forged cheques could amount to a usurpation of the account holder's rights. Lord Oliver stressed that, following the House of Lords' decision in *R* v *Morris* (above), it was not necessary for the prosecution to prove that the defendant had usurped all the rights of the owner, but simply that he had committed any assumption of any of the owner's rights. Precisely when the appropriation occurred in this case was not made clear. One view is that it could have occurred when the defendants made out the cheques and presented them; another is that it may not have occurred until the bank honoured them. In *R* v *Kohn* the Court of Appeal expressed the view that the theft did not occur until the transaction had gone through to completion, but it is submitted that the correct approach is that adopted in *Re Osman* [1988] Crim LR 611, where the Divisional Court held that theft (ie appropriation) occurred when the defendant dishonestly dispatched a telex instructing a New York bank to transfer funds from the bank account belonging to the company of which he was the chairman, to the bank account of another unconnected company, from whom he was to receive corrupt payments. Given the state of the existing law, the court regarded the question of where the appropriation had taken place as fully open. The court was (at the time) bound to follow the House of Lords' decision in *R* v *Morris* [1984] AC 320, to the extent that appropriation involved a usurpation of the owner's rights amounting to adverse interference with those rights, and on that basis concluded that a defendant appropriates another's bank balance when he issues a cheque on that account without authorisation. The theft is complete in law at that point, even though it may not be complete in fact until the account is debited. Hence the sending of the telexed instruction in the present case was the act of appropriation, and the theft had been committed at the place where it was dispatched. Following *Gomez* (below) reference to the unauthorised nature of the transaction would now be unnecessary.

If a defendant makes unauthorised use of a cheque book to draw cheques on an account which is not in credit, and in respect of which there is no overdraft facility, he cannot be charged with theft in relation to the account, for the simple reason that there is no property to appropriate: see *R* v *Kohn* (above). A charge of theft of the cheque itself may be considered, but this would not be without its complexities: see *R* v *Duru* [1973] 3 All ER 715. On the basis of *R* v *Navvabi* (above) it would seem to make no difference in this situation that the defendant not only makes unauthorised use of the cheque but, supports it with the accompanying cheque guarantee card.

It is submitted that in the majority of the situations considered above charges of either deception or forgery are likely to be more straightforward, and resort should only be had to theft where such offences cannot be made out.

17.3 Can a defendant appropriate property where he comes by it innocently?

Section 3(1) specifically provides that appropriation includes situations where a defendant comes by property innocently and later assumes the rights of the owner, although theft does not occur until the assumption of the rights is accompanied by dishonesty. Hence, in *Pilgrim* v *Rice Smith* [1977] 1 WLR 671, a shop assistant, in lawful possession of goods, was held to have appropriated them when she underpriced them and handed them to a friend for purchase at the lower price. Following *R* v *Gomez* (considered below) the assistant could be regarded as having appropriated the goods simply by handing them to the customer. The vital issue is that D's actions cannot become theft unless the assistant has a dishonest intent. A defendant who found property in the street, and on later discovering that it belonged to his neighbour resolved to keep it, would similarly be within s3(1).

Some protection is offered to the bona fide purchaser for value without notice, by s3(2) which provides:

> 'Where property or a right or interest in property is or purports to be transferred for value to a person acting in good faith, no later assumption by him of rights which he believed himself to be acquiring shall, by reason of any defect in the transferor's title, amount to theft of the property.'

Where, therefore, P buys stolen property from D, unaware that it is stolen, and he gives value for it, he will not be guilty of theft if he later discovers the truth and resolves to keep the property; neither will he incur any liability for handling stolen goods (see 23.5 and *R* v *Adams* [1993] Crim LR 72).

17.4 Can a defendant appropriate property even though the owner consents to his actions?

Lawrence *and* Morris

This question has arguably provoked the greatest difficulty in the interpretation of appropriation. Nowhere in s3 is it provided that the appropriation must be proved to have been without the owner's consent, although in the majority of cases it will have been. If, however, it is accepted that a defendant can appropriate with the owner's consent, the division between s1 theft, and s15 obtaining by deception, becomes blurred.

The House of Lords' decision in *Lawrence* v *MPC* [1972] AC 626 was, prior to *R* v *Gomez* (below), the main authority for the proposition that a defendant can appropriate even where the owner consents to the taking of property. The facts of *Lawrence* were very simple. An Italian student took a taxi ride for which the proper fare was 52p. He offered the defendant a £1 note, but the defendant said more money was needed, and proceeded to take a further £1 note and a £5 note from the student's open wallet. The question of the student's consent to this taking was never satisfactorily determined because he spoke very little English and had to give his evidence through an interpreter. Lawrence was convicted of theft and appealed unsuccessfully to the House of Lords. Viscount Dilhorne rejected the defendant's contention that he should have been charged under s15 and not s1. Not only did his Lordship take the view that the defendant could appropriate the £6 notwithstanding that the student might have consented to its taking, but that the defendant could appropriate the £6 as he became the owner of it. As mentioned above, an inescapable conclusion that results from this ruling is that the distinction between theft and obtaining property by deception, for all practical purposes, disappears. Nearly all cases of the latter would be chargeable as the former.

The problems created by *Lawrence* were not merely academic. Subsequent decisions of the lower courts indicated a reluctance to accept Viscount Dilhorne's approach. The decisions in *R* v *McPherson* [1973] Crim LR 191; *R* v *Meech* [1974] QB 549; *R* v *Skipp* [1975] Crim LR 114; and *Eddy* v *Niman* [1981] Crim LR 502, all turned upon a concept of appropriation which recognised the need for some unauthorised act on the part of the defendant. It is submitted that unauthorised in this context meant without the consent of the owner.

In *R* v *Skipp* the defendant collected three separate loads of produce intending not to return to Leicester with them, but to divert to another destination and sell them dishonestly. The defendant argued that he had committed theft each time he collected a load intending not to deliver it to its correct destination. The Court of Appeal held that the defendant had been rightly charged with one theft of the three loads on the back of his lorry. The theft took place when he diverted from the authorised route back to Leicester with dishonest intent; this was the defendant's first unauthorised act.

Similarly, it appeared that a shopper, even one having an intention to steal, did not do so simply by placing goods in the wire basket provided by the store, as these actions were authorised: see *Eddy* v *Niman* (above). By contrast, a customer was regarded as having appropriated goods in a store by placing them in her own bag, instead of the wire basket provided, because this was unauthorised: see *R* v *McPherson* (above).

In *R* v *Morris* [1983] 3 WLR 697 the House of Lords was presented with an opportunity to reflect on these difficulties, and possibly provide some degree of clarification. Their Lordships had to consider the extend to which label switching in supermarkets constituted theft. As Lord Roskill explained, the switching of price labels amounted to appropriation because it was an assumption by the defendant of the owner's right to determine what price the goods were to be sold at. If accompanied by mens rea it would be theft. Further, a defendant who committed theft by label switching might then proceed to commit the offence of obtaining property by deception where he paid the lower price for the goods at the checkout. In this sense label switching could also be seen as an attempt to commit s15.

In so far as it deals with the facts of the appeal, the decision in *R* v *Morris* was unobjectionable. Difficulties were caused, however, by Lord Roskill's more general observations on appropriation. His Lordship began by referring to *Lawrence* v *MPC* and re-affirming it as the guiding authority on appropriation. He then proceeded to deliver a speech somewhat at odds with what was decided therein. Lord Roskill envisaged appropriation as any assumption of any right of the owner, which had not been expressly or impliedly authorised by the owner, but which amounted to adverse interference with, or usurpation of, the owner's rights. The exclusion of expressly or impliedly authorised acts from the concept of appropriation was widely interpreted as excluding those acts to which the owner has consented, in direct contradiction to *Lawrence* v *MPC*.

Reconciling the irreconcilable

In the wake of *Morris*, judges, practitioners and students of criminal law were left with two House of Lords' decisions on appropriation which were in many respects irreconcilable. Generally, the academic view was that *R* v *Morris* was to be preferred to *Lawrence* v *MPC*. There was considerable doubt as to whether the passenger in Lawrence's taxi actually consented to the defendant taking the £6, in which case it is one of the most unremarkable examples of theft to have arisen in any magistrates' court. If the passenger was 'fooled' into allowing Lawrence to take the extra money then it might be said with some persuasion that Lawrence was wrongly charged with theft and should have been charged with obtaining the money by deception.

The Court of Appeal remained divided on the issue. In *R* v *Philipou* (1989) 89 Cr App R 290, it was held that where a defendant and his co-accused were the sole directors and shareholders of a company, he could be guilty of theft by removing funds from one of the company's bank accounts. O'Connor LJ expressed the view that it was obvious that Lord Roskill in *R* v *Morris* had not intended to insert the words 'without the consent of the owner' into the definition of appropriation under s3(1). His Lordship went on to suggest that it was the dishonesty with which an act was done that could operate so as to make the act relied upon an adverse appropriation of the owner's rights. It is submitted that the issue of appropriation need not have given rise to any difficulty in this case, since it is clear from *Attorney-General's Reference (No 2 of 1982)* [1984] 2 All ER 216, that where the shareholders and directors of a company act dishonestly in relation to the company, their consent to the dishonest acts cannot be imputed to the company, hence it cannot be contended that the company consents to these actions. In that sense the defendant's acts could easily have been regarded as an appropriation; the withdrawal of funds from the company's account was not an act which it expressly or impliedly authorised.

Conversely in *R* v *Fritschy* [1985] Crim LR 745 it was held that, as theft required proof of some overt unauthorised act on the part of the accused, he could not be guilty of stealing within the jurisdiction of the English courts where he had collected Krugerrands in London as directed even though he intended to make off with them once he reached continental Europe. The case is very much a re-affirmation of the approach in *Skipp* (above). Fritschy's unauthorised act would have occurred at the point at which he deviated from the delivery instructions, ie after leaving England.

Matters were further complicated by the contribution of the Court of Appeal (Civil Division) in *Dobson* v *General Accident Fire and Life Assurance Corporation plc* [1989] 3 All ER 927. The case concerned an action for breach of contract brought against the defendant insurance company which had refused to compensate the plaintiff under his household contents insurance policy. The plaintiff had advertised a gold watch and diamond ring for sale. A rogue, posing as a bona fide purchaser, visited his house to examine the goods, and agreed to buy them at the asking price of £5,950, payment to be by means of a building society cheque. It subsequently transpired that the cheque had been stolen and was worthless, but by this time the purchaser had disappeared. The plaintiff made a claim against the defendant insurers under his house contents policy which provided cover for his possessions in respect of theft. The defendants refused to make any payment contending that what had occurred could not amount to theft within s1(1) of the Theft Act 1968 because, inter alia, there could have been no appropriation of the property since the owner had consented to the purchaser taking the items. At first instance it was held that the plaintiff had been the victim of a theft, and this decision was upheld on appeal.

In dismissing the insurance company's appeal, the court held that the plaintiff had only intended to pass property in the goods in return for a valid building society cheque, hence when the goods were handed to the purchaser they were still property belonging to another as against him. Further, there could be an appropriation of the plaintiff's property even if he appeared to consent to its being taken by another, since the House of Lords' decision in *Lawrence* v *MPC* made it clear that there was no need, in proving theft, to establish that the taking had been without the owner's consent.

The final solution?

Inevitably the whole question, of whether or not appropriation involves an act done without the consent of the owner, has had to be reconsidered by the House of

Lords. The opportunity was provided by *R v Gomez* [1992] 3 WLR 1067, a case in which the defendant had obtained electrical equipment in exchange for worthless building society cheques. During the course of his trial the defendant made a submission that he should not be charged with theft as there had been no appropriation of the goods. This submission was based on the proposition that any such appropriation had to be without the consent of the owner, and that the owner in this case, through its agent, had expressly consented to the delivery of the goods. The trial judge rejected this submission, and the defendant changed his plea to guilty. Significantly, the Court of Appeal allowed his appeal, Lord Lane CJ commenting that since the transfer of the goods had been with the consent and express authority of the owner, there was no lack of authorisation and therefore no appropriation. The question certified for consideration by the House of Lords was stated as follows:

> 'When theft is alleged and that which is alleged to be stolen passes to the defendant with the consent of the owner, but that has been obtained by a false representation, has (a) an appropriation within the meaning of section 1(1) of the Theft Act 1968 taken place, or (b) must such a passing of property necessarily involve an element of adverse inference with or usurpation of some right of the owner?'

The choice for the House of Lords was, therefore, starkly laid out. *Lawrence* or *Morris*? That a majority of their Lordships should have opted for *Lawrence* in favour of *Morris* is a source of disappointment but not great surprise. Lord Keith confirmed that the defendant in *Morris* had committed an appropriation when he switched price labels, but went on to express the view that Lord Roskill's much cited dictum, to the effect that appropriation involved an act not expressly or impliedly authorised by the owner, was not be construed so as to suggest that only an unauthorised act would satisfy the requirements of s3(1). Lord Keith opted to expressly approve the earlier decision of the House of Lords in *Lawrence*, in particular Viscount Dilhorne's dictum that theft could be committed even where the owner consented to the defendant's taking of the property. His Lordship also expressed his full agreement with the views of Parker CJ in *Dobson v General Accident Fire and Life Insurance Corporation plc* to the effect that *Morris* cannot be taken to have overruled *Lawrence*. As Lord Keith put it:

> 'The actual decision in *Morris* was correct, but it was erroneous, in addition to being unnecessary for the decision, to indicate that an act expressly or impliedly authorised by the owner could never amount to an appropriation. There is no material distinction between the facts in *Dobson* and those in the present case. In each case the owner of the goods was induced by fraud to part with them to the rogue. *Lawrence* makes it clear that consent to or authorisation by the owner of the taking by the rogue is irrelevant.'

Was there any alternative?

Lord Lowry's powerful dissent in *R v Gomez* is worthy of close attention. He explains with admirable clarity the significance of the Criminal Law Revision

Committee's Report that presaged the enactment of the Theft Act 1968, and the sense in which the report supports his assertion that the intention of Parliament had been to maintain a fundamental distinction between theft and obtaining property by deception. This writer has considerable sympathy with the view that Parliament did intend s1 and s15 to have at least distinct, if not mutually exclusive, spheres of operation. As Lord Lowry concluded:

> 'To simplify the law, where possible, is a worthy objective but, my Lords, I maintain that the law, as envisaged in the [CLRC] report, is simple enough: there is no problem (and there would have been none in *Lawrence*, *Morris* and the present case) if one prosecutes under section 15 all offenders involving obtaining by deception and prosecutes theft in general under section 1. In that way some thefts will come under section 15, but no "false pretences" will come under section 1.'

With respect, Lord Keith's reasons for not consulting the CLRC Report are less than convincing. He stated:

> 'In my opinion it serves no useful purpose at the present time to seek to construe the relevant provisions of the Theft Act by reference to the report which preceded it ... [T]he decision in *Lawrence* was a clear decision of this House upon the construction of the word "appropriate" in section 1(1) of the Act, which had stood for 12 years when doubt was thrown upon it by obiter dicta in *Morris*. *Lawrence* must be regarded as authoritative and correct, and there is no question of it now being right to depart from it.'

What is the effect of Gomez?

The majority of their Lordships accept that the effect of the ruling in *Gomez* is to make nearly every case of obtaining property by deception, a case of theft too. Lord Browne-Wilkinson admits as much although he attempts to defend this conclusion by observing that there may still be exceptions:

> 'Take for example a man who obtains land by deception. Save as otherwise expressly provided, the definitions in sections 4 and 5 of the Act apply only for the purposes of interpreting section 1 of the Act: see section 1(3). Section 34(1) applies subsection (1) of section 4 and subsection (1) of section 5 generally for the purposes of the Act. Accordingly the other subsections of section 4 and section 5 do not apply to section 15. Suppose that a fraudster has persuaded a victim to part with his house: the fraudster is not guilty of theft of the land since section 4(2) provides that you cannot steal land. The charge could only be laid under section 15 which contains no provisions excluding land from the definition of property.'

One can perhaps be forgiven for speculating on how many such cases have come before the courts since 1968. With great respect it is submitted that this remaining exclusive role for s15 identified by his Lordship is in reality negligible. An interesting indication of parliamentary intent may be the change introduced by s26 of the Criminal Justice Act 1991, whereby the maximum sentence for theft was reduced to seven years imprisonment, whilst that for obtaining property by deception remained at ten. If the view of the majority is that nearly all cases under s15 can be charged as theft why should there be such a disparity in possible punishment? Is there something peculiarly culpable about obtaining land by deception that would warrant an extra three years incarceration?

Gomez also indicates the view to be adopted in respect of certain earlier Court of Appeal decisions. According to Lord Keith, both *Skipp* and *Fritschy* are now to be regarded as having been wrongly decided. Interestingly this means that he thinks that Skipp's conviction should have been quashed, whilst that of Fritschy should have been upheld.

The approach adopted in *Phillipou* (above) to abstraction of money from a limited company by a person in a position to give the consent of the company to the abstraction, was approved by both Lord Keith and Lord Browne-Wilkinson. It is a matter for speculation as to what extent, if at all, their Lordships were influenced by decisions such as that of Mr Justice Tucker, during the trial of Asil Nadir, where charges against the ex-chairman of Polly Peck International alleging theft totalling £119,000,000 were dropped because of the confusion as to whether his transfer of funds from a Polly Peck account to that of a subsidiary had the consent of the company.

Lord Browne-Wilkinson did observe, however, that in his view:

'The pillaging of companies by those who control them is now all too common. It would offend both common sense and justice to hold that the very control which enables such people to extract the company's assets constitutes a defence to a charge of theft from the company. The question in each case must be whether the extraction of the property from the company was dishonest, not whether the alleged thief has consented to his own wrongdoing.'

The position of shoppers in self-service stores is also worthy of note. Any assumption of any right of the owner can now be an appropriation of property, regardless of the intentions of either party. As Lord Browne-Wilkinson observed:

'For myself ... I regard the word "appropriation" in isolation as being an objective description of the act done irrespective of the mental state of either the owner or the accused.'

As a result, the honest shopper selecting goods in a supermarket now appropriates them, even though the goods cannot be placed in the trolley as requested by the store without such action by the shopper.

What of the customer who selects underpriced goods in a supermarket, intending to purchase them at the lower price if allowed to do so, and knowing the goods to be underpriced? When the matter came before the Divisional Court in *Dip Kaur* v *Chief Constable for Hampshire* [1981] 1 WLR 578, Lord Lane CJ held that there could be no theft until the defendant committed some act that only the owner would be allowed to perform, such as taking the shoes from the store. In that case the defendant had taken the shoes to the check-out and paid the lower, incorrect, price for them, and had been arrested on leaving the store. The Lord Chief Justice was of the view that by the time of her arrest property in the shoes had passed to the defendant, following the transaction at the check-out. That transaction had been vitiated by the cashier's mistake as to price, but in his Lordship's view the mistake could only render the contract voidable, and up to the time of the arrest the transaction had not been avoided. A few years later, however, the Lord Chief Justice was to change his views on this matter. When *R v Morris* came before him in the Court of Appeal, he expressed the view that, on reflection, *Dip Kaur* had been wrongly decided. It was now his Lordship's view that the defendant had appropriated the shoes when she had selected them. In the House of Lords, Lord Roskill stated that he was disposed to agree with the learned Lord Chief Justice. Lord Roskill went further, however, and expressed his distaste for the tendency to try and resolve issues of criminal liability by way of reference to:

> '... questions whether particular contracts are void or voidable on the ground of mistake or fraud or whether any mistake is sufficiently fundamental to vitiate a contract. These difficult questions should so far as possible be confined to those fields of law to which they are immediately relevant, and I do not regard them as relevant questions under the Theft Act 1968.'

The resolution of this problem, following *Gomez*, would now seem to lie in accepting that the selection of a wrongly priced item is an appropriation, shifting attention instead to the state of mind of the shopper. Any defendant with a passing knowledge of contract law would be tempted to claim that the price label is in any event no more than an invitation to treat, and that the customer is at liberty to select an item with the intention of making any offer he pleases at the check-out. Section 2(1)(a) of the 1968 Act (defendant's honest belief in a legal right) would seem relevant here. Failing that, would ordinary decent people consider such action dishonest (see *R v Ghosh*, considered in Chapter 18)?

Curiously, in *R v Gallasso* (1994) 98 Cr App R 284, a case decided by the Court of Appeal only a very short time after the House of Lords' decision in *Gomez*, Lloyd LJ made a number of comments suggestive of a desire to restrict the scope of *Gomez*. The appellant, a nurse caring for mentally disturbed adults, was entrusted with looking after the financial affairs of her patients, and in particular was authorised to withdraw money from their accounts in order to pay for their day-to-day requirements. When J, one of her patients, received a cheque for £4,000, the appellant opened a second account in his name and paid the cheque into that account. The appellant subsequently transferred £3,000 from this second account to J's first account, and £1,000 from J's second account to her own account. Some time later the appellant used a cheque for £1,800, that had been sent to J, to open a cashcard account in his name. The appellant was convicted of theft in respect of the transfer of £1,000 to her own account, and in respect of the cheque for £1,800 that she used to open the cashcard account. The appellant appealed successfully against conviction in respect of the cheque for £1,800 on the ground that she had not committed an appropriation. The Court of Appeal held that in opening the cashcard account the appellant was acting in a proper manner in relation to the cheque, in the sense that she was confirming J's right to the money rather than usurping it.

Whatever the appellant's secret dishonest intent, it could not convert her actions into an appropriation. With respect, the decision seems to be almost totally at odds with the rationale of *Gomez* as to the nature of appropriation, in that the court seems to be requiring some evidence of an overt act of adverse interference with the owner's rights for appropriation to be made out, raising the possibility that the Court of Appeal's decision is per incuriam. Clearly, if Gallasso is to be acquitted, the decision in *Fritschy* cannot be wrong. The fact that Gallasso was paying in the cheque, intending to divert funds later, whilst Fritschy had no intention of going to Switzerland with the Krugerrands, cannot be the basis of any sensible distinction. If the Court of Appeal is seriously seeking to reintroduce the distinction between those cases where the defendant carries off the property and those where he does not, Parliament may as well repeal the 1968 Act and start again, as these are the very problems it was designed to address. With respect it is submitted that, following *Gomez*, Gallasso appropriated the cheque when she took possession of it, regardless of her intent. If she had the mens rea for theft at the time, then the offence was made out. Perhaps a charge of attempted theft would have avoided these difficulties.

The duration of appropriation

In *R v Atakpu; R v Abrahams* [1993] 3 WLR 812, the Court of Appeal considered two issues; could property that had been appropriated by the defendant, be appropriated again each time he assumed the rights of the owner?; and, was appropriation a continuous act?

The appellants had hired cars in Germany using false documents, planning to sell the cars on returning to the United Kingdom, but were detained at customs on returning to the United Kingdom, and in due course charged with conspiring to steal the cars. Following a direction from the trial judge that an appropriation of the vehicles occurred within the United Kingdom, the appellants were convicted and subsequently appealed. The Court of Appeal, allowing the appeals, held that, applying *Gomez* (above), the appropriation of the cars took place in Germany even though the hire company was deceived into parting with the possession of them, and they had thus been stolen outside the jurisdiction. The theft was complete before the appellants returned. The court recognised that decisions such as those in *Meech* (above), and *Pitham and Hehl* (above), provided support for the proposition that there could not be a fresh appropriation every time the appellants subsequently dealt with the cars on their return to the jurisdiction. By contrast cases such as *Hale* (1978) 68 Cr App R 415 identified theft as a continuing act. Attempting to reconcile these various approaches Ward J, giving the judgment of the court, observed:

'... it would seem (1) theft can occur in an instant by a single appropriation but it can also involve a course of dealing with property lasting longer and involving several appropriations before the transaction is complete; (2) theft is a finite act – it has a beginning and it has an end; (3) at what point the transaction is complete is a matter for the jury to decide upon the facts of each case; (4) though there may be several appropriations in the course of a single theft or several appropriations of different goods each constituting a separate theft as in *Skipp*, no case suggests that there can be successive thefts of the same property (assuming of course that possession is constant and not lost or abandoned, later to be assumed again).'

Although the court regarded theft as a finite act, it recommended a flexible approach whereby the question of whether or not the theft was still taking place should be left to the jury, properly directed. The test of whether or not the defendants were still 'on the job' as propounded by Smith and Hogan (7th edn, 1992 p513), was endorsed by the court.

Presumably if the appellants had sold the cars in the United Kingdom they could have been indicted for handling stolen goods as, under s24 of the 1968 Act, it matters not where the theft producing the goods was committed, and they would no longer have 'been in the course of stealing'.

The Mens Rea of Theft

18.1 Dishonesty

18.2 Intention to permanently deprive

18.1 Dishonesty

A defendant can only be convicted of theft where his actions are found to be dishonest. It is this element in theft that results in any defendant charged with the offence having the right to trial by jury, regardless of how trivial the value of the property involved may be. A conviction for theft inevitably carries with it a slur on the defendant's character. It should be remembered that a defendant can be dishonest even where he does not act with a view to making a gain for himself or another. It is sufficient that he acts with a view to causing loss to the victim, this being the effect of s1(2) of the 1968 Act. Dishonesty is dealt with in s2 of the Theft Act 1968, but it only provides a partial, or negative, definition, and that this only applies to dishonesty in the context of theft, not deception or handling.

Section 2(1)(a)

Section 2(1)(a) provides that a person's appropriation of property belonging to another is not to be regarded as dishonest:

> '... if he appropriates the property in the belief that he has in law the right to deprive the other of it, on behalf of himself or of a third person.'

The test is subjective. The defendant's belief that he has in law the right to deprive another of property merely has to be honestly held, it does not have to be reasonable. This is confirmed by the Court of Appeal's decision in *R* v *Holden* [1991] Crim LR 478. As with all such subjective tests, the more outlandish the defendant's honest belief, the less likely the justices, or the jury, are to believe him. Further, the belief must relate to a legal right to deprive; hence if D wrongly thought property had passed to him from P under the terms of a contract, and he purported to sell the property on to X, his assumption of the rights of the owner would not be dishonest, provided his belief in the legal right to sell was genuine. In effect the defendant can rely on a mistake of civil (contract) law as a defence. It remains to be seen whether a defendant who believes he has a moral right to take property could bring himself within this subsection. It is submitted that it is more likely that he would be found not to have been dishonest under *R* v *Ghosh* (below).

Section 2(1)(b)

Section 2(1)(b) provides that a person's appropriation of property belonging to another is not to be regarded as dishonest:

> '... if he appropriates the property in the belief that he would have the other's consent if the other knew of the appropriation and the circumstances of it.'

The subsection might apply where D's car has run out of petrol, and D takes a can of fuel from his next-door neighbour P's garden. D has clearly appropriated property belonging to another and has intention to permanently deprive P of the petrol, but may be able to argue that he honestly believed P would have consented had he known. Again the test is subjective.

Section 2(1)(c)

Section 2(1)(c) provides:

> 'A person's appropriation of property belonging to another is not to be regarded as dishonest –
> (except where the property came to him as trustee or personal representative) if he appropriates the property in the belief that the person to whom the property belongs cannot be discovered by taking reasonable steps.'

The subsection will be of particular significance where the defendant finds property that has been lost by the owner (property that has been deliberately abandoned ceases to be property belonging to another within s5). Again, the test for the defendant's belief is subjective. As regards the question of what might be required by taking reasonable steps to discover ownership, this will depend partly on the identification available, the location in which it is found, and the value of the property. A defendant finding a £10 note in the street may well come within s2(1)(c), unless he has just seen it fall from the wallet of P who is walking in front of him. Similarly, if the defendant finds a suitcase containing £1,000,000 in the street, one would expect him to make considerable efforts to locate the owner. Nevertheless it should be kept in mind that the subsection is concerned with what the defendant views as reasonable steps: see further *R* v *Small* [1987] Crim LR 777 which affirms this latter point.

Section 2(2)

Section 2(2) provides:

> 'A person's appropriation of property belonging to another may be dishonest notwithstanding that he is willing to pay for the property.'

This subsection is included for the avoidance of doubt. Where D sees P's newspaper poking out of his letterbox, pulls out the newspaper, and leaves its price on P's doormat, D could still be guilty of theft. He has appropriated property belonging to another with intention to permanently deprive, and s2(2) states that he can still be regarded as dishonest; whether he is or not falls to be determined by the jury.

Dishonesty beyond s2

Should a defendant, who appropriates property belonging to another, intending to permanently deprive the other of it, knowing he has no legal right to do so, knowing that the owner does not consent, and knowing how to return the goods to the owner, nevertheless be able to escape liability for theft on the basis that he is not dishonest? The question is really asking whether a defendant who is unable to escape liability under s2(1), should nevertheless be able to contend that he is not dishonest. The answer must be yes. Whether certain behaviour is dishonest or not is a mixed question of law and morality, and one that has engendered considerable academic and judicial discussion. It is clear, however, that a defendant unable to bring himself within s2(1) may nevertheless escape liability because the jury do not regard his actions as blameworthy. Following *R v Feely* [1973] 1 QB 530, it is no longer permissible for a trial judge to withdraw the issue of dishonesty from a jury by directing them that, as a matter of law, the defendant's actions were dishonest. In cases where the defendant cannot avail himself of s2(1), and where there is nevertheless some debate as to whether or not his actions were dishonest, the matter should be left to the jury to determine, applying their own standards of common decency. The criticism of such an approach is that it may tend to play down the subjective element of dishonesty where the defendant contends that he believed he was behaving honestly. In this respect the Court of Appeal's decision in *R v Ghosh* [1982] 1 QB 1053, despite the fact that it was concerned with obtaining property by deception, may provide the 'model direction' for theft cases. The court held that in cases of doubt the jury should be directed in the following terms:

> 'Was the defendant dishonest according to the standards of ordinary decent people? If yes, did the defendant realise that what he was doing was dishonest by these standards?'

There is a rider to this test in *Ghosh* to the effect that the defendant is to be regarded as dishonest even where he believes his actions to be morally justified, if he nevertheless realises that ordinary decent people would regard it as wrong. A possible loophole in this new test is that a defendant may not have thought about whether ordinary decent people would have regarded his actions as dishonest, or even if he had, he may not have been able to tell. Further, the test does not remove the possibility of inconsistencies between juries, although it must be said that this latter problem is not the exclusive preserve of theft: see further *R v Forrester* [1992] Crim LR 79.

18.2 Intention to permanently deprive

The need for the prosecution to establish that the defendant intended to permanently deprive the owner of his property is what distinguishes borrowing from theft. Note that the owner does not in fact have to be permanently deprived of his property; it is sufficient that the defendant intended him to be so deprived. Where such intention is lacking, liability might still be imposed under s11 or s12 (see Chapters 19 and 20). Sections 6(1) and 6(2) do not provide a comprehensive definition of intention to permanently deprive, but should instead be regarded as 'deeming' sections which give an artificially extended meaning to the phrase. In the vast majority of situations the presence or absence of such a state of mind should be evident, recourse only being had to s6 in exceptional cases.

Section 6

Section 6(1) provides:

> 'A person appropriating property belonging to another without meaning the other permanently to lose the thing itself is nevertheless to be regarded as having the intention of permanently depriving the other of it if his intention is to treat the thing as his own to dispose of regardless of the other's rights: and a borrowing or lending of it may amount to so treating it if, but only if, the borrowing or lending is for a period and in circumstances making it equivalent to an outright taking or disposal.'

The subsection envisages two particular situations where D might be deemed to have intention to permanently deprive: where he treats the property as his own to dispose of regardless of the other's rights; and where he borrows the property in circumstances amounting to an outright taking.

Where D abandons property belonging to another he may be deemed to intend to permanently deprive that other of it, if the circumstances are such that there is little likelihood of the owner ever having the property returned to him. For example, D takes P's book and leaves it in a dustbin. D may hope that it is returned to P, but it is likely to be regarded as a disposal regardless of P's rights. Similarly where D takes P's book and sells it to X, D would be deemed to have intention to permanently deprive P, even though his only thought was of gaining money from X, although as with many similar examples of this nature, D might be more appropriately charged with obtaining property by deception from X. D will also be guilty of theft where he will only allow P to have his property back if he complies with some other condition, for example where he takes P's book and sells it back to P. D does not intend to permanently deprive P of the book, quite the contrary, but his behaviour will nevertheless bring him within the scope of s6(1): see *R v Coffey* [1987] Crim LR 498.

If D takes money intending to repay it at a later date, he is still to be regarded as having an intention to permanently deprive the owner of the money, since it is to be assumed that he will not be returning the exact same notes and coins: see *R v*

Velumyl [1989] Crim LR 299, although D could still contend that he was not dishonest given his intention to replace the money with an equivalent fund.

Some uncertainty arguably persists in relation to the meaning of the phrase '... to dispose of ...' as it is used in s6(1). In *DPP v Lavender* [1994] Crim LR 297, the respondent was charged with theft of two doors belonging to a local authority. He had taken the doors from a council property that was under construction, and used them to replace the damaged doors in his girlfriend's property, which was also owned by the same local authority. The Divisional Court held that under the first 'limb' of s6(1) the respondent could be described as having treated the doors as his own to dispose of regardless of the council's rights, as he had manifested an intention to treat them as his own by hanging them in a different property from that for which they were intended. This decision may, however, be difficult to reconcile with *R v Cahill* [1993] Crim LR 141, where the Court of Appeal took the view that 'to dispose of' implied a getting rid of the property by destroying or selling it. The court in the instant case would seem to be proceeding on the basis that s6(1) is satisfied if D acts in a manner that is inconsistent with P's rights. It is submitted that the approach of the Court of Appeal is to be preferred.

As indicated above, D may be deemed to have intention to permanently deprive where he borrows another's property for a period and in circumstances amounting to an outright taking. An example might arise where D takes P's video recorder and uses it for five years. D may have always intended to return it, but at the end of five years it may be of little practical use to P, given the wear and tear it has suffered, and its resale value will only be a fraction of what it was at the time it was taken. The subsection might also cover the situation where P owns a season ticket entitling him to enter the grandstand at Arsenal Football Club for 21 home league games and D takes the season ticket at the beginning of the season, uses it to attend the games, and returns it to P at the end of the season. Clearly P gets his ticket back, but the borrowing of it by D has, it is submitted, taken the 'value' out of it, and such conduct should amount to theft by virtue of s6(1). The question arises as to whether the same argument is sustainable where D only takes the ticket to get into one of the 21 games; in such a case P has hardly been deprived of his complete interest in the ticket. It may be more appropriate to charge D with theft of the chose in action which is represented by the ticket, ie the right to enter the grandstand for that game. The whole problem can be avoided if D is charged with obtaining services by deception contrary to s1(1) of the Theft Act 1978 when he uses the ticket to gain admission to the ground.

The requirement that a borrowing of property should result in its losing virtually all of its value before a defendant could be deemed to have intention to permanently deprive, was reaffirmed by the Court of Appeal in *R v Lloyd* [1985] QB 829. The appellants had taken prints of first run feature films from cinemas, copied them onto video tapes and returned the films to the cinemas in time for the next showing to the public. There was no evidence that the cinemas were ever prevented from showing the films at the advertised times. The convictions for theft of the films were quashed on the basis that there was insufficient evidence of intention to permanently deprive. The borrowing of the films did not amount to an outright taking in the circumstances, because they had not lost any of their value as films that could be shown to paying members of the public. The situation might have been different if the prints had been borrowed for three months and returned after most members of the public, who wanted to pay to see the film, had done so at other cinemas. The court further added that s6 was not to be interpreted so as to bring within the ambit of intention to permanently deprive anything which would not have been so regarded before 1968.

Special considerations apply where the property taken is a registered motor vehicle. Given the ease with which the ownership of abandoned vehicles can be traced, intention to permanently deprive may be virtually impossible to establish, hence the existence of the offence under s12 of the 1968 Act.

Stolen cheques

Questions have arisen as to whether a defendant, who takes a cheque book belonging to another and draws cheques on that person's account, can be charged with theft of the cheques. The problem arises from the fact that the cheques can be returned to the account holder once cashed. On the basis of *R* v *Duru* [1973] 3 All ER 715 a cheque represents a chose in action, and undergoes a fundamental change in legal status once it passes through the banking system; as Megaw LJ stated:

> 'So far as the cheque itself is concerned, true it is a piece of paper. But it is a piece of paper which changes its character completely once it is paid, because then it receives a rubber stamp on it saying it has been paid and it ceases to be a thing in action, or at any rate it ceases to be, in its substance, the same thing as it was before: that is, an instrument on which payment falls to be made.'

See further *R* v *Sobel* [1986] Crim LR 261, and *R* v *Downes* [1983] Crim LR 819.

Conditional intent

Does a defendant commit theft where he takes a painting because it might be valuable, intending to keep it if it is, discovers it is of little value and returns it to the owner? It might be argued that he has only a conditional intention to steal the painting, and as that condition is never fulfilled, he never has a present unconditional intention to permanently deprive the owner. Two decisions of the Court of Appeal, *R* v *Easom* [1971] 2 QB 315, and *R* v *Husseyn* (1977) 67 Cr App R 131, established that a conviction for theft was only sustainable where there was clear evidence that the defendant had a present intention to permanently deprive the owner. Problems were compounded by the fact that as the law then stood a defendant could not be charged with attempted theft where there was no property that he wanted to steal. Recourse was had to tortuous reasoning and dubious indictments in order to circumvent these difficulties, see *R* v *Bayley and Easterbrook* [1980] Crim LR 503, and *Scudder* v *Barrett* [1979] 3 WLR 591, but the major problems were removed by the enactment of the Criminal Attempts Act 1981 as interpreted by the House of Lords in *R* v *Shivpuri* [1986] 2 All ER 334. A defendant can now be charged with attempting to steal property he believed to be in existence, or of value, although problems may yet remain where the full offence of theft is charged, the prosecution can avoid difficulties if the charge does not particularise the property the defendant is alleged to have attempted to steal.

Section 6(2)

Section 6(2) provides:

> 'Without prejudice to the generality of subsection (1) above, where a person, having possession or control (lawfully or not) of property belonging to another, parts with the property under a condition as to its return which he may not be able to perform, this (if done for purposes of his own and without the other's authority) amounts to treating the property as his own to dispose of regardless of the other's rights.'

A defendant who takes another's property and pledges it with a pawnbroker without the owner's permission would probably come within s6(2). The defendant has parted with the property subject to a condition which he might not be able to perform, namely redeem the pledge by the appointed date. Again the effect is that the defendant is deemed to have intended to permanently deprive the owner of his property. Where a defendant is nevertheless positive that he will be able to redeem the pledge a jury might be persuaded to the view that his taking was not dishonest.

19

Sections 8, 9, 10 and 11 of the Theft Act 1968

19.1 Robbery

19.2 Burglary

19.3 Aggravated burglary

19.4 Section 11 of the Theft Act 1968

19.1 Robbery

Robbery is essentially an aggravated form of theft. The aggravating factor is the force used on the victim, or threats of force made, prior to or during the theft. Section 8(1) which creates the offence provides:

'A person is guilty of robbery if he steals, and immediately before or at the time of doing so, and in order to do so, he uses force on any person or puts or seeks to put any person in fear of being then and there subjected to force.'

It should be noted that a conviction for robbery will only be secured where all the elements of theft are established. In particular, a defendant charged with robbery can raise points of law by way of defence that would have been available had he been charged with theft. In *R* v *Robinson* [1977] Crim LR 173, the Court of Appeal held that a defendant should be found not guilty of robbery where he honestly believed he had a right in law to take the property, ie where the defendant came within s2(1)(a) of the 1968 Act (above).

The aggravated nature of robbery is also reflected in the punishment available to the court by s8(2) which provides:

'A person guilty of robbery, or of an assault with intent to rob, shall on conviction on indictment be liable to imprisonment for life.'

Use of force

The question of whether or not force has been used is one that should be left to the jury, the Court of Appeal so held in *R* v *Dawson* (1976) 64 Cr App R 170, where the

272

defendant had nudged the victim causing him to lose his balance so that his wallet could more easily be taken. As Lawton LJ observed:

> 'The choice of the word "force" is not without interest because under the Larceny Act 1916 the word "violence" had been used, but Parliament deliberately on the advice of the Criminal Law Revision Committee changed that word to "force". Whether there is any difference between "violence" or "force" is not relevant for the purposes of this case; but the word is "force". It is a word in ordinary use. It is a word which juries understand.'

The force can be used upon any person, not necessarily the owner or custodian of the property in question, thus confirming the decision of the House of Lords (under the previous law) in *Smith* v *Desmond Hall* [1965] AC 960, where the defendant was convicted of robbery after overpowering a night watchman in order to steal cash from an office some distance away.

The statute requires the force to be used 'on any person', but it may be sufficient for the defendant to use force on the victim's possessions in a way which affects the victim. In *R* v *Clouden* [1987] Crim LR 56, the defendant had pulled on the victim's handbag to wrench it from her hands. The Court of Appeal held that whilst a snatching of property without resistance from the owner, such as by a pickpocket, should not amount to robbery, the question of whether force had been used 'on any person' should be left to the jury. The defendant's appeal was dismissed.

There is no need for actual physical contact between robber and victim; it is sufficient that the victim is put in fear of immediate physical violence, or that some other person present is similarly put in fear. Were D to threaten P that unless P handed over £100 immediately, P's child X would be beaten on the way home from school later that day, the appropriate charge would be blackmail and not robbery, because X is not put in fear of force being used as he is not present when the threat is made, conversely P, who is present, is not being threatened with force. Presumably robbery is committed where D makes threats to P prior to stealing his property even though P is not frightened by them, as s8(1) covers the situation where D 'seeks to put any person in fear'.

The force must have been used by D, or he must be an accomplice to its use. Theft without knowledge of any violence having taken place is not robbery: see *R* v *Harris* (1988) The Times 4 March.

'In order to steal . . .'

The force, or threats of force, must be used in order to steal, as was held by the Court of Appeal in *R* v *Shendley* [1970] Crim LR 49; there is no such thing as robbery without violence. Hence where D attacks P in order to settle an argument, and having hit P to the ground finds his wallet to have fallen out, D will not be guilty of robbery should he run off with the wallet, because the force was not used by him with the intention of stealing.

Coincidence of force and stealing

Section 8(1) clearly provides that the force must be used immediately before, or during the course of, the theft, raising the question of for how long theft continues.

Where force, or threats of force are used prior to stealing, the requirement of immediacy must be met. It is submitted that where a threat of force is made at some time before the appropriation of property, the jury must be satisfied that the threat was still affecting the mind of the victim immediately before or during the theft. In short, there must be a continuing threat.

The theft that the use of force must precede or accompany will continue for as long as appropriation continues; this can be for a split-second, or an indeterminate length of time. In *Corcoran* v *Anderton* [1980] Crim LR 385, the defendant's appeal against conviction was dismissed by the Divisional Court on the ground that even though the victim had only been momentarily dispossessed of her property, where the defendant had tugged at her bag causing it to fall to the ground, there had been an appropriation accompanied by force. At the other extreme, the Court of Appeal in *R* v *Hale* (1978) 68 Cr App R 415 held that appropriation could be a continuing act; the point at which it ceased was to be determined by the jury on the facts of each case. Where, therefore, D steals property belonging to P, is discovered by P, and threatens P that unless he is allowed to escape without the police being called he will assault P, D will be guilty of robbery. The threats to P are made whilst the theft (appropriation) is continuing, and are made in order to accomplish the theft; see further *R* v *Atakpu* [1993] 3 WLR 812, in Chapter 17.

19.2 Burglary

The offence of burglary created by s9 replaces the old offences of 'breaking and entering', and much of the complexity that went with them. The section creates two forms of burglary: the first where the defendant enters as a trespasser with intent to commit one of four specified offences; the second where the defendant has entered as a trespasser and gone on to commit theft or grievous bodily harm. A person found guilty of burglary can be imprisoned for up to 14 years where the offence is committed in a building or part of a building used as a dwelling, or in other cases for a maximum of 10 years: s9(3)(a)(b). Common features of both forms of burglary are that the defendant must enter a building as a trespasser; these matters will be considered, therefore, before the two offences are considered separately.

'Building ... or part of a building'

Byles J, in *Stevens* v *Gourley* (1859) 7 CBNS 99 at 112, stated that a building was 'a structure of considerable size and intended to be permanent or at least to endure for a considerable length of time'. There is no requirement that the premises should be used for human occupation; in *B and S v Leathley* [1979] Crim LR 314 (a decision of Carlisle Crown Court) a large freezer container standing in a farmyard without foundations was held to be a building. In each case, whether or not a structure constitutes a building is a mixed question of law and fact to be determined by the jury after guidance from the trial judge. In *Norfolk Constabulary v Seekings and Gould* [1986] Crim LR 167, a lorry trailer which was used for storage, and to this end supplied with mains electricity, was held not to constitute a building. In this respect note also subs9(4) which provides:

> '(3) References in subsections (1) and (2) above to a building and the reference in subsection (3) above to a building which is a dwelling shall apply also to an inhabited vehicle or vessel, and shall apply to any such vehicle or vessel at times when the person having a habitation in it is not there as well as at times when he is.'

Reference to 'part of a building' covers the situation where D enters P's house with permission, but then enters P's bedroom, which he does not have permission to do. D would not have committed burglary on first entering the house, but may have done so, subject to what follows below, on entering the bedroom. The Court of Appeal decision in *R v Walkington* (1979) 68 Cr App R 427 further illustrates the point. The defendant had entered a department store during opening hours, and had approached a three-sided partition that surrounded a till on the middle of the shop floor. He proceeded to stand inside the partitioned area and opened the till drawer to see if it contained any money for him to steal. The Court of Appeal held that the area inside the partition represented a 'part of a building' from which the public had been impliedly excluded. The defendant being aware of this had been correctly convicted under s9(1)(a) of entering part of a building as a trespasser with intent to steal.

'Enters ... or ... having entered'

The defendant must enter, or have entered, a building in order to be guilty of burglary. Failure to enter may still leave the possibility of an attempt charge. Placing a key in a lock, or the blade of a knife inside a window, will not be enough. On the basis of the Court of Appeal decision in *R v Collins* [1972] 2 All ER 1105, the entry must be 'substantial and effective'. What constitutes such an entry will depend on the circumstances, but in *R v Brown* (1985) The Times 31 January, the Court of Appeal held that leaning into a broken shop window to extract goods must be enough for burglary. Watkins LJ rejected as an 'astounding proposition' any suggestion that this was not the case.

' ... as a trespasser'

In civil law A commits a trespass upon B's land, where he enters upon that land without B's permission. B will of course only be able to recover damages where A actually causes him some loss. The civil law concept of trespass is at the heart of the crime of burglary, and in simple terms it could be said that D enters a building owned by P as a trespasser, either where D has no express or implied permission from P to do so, or D exceeds the express or implied permission granted by P.

In *R* v *Collins* (above), the Court of Appeal confirmed that trespass, for the purposes of the Theft Act 1968, does require proof of mens rea. The appellant sought to challenge his conviction for burglary contrary to s9(1)(a), on the ground that he believed that he had been given permission to enter the house in question by the owner's daughter. Edmund-Davies LJ observed that:

> '... there cannot be a conviction for entering premises "as a trespasser" within the meaning of section 9 of the Theft Act unless the person entering does so knowing that he is a trespasser and nevertheless deliberately enters, or, at the very least, is reckless as to whether or not he is entering the premises of another without the other party's consent.'

It is submitted that the recklessness envisaged here is 'subjective' as in *R* v *Cunningham* [1957] 2 QB 396, and not 'objective' as in *R* v *Caldwell* [1982] AC 341, hence D might escape liability where he stopped to consider the risk that he might be trespassing, but went on to dismiss it as negligible.

The court went on to reject the proposition that a defendant could enter a building with permission, but then become a trespasser within s9 simply by exceeding the permission that he had been given, for example by deciding *after* entry to rape or steal. As Edmund-Davies LJ observed:

> '... we are entirely in agreement with the view ... that the common law doctrine of trespass ab initio has no application to burglary under the Theft Act 1968.'

It might be different, of course, where D is invited into P's house for tea, and D accepts the invitation, intending to steal silverware from P's lounge whilst P is out of the room. Provided D has this secret dishonest intent at the time of his entry into P's house, he will be trespassing, as he will be entering for a purpose in excess of his permission to do so. In *R* v *Smith and Jones* [1976] 3 All ER 54, the appellants, who had visited the house of Smith's father and stolen his television set, were convicted under s9(1)(b) and appealed on the basis that they had permission to go into the house and thus could not have been trespassing. The court held that the defendants were rightly convicted under s9(1)(b), on the basis that a person enters a building as a trespasser where he realises he has exceeded his permission, or is reckless as to whether he has done so. The defendants might have had permission to enter the house for normal domestic purposes, but not to enter in the middle of the night to steal. Confirming that the decision in *R* v *Collins* (above), had added to the concept of trespass as a civil wrong the mental element of mens rea, James LJ observed:

> '... it is our view that a person is a trespasser for the purpose of section 9(1)(b) of the Theft Act 1968, if he enters premises of another knowing that he is entering in excess of the permission that has been given to him, or being reckless as to whether he is entering in excess of the permission that has been given to him to enter, providing the facts are known to the accused which enable him to realise that he is acting in excess of the permission given or that he is acting recklessly as to whether he exceeds that permission ...'

In *R* v *Collins*, a further point was raised by the prosecution, to the effect that the daughter, not being the tenant or occupier of the dwelling-house and her mother being apparently in occupation, could not have extended an effective invitation to the appellant to enter. Regardless of the position in the law of tort, the court regarded the application of such a proposition in criminal law as 'unthinkable'.

Section 9(1)(a)

Section 9(1)(a), which creates the first form of burglary, provides:

> 'A person is guilty of burglary if –
> he enters any building or part of a building as a trespasser and with intent to commit any such offence as is mentioned in subsection (2) below.'

Subsection (2) (as amended by the Criminal Justice and Public Order Act 1994, Schedule 10, para 26) further provides:

> 'The offences referred to in subsection (1)(a) above are offences of stealing anything in the building or part of a building in question, of inflicting on any person therein any grievous bodily harm or raping any person therein, and of doing unlawful damage to the building or anything therein.'

A defendant can incur liability under s9(1)(a) for entering as a trespasser with intent to steal, regardless of whether there is any property to steal in the building. The Court of Appeal's ruling in *Attorney-General's References (Nos 1 & 2 of 1979)* [1979] 2 WLR 578 establishes that the essence of the offence is the defendant's state of mind at the time of entry; the intent to steal can exist quite independently of any property that he can, or wants to, steal.

The offence of inflicting grievous bodily referred to in s9(2) is assumed to be that under s18 of the Offences against the Person Act 1861, given that the defendant is required to have a specific intent to commit the offence.

Section 9(1)(b)

Section 9(1)(b) provides:

> 'A person is guilty of burglary if having entered any building or part of a building as a trespasser he steals or attempts to steal anything in the building or that part of it or inflicts or attempts to inflict on any person therein any grievous bodily harm.'

Note that the defendant does not need to have had the intention to steal or inflict grievous bodily harm when he entered the building as a trespasser; such intent can be formed subsequent to entry. Curiously, the infliction of grievous bodily harm under s9(1)(b) does not have to constitute an offence, it simply requires D to have inflicted or attempted to inflict grievous bodily harm upon P. The Court of Appeal in *R* v *Jenkins* [1983] 1 All ER 1000 contemplated that a defendant would be guilty under s9(1)(b) where he entered a house as a trespasser and was observed by an occupant of whose presence he was unaware. Should the occupant suffer a stroke as a result of this shock, the defendant would have inflicted grievous bodily harm regardless of his lack of mens rea. The House of Lords, although allowing the defendant's appeal, in *R v Jenkins* [1983] 3 All ER 448, did not dissent from the above analysis of s9(1)(b).

This unsatisfactory state of affairs is adverted to in the Law Commission's draft code, which restates, in code terminology, the offence of burglary. Clause 147 provides (inter alia) that a person commits burglary if, having entered a building as a trespasser, he commits in the building an offence of causing serious personal harm. The causing of such harm, as indicated by clauses 70 and 71 of the Code, would require proof of either intention or recklessness. As the commentary upon clause 147 explained:

> 'This clause takes the opportunity to correct a plain and unintended error in s9 of the Theft Act 1968. Section 9(1)(a) expressly requires entry as a trespasser with intent to commit an "offence". But s9(1)(b) does not expressly require the infliction of grievous bodily harm, which may convert a trespassory entry into burglary, to be an offence; if paragraph (b) were taken literally, burglary could be committed accidentally by someone in a building as a trespasser. This anomaly is an accident of the parliamentary proceedings on the Theft Bill. Our draft eliminates the error, consistently with known parliamentary intention and, we believe, uncontroversially.' [Vol II para 16.8]

19.3 Aggravated burglary

The offence of aggravated burglary is created by s10(1) of the 1968 Act which provides:

> 'A person is guilty of aggravated burglary if he commits any burglary and at the time has with him any firearm or imitation firearm, any weapon of offence, or any explosive; and for this purpose –
> a) "firearm" includes an airgun or air pistol, and "imitation firearm" means anything which has the appearance of being a firearm, whether capable of being discharged or not; and
> b) "weapon of offence" means any article made or adapted for use for causing injury to or incapacitating a person or intended by the person having it with him for such use; and
> c) "explosive" means any article manufactured for the purpose of producing a practical effect by explosion, or intended by the person having it with him for that purpose.'

A defendant convicted of the offence on indictment may be sentenced to a maximum of life imprisonment.

The definition of firearm seems to be largely in line with that given under the Firearms Act 1968. Weapon of offence would cover a wide range of articles such as knuckle dusters, coshes, flick knives, razors, pickaxe handles and so on. See *Gibson v Wales* [1983] 1 All ER 869; *R v Simpson* [1984] Crim LR 39. Explosives can be defined with reference to the Explosives Act 1875.

The defendant must be proved to have had the weapon with him at the time the burglary is committed. In the case of a s9(1)(a) burglary this is the moment of entry as a trespasser with intent. In the case of s9(1)(b), it is the moment when the offence of theft or grievous bodily harm is attempted or committed: see *R v Francis* [1982] Crim LR 363.

Following *R* v *Stones* [1989] 1 WLR 156 it appears that it will not avail a defendant charged under s10 to contend that, despite his possession of a weapon at the time of the burglary, it had not been his intention to use it. The Court of Appeal held that s10 merely required that the appellant had with him a weapon of offence at the time of the burglary. Applying the mischief rule, the court felt that what Parliament sought to prevent was the commission of burglary by a defendant who might be tempted to use any weapon of offence in his possession if challenged or opposed during the course of a burglary.

These matters were reviewed in *R* v *Kelly* (1992) 97 Cr App R 245. The prosecution case was that the appellant had used a screwdriver to gain access to the house in question, and on being disturbed by the occupant had ordered him to unplug a video recorder. It was further alleged that the appellant had then pushed the screwdriver into the occupant's ribcage and made off. The appellant was subsequently apprehended and stated in evidence that he had never taken the screwdriver out of his pocket during the burglary. Rejecting a submission of 'no case', the trial judge ruled that the key question was whether or not the appellant had had the screwdriver with him as a weapon of offence at the time of the burglary (ie under s9(1)(b), at the time the video recorder was stolen). On this basis he was satisfied that the appellant had induced the occupant to unplug the video recorder by taking out his screwdriver. In summing up, the trial judge directed the jury that the offence was made out if the appellant had with him at the time of the burglary a weapon with which he intended to inflict injury should the need arise. Dismissing the appeal, the Court of Appeal held that s10(1) of the 1968 Act was specifically concerned with the use of a weapon which made the offence of burglary more serious. The screwdriver was a weapon of offence if the appellant intended to use it to injure the occupant. Given that the burglary occurred at the moment when the appellant stole the video recorder, the only remaining issue was whether or not the appellant had the weapon with him at this time. It would seem that, on the basis of the *Kelly*, D could incur liability under s10(1) where he enters a building unarmed, steals property, is disturbed by the occupant, and picks up an ashtray and assaults the occupant with it. One might ask if this was what Parliament intended? D might argue that the offence of burglary is in fact made out under s9(1)(b) once he has attempted to steal property, thus in the example given, use of the weapon is not 'at the time' of the burglary. The decision in *Hale* (above) suggests, however, that the court would regard the burglary as continuing for at least as long as D was appropriating the property within the building.

19.4 Section 11 of the Theft Act 1968

The Criminal Law Revision Committee envisaged the offence created by s11 as covering situations where a defendant removes an item, from a public exhibition or an art gallery to which the public has access, but lacks any intention to permanently deprive the owner of the item. The Committee sought to avoid extending theft to include temporary deprivation, or creating a general offence of temporary deprivation. Section 11(1) provides:

> '11(1) Subject to subsections (2) and (3) below, where the public have access to a building in order to view the building or part of it, or a collection or part of a collection housed in it, any person who without lawful authority removes from the building or its grounds the whole or part of any article displayed or kept for display to the public in the building or that part of it or in its grounds shall be guilty of an offence.'

The maximum sentence available following conviction on indictment is five years imprisonment. Note that the offence may be a suitable alternative charge where the elements necessary for s1 theft, or s9 burglary cannot be made out. A defendant who removes items from a public exhibition and refuses to return them unless the owner or some other person fulfils a condition (such as payment of a sum of money to charity) could be charged with theft, contrary to s1, on the basis (inter alia) that he can be deemed to have intention to permanently deprive within s6(1), or blackmail contrary to s21, on the basis that he is making a demand that is unwarranted, accompanied by menaces, with a view to gain or another's loss.

'Building to which the public have access in order to view ...'

The building must be one that the general public have been invited to enter, and not simply some section of the public. The owner's purpose in inviting the public must be to enable them to view the building itself or a collection housed in it. Section 11(2) provides:

> 'It is immaterial for purposes of subsection (1) above, that the public's access to a building is limited to a particular period or particular occasion; but where anything removed from a building or its grounds is there otherwise than as forming part of, or being on loan for exhibition with, a collection intended for permanent exhibition to the public, the person removing it does not thereby commit an offence under this section unless he removes it on a day when the public have access to the building as mentioned in subsection (1) above.'

As to the meaning of 'collection' s11(1) further provides:

> ' "Collection" includes a collection got together for a temporary purpose, but references in this section to a collection do not apply to a collection made or exhibited for the purpose of effecting sales or other commercial dealings.'

Where the public are admitted to a commercial gallery, therefore, an offence would not be committed within s11, where one of the paintings on display is 'borrowed'.

Clearly an offence is not committed where a defendant borrows items from a building which is open to the public but not for the purposes listed in s11(1). In *R* v *Barr* [1978] Crim LR 244, therefore, no offence under s11 was committed by a defendant who removed a cross which was on display in a church for devotional purposes.

Provided that articles are exhibited within a building, liability extends to the removal of articles from the grounds of the building which also form part of the exhibition.

Mens rea

The defendant must intend to remove the article in question, knowing he does not have the consent of the owner, or other lawful authority to do so; in this regard s11(3) provides:

> 'A person does not commit an offence under this section if he believes that he has lawful authority for the removal of the thing in question or that he would have it if the person entitled to give it knew of the removal and the circumstances of it.'

Note that there is no requirement that the prosecution prove the defendant to have acted dishonestly.

20

Sections 12, 13, 21 and 25 of the Theft Act 1968

20.1 Taking a conveyance

20.2 Aggravated vehicle taking

20.3 Dishonestly abstracting electricity

20.4 Blackmail

20.5 Going equipped

20.1 Taking a conveyance

Section 12 replaces the old offence of 'taking and driving away' with a wider offence of 'taking a conveyance'. In common with ss11 and 13, no intention to permanently deprive the owner need be proved on the part of the defendant. Where a defendant is charged with theft of a conveyance contrary to s1, the jury may return a verdict of 'not guilty as charged' and substitute a verdict of guilty in respect of the lesser included offence under s12 (see s12(4)).

Section 12(1) provides:

'Subject to subsections (5) and (6) below, a person shall be guilty of an offence if, without having the consent of the owner or other lawful authority, he takes any conveyance for his own or another's use or, knowing that any conveyance has been taken without such authority, drives it or allows himself to be carried in or on it.'

In the majority of situations a defendant charged with the offence will simply have been 'stealing a ride', in that he takes a conveyance from point 'A' without the owner's consent and leaves it at point 'B'. One of the difficulties in making such conduct theft in respect of motor vehicles is proof of any intention to permanently deprive. Even where D takes the victim's vehicle in Cornwall and leaves it in Newcastle-upon-Tyne, he will still deny intention to permanently deprive on the basis that he knew the vehicle would be returned to the owner once its registration number was traced on computer records held at DVLC. A charge of theft might be more viable where the defendant takes a vehicle and destroys it, ships it out of the country, or changes its chassis number and registration plates, and sells it.

Section 12(5) makes separate provision in respect of pedal cycles where it states:

'Subsection (1) above shall not apply in relation to pedal cycles; but, subject to subsection (6) below, a person who, without having the consent of the owner or other lawful authority, takes a pedal cycle for his own or another 's use, or rides a pedal cycle knowing it to have been taken without such authority, shall on summary conviction be liable to a fine not exceeding fifty pounds.'

The maximum punishment available for the offence under s12(1) following trial on indictment is three years imprisonment.

'Conveyance'

Section 12(7)(a) provides:

' "Conveyance" means any conveyance constructed or adapted for the carriage of a person or persons whether by land, water or air, except that it does not include a conveyance constructed or adapted for use only under the control of a person not carried in or on it, and "drive" shall be construed accordingly.'

This definition would seem to exclude goods vehicles where no provision is made for the person controlling the vehicle to sit on it. A goods trailer might fall within this category, as might some electric milk floats which are operated by a person walking alongside. *Neal* v *Gribble* [1978] RTR 409 is authority for the proposition that a horse is not a 'conveyance' within s12, although a horse-drawn vehicle would seem to be within the definition.

'Takes ... drives ... or allows himself to be carried'

Whilst a defendant will incur liability by driving another's conveyance without consent, it is clear that liability does not depend upon the conveyance being 'taken away'. For a 'taking' within the section there must be some movement of the conveyance, even if only for a short distance. The decision to prosecute should be based, it is submitted, on whether an owner has suffered some, albeit temporary, deprivation of his property. Where there is no movement of the conveyance, a charge of attempt may still be appropriate: see *R* v *Bogacki* [1973] QB 832. Similarly, where a defendant is charged under s12 on the basis that as a passenger, he 'allowed himself to be carried', some movement of the vehicle must be established: see *R* v *Miller* [1976] Crim LR 147, and *R* v *Diggin* [1980] Crim LR 656.

'For his own or another's use ...'

Where the charge alleges a taking of the conveyance by the defendant, the prosecution must prove that this was for his own, or another's use. Notwithstanding the questionable decision of the Court of Appeal in *R* v *Pearce* [1973] Crim LR 321, it is submitted that the prosecution must prove that the defendant has used the vehicle in question as a conveyance, ie he has been transported by it, or has enabled another person to be transported on it. This view is supported by a number of authorities.

In *R v Bow* (1976) 64 Cr App R 54 the Court of Appeal held that the appellant had taken a conveyance for his own use, when he had sat in the driver's seat, released the handbrake, and steered it downhill for 200 yards in order to prevent it from causing any further obstruction to a road across which it had been parked. Despite his motives, and the fact that he had not started the engine, the defendant had used the vehicle as a conveyance. Where a defendant pushed a woman's car around a corner as a practical joke, the intention being to give the impression that it had been stolen, the Court of Appeal held that the defendant was not guilty within s12. He had not actually sat in the car and used it as a conveyance: see *R v Stokes* [1982] Crim LR 695. Finally, in *R v Dunn and Derby* [1984] Crim LR 367, a judge directed a jury at Snaresbrook Crown Court to acquit, where a defendant who was charged under s12 admitted wheeling a motor-cycle 40 yards without the owner's consent so that he could inspect it more closely under a street light. The Crown conceded that by pushing the motorbike and not riding on it the defendant had not used the vehicle as a conveyance.

'Without the consent of the owner ...'

In general terms, where a defendant takes a vehicle without permission he will not have the consent of the owner. If a defendant removes a victim's car from outside his house and drives it to a spot five miles away without first having secured the owner's consent, he will be liable under s12. Similarly where a defendant has limited permission to take a conveyance, for example to deliver his employer's goods and then return the vehicle to his place of work, a deviation from the permitted route could be a taking without consent. In this latter example it may be argued that the employer impliedly consents to some reasonable deviation – it will be a matter of degree in each case. That such activity can amount to an offence within s12 is evidenced by two authorities. First, *R v Phipps and McGill* [1970] RTR 209, a defendant was given permission to drive the owner's car to a London station. The defendant did so, but then decided to drive to a south coast resort in the car without obtaining any further permission. The Court of Appeal held this second taking to be without the owner's consent. Secondly, in *McKnight v Davies* [1974] RTR 4 the defendant lorry driver was held to have taken his employer's lorry without consent when, instead of returning it to his employer's place of business at the end of the working day, he drove to a public house.

As Lord Widgery CJ observed :

'The difficulty ... is in defining the kind of unauthorised activity on the part of the driver, whose original control is lawful, which will amount to an unlawful taking for the purpose of section 12. Not every brief, unauthorised diversion from his proper route by an employed driver in the course of his working day will necessarily involve a "taking" of the vehicle for his own use. If, however, as in *R v Wibberley* [1966] 2 QB 214, he returns to the vehicle after he has parked it for the night and drives it off on an unauthorised errand, he is clearly guilty of the offence. Similarly, if in the course of his working day, or otherwise while his authority to use the vehicle is unexpired, he appropriates it to his own use in a manner which repudiates the rights of the true owner, and shows that he has assumed control of the vehicle for his own purposes, he can properly be regarded as having taken the vehicle within section 12.'

Deception and consent

A difficulty arises where the defendant obtains consent from the owner to his taking a vehicle, as a result of some deception he has exercised on the owner. For example, D rushes into his neighbour's house and asks to borrow his neighbour P's car to take his sick wife to hospital. P agrees. In fact D intends to use the car to drive himself to the cinema, and he does so. Has D taken the car without consent? Two authorities seem to suggests that there would be no liability under s12. In *R v Peart* [1970] 2 QB 672 the defendant had asked the owner of a car for permission to drive it to Alnwick, a nearby town, and this was granted. The defendant drove the car to Burnley, as he had always intended, and did not return the car until the following day. The Court of Appeal allowed his appeal against conviction under s12, holding that no offence was committed where a defendant obtained consent by deception. This seemingly odd decision is explained by reference to the court's reluctance to create an offence of obtaining property by deception without intention to permanently deprive the owner. It was felt that to do so would both unnecessarily complicate the offence, and to go against the wishes of the legislature. Secondly, in *Whittaker v Campbell* [1983] 3 WLR 676, the Divisional Court developed this view further by holding that provided the owner had given de facto consent to the taking of his vehicle, it mattered not that the consent was obtained by deception or even fraud. The defendant in this case had hired a vehicle after producing another man's driving licence to the owner. In allowing the appeal against conviction under s12, Robert Goff LJ contended that there could be no liability, even where the defendant's deception induces the owner to make a 'fundamental mistake', for example as to identity. Again the underlying reasoning is the reluctance to create an offence of obtaining property by deception in the absence of any intention to permanently deprive the owner.

A conclusion can thus be reached, that where a defendant simply takes a vehicle without asking for permission, or has permission to use it in a particular way and having done so he decides, without seeking further permission, to make some different use of the vehicle, he may well incur liability under s12. Where, on the other hand, the defendant deliberately exercises some fraud or deception from the outset and obtains some de facto consent from the owner, he does not incur liability because he does have some 'consent' – despite the fact that many might regard the latter behaviour as more dishonest.

Mens rea

The defendant must know that the owner does not consent to the taking, or know that the conveyance has been taken without the owner's authority. The owner, for these purposes, being defined by s12(7)(b):

> '"Owner" in relation to a conveyance which is the subject of a hiring agreement or hire-purchase agreement, means the person in possession of the conveyance under that agreement.'

Section 12(6) provides further in relation to mens rea:

> 'A person does not commit an offence under this section by anything done in the belief that he has lawful authority to do it or that he would have the owner's consent if the owner knew of his doing it and the circumstances of it.'

In relation to this latter provision, the Court of Appeal held in *R v Clotworthy* [1981] Crim LR 501, that the test to be applied was subjective. What was vital was that the defendant believed he had lawful authority, or would have had the consent of the owner, not that he actually had such authority or would have had such consent. The more unreasonable the defendant's belief, the less likely the jury are to accept his evidence. It would appear that a drunken mistake by a defendant that the car he is driving is his own will not provide the basis for a defence under s12(c): see *R v Gannon* (1988) 87 Cr App R 254.

20.2 Aggravated vehicle taking

The Aggravated Vehicle Taking Act 1992 was Parliament's response to the problem of cars being taken without the consent of the owner, and used to cause serious injury or damage to property. The offence builds upon the elements of s12 of the Theft Act 1968, by introducing a new s12A.

Under the aggravated offence, a person will incur liability if he commits the basic offence under s12 and it is proved, at any time after the vehicle was unlawfully taken and before it was recovered, the vehicle was driven dangerously in a public place, damage was caused to the vehicle, or due to such driving accidental injury occurred to any person or harm was caused to any property other than the vehicle. Hence in *Dawes v DPP* [1994] Crim LR 604, the appellant was convicted of the aggravated offence where he had unknowingly taken a vehicle adapted by police to trap 'joyriders', the vehicle having been fitted with devices that caused the engine to cut out after it had been driven 30 yards and activated the central locking, thus trapping the appellant within. He caused damage whilst trying to break out of the car. The court held that his detention within the car had not been unlawful, thus he had not been entitled to use force in order to free himself. The Act provides for a maximum penalty of five years' imprisonment following conviction.

A defendant can escape liability, the burden of proof being upon him, by establishing either that the dangerous driving, accident or harm was caused prior to the unlawful taking under s12, or that he was neither in, nor in the vicinity of, the vehicle when these events occurred.

It should be borne in mind that any defendant causing damage to property, or injury to others could, in any event, be charged under the Criminal Damage Act 1971, or with a range of common law and statutory assaults, as appropriate.

20.3 Dishonestly abstracting electricity

The offence of abstracting electricity is created by s13 of the Theft Act 1968 which states:

> 'A person who dishonestly uses without due authority, or dishonestly causes to be wasted or diverted, any electricity shall on conviction on indictment be liable to imprisonment for a term not exceeding five years.'

Such activity cannot be brought within the scope of theft because electricity is not property within the definition provided by s4 of the 1968 Act: see *Low* v *Blease* (1975) 119 Sol Jo 695. It would appear that the electricity can come from a mains supply or from a battery. Dishonest use of a private telephone line could arguably be within the scope of the offence under s13, as could the insertion of foreign coins of little value in a washing machine or car wash. Similarly, unauthorised use of a photocopier would involve liability, and possibly a charge of theft of the paper obtained. Following *R* v *McCreadie and Tume* [1992] Crim LR 872, it would appear that the test for abstraction is to ask whether but for the defendants' actions the electricity would have been consumed? If the answer is 'no' the actus reus is made out.

The result is that in the not infrequent case of squatters consuming electricity on a metered supply in a dwelling, the prosecution does not have to provide proof of any tampering with the meter.

The mens rea required would appear to be that the defendant knows he is abstracting electricity, and is dishonest at the time he does this. It is submitted that the meaning of dishonesty here is that provided by the Court of Appeal in *R* v *Ghosh* [1982] QB 1053. In *R* v *McCreadie* (above), the Court of Appeal, approving the use of *Ghosh* in the context of this offence, felt that the appellants' defence (that they were intending to pay the bill when it arrived), was undermined by the evidence that they had not notified the electricity company of their occupation, that they were moving out when the police arrived, and that they had not notified the electricity company of their impending departure.

20.4 Blackmail

The offence of blackmail existed before 1968 in a variety of offences under the Larceny Act 1916. The essence of the offence is that the defendant makes an unwarranted demand with menaces. Section 21(1) of the Theft Act 1968 provides:

> 'A person is guilty of blackmail if, with a view to gain for himself or another or with intent to cause loss to another, he makes any unwarranted demand with menaces; and for this purpose a demand with menaces is unwarranted unless the person making it does so in the belief:
> a) that he has reasonable grounds for making the demand; and
> b) that the use of the menaces is a proper means of reinforcing the demand.'

A defendant convicted of blackmail on indictment may be sentenced to up to 14 years imprisonment.

Demand

The demand, which lies at the heart of blackmail, can be in the form of words, actions or omissions, and can be express or implied. In *R v Collister and Warhurst* (1955) 39 Cr App R 100, two police officers discussed, within earshot of the victim, that payment of some money might lead them to drop what were in any event bogus indecency charges against the victim. It was obvious to the victim, and would have been obvious to a reasonable man, that a demand was being made even though it was never directly addressed to the victim.

It should be remembered that the offence does not require proof that the demand ever reaches the victim. Blackmail is, in a sense, an inchoate offence, raising the nice question of whether there is such an offence as attempted blackmail. Such an offence may exist in theory but will, it is submitted, be of slight practical importance.

The question of demands made by way of letter delivered by the Post Office was considered by the House of Lords in *Treacy v DPP* [1971] AC 537. The defendant had posted a letter containing unwarranted demands with menaces to a woman in Germany. By a majority their Lordships took the view that the demand, for the purposes of blackmail, had been made when the letter was posted in England, and thus the English courts had jurisdiction over the offence. Lord Diplock was willing to go further and suggest that had the letter been posted in Germany and received by a victim in England, then the English courts would still have had jurisdiction on the basis that the demand continues to be made once the letter has been sent, and would thus be 'made' in England as well as Germany.

With menaces

It has been suggested, by Cairns LJ in *R v Lawrence* (1971) 57 Cr App R 64, that 'menaces' is an ordinary English word which would normally call for no elaboration on the part of a trial judge, unless there were exceptional circumstances where what would not normally be menacing to an ordinary person, was menacing to the victim. Lord Wright, in *Thorne* v *Motor Trade Association* [1937] AC 797 stated that:

'I think the word "menace" is to be liberally construed and not as limited to threats of violence but as including threats of any action detrimental to or unpleasant to the person addressed. It may also include a warning that in certain events such action is intended.'

It is submitted that this is wide enough to include threats to reveal a person's criminal record, adultery, medical details, or to adversely affect an individual's business or property.

The test applied to determine whether or not menaces have been established, is that laid down by the Court of Appeal in *R* v *Clear* [1968] 1 QB 670 (a case decided under the Larceny Act 1916). It was suggested that the actions of the defendant should be considered in the light of the effect they would have on the ordinary person of reasonable fortitude. This test may have to be modified, however, where the victim is unusually timorous or brave. In *R* v *Garwood* [1987] 1 All ER 1032 Lord Lane CJ held that if the victim was not influenced by the menaces, but the evidence was that an ordinary person of normal stability would have been, then the menaces were made out. On the other hand, where the threats did affect the victim, but would not have so influenced the reasonable person of normal stability, menaces were made out where the defendant nevertheless realised the effect of his actions on the victim.

Again, regard should be had to s21(2) which provides (inter alia) that it is immaterial whether the menaces relate to action to be taken by the person making the demand. Common sense dictates that there will be some demands which are of such a trivial or lighthearted nature that no menaces can sensibly be implied. Such a situation arose in *R* v *Harry* [1974] Crim LR 32 where a student had suggested to a shopkeeper that if he were to make a £50 contribution to the college's Rag Week fund, the shop would be 'immune' from Rag Week activities. The trial judge ruled that he was not satisfied that there were any menaces within the meaning of the Act.

'With a view to gain or loss (etc)'

Although s21(2) provides that the nature of the act or omission demanded is immaterial, s21(1) clearly states that the demand must be made by the defendant either with a view to gain for himself or another, or with intent to cause loss to another. Thus were D to say to P, 'let me have sex with you or I will tell your mother that you secretly had an abortion', D would not be committing an offence of blackmail because his demand would not be made with a view to gain or causing another loss. (Although if he proceeds with the plan and has intercourse with P he may be guilty of rape.) The concept of 'gain' and 'loss' is given an artificially wide meaning by s34(2)(a) of the Theft Act 1968 which provides:

'For purposes of this Act:
a) "gain" and "loss" are to be construed as extending only to gain or loss in money or

other property, but as extending to any such gain or loss whether temporary or permanent; and

i) "gain" includes a gain by keeping what one has, as well as a gain by getting what one has not; and

ii) "loss" includes a loss by not getting what one might get, as well as a loss by parting with what one has.'

The effect of s34(2)(a) is to bring within the scope of blackmail situations such as where D threatens to reveal P's adultery to P's wife, unless P repays D the £100 which he owes him; this demand is made by D with a view to 'gain' even though D is trying to recover that to which he had a right in any event. Similarly an offence may be committed where D makes such a threat to P unless P relinquishes his right to sue D for money owed by D to P; here P's 'loss' is not getting what he might get. See *R v Parkes* [1973] Crim LR 358. In *R v Bevans* (1988) 87 Cr App R 64, D was convicted of blackmail, after he had threatened to shoot a doctor if he did not provide D with a pain-killing morphine injection, on the basis that his demand had been made with a view to gain. As Jones J observed:

'It seems difficult, if not impossible, to argue that the liquid which constituted the substance which was to be injected into the appellant's body was not property. It clearly was. There has been no dispute but that if an ampoule containing the liquid had been handed over to the appellant instead of being transferred to a syringe and injected into his body, he would have got property in that sense. This Court can see no difference between the liquid being contained in the syringe before it is passed into his body and the liquid being contained in an ampoule. There can be no question but that that morphine was property ... It is nothing to the point that his ultimate motive was the relief of pain through the effect which that morphine would have upon his bodily processes. It was pointed out in the course of argument that someone may very well demand a bottle of whisky. His ultimate motive may simply be to get drunk, that is to drink it all himself and to get drunk. That does not detract in any way from the proposition that in fact he would be demanding property in the form of the bottle of whisky and in particular the bottle's contents. By analogy exactly the same argument must apply here. This demand, which was a demand for an injection of morphine, involved two things: first of all it involved the passing of a drug to him, and secondly it involved the service by the doctor of actually carrying out the injection. The fact that he was gaining the service does not in any way mean that he was not gaining the property which consisted of the morphine. There is no suggestion anywhere in the Act that the gain must be exclusively directed to one particular object.'

Unwarranted

A demand will be unwarranted unless the defendant makes it in the belief that he has reasonable grounds for so doing, and in the belief that the use of the menaces is a proper means of reinforcing the demand. The test is prima facie subjective, in that the defendant's belief does not have to be reasonable, although the more unreasonable it is the less likely the jury are to believe him. Further, note that both states of mind have to be established.

The defendant may honestly believe that there are grounds for making the demand for any number of reasons. He does not have to establish any particular legal, moral or factual basis for his belief; he will nevertheless have to provide evidence upon which a jury can act, that he honestly believed such grounds to exist. The fact that the defendant was owed money by the victim, or had been in some other way disadvantaged by the victim, might provide such evidence. The nature of what is demanded by the defendant may be relevant here.

The subjective nature of this provision, particularly as regards the defendant's belief that menaces were appropriate in the circumstances, may be problematic. Where the defendant has very low moral standards he may regard as 'proper means' methods which a reasonable person would find outrageous. Perhaps the problem is more theoretical than real in that the jury would convict in such a situation. In any event, an important limitation was introduced by the Court of Appeal in *R* v *Harvey* (1980) 72 Cr App R 139. The defendant had threatened to kill, maim, and rape members of the victim's family if he did not return £20,000 that he had obtained from D by deception. The trial judge directed the jury that as a matter of law such threats could not be a 'proper' means of enforcing his demand for the return of the money. The Court of Appeal upheld this ruling, emphasising that a defendant could not claim that the means adopted were 'proper' whilst he also knew that they would involve the commission of serious criminal offences. On the facts there was little doubt that D had been aware that the means adopted would have involved the commission of serious crimes, and although the court did feel that the trial judge had erred in leaving this issue to the jury, the proviso was applied. As Bingham J observed:

'In order to exonerate a defendant from liability his belief must be that the use of the menaces is a "proper" means of reinforcing the demand. "Proper" is an unusual expression to find in a criminal statute. It is not defined in the Act, and no definition need be attempted here. It is, however, plainly a word of wide meaning, certainly wider than (for example) "lawful". But the greater includes the less and no act which was not believed to be lawful could be believed to be proper within the meaning of the subsection. Thus no assistance is given to any defendant, even a fanatic or a deranged idealist, who knows or suspects that his threat, or the act threatened, is criminal, but believes it to be justified by his end or his peculiar circumstances. The test is not what he regards as justified, but what he believes to be proper. And where, as here, the threats were to do acts which any sane man knows to be against the laws of every civilised country no jury would hesitate long before dismissing the contention that the defendant genuinely believed the threats to be a proper means of reinforcing even a legitimate demand.'

Blackmail and robbery

In some situations there may be an overlap between robbery and blackmail. The highwayman who points his gun at the victim and declares 'your money or your life' and thus induces him to hand over valuables doubtless commits robbery contrary to s8 of the Theft Act 1968, but also blackmail. What separates the two offences, amongst other things, is that s8 requires a person to be put in fear of being 'then and there subjected to force'. As indicated in Chapter 19, if D demands money from P saying that if it is not paid P's child will be beaten up leaving school that day, D will be guilty of blackmail, but not robbery, no one is put in fear of being then and there subjected to violence.

Blackmail and handling

Note that for the purposes of s24(4) of the Theft Act 1968 goods obtained as a result of blackmail are regarded as stolen for the purposes of handling stolen goods.

20.5 Going equipped

Section 25 of the Theft Act 1968 creates the offence of 'going equipped'; it provides:

> 'A person shall be guilty of an offence if, when not at his place of abode, he has with him any article for use in the course of or in connection with any burglary, theft or cheat.'

The offence carries a maximum sentence of three years imprisonment following conviction on indictment. The offence is clearly designed to cover situations where a defendant is searched and found to have a collection of skeleton keys in his possession for which he cannot provide a satisfactory explanation, a number of credit cards or cheque books the names upon which do not correspond to his own, and the defendant whose car is found to contain housebreaking implements such as a crowbar, 'jemmy' or other such items.

It should be noted that the offence is aimed at the defendant who has such items intending to use them in the course of committing offences outlined below. It is not an offence within the section to be in possession of such items merely because they have been used in the course of committing such offences: see *R* v *Ellames* [1974] 3 All ER 130.

In theory, s12 could be charged as an alternative to attempted theft or deception where D is in possession of the relevant equipment at the time of the attempt. See *DPP* v *Minor* [1988] Crim LR 55.

'When not at his place of abode ...'

The offence is preparatory in its nature, nevertheless the defendant does not commit any offence where he has the relevant articles at his dwelling place, regardless of his mens rea. As soon as the defendant leaves his home with the tools and has the necessary mens rea, an offence within the section may be committed. A defendant having such articles at his place of work might, therefore, incur liability.

In *R* v *Bundy* [1977] 1 WLR 914, the Court of Appeal considered the case of a defendant found to have housebreaking tools in his car, but who claimed not to be guilty under s25, since the car was also his 'place of abode', the defendant having no other house. The court held that whilst the car might be his place of abode when he was using it as such (eg sleeping in it), when he was using it as a car, he was committing an offence within the section.

'*Has with him . . .*'

This expression implies that the defendant has an article within his possession or control. A defendant has an article in his control if he is able to gain access to it quickly, for example, the driver of a vehicle who has tools in the boot of his car. Note that s25(3) provides:

> 'Where a person is charged with an offence under this section, proof that he had with him any article made or adapted for use in committing a burglary, theft or cheat shall be evidence that he had it with him for such use.'

In *R* v *McAngus* [1994] Crim LR 602 the applicant took two undercover fraud investigators to a bonded warehouse and showed them a number of shirts which falsely purported to be of a brand manufactured in the United States. The prosecution case was that he had agreed to sell the shirts to the officers. The applicant, who was due to be extradited to the United States on a charge of going equipped, applied unsuccessfully for a writ of habeus corpus on the ground, inter alia, that he had not had the shirts 'with him' as required by the wording of s25 of the Theft Act 1968. There might, it is submitted, be some debate as to whether the applicant, although obviously not at his place of abode, was actually *going* equipped on these facts. The Criminal Law Revision Committee report that presaged the 1968 Act envisages an offence being committed where D starts out on his journey to commit one of the specified offences whilst in possession of the prohibited articles. On the basis that any ambiguities should be construed in favour of the accused it is submitted that there is an arguable case that the present decision offends at least the spirit of s25 if not the letter.

'*Any article for use in the course of or in connection with any burglary theft or cheat*'

The offence is potentially very wide given the use of the phrase 'any article'. Its effect is narrowed, however, by reference to the offences that the defendant must be proved to have had in mind. Some common sense should also be exercised in the application of the section. For example, a defendant on his way to commit a burglary may be wearing a shirt and trousers. He intends to wear them (it is hoped!) whilst committing the burglary, but it would seem to be straining the wording of the section to say that they are 'articles for use in the course of the burglary'. The point is that the defendant would have been wearing the clothes anyway. A more difficult question arises where the defendant is wearing gloves, or a balaclava helmet. Is he wearing these items because he is cold, or to avoid detection?

The section contemplates that the articles are to be used in connection with the following offences:

1. Burglary (see Chapter 19);
2. Theft (see Chapters 16, 17 and 18); and for these purposes theft includes an offence under s12 of the Theft Act 1968 (see Chapter 20);

3. Cheat.

For these purposes 'cheat' means an offence under s15 Theft Act 1968. Considerable difficulties have arisen as to what approach should be taken by the courts in determining whether a defendant in possession of certain items would have actually deceived another person by use of the items. In *R v Rashid* [1977] 2 All ER 237, the Court of Appeal held that a defendant British Rail steward who was caught boarding a train in possession of bread and tomatoes that he intended to sell to passengers as his own, pocketing the proceeds, was not going equipped to 'cheat' on the basis that it could not be said that the British Rail passengers could not have bought his food had they known the truth. In short, the court was not satisfied that Rashid's deception would have been operative on the passengers – a point it was necessary for the prosecution to establish for liability under s15 (the 'cheat').

Conversely in *R v Doukas* [1978] 1 All ER 1061, the Court of Appeal held that the defendant hotel wine waiter was guilty of going equipped to cheat where he was stopped entering the hotel for work, carrying two bottles of wine that he intended to sell to hotel diners as being the hotel's and pocketing the proceeds. The evidence was that the hotel diners would not have knowingly participated with Doukas in a fraud on the hotel; his deception as to the origin of the wine would have been operative. This decision was subsequently followed by the Court of Appeal in *R v Corboz* [1984] Crim LR 629, on facts very similar to those arising in *R v Rashid* (above).

More recently the matter has come before the House of Lords as a subsidiary issue in *R v Cooke* [1986] AC 909, which concerned an alleged agreement between the defendant and others to supply British Rail passengers with their own food; the facts again being very similar to *R v Rashid* and *R v Corboz* (above). Regarding the question of whether the defendant should have been charged with conspiracy to commit an offence contrary to s25, it was held that there was no evidence to show that British Rail passengers would have refused to purchase the food supplied by the defendant had they known of its origin. In the view of Lord Mackay, whether or not the 'cheat' element of the s25 offence is made out is a question for the jury based on the evidence of the attitude and understanding of those receiving the supplies.

Difficulties remain, however, as exemplified by the Court of Appeal's decision in *R v Whiteside and Antoniou* [1989] Crim LR 436. The appellants were arrested selling 'pirate' cassette tapes of popular recording artists, and convicted of going equipped for cheating. The appellants claimed in evidence that if any customer had enquired into the provenance of the tapes they would have admitted that they were not authorised copies. Before the Court of Appeal they contended first, that there was no direct evidence that they had intended to cheat any member of the public, secondly that the trial judge had been wrong to raise issues relating to the Copyright Act when directing the jury on dishonesty, and thirdly that the trial judge had erred in directing the jury that the obtaining of property by deception (the cheat) could be wholly or partly as a result of the appellants' actions.

Whilst the court allowed the appeal by concurring with the second and third contentions, it held that the tapes bore a close resemblance to the 'genuine' article, and the appellants had done nothing to indicate to the public generally that they were not authorised copies, hence the jury had been entitled to infer the intention to 'cheat' the public. This conclusion is perhaps debatable, since potential customers would not have been deceived as to the nature of the music recorded on the tapes, and there was no evidence that the quality of the recordings was any worse than that of the authorised versions. The only deception, therefore, would have been as to whether the permission of the copyright owner had been obtained prior to making the copies. Such a deception could only become operative if it could be shown that a potential customer would not have bought one of the tapes had he known that its production had involved breaches of the Copyright Act, thus raising exactly the same problem as that in *R* v *Doukas*, and *R* v *Cooke*.

Mens rea

The defendant must know he is not at his place of abode, and must know that he has the relevant articles 'with him'. It is in the nature of the offence that the defendant will almost invariably know the nature of the articles. That knowledge of the presence of the articles is necessary is, it is submitted, evidenced by *R* v *Lester and Byast* (1955) 39 Cr App R 157, a decision under the former law. Further, the defendant must intend to use the said articles in the course of one of the offences discussed above. If, therefore, a defendant intends to use a stolen membership card to obtain services by deception, contrary to s1 Theft Act 1978, he would not be guilty under s25.

In *R* v *Ellames* (above) the Court of Appeal held that a defendant could be convicted under s25 even though he does not have a specific theft or burglary in mind. Any theft or burglary will suffice. Further, in *R* v *Hargreaves* [1985] Crim LR 243, the Court of Appeal held that an intention to use an article in the course of a theft, cheat or burglary, should the opportunity present itself, would also be sufficient mens rea. The defendant's appeal was allowed however, on the basis that the jury might have been misled by the judge's direction into thinking that a defendant had the necessary mens rea even where he had not decided whether or not to use the article should the opportunity to commit one of the above offences present itself.

Sections 15, 16, 17 and 20 of the
Theft Act 1968

21.1 Section 15   Obtaining property by deception
21.2 Section 16   „   pecuniary advantage by deception
21.3 Section 17   False accounting
21.4 Section 20   ~~Dishonestly destroying~~ – – – – a valuable security

21.1 Section 15

Section 15(1) creates the offence of obtaining property by deception. It provides:

> 'A person who by any deception dishonestly obtains property belonging to another, with the intention of permanently depriving the other of it, shall on conviction on indictment be liable to imprisonment for a term not exceeding ten years.'

Prior to the House of Lords' decision in *R v Gomez* [1993] AC 442, it was possible to identify quite distinct roles for the offences of theft and obtaining property by deception, on the basis that the former required proof of an unauthorised assumption of the owner's rights (as was suggested by Lord Roskill in *R v Morris*), whilst the latter involved the owner consenting to the property being taken, but only because of the defendant's deception. In the light of *Gomez*, as explained in Chapter 17, the offence of theft can now cover the vast majority of situations that would previously have only fallen within s15, as there is no need for the prosecution to prove that the defendant's appropriation of the property was without the owner's consent.

'Property belonging to another'

Property for these purposes has a meaning broadly similar to that provided in s4 for the purposes of theft, with some extension as regards land. Section 34(1) states that ss4(1) and 5(1) relating to property belonging to another should apply generally for the purposes of the 1968 Act. A situation analogous to that in *R v Turner (No 2)* [1971] 2 All ER 441 may arise therefore where D obtains his own property from P, who has lawful possession of it.

'Obtains'

Subsection 15(2) provides:

> 'For the purposes of this section a person is to be treated as obtaining property if he obtains ownership, possession or control of it and "obtains" includes obtaining for another or enabling another to obtain or to retain.'

It is clear from the above that the offence is committed where D induces P to loan property, make a gift of it, or sell it to D, provided D has the necessary mens rea at the time. Further, it would be an offence for D to deceive P into giving property to a third party, or allowing a third party to retain such property. It is submitted that were D to deceive P into permitting D to retain property of which D already had possession or control, the appropriate charge would be one of theft, by virtue of s3(1). Where D already has ownership (albeit a voidable title) and he deceives P into allowing him to retain it, the situation is less clear. Theft may be inappropriate on the basis that the property no longer belongs to another, unless it can be argued that P retains an equitable interest within s5(1). A charge under s15 may be impossible on the basis that subs(2) does not contemplate such a situation.

Jurisdictional problems can arise where a deception is exercised in one country in order to obtain property in another. Where D is abroad and he communicates his deception to persons within the jurisdiction of the English courts, an offence, or an attempt, will have been committed within the jurisdiction. See *R* v *Baxter* [1972] QB 1; *DPP* v *Stonehouse* [1978] AC 55. The English courts will also normally have jurisdiction where D in England communicates a deception to P who is abroad, and as a result receives property belonging to P in England. See *R* v *Tirado* (1974) 59 Cr App R 80, which the Court of Appeal stated was to be preferred to *R* v *Harden* [1963] 1 QB 8.

Given the above, the Court of Appeal decision in *R* v *Thompson* [1984] 1 WLR 962 seems rather difficult to support. The defendant, whilst employed as a computer operator at a bank in Kuwait, had instructed the bank's computer to transfer amounts from customers' accounts to a savings account he had opened for himself at another Kuwaiti bank. On his return to England, the defendant requested that the balance of his savings account should be transferred by telex to his accounts in England. The Court of Appeal, applying the proviso to s2(1) Criminal Appeal Act 1968, upheld the defendant's conviction under s15, rejecting his contention that if there had been an obtaining it occurred in Kuwait. The decision has been criticised on the basis that when the money was transferred in Kuwait from the defendant's employer to his own account, he obtained a chose in action, but not by deception as machines cannot be deceived. Further, when the request was made from England, to transfer the money from Kuwait, the defendant may have been exercising a deception, but what he was obtaining was a chose in action (bank balance) that belonged to himself. The Court of Appeal insisted, however, that a debt brought about by fraud could not be regarded as a chose in action, a finding which raises the broader question as to, what the defendant did obtain.

chose in action ?

'By deception ...'

Deception is in part defined by s15(4) which provides:

> 'For purposes of this section "deception" means any deception (whether deliberate or reckless) by words or conduct as to fact or as to law, including a deception as to the present intentions of the person using the deception or any other person.'

Where the deception is in the form of words, the statement must obviously be untrue, and the burden of proving this rests upon the prosecution. In some instances the truthfulness or otherwise of a statement can only be established by reference to facts known to the defendant, for example, the defendant's statement to prospective purchasers that certain goods are 'the cheapest in town'. In such a case the onus is on the defendants to prove something within their personal knowledge: see *R* v *Mandry and Wooster* [1973] 3 All ER 996.

A statement alleged to constitute a deception must be one of fact or law, whether this is the case is a matter to be determined by the jury: see *R* v *Banaster* [1979] RTR 113. On this basis, it would appear that a statement of opinion by the defendant cannot constitute a deception, even though it may result in a victim parting with his property at an undervalue. Distinguishing between a statement of fact and one of opinion can clearly cause difficulty. The decision of Nottingham Crown Court in *R* v *King* [1979] Crim LR 122 suggests that a defendant who knows a representation, such as the odometer reading on a motor car, to be untrue, but who states that it 'may be incorrect' implies that as far as he knows it is correct, and thus commits a deception. The Court of Appeal's decision in *R* v *Silverman* [1987] Crim LR 574 suggests that a relevant factor may be the nature of the relationship existing between the parties. Clearly if a defendant presenting a grossly excessive quotation accompanies it with an assertion to the effect that he will only be making a modest profit, he will be perpetrating a misrepresentation of fact. If, as in *Silverman*'s case, a relationship of mutual trust had been built up over a long period of time, the court may conclude that the appellant's silence as to the excessive nature of the charges comprises part of the deception inducing payment.

It is submitted that an expression of opinion which is not genuinely held should be regarded as a misrepresentation of the present intentions of the persons expressing the opinion: see further *R* v *Jeff and Bassett* (1966) 51 Cr App R 28.

There is no clear authority under the 1968 Act as to whether silence, or as JC Smith puts it, 'an omission to undeceive', can constitute deception. As a matter of civil law, silence can amount to a misrepresentation.

In any event, the conduct accompanying silence can amount to a deception. In so providing, s15(4) affirms much older decisions such as that in *R* v *Barnard* (1837) 7 C & P 784, where the defendant obtained goods on credit by false pretences (deception) in that he dressed up as an undergraduate in a fellow-commoner's cap and gown.

The significance of conduct as a deception rests with what the conduct implies. In *DPP* v *Ray* [1974] AC 370, the defendant had ordered a meal in a restaurant and had consumed it with an honest state of mind. He then discovered his inability to pay for the meal and remained silent as to this change in circumstances. The defendant waited until the dining area was clear of waiters before running out. The House of Lords held that the defendant had exercised a deception by remaining seated in the restaurant having decided not to pay. His remaining in this position created the implied and continuing representation that he was an honest customer who intended to pay the bill, thus inducing the waiters to leave the dining area unattended, giving him the opportunity to run off without paying. What can be implied from any given conduct clearly depends upon the facts of each case. In *R v Williams* [1980] Crim LR 589, where the defendant had been tendering obsolete Yugoslavian dinar notes at a bureau de change and obtaining sterling in exchange, the Court of Appeal held that implicit in the tendering of the notes was the representation that it was valid currency having an equivalent sterling value.

If a defendant makes a statement of fact or law, which he believes to be untrue, but which unknown to him is truthful, he could, despite the fact that there is in reality no deception, be convicted of attempting to obtain property by deception, on the basis that he has taken steps that he believes to be more than merely preparatory to obtaining property by deception; see s1(1) Criminal Attempts Act 1981, as interpreted in *R v Shivpuri* [1986] 2 WLR 988. In this respect it is submitted that the defendant in cases such as *R v Deller* (1952) 36 Cr App R 184, (wherein it was held that the defendant could not be guilty of obtaining by false pretences because the car he was selling was, unknown to him, free from encumbrances), would now be guilty of an attempt: but see further *R v Wheeler* (1990) The Times 5 December.

The deception must be operative

The deception must cause the obtaining of property; to this end the deception must precede the obtaining of property. Thus in *R v Collis-Smith* [1971] Crim LR 716, a defendant who had put petrol into his car, and then falsely told the attendant that his employer would be paying for the petrol, was successful in his appeal against conviction under s15(1) on the basis that his deception did not arise until after the property in the petrol had passed to him. The appropriate charge in such a case would be an offence under s2 of the Theft Act 1978.

Assuming that the deception arises prior to the obtaining of the property, the question of causation necessitates the application of a 'but for' test. But for the deception would the defendant have obtained the property? If the answer is 'no' the deception is operative, if 'yes' then the deception is not operative because the defendant would have got the property anyway. Even where a deception is found not to be operative, the defendant might nevertheless be guilty of an attempt provided the required mens rea is present. The deception must operate on a human mind, in law a machine cannot be deceived: see *Davies v Flackett* (1972) 116 SJ 526. Where D places a worthless token in a machine and extracts a bar of chocolate he cannot therefore be charged under s15, but can be charged with theft. More difficult is the situation where D uses a worthless token to operate a machine that provides a service, such as a car wash. He cannot be charged with obtaining services by deception because a machine cannot be deceived, and he cannot be charged with theft because he does not obtain any property. The only appropriate charge would appear to be dishonestly abstracting electricity contrary to s13. In some cases, however, the facts themselves reveal that the deception can have been the only reason for the defendant being given the property; hence in *Etim* v *Hatfield* [1975] Crim LR 234, where the defendant had made a false statement to a Post Office clerk in order to obtain supplementary benefit, the court held that it was a necessary inference from the facts that the deception induced the payment, there being no other conceivable reason. Ultimately the question of whether the deception has been operative is one of fact for the jury: see *R* v *King and Stockwell* [1987] Crim LR 398.

In *R* v *Hamilton* [1990] Crim LR 806, the Court of Appeal considered the case of an appellant who had forged the authorising signature on a number of stolen company cheques, paid them into a building society account, and withdrawn cash by signing withdrawal slips. He was convicted of, inter alia, obtaining or attempting to obtain property by deception, on the basis that he had falsely represented that the balance in the building society account was genuine and that he was entitled to withdraw the sums therefrom. On appeal, counsel for the appellant contended that there had been no representation, and therefore no false representation, ie deception, since the completion of a withdrawal slip effectively involved the appellant in saying nothing more than 'give me the money', and that there had been no representations as to the source of funds credited to the account; neither was there any representation as to his entitlement to the sum claimed. In dismissing his appeal, the court held that, given that the appellant had dishonestly induced the bank to make the credit entries in his favour by using the stolen cheques, the primary question was as to what representations, if any, should be inferred from his act of presenting the withdrawal slip. It rejected the submission that presentation of the withdrawal slip meant no more than 'give me the money'. The money in the account was identified by means of the number on the slip, and the appellant's presentation of it was a representation to the bank that he was the person entitled to withdraw funds from the account. A jury could infer from his conduct that he was representing that he was the person to whom the bank was indebted in respect of the account, and by demanding withdrawal of a stated sum he necessarily represented that the bank owed him that amount. In arriving at this conclusion the court relied upon passages from *Joachimson* v *Swiss Bank Corp* [1921] 3 KB 110 at p127, to the effect that the relationship between a bank and its customers, in regard to deposit and current accounts, was that of debtor and creditor, with a condition that the debt only became payable by the bank upon a proper demand being made at the branch where the amount was held. The appellant had no right to demand payment of any money from the account. When the building society had received payment in respect of the cheques from the drawer's bank, it had done so under a mistake of fact, on discovery of which the money became repayable to the paying bank. The court further expressed its view that although the authorities dealing with representations made by those drawing cheques could be distinguished, because of the involvement of a third party, the present situation was analogous to that of an individual seeking to withdraw cash from his own account by means of a cheque payable to 'self' or cash.

The decision raises a number of interesting questions. Suppose that D steals £1,000 and places it in a deposit account at a bank. Does he commit an offence of deception when he requests the bank to deliver up the money? Can this example be distinguished from the above case? How would the situation differ, if at all, if D forged £1,000 in £10 notes and paid them into a deposit account? What offence would he commit in requesting the withdrawal of an equivalent sum? Note that the appellant had also sought to challenge his conviction on two further grounds. First, the contention that the bank clerk had not been induced to hand over money in response to the withdrawal slip, but by checking D's balance on a VDU screen. The court held that a representation only has to be a cause of the obtaining, not the sole cause, and that the presentation of the slip at least caused the clerk to check the screen. Secondly, the appellant pointed to the fact that the clerk had not been called to give evidence to the effect that he would not have paid out if he had known the true situation. In rejecting this contention it would appear that the court regarded it as an irresistible inference, following *R v Lambie* (considered below), that the clerk would not have paid out funds had he known the truth.

Deception, cheques and credit cards

If a defendant uses his own cheque book and cheque card to buy goods costing less than £50, having been informed by his bank that he must not write any cheques because he is overdrawn, he will be guilty of deception. He has represented that he has authority to write cheques when in fact he does not. The difficulty lies in establishing that this deception induces the retailer to part with the goods, because he knows (provided the conditions of use are met) that he will be reimbursed by the defendant's bank in accordance with the bank guarantee inscribed on the cheque card. Reimbursement by the bank is in no way dependent on there being any funds in the defendant's account. The defendant may thus argue that it is not his deception that induces the retailer to accept the cheque in return for goods, but the guarantee offered by the bank. Reference to 20.10 (above) reveals that the same problem arises in respect of defendants charged with 'going equipped to cheat'. See *R v Rashid* [1977] 2 All ER 237; *R v Doukas* [1978] 1 All ER 1061.

The problem was addressed by the House of Lords in *Metropolitan Police Commissioner v Charles* [1977] AC 177. The appellant had drawn cheques, supported by his cheque guarantee card, on his current account for amounts in excess of his agreed overdraft. The cheques had been exchanged for gaming chips in a casino. He was convicted on a number of counts alleging that he had obtained a pecuniary advantage (being allowed to borrow by way of overdraft) by deception, contrary to s16(1) of the Theft Act 1968, and appealed unsuccessfully to the House of Lords.

Lord Edmund-Davies identified the representations made by the drawer of a cheque, using a cheque guarantee card as follows:

> 'By drawing the cheque the accused represented that it would be met, and by producing the card so that the number thereon could be endorsed on the cheque he in effect represented, "I am authorised by the bank to show this to you and so create a direct contractual relationship between the bank and you that they will honour this cheque." The production of the card was the badge of the accused's ostensible authority to make such a representation on the bank's behalf.'

Notwithstanding that the appellant's representations were false, as he had no such authority, it was contended that his deception was not operative, as the manager of the casino would have accepted the cheques in any event, because payment by the bank was guaranteed through use of the card.

Despite the casino manager's assertions that where a cheque guarantee card was used no inquiries were made as to the client's credit-worthiness, and that the relationship between the client and his bank was 'irrelevant', Lord Edmund-Davies sought to stress that:

> '... [the manager] made clear that the accused's cheques were accepted *only* because he produced a cheque card, and he repeatedly stressed that, had he been aware that the accused was using his cheque book and cheque card "in a way in which he was not allowed or entitled to use [them]" no cheque would have been accepted. The evidence of that witness, taken as a whole, points irresistibly to the conclusions (a) that by this dishonest conduct the accused deceived [the manager] in the manner averred in the particulars of the charges and (b) that [the manager] was thereby induced to accept the cheques because of his belief that the representations as to both cheque and card were true.'

The deception, therefore, became operative because the House of Lords concluded that the casino would not have accepted the cheques supported by the cheque card had the truth been known. The problem, of course, is that on the facts there was no evidence that the casino manger was aware of the lack of authority. The decision therefore rests upon an assumption as to how the payee would have responded. The decision is also questionable in the sense that the relationship between the defendant and his bank is entirely private. Were a retailer to enquire of a customer whether or not he had permission to use his cheque card, the customer could quite understandably refuse to answer. It is submitted that the inference drawn in *Charles* is a necessary one in order to make the section effective.

The corresponding difficulty in relation to credit cards arose in *R v Lambie* [1981] Crim LR 712. The appellant used her own credit card to buy goods totalling less than £50, knowing she was in excess of her spending limit. Despite the shop assistant's evidence that she had made no assumptions whatsoever as regards the appellant's authority to use the card, the appellant's conviction under s16(1) (the charges were based on events taking place before the 1978 Act came into force) was upheld by the House of Lords on the basis that if the shop assistant had known the truth she would not have accepted the credit card in payment, hence the use of the card was an operative deception. Again the problem here is that the shop assistant did not know of the lack of authority, so the House of Lords had to resort to assumptions as to how she would have acted in order to make the deception operative. The defendant in such a case could, of course, call the retailer or shop assistant to give evidence that he was prepared to accept the credit card in full knowledge of the D's lack of authority, but the retailer is unlikely to want to run the risk of becoming an accomplice to the D's fraud on the credit card company.

It is clear from *Charles* that a defendant who uses a cheque book and a cheque card without authority commits an offence under s16, by obtaining a pecuniary advantage (being allowed to borrow by way of overdraft) by deception. It matters not that the deception is exercised on the retailer, and the pecuniary advantage obtained from the bank. As Lawton LJ observed in *R v Kovacks* [1974] 1 WLR 370 at p373:

> 'Section 16(1) does not provide either expressly or by implication that the person deceived must suffer any loss arising from the deception. What does have to be proved is that the accused by deception obtained for himself or another a pecuniary advantage. What there must be is a causal connection between the deception used and the pecuniary advantage obtained.'

What other offences might such a defendant commit? Prima facie he also obtains property by deception from the retailer, or possibly services contrary to s1(1) of the 1978 Act, yet the defendant might well contend that, since the cheque was bound to be honoured by the bank, he was not dishonest vis-à-vis the retailer, as he knew he would not suffer any financial loss. In reality, the retailer is unlikely to be interested in pressing a charge under s15, if indeed he ever learns of the defendant's criminality.

Lambie was charged with an offence contrary to s16 of the 1968 Act which has since been abolished, thus raising the question as to which offence would now be appropriate should the circumstances recur. It seems inappropriate to describe a credit card account as an overdraft, thus rendering a charge under the remaining sections of s16 impossible. Perhaps the answer is to charge the defendant with obtaining the services of the credit card company by deception, but it would have to be established that the service was one in respect of which payment was required; see further 22.1. One remaining possibility is that of charging the defendant with dishonestly, by deception, securing the remission of a liability, contrary to s2(1)(a) of the 1978 Act, but again the problem of dishonesty may arise as the defendant is using his or her own credit card: see further 22.2.

Remoteness

There will be no liability under s15(1) where the deception is too remote from the obtaining of property. If D gives false details that enable him to enter a race which he then wins, as a result of which he is awarded a prize, he will not be guilty of obtaining the prize by deception. The prize is obtained as a result of winning the race, not the deception by which he gained entry to it: see *R v Button* [1900] 2 QB 597. Similarly where D deceives P into allowing him to place bets on horses which subsequently win. D receives the winnings because the horses he backed have won, not because of his deception: see *R v Clucas* [1949] 2 KB 226. Whilst s16 of the 1968 Act (see below) does cover some of these problems, difficulties can arise in cases such as *R v Miller* [1992] Crim LR 744, where the appellant, having posed as an authorised taxi driver, charged passengers ten times the normal rate for a journey from airports to central London. Despite the Court of Appeal's assertion that the convictions for obtaining the fares by deception could stand as long as the various deceptions alleged in the indictment could be said to be the cause of the money being handed over, there remained the point that the passenger paying the money at the end of the journey may have done so knowing that he was being swindled. Following the House of Lords' decision in *R v Gomez* (see 17.4), it might be the case that a charge of theft would be more appropriate in circumstances such as these.

Mens rea

The mens rea required for s15 involves proof of dishonesty and deception.

Deception

Section 15(4) states that the defendant must intend to deceive or be reckless as to whether he deceives. In *R v Staines* (1974) 60 Cr App R 160 the Court of Appeal accepted that reckless in this context involved more than simple carelessness, or negligence on the part of the defendant, and amounted to indifference as to whether a statement was true or false. It is submitted that the *Cunningham* test for recklessness should continue to be used, that is, a defendant should only be found to have been reckless where he is aware of the risk that he may deceive another, but goes on to take that risk. In any event, it seems unlikely that a defendant could have failed to realise that there was an obvious risk that he might be deceiving another and yet at the same time be dishonest. This view is supported by *Large v Mainprize* [1989] Crim LR 213. Simply because the evidence reveals an intentional or reckless deception does not mean that the jury would therefore be entitled to assume dishonesty. The two matters must be assessed independently: see *R v Feeny* (1992) 94 Cr App R 1.

Dishonesty

Unlikely dishonesty in theft, to which s2(1) of the 1968 Act applies, there is no negative definition of dishonesty applicable to deception offences. In cases of doubt the Court of Appeal's decision in *R v Ghosh* [1982] 1 QB 1053 should be referred to: see further 18.1, although a *Ghosh* type direction is not necessary in every case. In *R v Price* (1990) 90 Cr App R 409, the appellant's defence to a number of deception charges was that he believed himself to be the beneficiary of a trust fund, and shortly expected to receive £100,000. In directing the jury as to dishonesty the trial judge had not referred to the direction set out in *R v Ghosh* (1982) 75 Cr App R 154, but had invited the jury to draw an analogy between the appellant and Billy

Bunter, on the basis that the latter had always been depicted as persuading others to lend him money on the strength of a postal order which was always going to arrive but which never materialised. Dismissing the appeal, the court expressed the view that in cases such as the present the *Ghosh* direction was unnecessary, as there was no evidence that the appellant believed that what he was alleged to have done was in accordance with the ordinary person's idea of honesty. The judge's references to the Billy Bunter stories were not unfair given the hopelessness of the defence case. Where it is necessary to resort to *Ghosh* a trial judge would be wise to use the ipsissima verba of Lord Lane CJ in *Ghosh,* rather than resorting to a paraphrase of the model direction: see *R* v *Vosper* (1990) The Times 26 February: *R* v *Melwani* [1989] Crim LR 565; *R* v *O'Connell* (1992) 94 Cr App R 39; and *R* v *Lightfoot* (1993) 97 Cr App R 24.

Intention to permanently deprive. Section 15(3) provides:

> 'Section 6 above shall apply for purposes of this section, with the necessary adaptation of the reference to appropriating, as it applies for purposes of section 1.'

Hence a defendant charged under s15 may be deemed to have intention to permanently deprive in those situations outlined at 18.2 (above).

In *R* v *Mitchell* [1993] Crim LR 788, the appellant, in the course of his work as a theatre manager, asked various businesses, including two advertising agencies, to issue invoices to the theatre in advance of work being carried out. He explained to them that the theatre would transfer the money by cheque to be held against future orders and thus avoid a budget surplus. The appellant then set up a company of his own and invoiced the agencies, asking them to transfer to his company the money that had been transferred to them by the theatre. The agencies refused to make the transfers requested and returned the sums involved to the theatre. The appellant was convicted of obtaining the cheques by deception from the theatre and attempting to obtain the cheques by deception from the agencies. On appeal he argued that he could not have intended to permanently deprive the theatre of the cheques as cheque forms, as they would be returned to the drawer's bank in the normal course of clearing. Further, he could not have intended to permanently deprive the theatre of property in the form of a chose in action (ie the right to sue on the cheques) as that right could not be vested in the drawer of a cheque and had thus never been property belonging to another. Dismissing his appeal, the Court of Appeal held that the appellant could be deemed to have intended to permanently deprive the theatre of the cheques, either on the basis that when the cheque was returned having been cashed it would be a substantially different document (ie one on which payment could not longer be enforced: see *Duru* (1973) 59 Cr App 151), or because the appellant was only willing to return the cheque subject to a condition (ie that he obtained payment on them), and he was thus treating the cheques as his own to dispose of regardless of the theatre's rights. It is submitted that there may be difficulty in sustaining the argument that the appellant obtains property (in the form of the piece of paper comprising the cheque) by deception, as it will be returned to the bank, albeit with various endorsements upon it. The real nature of the criminality lies in what the cheque represents, the right to draw money on a particular account. If P, the account holder, draws a cheque in favour of D, he is creating intangible property belonging to D, the right to draw money from the account. By definition this intangible property has never belonged to P, and cannot unless D endorses the cheque in favour of P. To rely on s6(1) of the Theft Act 1968, to the effect that the appellant is in the same position as D who takes P's property and sells it back to him, does perhaps place a greater strain on the section than it can withstand. When the cheque is returned to P it is not analogous to him 'buying back' his property as he never owned the chose in action in the first instance.

21.2 Section 16

Section 16(1) creates the offence of obtaining a pecuniary advantage by deception; as amended it provides:

> 'A person who by any deception dishonestly obtains for himself or another any pecuniary advantage shall on conviction on indictment be liable to imprisonment for a term not exceeding five years.'

Actus reus

As with s15, the obtaining (in this case of a pecuniary advantage) must be as a result of a deception exercised by the defendant. Section 16(3) provides that for the purposes of s16 'deception' should have the same meaning as in s15. See generally, therefore, 21.1 above.

Pecuniary advantage has a very precise meaning within s16. It would appear to cover the following:

1. Being allowed to borrow by way of overdraft. See *MPC* v *Charles* (above). Where D pays for goods or services by way of a cheque drawn on his own account having been instructed by his bank not to do so, he will not commit an offence under s16 unless the cheque is supported by his cheque guarantee card and the bank, as a result, has to debit the amount of the cheque from D's account, thus increasing his overdraft; see *R* v *Bevan* [1987] Crim LR 129. If no cheque guarantee card is used, the bank will not increase D's overdraft because it will refuse to honour his cheque. A charge of attempt may be sustainable on such facts.
2. Taking out a policy of insurance or annuity contract, or obtaining an improvement of the terms on which the defendant is allowed to do so. Liability would arise if D were to lie about his age or health to P, an insurance company. Should D receive a payment under any subsequent policy, he could not be charged under s15 because the deception is too remote from his obtaining of property, hence the existence of this form of liability under s16.

3. Being given an opportunity to earn remuneration or greater remuneration in an office or employment. Again this is a situation that would fall outside s15. If D lies about his qualifications, and secures a job as a result, the money he receives is paid because of the work he does, not because of the lies he has told; the deception is too remote from the obtaining of property. The job is, therefore, the pecuniary advantage obtained by deception. There has been some debate as to whether this provision applied to those obtaining remunerative work as independent contractors. It was thought, for example, that if D falsely claimed to be a tree surgeon and was paid to remove P's tree, he did not obtain an 'office or employment' by deception: see further the prosecution's reliance on s15 in *R* v *King and Stockwell* [1987] Crim LR 398. Exactly what Parliament did intend in enacting this aspect of s16 may be unclear, as it was not included in the original draft Bill, but added as the legislation progressed through Parliament. Hence the matter is not adverted to in the Criminal Law Revision Committee's Report that led to the enactment of the 1968 Act.

Some clarification is provided, however, by the Court of Appeal's decision in *R* v *Callender* [1992] 3 All ER 51. The appellant agreed to prepare accounts for a number of small businessmen, having falsely held himself out as being professionally qualified to do so. In dismissing his appeal against conviction under s16, Wright J, on behalf of the Court of Appeal, observed:

> 'We have come to the clear conclusion that Parliament, in adopting the phrase "office or employment", intended section 16(1) of the Acts of 1968 to have a wider impact than one confined to the narrow limits of a contract of service. A small indication is the use of the word "remuneration", which is a wide term, and the absence of any reference to salary or wages ... It seems to us that it is a perfectly proper use of ordinary language and as such to be readily understood by ordinary literate men and women to say of a person in this appellant's position that his services as an accountant were "employed" by his customers, and that this state of affairs is properly to be described by the word "employment".'

The court seems to have been motivated by a desire not to create a gap in the law which would permit dishonest people, by arranging their affairs so that they could come within the definition of 'self-employed', to escape conviction and punishment for their deceitful conduct.

4. Being given the opportunity to win money by betting. This brings within s16 situations such as that in *R* v *Clucas* [1949] 2 KB 226.

Mens rea

Section 16 requires that the defendant should intend to deceive or be reckless as to whether he deceives another. Note that the deception can be exercised on X, although the pecuniary advantage is obtained from P. (See *Charles* and *Lambie* above). The defendant must also be dishonest at the time of obtaining the pecuniary advantage; for more detail see 21.1 above.

21.3 Section 17

Section 17(1) which creates the offence of false accounting provides:

> 'Where a person dishonestly, with a view to gain for himself or another or with intent to cause loss to another –
> a) destroys, defaces, conceals or falsifies any account or any record or document made or required for any accounting purpose; or
> b) in furnishing information for any purpose produces or makes use of any account, or any such record or document as aforesaid, which to his knowledge is or may be misleading, false or deceptive in a material particular;
> he shall, on conviction on indictment, be liable to imprisonment for a term not exceeding seven years.'

Actus reus

A document made or required for any accounting purpose is interpreted as one required for financial accounting. Accounting need not be the sole purpose for which the document is produced provided it is one of the purposes. Section 17(2) provides further:

> 'For purposes of this section a person who makes or concurs in making in an account or other document an entry which is or may be misleading, false or deceptive in a material particular, or who omits or concurs in omitting a material particular from an account or other document, is to be treated as falsifying the account or document.'

In *Edwards* v *Toombs* [1983] Crim LR 43 it was held that a turnstile operator, who allowed two persons into a stadium whilst only recording the entry of one, had falsified a record for the purposes of the offence. Similarly, it is submitted, an offence under s17 would be committed by a cashier failing to ring up the full amount tendered by a customer, where the cashier intended to remove the amount under-rung sometime later when an opportunity presented itself: see *R* v *Monaghan* [1979] Crim LR 673, and *R* v *Golecha* [1989] 3 All ER 908.

Further in *R* v *Scott-Simmonds* [1994] Crim LR 933, the Court of Appeal confirmed that the word 'account' was to be given its ordinary meaning and, following *Attorney-General's Reference (No 1 of 1980)* (1980) 72 Cr App R 60, was to be interpreted widely, as it had been the intention of Parliament that the offence should extend to the preparation of accounts as well as the alteration of existing accounts. See chapter 26, section 26.9, for further details.

Mens rea

The prosecution must prove dishonesty, as in *R* v *Ghosh* (above), and that D acted with a view to gain for himself or another, or with intent to cause loss to another. See s34(2)(a), as explained at 20.7 above. In respect of s17(1)(b), the defendant must know that the document is or may be misleading, false or deceptive in a material detail, or he must be at least subjectively reckless in this regard.

21.4 Section 20

Section 20(1) creates the offence of dishonestly destroying, defacing or concealing a valuable security with a view to gain or intent to cause loss to another. Section 20(2) creates the offence of dishonestly securing the execution of a valuable security by deception, with a view to gain or intent to cause loss to another. Both offences carry a maximum possible sentence of seven years imprisonment. They can to some extent be seen as preparatory offences in that liability can arise without any advantage having been obtained. As indicated below the offence under s20(2) has been used in respect of two particularly common forms of criminal activity, mortgage fraud, and unauthorised use of cheques and credit cards. Since the enactment of s12 of the Criminal Justice Act 1987 it may be preferable, where the evidence reveals an agreement to indulge in such activities, to proceed with a charge of common law conspiracy to defraud.

What is a valuable security?

Section 20(3) provides that:

> '... valuable security means any document creating, transferring, surrendering or releasing any right to, in or over property, or authorising the payment of money or delivery of any property, or evidencing the creation, transfer, surrender or release of any such right, or the payment of money or delivery of any property, or the satisfaction of any obligation.'

With the inevitable move towards computerisation of banking transactions, arguments have developed as to whether or not the offence created by s20(2) can be used against defendants who dishonestly procure the electronic transfer of funds. In *R* v *Bolton* (1991) 94 Cr App R 74, the Court of Appeal quashed the appellants' convictions under s20(2) on the ground, inter alia, that the term 'document' as it was used in s20(3) could not be so widely construed as to include a telegraphic transfer of mortgage funds by a building society. The court also rejected the submission that the bank statement indicating that the transfer had taken place could be regarded as a valuable security for the purposes of the offence. It was willing to accept, however, that a mortgage deed would fall within the scope of the subsection. See further *R* v *IK Dhillon and GS Dhillon* [1992] Crim LR 889.

    R v *King* [1991] Crim LR 906 also raised the problem of fraudulent mortgage applications. On this occasion the funds were to be transferred from the paying customer's bank account to the appellant's by means of a 'CHAPS' (Clearing House Automated Payments System) order. The appellant's contention was that such an order could not constitute a valuable security since it did not create any right to property (on the basis that it could not be sued on by someone outside the bank), but merely authorised activity which might lead to the creation of property. In rejecting this argument, the Court of Appeal held that a CHAPS order, once processed, did effect a transfer of intangible property (money in the paying customer's account) to the payee. In addition it created property, in that the payee now possessed a chose in action, and evidenced the creation and transfer of property. With respect, this may be seen as an attempt to reach the 'right' result by rather dubious means. The court appears to hold that there is at once the transfer and creation of property. It would seem that these concepts are mutually exclusive. If the property in question is the right to sue the bank on the credit balance of the account, once the paying customer's CHAPS order is executed, his right to sue his bank in respect of the sum specified in the order is destroyed, and a new right, belonging to the payee, to sue his bank in respect of the sum now credited to his account is created. The difficulty that remains is that s20(3) specifically refers to documents which create rights to or over property, or evidence the creation of such rights. As JC Smith suggests in his commentary upon the case at p909, if the CHAPS order '... creates the property it does not create a right in or over property'. See further *R* v *Benstead* [1982] Crim LR 456. The courts have shown reluctance to extend this approach. In *R* v *Manjdadria* [1993] Crim LR 73, a case confirming that a telegraphic transfer of funds is not a valuable security, the Court of Appeal expressed the view that *R* v *King* was to be regarded as a decision defining the extreme limits of what could constitute a valuable security.

Section 20(1), is wider in ambit than s20(2). In addition to dealing with valuable securities, it can be used to charge the defendant who destroys or defaces testamentary documents, or original documents filed with a court of law or government department.

What constitutes execution?

The Court of Appeal's ruling in *R* v *Beck* (1985) 80 Cr App R 355, to the effect that 'execution' was not to be construed in a restricted sense, has not been followed in subsequent decisions. In *R* v *Nanayakkara* (1987) 84 Cr App R 125, the trial judge's ruling, that execution in the form of 'acceptance' under s20(2) meant merely taking into possession, was rejected by Lord Lane CJ, on the ground that an examination of the legislative history of the provision revealed that 'acceptance' had been used in its technical sense in previous enactments, and there was no evidence to suggest that s20(2) was using the term in any different sense. This restrictive interpretation now has the approval of the House of Lords, following the decision in *R* v *Kassim* (1991) 93 Cr App R 391. In that case the appellant had opened a number of bank accounts having given false particulars to the bank, and subsequently used the cheque books and cheque cards with which he had been issued to obtain sums of money and goods from third parties. The prosecution could have tried to charge the appellant with offences contrary to s15 of the 1968 Act, but as Lord Ackner observed:

'... I fully appreciate that the current use of cheque guarantee cards and credit cards does give rise to problems where charges are brought under s15 in cases where the representation alleged is that the defendant was authorised to use his card, when he knew he was not because, for example, his account is overdrawn. However, since the whole object of the card is to relieve the tradesman from concerning himself with the relationship between the customer and his own bank, the tradesman may well not care whether or not the customer was exceeding the authority accorded to him by his own bank. All he will be concerned with is that the conditions on the card are satisfied. Such cases obviously give rise to the difficulty of establishing an operative deception. This problem cannot, however, be overcome by overstraining the meaning of the word "execution" as used in s20(2).'

Lord Ackner concluded that a defendant who presents a cheque for payment knowing he will not have funds to meet it falls outside the scope of s20(2) because, although he seeks financial gain for himself, the dishonest means by which he intends to achieve this is not by the cancellation or destruction of the cheque (ie the execution of it), since he will have achieved the sought after financial gain prior to the cheque's destruction or cancellation. As his Lordship succinctly put it:

'The subsection contemplates acts being done to or in connection with such documents. It does not contemplate and accordingly is not concerned with giving effect to the documents by the carrying out of the instruction which they may contain, such as the delivery of goods or the payment out of money.'

The mental element

The offences under s20 require proof of dishonesty, as to which see the guidelines in *R v Ghosh*, considered at 18.1. Similarly, deception bears the meaning provided by s15(4), considered above at 21.1. The proof of the defendant's 'view to gain' etc, is governed by s34(2)(a), considered at 20.7.

22

The Theft Act 1978

22.1 Section 1   *Obtaining service by deception.*
22.2 Section 2   *Evasion of a liability by deception*
22.3 Section 3   *Making off without payment*

22.1 Section 1

Section 1(1) of the Theft Act 1978 creates the offence of obtaining services by deception. Services can clearly be of economic value, and it is right that they should be protected by criminal law. Section 1 provides:

> 'A person who by any deception dishonestly obtains services from another shall be guilty of an offence.'

Section 4(2)(a) states that a defendant convicted on indictment for this offence can be sentenced to a maximum of five years imprisonment. Note that a defendant who commits this offence may also incur liability under ss2 and 3 of the 1978 Act considered below.

Actus reus

The Act provides no detailed definition of services, although s1(2) does provide a partial definition where it states:

> 'It is an obtaining of services where the other is induced to confer a benefit by doing some act, or causing or permitting some act to be done, on the understanding that the benefit has been or will be paid for.'

The requirement that the provision of the service should be a 'benefit' to the defendant should not be construed too narrowly. Whether or not a service is beneficial is a matter of taste; for example tattooing, being given a 'mohican' haircut, or having one's car sprayed purple. It is submitted that a service is a benefit if it is something that an individual would be willing to pay for, or alternatively if it would be sufficient consideration to support a contract. The matter has produced little in the way of illuminating authority. In *R v Halai* [1983] Crim LR 624, the defendant drew cheques on his bank account, in which there was only £28, to pay for a building society survey of a property he wished to buy, to open a savings account at the building society, and he misrepresented his employment status in order to try and obtain a mortgage advance from the building society. The Court of Appeal held that in respect of the property survey, the defendant had been rightly convicted under s1, the cheque was the deception (the defendant representing that it would be met on presentation, which was not true). The provision of the survey was a benefit to the defendant, not only because it was an essential step in his obtaining a mortgage, but also because it was provided on the understanding that it would be paid for. The provision of a savings account was not a service, however, because even if it was a benefit to the defendant, it was not one for which the building society made any charge and thus fell outside the scope of s1(2). More questionable was the court's decision that a mortgage advance was not a service because it was a lending of money for the purchase of a property. The advance would have been to the defendant's benefit, and there would have been no question of his not having to pay for it through interest payments. The defendant could of course have been charged under s15, but this cannot mean a charge under s1 of the 1978 Act was unsustainable. The offences are not mutually exclusive. Further doubt is cast on aspects of *R* v *Halai* by the later Court of Appeal decision in *R* v *Widdowson* [1986] Crim LR 233, wherein it was held that a hire-purchase agreement was a service and could be distinguished from a mortgage advance, but the court did not provide a detailed explanation for this. It is submitted that *R* v *Widdowson* is rightly decided, and that (on this point) *R* v *Halai* is wrong, in that hire-purchase agreements and mortgage advances should be regarded as services within s1(2). Although not called upon to deal directly with this issue, the Court of Appeal, in *R* v *Teong Sun Chuah* [1991] Crim LR 463, stated that *Halai* bore all the hallmarks of being per incuriam.

The words 'on the understanding that the benefit has been or will be paid for' which appear in s1(2) have the effect of excluding gratuitous services from the scope of the offence. Clearly, a service provided free of charge is not one for which payment will have been made or be expected. Hence where D persuades a taxi driver P to give him a free ride after telling him a false 'hard luck' story, he will not be committing an offence within s1. The important point to bear in mind is that P is under no illusion as to whether he will be paid for providing the journey. Should he not wish to provide it for free, he can simply refuse. In such a case D may be guilty of an offence under s2(1)(c) (see below).

The requirement that the service should not be one that is gratuitous may have some interesting consequences. In *R* v *Atwal* [1989] Crim LR 293, for example, the trial judge directed the jury at Knightsbridge Crown Court that to obtain an American Express credit card by deception could be an offence under s1(1) of the 1978 Act, because an annual fee is charged in respect of membership, but no such offence would be made out where the defendant had exercised a deception in order to obtain a Visa or Access card, for which, at the time no charge was made. Note the difficulties inherent in charging the defendant with obtaining property (ie a card) by deception, given the need to establish intention to permanently deprive under s15 of the 1968 Act.

There is nothing in s1(2) to expressly exclude from the definition of services acts which are contrary to law or against public policy, such as where D induces P to whip him in order to satisfy a particular sexual preference, or where D induces P, a prostitute, to have sex with him. In the absence of authority the point must remain open, although as a matter of construction, the fact that Parliament has expressly provided for this matter in relation to 'making off without payment' (see s3(3)) perhaps suggests that such acts are not to be excluded from the definition of services.

The obtaining of services must be by deception. The deception must therefore precede the obtaining of the service, and must be operative in the sense that it induces the provision of the service. See further 21.1 (above). Further, s5(1) of the 1978 Act provides:

'For the purposes of sections 1 and 2 above "deception" has the same meaning as in section 15 of the Theft Act 1968, that is to say, it means any deception (whether deliberate or reckless) by words or conduct as to fact or as to law, including a deception as to the present intentions of the persons using the deception or any other person; and section 18 of that Act (liability of company officers for offences by the company) shall apply in relation to sections 1 and 2 above as it applies in relation to section 15 of that Act.'

Any suggestion that the deception must relate to payment is to be rejected. In the majority of cases the deception will relate to payment, such as where D sits in a barber's chair having no intention of paying for his haircut, but by his conduct he induces the barber to provide the service. The situation where D produces a false driving licence in order to hire a car is also covered, even though D pays in full for the hire. The provision of car hire is a service within s1(2) because it is a benefit to D provided on the understanding that he will pay for it: see *R* v *Adams* [1993] Crim LR 525.

Mens rea

The defendant must be dishonest at the time of obtaining the service. The test in *R* v *Ghosh* is to be used (see 18.1). The defendant must have the mens rea for deception, which is intention or recklessness, see s5(1) (above) and 21.1. There is clearly no need here for any intention to permanently deprive since once the service has been provided its economic value has been passed to the defendant.

22.2 Section 2

Section 2 of the Theft Act 1978 creates three offences concerned with the defendant's evasion of a liability by deception. On the basis of *R* v *Holt and Lee* [1981] 2 All ER 834 (discussed below) it is submitted that the three offences are not mutually exclusive.

Section 2(1)(a)

Section 2(1)(a) provides:

> '... where a person by any deception dishonestly secures the remission of the whole or part of any existing liability to make a payment, whether his own liability or another's, he shall be guilty of an offence.'

The deception must precede the securing of the remission of liability, and must cause it: see further 21.1 (above) and s5(1) of the 1978 Act.

The liability referred to must be an existing legal liability to pay, in the sense that it is legally enforceable. Section 2(2) further provides that liability should not be interpreted as extending to a liability that has not been accepted or established to pay compensation for some wrongful act or omission, such as where D deceives P into believing that he cannot sue D for damages in respect of an accident caused by D's negligence. This restriction on the definition of liability applies equally to all three offences under s2(1). The fact that a liability to pay might only be enforced by a court order, such as one arising under an improperly executed credit agreement, does not prevent it from being an existing liability for the purposes of s2(1): see *R v Modupe* [1991] Crim LR 530.

The requirement in s2(1)(a) that the defendant must have 'secured the remission' of the liability in question means something more than that he has persuaded the creditor by deception to relieve him of liability, partly because such activity is amply catered for under s2(1)(b), but also because of the absence of the need to prove any intention to make permanent default under s2(1)(a). A defendant who secures the remission of a liability would therefore be one who succeeds in extinguishing his legal liability to pay, so that the creditor could not pursue him for payment. Such a situation can arise where D owes P £100 repayable on June 23rd, and P agrees to accept £80 in full settlement of the debt on June 20th. The earlier repayment, albeit of a lesser sum, constitutes consideration which supports P's promise not to claim the remaining £20. D has here secured the remission of his liability to pay the £20. If D were to have induced such an agreement by P by falsely telling him that he was emigrating to Australia on June 21st and that if P waited until the 23rd June he would receive nothing, it might be contended that D had now committed an offence contrary to s2(1)(a) on the basis that he had now secured the remission of his liability to pay the remaining £20 by deception. The problem is whether, as a matter of civil law, D can ever have wiped out his legal liability to pay a debt where he has exercised a deception. It could be argued that his fraud renders P's agreement void and of no effect, or at least that P's agreement is voidable, and that as soon as P discovers the truth he can sue D for the remaining £20. If this interpretation is correct it becomes difficult to see what situations, if any, s2(1)(a) can apply to.

Notwithstanding this difficulty, the Court of Appeal in *R v Jackson* [1983] Crim LR 617 held that a defendant committed the offence where he paid for petrol with a stolen credit card. The existing liability was to pay for the petrol that he had put into the tank of his motorbike. The deception was the use of another person's card. The use of the card induced the petrol station to look to the credit card company for payment, not the defendant, and the credit card company would be contractually bound to reimburse the petrol station provided the conditions of using the card had been met. On this basis the court felt that Jackson had secured the remission of his liability to pay for the petrol. It is submitted that the defendant might have been more appropriately charged under s2(1)(b) or s3 of the 1978 Act (see below). He could not really be said to have wiped out his legal liability to pay for the petrol. If for any reason the credit card company had refused to reimburse the petrol station, the proprietors would have wanted, if at all possible, to recoup payment from the defendant.

The mens rea required for s2(1)(a), which is common to all three offences under s2, is that the defendant should be dishonest, see 18.1, and intend to deceive or be reckless as to whether he deceives, see Chapter 21.1 and s5(1) of the 1978 Act. Given that the section requires proof of the defendant securing the remission of a liability, any further requirement of proof that the defendant intended to make permanent default would be pointless.

Section 2(1)(b)

Section 2(1)(b) provides:

> 'Where a person by any deception with intent to make permanent default in whole or in part on any existing liability to make a payment, or with intent to let another do so, dishonestly induces the creditor or any person claiming payment on behalf of the creditor to wait for payment (whether or not the due date for payment is deferred) or to forgo payment, he shall be guilty of an offence.'

The observations concerning deception and dishonesty made above in relation to s2(1)(a) apply equally to the offence under s2(1)(b). It is aimed at the defendant who seeks to delay repayment of a debt by lying to his creditor, whilst not having any real intention of ever repaying the money. Where D owes P £20, the date for repayment having passed, and D falsely tells P that he has been robbed and will not have the money to repay P until next week, D commits an offence under s2(1)(b) if P accepts this story and D never intends to repay. P has been induced by D's deception to wait for payment. Similarly if P were to be persuaded by D's lies to let him off the debt altogether, P would then have been induced to forgo payment. Note that the section also caters for the situation where D acts with intent to let another person make permanent default on an existing liability.

The Court of Appeal decision in *R v Holt and Lee* [1981] 2 All ER 834 illustrates the operation of the section. The defendants had consumed a meal in a restaurant and decided that when the waitress presented the bill for payment they would tell her that they had already paid another waitress (which was untrue) and on being left unattended would make good their escape. The defendants were overheard planning their crime by an off-duty policeman who was dining at a nearby table and he promptly arrested them. The court held that the defendants had been rightly convicted of an attempt to commit an offence under s2(1)(b). Had the plan succeeded, the waitress acting as agent of the creditor would have been induced by their deception to forgo payment for the meal, their mens rea being evident.

Section 2(3) provides:

> 'For purposes of subsection (1)(b) a person induced to take in payment a cheque or other security for money by way of conditional satisfaction of a pre-existing liability is to be treated not as being paid but as being induced to wait for payment.'

Thus where D induces P to take a cheque D knows to be worthless, in that it will be dishonoured on presentation, in payment for a liability, and D has the appropriate mens rea, D will be guilty of an offence under s2(1)(b). The purpose of s2(3) is to replace the common law rule that acceptance of a cheque amounts to a conditional payment, suspending the creditor's remedies until the cheque has been paid or dishonoured. Such a rule might make it difficult to show that P had been induced to wait for or forgo payment (but see also *R v Andrews and Hedges* [1981] Crim LR 106).

The mens rea required for s2(1)(b) is dishonesty and deception (see 22.2 above) and in addition the defendant must have an intention to make permanent default on the existing liability, which in simple terms means an intention never to pay the debt. Where the charge alleges that D acted with intent to let another person default on their liability, the trial judge should be careful to direct the jury that the conduct of D that might be regarded as dishonest where he acted for his own benefit might not necessarily be so regarded where he acted for another: see *R v Attewell-Hughes* (1991) 93 Cr App R 132.

Section 2(1)(c)

Section 2(1)(c) states:

> 'Where any person by any deception dishonestly obtains any exemption from or abatement of liability to make a payment he shall be guilty of an offence.'

Liability has the same meaning here as it does for the other two offences under s2, but unlike them encompasses also future liabilities. This point was emphasised by the Court of Appeal in *R v Firth* (1989) 91 Cr App R 217. The appellant, a consultant gynaecologist/obstetrician who had treated both private and NHS patients at hospitals within the Mid Downs Area Health Authority, had an arrangement with the Authority under which he would inform them if an antenatal test, or hospital bed, was being provided for one of his private patients. In such cases the appellant would be responsible for paying the Authority and could recoup the charges from his patient at a later stage. A number of specimen charges had been brought against the appellant alleging that, contrary to s2(1)(c) of the Theft Act 1978, he had dishonestly by deception obtained exemption from a liability by not informing the Authority that certain patients receiving treatment in its hospitals were his private patients and not NHS patients. He appealed against conviction on the grounds, inter alia, that the offence contrary to s2(1)(c) could not be committed by omission, and that at the time of the alleged deception, there had been no existing liability to make a payment.

As to the first of those grounds, the court declared that it was satisfied that if, under the arrangement with the Authority, it had been incumbent upon the appellant to inform the hospital of the status of a particular patient, and as a result of his failure to do so he was not billed for treatment as he otherwise would have been, the requirements of the section were made out. This duty to inform the hospital of the status of his patients receiving treatment presumably arose from the appellant's contract with the hospital, but the point is not clearly explained in the course of the Lord Chief Justice's judgment. His Lordship appears to have been happy to accept the prosecution assertion that this was the case. Given that such a contractual duty did exist, there is no doubt that the offence could be committed by omission.

As to the second ground, the court regarded it as significant that ss2(1)(a), and 2(1)(b) of the 1978 Act expressly required the prosecution to establish an existing liability that a defendant had tried to evade whilst s2(1)(c) was silent on this point. Their Lordships did not think that this omission had been accidental, but was evidence that, in relation to s2(1)(c), Parliament had not intended that any existing liability need be shown at the time of the deception. The subsection applied equally, therefore, to future liabilities such as that in the present case. Deception should be interpreted in the same way here as it is under the other s2 offences.

By virtue of s2(4) 'obtains' in s2(1)(c) includes obtaining for another or enabling another to obtain.

The mens rea required is dishonesty and deception, see 22.2 above. No intention to make permanent default need be established.

The major difficulty with s2(1)(c), as with s2(1)(a), is in determining its sphere of operation, since strictly construed, it is hard to see how a defendant would ever gain genuine exemption from a liability where he has exercised a deception. As soon as the deception is discovered he will become liable to pay the full amount due. It may be more sensible to view the offence as one of deceiving a prospective or actual creditor into believing that only a reduced payment, or even no payment at all, is due from the defendant. Such an interpretation is supported by the Court of Appeal decision in *R v Sibartie* [1983] Crim LR 470, where the defendant's conviction for attempted evasion of a liability by deception was upheld, following his showing of an invalid travel ticket to a London Underground ticket inspector in the hope that she would be tricked into letting the defendant pass on to the next stage of his journey. Had his scheme worked the defendant would not have gained exemption from his liability to pay the full fare but would have persuaded the inspector that no further payment was due from him. It is arguable that the defendant was also guilty of an attempt to commit an offence under s2(1)(b).

22.3 Section 3

Section 3(1) of the Theft Act 1978 creates the offence of making off without payment. It provides:

'Subject to subsection (3) below, a person who, knowing that payment on the spot for any goods supplied or service done is required or expected from him, dishonestly makes off without having paid as required or expected and with intent to avoid payment of the amount due shall be guilty of an offence.'

The offence is aimed at the defendant who, for example, drives to a petrol station and fills the tank of his car, intending all the time to pay, but having taken the petrol decides not to pay, and drives off without exercising any deception as to his intentions. He cannot be guilty of theft because his appropriation of the petrol was not dishonest, and when he drives from the petrol station property in the petrol has passed to him. Neither does he obtain the petrol by deception. Clearly, however, he will have committed an offence contrary to s3.

Actus reus

The offence applies equally to goods and services for which payment has not been made. However a restriction is introduced by s3(3) which provides:

'Subsection (1) above shall not apply where the supply of the goods or the doing of the service is contrary to law, or where the service done is such that payment is not legally enforceable.'

Hence if D were to run out of a brothel without paying for the sexual intercourse he has just had with a prostitute P he would not incur any liability under s3(1). Similarly where D is under no liability to pay P for a service performed or goods supplied, because P is in breach of contract, no liability under s3(1) can arise. This latter point was reaffirmed by the Divisional Court in *Troughton* v *Metropolitan Police* [1987] Crim LR 138, when the defendant's conviction for making off without paying for a taxi journey was quashed on the basis that payment for the journey was unenforceable under s3(3) because the taxi driver was in breach of a contract of complete obligation, having failed to take the defendant to his required destination.

There must be evidence of D having 'made off'. The phrase suggests a departure at high speed, but obviously this is not necessary for conviction. The most effective departure by one seeking to avoid payment is likely to be one that is quiet and unobtrusive. Although the statute does not make clear exactly where the making off must occur, it should be noted that D must be shown to have made off knowing that payment on the spot is required, thus it will normally arise after a service has been provided (as is made clear by s3(2)) or after goods have been supplied (eg food in a restaurant or petrol at a filling station). In *R* v *McDavitt* [1981] Crim LR 843, where D ran from his table at a restaurant without having paid for his meal, the court held that for the completed offence there would have to be evidence that D had left the premises altogether. Where, as in *R* v *McDavitt,* a defendant is apprehended before exiting from the premises, the appropriate charge could be one of attempt.

The issue was considered in *R* v *Aziz* [1993] Crim LR 708, where the appellant was one of two men who had called a taxi to take them to a nightclub. On arrival at the destination the driver asked for the correct fare, which was £15, but the appellant and his companion contested the amount due, and offered to pay £4. The driver surmised that his passengers were was not going to pay and started to drive them back to the point from which they had been collected, but en route decided to drive them to a police station. The appellant and his companion began to damage the car's fittings, and the driver pulled into a petrol station and asked the attendant to call the police, at which the appellant made off. Upholding his conviction under s3, the Court of Appeal noted that the phrase 'knowing that payment on the spot ... is expected' was a reference to the defendant's state of mind, and not to a specific location. It was sufficient that the requirement to pay had come into existence, and that the defendant was shown to have made off from the place where payment would normally be made. In the case of a taxi journey, the place for payment could be inside the cab, or standing outside the cab. Presumably the requirement to pay did not come into existence until the driver in this case had taken the appellant to his requested destination, see *Troughton* v *MPC* (above), but at any time after that, payment could be demanded, hence making off at any time after reaching the destination could form the basis of the offence.

The defendant must have made off 'without having paid as required and expected', an expression that may be somewhat ambiguous now. Failing to make any payment at all would clearly satisfy this requirement, as would the leaving of an inadequate amount, foreign currency, or counterfeit notes. It is submitted that the phrase also encompasses the defendant who pays for goods or services using another person's cheques or credit card, although there may be other more appropriate offences in such cases. More questionable is the situation where the defendant uses his own cheques supported by his cheque guarantee card, or his own credit card knowing he does not have authority to do so because he has reached or already exceeded his overdraft or credit limit. It could be argued on the basis of *MPC* v *Charles* [1976] 1 All ER 659 and *R* v *Lambie* [1981] 1 All ER 332 (see 21.1 above) that the retailer would not accept the cheque or credit card in payment if he knew that the defendant had no authority to use these items, but s3 is not a deception offence, and given that payment is guaranteed, it is submitted that a defendant who acts in this way does pay as required and expected. The same probably cannot be said of the defendant who draws a cheque on his own account to pay for goods or services, which is not supported by a cheque guarantee card and which he knows will not be honoured when presented for payment. A worthless cheque is not payment as required and expected, and there should be liability under s3: see further, *R* v *Brooks and Brooks* (1982) 76 Cr App R 66.

Mens rea

The defendant must know that payment on the spot for any goods supplied or service done is required or expected from him, and in this respect s3(2) provides that 'payment on the spot' includes payment at the time of collecting goods on which work has been done or in respect of which service has been provided. D will escape liability therefore, if he leaves a restaurant without paying in the honest belief that his companions who remain at the table will pay his share of the bill, or where he believes that the goods or services are provided free of charge, or where he believes that the goods or services are being supplied on credit, and that payment will not be due until some later date: see further *R* v *Brooks and Brooks* (1982) 76 Cr App R 66.

The defendant must be dishonest at the time of his making off; where necessary the test in *R* v *Ghosh* [1982] QB 1053 is applicable, see 18.1.

The House of Lords, in *R* v *Allen* [1985] AC 1029, ruled that the requirement in s3(1), that D should be proved to have intended to avoid payment, should be interpreted so as to require proof of an intention to permanently avoid payment. The defendant had stayed at a hotel for nearly a month and left without paying the bill, but contacted the hotel a few days later and explained he was in financial difficulties and would return to the hotel to collect his belongings and leave his passport as security. When he did so he was arrested and charged with an offence contrary to s3(1). The trial judge directed the jury that the intent to avoid payment merely referred to the time when payment should have been made 'on the spot' and the defendant was convicted. Lord Hailsham was content to endorse the reasoning adopted by Boreham J in the court below, to the effect that, if intent to avoid payment meant no more than an intention to delay or defer payment of the amount due, it added little to the other elements. Anyone who knew that payment on the spot was expected or required of him and who dishonestly made off without paying as required or expected must have had at least an intention to delay or defer payment. Thus the conjoined phrase 'and with intent to avoid payment of the amount due' added a further ingredient: an intention to do more than delay or defer, an intention to evade payment altogether. Lord Hailsham was also of the view that if Parliament had intended to create an offence involving intention only to delay payment it would have said so in more explicit terms. Support for the House of Lords' view is provided by the Criminal Law Revision Committee's Thirteenth Report (*Section 16 of the Theft Act 1968*) (Cmnd 6733 (1977)), which led to the passing of the 1978 Act. Paragraphs 18 states:

> '... there was general support for our suggestion that where the customer knows that he is expected to pay on the spot for goods supplied to him or services done for him it should be an offence for him dishonestly to go away without having paid and intending never to pay.'

Whilst it is encouraging to see the House of Lords construing the ambiguity in the statute in favour of the accused, the ruling does reveal the limited protection that s3 offers to taxi drivers, restauranters and owners of filling stations, as anyone making off without payment, if subsequently apprehended, can claim that they *did* intend to pay at some later date. Liability may well then depend upon the plausibility of the defendant's evidence.

23

Handling Stolen Goods

23.1 Introduction

23.2 Stolen goods

23.3 Modes of handling

23.4 Mens rea

23.5 Innocent receipt and subsequent mens rea

23.1 Introduction

Section 22(1) of the Theft Act 1968 creates the offence of handling stolen goods, replacing offences under the Larceny Acts of 1861 and 1916 which had previously represented the law. As may be seen from what follows, the 1968 Act may have replaced the old law, but it is an area that still bristles with complexities due in no small part to the form in which the offence is drafted. Section 22(1) provides:

'A person handles stolen goods if (otherwise than in the course of the stealing) knowing or believing them to be stolen goods he dishonestly receives the goods, or dishonestly undertakes or assists in their retention, removal, disposal or realisation by or for the benefit of another.'

The maximum punishment for handling following conviction on indictment is 14 years imprisonment. The rationale behind punishing handlers more severely than thieves is that were it not for the existence of handlers (or 'fences') there would be little theft of an organised nature.

23.2 Stolen goods

The combined effect of a number of provisions in the 1968 Act is that the term 'stolen goods' has acquired a meaning peculiar to the offence.

Goods

Section 34(2)(b) provides:

' "Goods", except in so far as the context otherwise requires, includes money and every other description of property except land, and includes things severed from the land by stealing.'

323

The phrase 'and every other description of property' is presumed to encompass choses in action as well as tangible property. Were it to be otherwise it might prove impossible to convict a defendant of handling stolen goods where money had been stolen by the thief, paid into the thief's bank account, and then transferred via a bank credit to the defendant's bank account. The chose in action, the bank balance, clearly represents the original stolen money. See further *R* v *Pitchley* (1973) 57 Cr App R 30; *Attorney-General's Reference (No 4 of 1979)* (1980) 71 Cr App R 341.

Stolen

The question of whether or not goods are 'stolen' for the purposes of s22(1) is best approached in three stages. Section 24(4) provides:

> 'For purposes of the provisions of this Act relating to goods which have been stolen (including subsections (1) to (3) above) goods obtained in England or Wales or elsewhere either by blackmail or in the circumstances described in s15(1) of this Act shall be regarded as stolen; and "steal", "theft" and "thief" shall be construed accordingly.'

Note that the goods must have been obtained as a result of one of the three offences (theft, obtaining property by deception, or blackmail) having been committed. It is not enough that the defendant believes the goods to have been stolen: see *R* v *Porter* [1976] Crim LR 58. In such a case, however, the defendant might still be convicted of attempting to handle stolen goods on the basis that he believes them to have been stolen, even though they have not: see below.

If s24(4) is satisfied, it is necessary to ensure that the goods have not ceased to be stolen for the purposes of s22(1) by operation of s24(3) which provides:

> 'But no goods shall be regarded as having continued to be stolen goods after they have been restored to the person from whom they were stolen or to other lawful possession or custody, or after that person and any other person claiming through him have otherwise ceased as regards those goods to have any right to restitution in respect of the theft.'

Hence if goods are restored to the possession of the person entitled to possess them they cease to be stolen. Similarly if they are placed in police custody; but this in itself raises the difficult question of what constitutes police custody. In *Haughton* v *Smith* [1975] AC 476, a lorry loaded with tins of meat ceased to be stolen when police stopped the vehicle, and climbed aboard, hiding themselves in the trailer, intending to ambush other members of a criminal gang when they came to unload the contents of the lorry. On the other hand, in *Attorney-General's Reference (No 1 of 1974)* [1974] 1 QB 744 the Court of Appeal were unwilling to conclude that a police officer, who had spotted what he thought might be stolen goods inside a car and who as a consequence had removed the car's rotor arm thus immobilising the car, had taken lawful possession and custody of the car. He had kept it under observation so that he could question the driver when he returned, but the court ruled that the matter was one that should have been left to the jury on the facts. Essentially it was a question of what the police officer had intended at the time.

Where goods cease to be stolen because of the operation of s24(3), but the defendant fails to realise this and handles goods believing them to be stolen, he can be charged with attempting to handle stolen goods, contrary to s1(1) Criminal Attempts Act 1981. The House of Lords' decision in *Anderton* v *Ryan* [1985] 2 WLR 968, which had suggested that there could be no charge of attempted handling in the absence of proof that goods were actually stolen, has been overruled by a more recent decision of their Lordships in *R* v *Shivpuri* [1986] 2 WLR 988. The problem should now be dealt with by asking: 'Did the defendant take steps that he believed were more than merely preparatory to the commission of the offence of handling stolen goods?' Such a belief can exist regardless of whether or not the goods are stolen.

Further, s24(3) refers to goods ceasing to be stolen for the purposes of s22(1) where the owner ceases to have any right of restitution in respect of those goods. The law relating to restitution is a large and complex topic, an explanation of which would be neither suitable or practical in a work of this nature. A relatively simple illustration of the subsection's operation can, however, be given by the following example.

A obtains property by deception from P, for example having purchased goods by drawing a worthless cheque. A obtains voidable title to the goods. Now suppose that before P takes any effective steps to avoid this transaction, A sells the goods on to B, a bona fide purchaser for value without notice. It is submitted that in such a case P would have lost his right to restitution, and even if B later discovers the origin of the goods, B cannot be guilty of handling because the goods cease to be stolen by virtue of s24(3).

Section 24(2) is the third provision that may need satisfying in determining when goods are stolen. It deals with the situation where stolen property has changed hands and been exchanged for other forms of property. It states:

> 'For purposes of those provisions references to stolen goods shall include, in addition to the goods originally stolen and parts of them (whether in their original state or not) –
> a) any other goods which directly or indirectly represent or have at any time represented the stolen goods in the hands of the thief as being the proceeds of any disposal or realisation of the whole or part of the goods stolen or of goods so representing the stolen goods; and
> b) any other goods which directly or indirectly represent or have at any time represented the stolen goods in the hands of a handler of the stolen goods or any part of them as being the proceeds of any disposal or realisation of the whole or part of the stolen goods handled by him or of goods so representing them.'

Despite appearances, the aim and effect of s24(2) is to limit the scope of handling stolen goods. For goods to be stolen they must be, or have been, in the hands of a thief or handler and directly or indirectly represent the stolen goods in whole or part. The original stolen property will remain stolen throughout any scheme of handling until the provisions of s24(3) come into play. Section 24(2) is of more significance where a defendant knowingly deals with the proceeds of the original stolen goods. The extent to which s24(2) can actually restrict the scope of handling is illustrated by the following example.

A steals a car from P and sells it to B for £500. A then gives £100 of this money to C, who is innocent as to its origin. C spends the £100 on a watch, then discovers the truth and resolves to keep it. The complexities of innocent receipt and subsequent mens rea are considered below at 23.5, but for present purposes it should be noted that the watch purchased by C is not stolen property. It does indirectly represent the stolen car (the original stolen property) but it has not been in the hands of a thief or a handler, and is not in the hands of a thief or handler. It would be otherwise had C realised the source of the money before buying the watch.

A particular difficulty arises in the case of stolen money put into bank accounts. In *R* v *Pitchley* (above) the defendant's son stole £150, which the defendant placed in his Post Office savings account. The defendant later learnt of the source of the money and after a few days informed the police. The defendant was convicted of assisting in the retention of the money for the benefit of his son, a decision upheld by the Court of Appeal. The decision has been criticised on the basis that when the money was paid into the account it became a different type of property, namely a debt, or chose in action, and as such ceased to be stolen because it had not been and was not in the hands of a thief or handler in that form. This must provoke a further question which is, can a chose in action ever be in the hands of a thief or handler? It is submitted that where stolen money, or the proceeds of selling stolen goods are paid into bank accounts, the phrase 'in the hands of a thief or handler' should be interpreted as meaning under the control and direction of a thief or handler.

Suppose then that A steals £500 from P and puts the money in his bank account, and then writes B a cheque for £100, B being aware of A's theft. Can B be charged with receiving stolen property? The difficulty lies, of course, in determining whether the £100 represents part of the proceeds of the £500 originally stolen. Where A's account is at zero before the £500 is paid in, there is little difficulty, but where the previous balance was £200, there is no way of determining whether the £100 comes from A's legitimate money or the stolen money. In *Attorney-General's Reference (No 4 of 1979)* (1980) 71 Cr App R 341, the Court of Appeal suggested that in such a case, no charge of handling could be brought against B, until the balance of A's account fell below £500, and A had drawn a cheque in B's favour. Only then could it be assumed that the payments made to B represented the original stolen money. Further the mere receiving of a cheque by B would not be sufficient to amount to any more than an attempt to receive stolen goods. The full offence would not be committed until the cheque was presented for payment and the amount credited to his account, because only then would A's bank balance be affected.

23.3 Modes of handling

Section 22(1) creates several different modes of handling such as receiving, removing, retaining and so on. The Court of Appeal held in *R* v *Nicklin* [1977] 2 All ER 444 that a defendant could be charged on an indictment which simply alleged handling without particularising the mode. Where an indictment does particularise a mode of handling, however, such as receiving, the defendant cannot be convicted of a different form, such as assisting in the removal of goods.

Receiving

Receiving, and arranging to receive, are the only modes of handling that can be charged where the defendant does not act for the benefit of another or assist another to deal with the property. The most obvious instances are where the defendant takes stolen property into his possession or control for his own use. It is not necessary to show, however, that the receiving is for the benefit of the defendant, and *Haughton v Smith* (above) is evidence that it is sufficient for the defendant to have taken control of goods.

The two forms of handling

It is apparent from the decision of the House of Lords in *R v Bloxham* [1982] 1 All ER 582 that the modes of handling fall into two forms. On the one hand the defendant might receive, or arrange to receive. On the other hand the defendant might undertake the retention, removal, disposal, or realisation of stolen goods for another's benefit or assist in the retention, removal, disposal, or realisation of stolen goods by another person, or for the benefit of another.

Removal would simply involve transportation or movement of the stolen goods from one point to another. For example, D entrusts stolen goods to X, who does not know they are stolen. Later D informs X of the truth and requests X to take the goods to Y's house, which X does. X cannot be charged with receiving stolen property because he lacked mens rea at the time of receipt, but he clearly undertakes the removal of stolen goods for another's benefit with mens rea.

Realisation involves the defendant in the sale or exchanging of stolen property. Placing stolen cash in a bank account is arguably the realisation of stolen property on the basis that tangible property has been changed into intangible property, a debt. Disposal would encompass such activity as burying or destroying stolen property.

Retention, according to the Court of Appeal in *R v Pitchley* (above) should be given its ordinary dictionary meaning of 'keep possession ... not lose, continue to have', and the court proceeded to hold that the defendant had assisted in the retention of money stolen by his son, by permitting it to remain in his savings account. The decision raises the question of to what extent a defendant may be guilty of retention by omission. In *R v Brown* [1970] 1 QB 105, the Court of Appeal held that a defendant, who had told police searching for stolen property in his flat that he knew nothing of any stolen property and that they should 'get lost' might not necessarily be guilty of assisting in the retention of stolen goods. The failure of the defendant to reveal the presence of stolen goods was evidence of his guilt but not conclusive proof. Given that the defendant is not under a legal duty to inform the police of such matters, the decision is clearly correct. The situation might be rather different where the defendant deliberately misleads the police. In *R* v *Kanwar* [1982] Crim LR 532, the Court of Appeal held that the defendant who had lied to the police as to the origin of goods in her house that had in fact been stolen and stored there by her husband, was held to have assisted in their retention by him.

Strange as it may seem, although a defendant can be guilty of retention by misleading the police, he or she will not necessarily incur liability simply by using goods known to be stolen. In *R* v *Sanders* (1982) 75 Cr App R 84 the defendant had used a fan heater and battery charger at premises owned by his father, knowing that his father had stolen the items. The Court of Appeal allowed his appeal against conviction for handling the stolen goods by assisting in their retention, on the basis that mere use of the goods knowing them to be stolen was not enough; it had to be proved that the defendant had assisted in the retention in some way, for instance by making them more difficult to identify or holding them pending their ultimate disposal.

Arranging

Section 22(1) creates yet further modes of handling by making it an offence to arrange to receive, arrange to undertake the removal, realisation, disposal, retention of stolen goods for another's benefit, or arrange to assist in the removal, realisation, disposal or retention of stolen goods by another person. The effect is to create an inchoate form of handling akin to conspiracy, which is indeed what it will become if 'another party' to the arrangement has the requisite mens rea. Liability depends upon the goods being stolen when the arrangement is made, although as with other forms of inchoate liability, there is no need for the arrangement to be carried out. The need for the goods to have been stolen before any such arrangement can found a conviction was reiterated by the Court of Appeal in *R* v *Park* [1988] Crim LR 238.

'For the benefit of another'

From the above it will have been seen that the so-called second form of handling requires the defendant to act in the assistance of another person or undertake action for another's benefit. It is this latter provision which has caused some uncertainty. The principal authority on the point is the House of Lords' decision in *R* v *Bloxham* (above). The defendant bought a car at a bargain price. He later discovered that it was stolen, and sold it on cheaply to an unknown person. The defendant was charged with assisting or undertaking the realisation of stolen property by another person or for another's benefit. In holding that this activity fell outside the scope of handling as defined by s22, Lord Bridge observed:

> 'The critical words to be construed are "undertakes ... their ... disposal or realisation ... for the benefit of another person". Considering these words first in isolation, it seems to me that, if A sells his own goods to B, it is a somewhat strained use of language to describe this as a disposal or realisation of the goods for the benefit of B. True it is that B obtains a benefit from the transaction, but it is surely more natural to say that the disposal

or realisation is for A's benefit than for B's. It is the purchase, not the sale, that is for the benefit of B. It is only when A is selling as agent for a third party C that it would be entirely natural to describe the sale as a disposal or realisation for the benefit of another person ... the words cannot ... be construed in isolation. They must be construed in their context, bearing in mind ... that the second half of the subsection creates a single offence which can be committed in various ways ... the ... words contemplate four activities (retention, removal, disposal, realisation). The offence can be committed in relation to any one of these activities in one or other of two ways. First, the offender may himself undertake the activity *for the benefit of* another person. Secondly, the activity may be undertaken *by* another person and the offender may assist him. Of course, if the thief or an original receiver and his friend act together in, say, removing the stolen goods, the friend may be committing the offence in both ways. But this does not invalidate the analysis and if the analysis holds good, it must follow, I think, that the category of other persons contemplated by the subsection is subject to the same limitations in whichever way the offence is committed. Accordingly, a purchaser, as such, of stolen goods, cannot, in my opinion, be "another person" within the subsection, since his act of purchase could not sensibly be described as a disposal or realisation of the stolen goods *by* him. Equally, therefore, even if the sale to him could be described as a disposal or realisation for his benefit, the transaction is not, in my view, within the ambit of the subsection.'

On this basis Bloxham would, presumably, have been guilty had he instructed the purchaser to pay over the purchase money direct to some third party, as this would have been a realisation for another's benefit. Although Bloxham would have been protected from any liability for theft, in relation to the car, by s3(2) of the 1968 Act, it is conceivable that he might have been charged with obtaining the proceeds of the sale by deception, if the purchaser bought the car on the basis that it had not been the subject of a theft.

'Otherwise than in the course of stealing'

This phrase appears in parenthesis in s22(1) and is there in order to avoid, to some extent, an overlap in liability between thieves and handlers, bearing in mind the greater maximum penalty that might be imposed on the latter. The provision nevertheless creates two particular difficulties.

When does stealing end and handling commence? If A picks P's pocket and immediately hands the contents to B who is standing next to him, is A guilty of theft and B of handling, or is B an accomplice to A's theft? The answer rather depends on the approach taken to appropriation. In *R* v *Pitham and Hehl* (1977) 65 Cr App R 45, the view was taken that appropriation was an instantaneous act; thus if A offered to sell P's goods to B, both A and B knowing that they had no right to be dealing with P's goods in this way, A would be guilty of theft as soon as the offer to sell was made, and B would be guilty of arranging to receive as soon as he accepted. The theft by A would be complete on the making of the offer, thus B's acceptance would be otherwise than in the course of stealing. The contrary view of appropriation is illustrated in the Court of Appeal's decision in *R* v *Hale* (1978) 68 Cr App R 415, wherein it was held that appropriation was a 'continuing act' that began when the defendant assumed the rights of the owner; where it ended was a matter to be determined on the facts by the jury. It is generally agreed that unless this latter interpretation is adopted, the 'otherwise than in the course of dealing' provision becomes of little use.

The second difficulty is in determining to whom the phrase applies. Clearly the original thief, but what of those who knowingly deal with the stolen property subsequently? The problem arises from the fact that nearly all those who handle stolen property also commit theft of it, in the sense that they dishonestly assume the rights of the owner with intention to permanently deprive the owner of it. Were the provision to be applied strictly it would be virtually impossible to convict anyone of handling stolen goods because they would be acting *within* the course of stealing. The problem may be, however, more apparent than real. The decision of the Court of Appeal in *R* v *Sainthouse* [1980] Crim LR 506 suggests that the 'course of stealing' should be restricted to the initial theft by which the goods become 'stolen'. Thus subsequent handlers can also be charged as thieves and vice-versa, the limitation having no application to them. See also *R* v *Dolan* (1976) 62 Cr App R 36. The prosecution do not have a positive duty to prove that a (subsequent) handling is otherwise than in the course of stealing, see *R* v *Cash* [1985] Crim LR 311, and *Attorney-General for Hong Kong* v *Yip Kai Foon* [1988] 1 All ER 153.

23.4 Mens rea

Dishonesty

The defendant's dishonesty must coincide with and relate to his mode of handling. There are no particular provisions in s22 relating to dishonesty (unlike theft), hence the question is one for the jury to decide on the facts. The Court of Appeal decision in *R* v *Roberts* [1986] Crim LR 122 suggests that whilst the test in *R* v *Ghosh* (see 18.1) can be used, it should only be resorted to when there is a real case for so doing, ie the defendant must have raised the defence that he did not realise that anybody would regard what he was doing as dishonest. See further to the same effect in *R* v *Brennen* [1990] Crim LR 118.

'Knowledge or belief that the goods are stolen'

In addition to dishonesty, the prosecution must prove that the defendant knew or believed the goods to be stolen at the time of handling, and the moment of handling should be particularised in the direction to the jury: see *R* v *Brook* [1993] Crim LR 455. In *Atwal* v *Massey* (1971) 56 Cr App R 6, the Court of Appeal sought to make clear that the correct approach to 'belief' was to apply a subjective test. As Lord Widgery CJ observed:

'If when the justices said that the appellant ought to have known that the kettle was stolen they meant that any reasonable man would have realised that it was stolen, then that was not the right test. It is not sufficient to establish an offence under section 22 that the goods were received in circumstances which would have put a reasonable man on his enquiry. The question is a subjective one: was the appellant aware of the theft or did he believe the goods to be stolen or did he, suspecting the goods to be stolen, deliberately shut his eyes to the consequences?'

As James LJ pointed out, however, in *R v Griffiths* (1974) 60 Cr App R 14, great care should be taken by a trial judge, directing a jury on the basis of *Atwal v Massey*, to avoid confusion between the mental element of knowledge or belief and the approach by which the jury may arrive at a conclusion as to knowledge or belief. He commented:

'To direct the jury that the offence is committed if the defendant, suspecting that the goods were stolen, deliberately shut his eyes to the circumstances as an alternative to knowing or believing the goods were stolen is a misdirection. To direct the jury that, in common sense and in law, they may find that the defendant knew or believed the goods to be stolen, because he deliberately closed his eyes to the circumstances, is a perfectly proper direction.'

The question, therefore, is not whether a reasonable man in the circumstances would have believed the goods to be stolen, but whether the defendant actually did so. Where there was evidence that should have made the defendant suspicious, and it appeared that he deliberately turned a blind eye to this, the jury could infer from this that he believed the goods to be stolen, but it is not to be equated with such belief. It is certainly a misdirection to tell a jury that a defendant can be treated as having 'belief' where he thinks goods are probably stolen: see *R v Reader* (1978) 66 Cr App R 33; *R v Lincoln* [1980] Crim LR 575; *R v Stagg* [1978] Crim LR 227; *R v Grainge* [1974] 1 All ER 928; and *R v Toor* [1987] Crim LR 122.

R v Brook (above) indicates the dangers where the trial judge seeks to embellish the standard 'subjective' direction. In that case the trial judge had directed that jury that the fact that there was no reasonable conclusion other than that the contents of a bag in the appellant's possession comprised stolen goods was a factor that might assist them in deciding whether or not the appellant knew or believed the goods to be stolen. The Court of Appeal held that the trial judge had erred in introducing an unwarranted element of objectivity in relation to the mens rea to be proved. The fact that an objective observer would have concluded that the goods were undoubtedly stolen was irrelevant given that the test for mens rea was subjective. In the light of the above one might be tempted to ask whether or not the law should be amended to permit the jury to consider evidence as to whether or not it was reasonable for such a belief to be held. By way of analogy consider the approach in rape to the defendant's honest belief that a woman was consenting to sexual intercourse, where s1(2) of the Sexual Offences (Amendment) Act 1976 provides that:

'... if at a trial for a rape offence the jury has to consider whether a man believed that a woman was consenting to sexual intercourse, the presence or absence of reasonable grounds for such a belief is a matter to which the jury is to have regard, in conjunction with any other relevant matters, in considering whether he so believed.'

Recent possession

Where a defendant is found to have been in possession of stolen property and gives no explanation or at least no satisfactory explanation for its presence, the jury will be told of the short passage of time between the reporting of the theft and the finding of the defendant in possession of the stolen goods, and is entitled to infer from this evidence that the defendant acquired the goods knowing or believing them to be stolen.

23.5 Innocent receipt and subsequent mens rea

Where a defendant receives stolen property innocently but later discovers it to have been stolen, he cannot be charged with receiving stolen property because he was innocent at the time of receipt; non-coincidence of mens rea and actus reus. Whether he will incur liability subsequent to his discovering the truth depends upon whether he gave value for the property, and what he does with it.

Where the defendant receives stolen property innocently as a gift and then discovers the truth, he is likely to incur liability of some sort if he does anything other than restore it to lawful custody. If he decides to keep the property for himself, he cannot be guilty of handling, for although the goods are stolen he does not assist in or undertake the retention of the goods by another, or for another's benefit. He would, however, be guilty of theft by virtue of s3(1), in that he has come by the property innocently and later assumed the rights of the owner by keeping it. If he decides to sell or dispose of the property he will not be guilty of handling, see *R* v *Bloxham* (above) because this will not be 'by another' or 'for another's' benefit. He will be guilty of theft as above in that the sale or disposal will be an appropriation of another's property.

Where the defendant gives value for the property and then discovers the truth, he will be protected from liability for theft regardless of how he deals with the property, on the basis of s3(2) which provides that:

'Where property or a right or interest in property is or purports to be transferred for value to a person acting in good faith no later assumption by him of rights which he believed himself to be acquiring shall, by reason of any defect in the transferor's title, amount to theft of the property.'

Given *R* v *Bloxham* (above) the defendant should also escape liability for handling in that his removal, retention, disposal, or realisation of the property will not be 'by or for the benefit of another': see further *R* v *Wheeler* (1991) 92 Cr App R 279.

24

Forgery and Counterfeiting Act 1981

24.1 Introduction

24.2 The offence of forgery

24.3 The offences of copying and using false instruments

24.4 The offences of counterfeiting notes and coins

24.5 Other offences relating to counterfeit notes and coins

24.1 Introduction

The Forgery and Counterfeiting Act 1981 ('the 1981 Act') resulted largely from the Law Commission's Working Paper No 26 (1970) and the Commission's Report (No 55) (1973). Section 13 of the 1981 Act states that the offence of forgery at common law is abolished, hence pre-1981 authorities cease to be binding, but may still be regarded as persuasive in the interpretation of the new law. The Forgery Act 1913, and the Coinage Offences Act 1936 are repealed. The long title of the 1981 Act provides that it has been enacted to:

> '... make fresh provision for England and Wales and Northern Ireland with respect to forgery and kindred offences; to make fresh provision for Great Britain and Northern Ireland with respect to the counterfeiting of notes and coins and kindred offences; to amend the penalties for offences under s63 of the Post Office Act 1953; and for connected purposes.'

Part I of the Act deals with 'forgery and kindred offences', Part II with 'counterfeiting and kindred offences'.

It should be borne in mind that the use of forged and counterfeited articles will frequently involve a defendant in liability for theft or obtaining property by deception. The 1981 Act introduces liability at an earlier stage, for example for the making or possession of such articles, behaviour which would be unlikely to amount to even an attempt to steal or obtain by deception.

333

24.2 The offence of forgery

Section 1 of the 1981 Act provides:

> 'A person is guilty of forgery if he makes a false instrument, with the intention that he or another shall use it to induce somebody to accept it as genuine, and by reason of so accepting it to do or not to do some act to his own or any other persons's prejudice.'

The maximum penalty that can be imposed following conviction on indictment is ten years imprisonment (s6(2)).

Actus reus

Section 1 requires the 'making' of a false instrument. Section 9(2) provides further detail of what this entails where it states:

> 'A person is to be treated for the purposes of this Part of this Act as making a false instrument if he alters an instrument so as to make it false in any respect (whether or not it is false in some other respect apart from that alteration).'

The change here from the previous law under the Forgery Act 1913 is that the alteration does not have to relate to a material particular – an alteration making the instrument false in any respect will suffice.

The meaning of 'instrument' for the purposes of Part I of the 1981 Act is defined by s8(1) which provides:

> 'Subject to subsection (2) below, in this Part of this Act "instrument" means –
> a) any document, whether of a formal or informal character;
> b) any stamp issued or sold by the Post Office;
> c) any Inland Revenue stamp; and
> d) any disc, tape, sound track or other device on or in which information is recorded or stored by mechanical, electronic or other means.'

Subsection (2) excludes currency notes from the meaning of 'instrument'. The definition of 'instrument' does not, therefore, extend to include counterfeit goods such as imitation Cartier watches, or a fake Stradivarius, but would cover a document which purported to be a certificate stating that such items were genuine. With regard to the facts of *R* v *Donelly* (below) jewellery would not be an 'instrument', but a valuation certificate would be.

In *R* v *Gold and Shifreen* [1988] 2 All ER 186 the House of Lords held that the Act did not extend to cover the practice of 'hacking' into computer programs because, inter alia, no false instrument was created in order to do so.

The most complex requirement of actus reus is that the instrument should be false. The meaning of false is given an exhaustive definition by s9(1)(a)–(h) which provides:

> 'An instrument is false for the purposes of this Part of this Act –
> a) if it purports to have been made in the form in which it is made by a person who did not in fact make it in that form; or
> b) if it purports to have been made in the form in which it is made on the authority of a

person who did not in fact authorise its making in that form; or

c) if it purports to have been made in the terms in which it is made by a person who did not in fact make it in those terms; or

d) if it purports to have been made in the terms in which it is made on the authority of a person who did not in fact authorise its making in those terms; or

e) if it purports to have been altered in any respect by a person who did not in fact alter it in that respect; or

f) if it purports to have been altered in any respect on the authority of a person who did not in fact authorise the alteration in that respect; or

g) if it purports to have been made or altered on a date on which, or at a place at which, or otherwise in circumstances in which, it was not in fact made or altered; or

h) if it purports to have been made or altered by an existing person but he did not in fact exist.'

The Law Commission noted in its report (No 55) (para 43) that:

'The essential feature of a false instrument in relation to forgery is that it is an instrument which "tells a lie about itself" in the sense that it purports to be made by a person who did not make it (or altered by a person who did not alter it) or otherwise purports to be made or altered in circumstances in which it was not made or altered. Falsity needs to be defined in these terms to cover not only, for example, the obvious case of forging a testator's signature to a will, but also the case where the date of a genuine will is altered to make it appear that the will was executed later than it in fact was, and therefore after what in truth was the testator's last will.'

As Blackburn J stated in *R* v *Windsor* (1865) 10 Cox CC 118 at 123:

'Forgery is the false making of an instrument purporting to be that which it is not, it is not the making of an instrument which purports to be what it really is, but which contains false statements. Telling a lie does not become a forgery because it is reduced into writing.'

The following example illustrates the distinction. If D is applying for a means-tested welfare benefit and fills in an application form falsely stating that he has no savings, he may be attempting to obtain property by deception, but the application form does not thereby become a 'false instrument'. Were D to purchase a rent book, however, and register within it payments to his landlord for rent, which had never been paid, accompanied by an imitation of his landlord's signature, then the rent book would be 'telling a lie about itself', and would constitute a 'false instrument' within Part I of the Act.

Subsection (a) would clearly cover the case where D applies for a job and produces a reference which purports to have been written by his previous employer, but which has in fact been written by D, or some other person, without the employer's authority; where the reference purports to have been written on the authority of the previous employer it would fall under subsection (b). Subsections (c) and (d) would cover a reference that had been made by D's previous employer, but which had been altered in some respect by D, for example by substituting a much higher figure as his leaving salary.

Subsections (e) and (f) would relate to unauthorised alterations; for example where D, having enjoyed a meal in a restaurant, receives a bill from the waiter which he alters to a lower amount, the bill would have been 'altered ... by a person who did not in fact alter it'. It would be different had the waiter been deliberately failing to enter items at the correct price on the bill so that an accomplice D could receive a cheap meal. Here the bill would simply have been inaccurate, not false (subject to s9(1)(g) (below)) because it was made by the person authorised to do so. Similarly if the waiter were to alter a correctly made up bill in D's favour.

The ambit of subs (g) was considered by the Court of Appeal in *R v Donelly* (1984) 79 Cr App R 76. The appellant, the manager of a jewellery store, had drawn up a valuation certificate in relation to jewellery which did not exist, the purpose being to enable another man, with whom he was collaborating, to defraud an insurance company. The appellant contended that the document was not 'false' within the meaning of the Act. The court held that the certificate came within subs (g) because it purported 'to have been made ... otherwise in circumstances in which it was not in fact made.' On the facts it purported to have been made following the examination of certain jewellery which did not in fact exist; therefore it told a lie about itself, the circumstances in which it had been made. Had the jewellery in fact existed and the appellant simply overvalued it for insurance purposes, the document would not have been false, simply inaccurate.

Despite being subject to considerable academic criticism the decision *Donelly* was applied in *R v Jeraj* [1994] Crim LR 595. The appellant, the manager of a branch of an Indian bank, met two men at a London hotel and, following discussions, signed a document on bank notepaper. The prosecution alleged that the letter amounted to verification of his bank's endorsement of a letter of credit drawn by the Banco Unidyn de Bolivia, the prosecution case being that the letter of credit and the Banco Unidyn de Bolivia never existed and that the document signed by the appellant was part of a banking fraud that would be perpetrated in the United States. The appellant contended that he had been duped by the two men and had signed the document merely as confirmation that he had seen a letter of credit that had been drawn up in a form acceptable to his bank. Upholding his conviction, the court ruled that the trial judge had rightly ruled that the document could amount to a forgery within s9(1)(g) of the Forgery and Counterfeiting Act 1981 on the basis that it purported to have been made in circumstances in which it was not in fact made. See chapter 26, section 26.10, for further details. See further *R v Warnford and Gibbs* [1994] Crim LR 753.

Finally, subs (h) brings within it the definition of 'false' instruments which purport to have been made or altered by an existing person who does not in fact exist. The provision causes great difficulty where a person acts under an alias. If D fills out an application form using the alias 'Mickey Mouse', is the form a forgery? Mickey Mouse may be a fictitious character, but D 'alias Mickey Mouse' is a real person. The problem arose under the old law in *R v Hassard and Devereux* [1970] 2 All ER 647, where the Court of Appeal held that the drawing of a cheque on an account opened in a false name (using a stolen cheque) was a forgery in that it 'purported to be made by a fictitious person'. The decision has been criticised for the reasons given above, and now seems untenable in the light of the House of

Lords' decision in *R* v *Moore* [1987] 3 All ER 825. Moore had come into possession of a cheque for £5,303.23, made payable to an 'M. R. Jessel'. He opened a building society account using the name 'M. R. Jessel', and ten days later withdrew £5,000, using a withdrawal form made out in the name of the payee. Moore was convicted of making a false instrument, namely the withdrawal form, and the point of law certified for the House of Lords was whether or not the instrument became false within s9 of the 1981 Act because Moore had used someone else's name to open the account, and complete the withdrawal form. The House of Lords held that the conviction would have to be quashed. The withdrawal form did not tell a lie about itself. It purported to have been made by the person who had opened the account, ie the defendant using the name 'M. R. Jessel', and in that respect it was entirely accurate. The withdrawal form did not purport to have been made by the original payee in whose name the cheque had been drawn to open the account.

Mens rea

Beyond a basic intention to make a false instrument, s1 requires a specific intent on the part of the defendant that the false instrument should be used to induce another to accept it as genuine and thereby act, or fail to act, to their own or another's prejudice.

The requirement that some other person be induced to accept the false instrument as genuine is given an extended meaning by s10(3) which provides:

'In this Part of this Act references to inducing somebody to accept a false instrument as genuine, or a copy of a false instrument as a copy of a genuine one, include references to inducing a machine to respond to the instrument or copy as if it were a genuine instrument or, as the case may be, a copy of a genuine one.'

Where the subsection applies, the act or omission intended to be induced by the machine responding to the instrument or copy shall be treated as an act or omission to a person's prejudice (s10(4)).

Section 10 provides an exhaustive definition of what, for the purposes of Part I of the Act, constitutes a person acting (or failing to act) to their prejudice, where it provides in subs(1) that:

'Subject to subsections (2) and (4) below, for the purposes of this Part of this Act an act or omission intended to be induced is to a person's prejudice if, and only if, it is one which, if it occurs –
a) will result –
i) in his temporary or permanent loss of property; or
ii) in his being deprived of an opportunity to earn remuneration or greater remuneration; or
iii) in his being deprived of an opportunity to gain a financial advantage otherwise than by way of remuneration; or
b) will result in somebody being given an opportunity –
i) to earn remuneration or greater remuneration from him; or
ii) to gain a financial advantage from him otherwise than by way of remuneration; or
c) will be the result of his having accepted a false instrument as genuine, or a copy of a false instrument as a copy of a genuine one, in connection with his performance of any duty.'

Loss for the purposes of this section includes not getting what one might get as well as parting with what one has (s10(5)). In *R v Utting* [1987] 1 WLR 1375, the Court of Appeal had an opportunity to consider the scope of s1 in relation to mens rea. The defendant had produced a false document with the intention that the police should accept it as genuine, and take no further steps to prosecute him for theft. He was convicted of forgery contrary to s1 and appealed on the basis that the act or omission that he intended the document to induce, namely his non-prosecution, was not within the meaning of 'an act or omission ... to a person's prejudice' in s10, and further that the offence was only made out where the victim of the forgery would have acted to his prejudice, or some person other than the perpetrator would have done so. The court held that these submissions were well founded. The forger could not be 'any other person' within s1, otherwise it would be an offence for the forger to make a false instrument with the intention of inducing someone to accept it as genuine and thereby do an act to the prejudice or harm of the forger himself. This cannot have been the intention of Parliament. The court thought it remarkable that the non-prosecution should be regarded as being to the defendant's prejudice. The court went on to point out that the situation might have been different had the charge against the defendant proceeded on the basis that the act or omission would have been to the prejudice of the police within s10(1)(c), but that was not the basis of the charge here. See further *R v Garcia* (1987) 87 Cr App R 175.

As a matter of law, a person does not act to his own or another's prejudice simply by performing an enforceable duty, or refraining from an action which he is not entitled to take anyway. Section 10(2) provides:

'An act which a person has an enforceable duty to do and an omission to do an act which a person is not entitled to do shall be disregarded for the purposes of this Part of this Act.'

Hence, if D is owned money by P and D forges a letter which puts pressure on P to repay, D does not induce P to act to his prejudice, as his duty to repay the money is enforceable at law. See *R v Parkes* (1910) 74 JP 210. The matter has been considered on two occasions by the Court of Appeal since 1981.

First, in *R v Campbell (Mary)* (1985) 80 Cr App R 47, the appellant endorsed a cheque for her friend by forging the payee's signature and paying it into her own account. She then took out an equivalent amount in cash from her account and gave it to her friend. The appellant was convicted under s1 of the 1981 Act. The Court of Appeal, dismissing the appeal, held that the appellants's argument in reliance on s10(2), to the effect that the bank was under a duty to pay out on the cheque, and that she had not, therefore, intended that the bank should act to its prejudice, was to be rejected. The bank only had a duty to pay out on a valid instrument, thus s10(2) was of no relevance. The actions of the appellant were to the bank's prejudice by reference to s10(1)(c), because the bank accepted the cheque in connection with the performance of a duty. It should be further noted that the defendant would have had mens rea even if she had believed her friend had a right to the amount of money represented by the cheque, because she must have known that in any event the bank would not be willing to pay out on a fraudulently endorsed cheque.

Secondly, in *R v Tobierre* [1986] Crim LR 243, the appellant was convicted under s3 of the 1981 Act (see below), having signed a child allowance book in his wife's name, failing to report the fact that his wife and children were abroad, living in St Lucia. The Court of Appeal quashed the conviction due to the trial judge's failure to give an adequate direction on intention. It was held that s3 and s10 of the Act, when read together, required proof of two states of mind; an intention to induce another to accept an instrument as genuine, and an intention that the other person should act or omit to act to his own or some other person's prejudice. The jury should have been directed to consider whether the appellant believed that he had authority to sign on his wife's behalf, and if he did believe this, whether he believed as a consequence that the Secretary of State was under a duty to pay out within s10(2). Had the defendant so believed he would not have had the necessary intention to cause another to act to his own or some other person's prejudice. Such an interpretation, it is submitted, goes some way towards alleviating possible injustices under the Act, given the absence of any need to establish dishonesty.

24.3 The offences of copying and using false instruments

Section 2 creates the offence of copying a false instrument, by providing:

'It is an offence for a person to make a copy of an instrument which is and which he knows or believes to be, a false instrument, with the intention that he or another shall use it to induce somebody to accept it as a copy of a genuine instrument, and by reason of so accepting it to do or not to do some act to his own or any other person's prejudice.'

The maximum penalty following conviction on indictment is ten years' imprisonment.

The section puts it beyond doubt that it is now an offence to photocopy a false instrument with the requisite mens rea.

Section 3 makes it an offence to use a false instrument. It provides:

'It is an offence for a person to use an instrument which is, and which he knows or believes to be, false, with the intention of inducing somebody to accept it as genuine, and by reason of so accepting it to do or not to do some act to his own or any other person's prejudice.'

Note that this offence was the subject of the charge in *R v Tobierre* (above). Penalty as for s2.

Section 4 creates the offence of using a copy of a false instrument by providing:

'It is an offence for a person to use a copy of an instrument which is, and which he knows or believes to be, a false instrument, with the intention of inducing somebody to accept it as a copy of a genuine instrument, and by reason of so accepting it to do or not to do some act to his own or any other person's prejudice.'

24.4 The offences of counterfeiting notes and coins

The offences of making counterfeit notes and coins are created by s14, which provides:

> '14(1) It is an offence for a person to make a counterfeit of a currency note or of a protected coin, intending that he or another shall pass or tender it as genuine.
> (2) It is an offence for a person to make a counterfeit of a currency note or of a protected coin without lawful authority or excuse.'

Section 14(1) is the more serious offence by virtue of the ulterior intent; it carries with it a maximum sentence of ten years imprisonment following conviction on indictment. Section 14(2) carries a maximum of two years imprisonment following conviction on indictment.

Actus reus

The meaning of 'currency note' and 'protected coin' where those phrases are used in Part II of the Act, is provided by s27 which states:

> '27(1) In this Part of this Act –
> "currency note" means –
> a) any note which –
> i) has been lawfully issued in England and Wales, Scotland, Northern Ireland, any of the Channel Islands, the Isle of Man or the Republic of Ireland; and
> ii) is or has been customarily used as money in the country where it was issued; and
> iii) is payable on demand; or
> b) any note which –
> i) has been lawfully issued in some country other than those mentioned in paragraph (a)(i) above; and
> ii) is customarily used as money in that country; and "protected coin" means any coin which –
> a) is customarily used as money in any country; or
> b) is specified in an order made by the Treasury for the purpose of this Part of this Act.'

Section 28 provides the definition of 'counterfeit' for the purpose of Part II of the Act. It states:

> '28(1) For the purposes of this Part of this Act a thing is a counterfeit of a currency note or of a protected coin –
> a) if it is not a currency note or a protected coin but resembles a currency note or protected coin (whether on one side only or on both) to such an extent that it is reasonably capable of passing for a currency note or protected coin of that description; or
> b) if it is a currency note or protected coin which has been so altered that it is reasonably capable of passing for a currency note or protected coin of some other description.
> (2) For the purposes of this Part of this Act –
> a) a thing consisting of one side only of a currency note, with or without the addition of other material, is a counterfeit of such a note;
> b) a thing consisting –
> i) of parts of two or more currency notes; or
> ii) of parts of a currency note, or of parts of two or more currency notes, with the addition of other material,
> is capable of being a counterfeit of a currency note.

(3) References in this Part of this Act to passing or tendering a counterfeit of a currency note or a protected coin are not to be construed as confined to passing or tendering it as legal tender.'

Mens rea

Section 14(2) is arguably an offence of basic intent requiring only that the defendant intended to produce the prohibited articles. Section 14(1) requires a further, or ulterior, intent to pass such notes or coins as genuine.

24.5 Other offences relating to counterfeit notes and coins

Section 15 creates various ways by which criminal liability can arise from passing counterfeit notes and coins (note s28(3) above). It provides:

'15(1) It is an offence for a person –
a) to pass or tender as genuine any thing which is, and which he knows or believes to be, a counterfeit of a currency note or of a protected coin; or
b) to deliver to another any thing which is, and which he knows or believes to be, such a counterfeit, intending that the person to whom it is delivered or another shall pass or tender it as genuine.
(2) It is an offence for a person to deliver to another, without lawful authority or excuse, any thing which is, and which he knows or believes to be, a counterfeit of a currency note or of a protected coin.'

The maximum penalties following conviction on indictment are ten years imprisonment for s15(1), and two years for s15(2).

Section 16 creates two offences concerned with having custody of, or control over, counterfeit notes and coins. It provides:

'16(1) It is an offence for a person to have in his custody or under his control any thing which is, and which he knows or believes to be, a counterfeit of a currency note or of a protected coin, intending either to pass or tender it as genuine or to deliver it to another with the intention that he or another shall pass or tender it as genuine.
(2) It is an offence for a person to have in his custody or under his control, without lawful authority or excuse, any thing which is, and which he knows or believes to be, a counterfeit of a currency note or of a protected coin.
(3) It is immaterial for the purposes of subsections (1) and (2) above that a coin or note is not in a fit state to be passed or tendered or that the making or counterfeiting of a coin or note has not been finished or perfected.'

Penalties for ss16(1) and 16(2) are as for ss15(1) and 15(2) respectively.

Section 17 creates three offences relating to the making or possession of counterfeiting equipment. It provides:

'17(1) It is an offence to make, or to have in his custody or under his control, any thing which he intends to use, or permit any other person to use, for the purpose of making a counterfeit of a currency note or of a protected coin with the intention that it be passed or tendered as genuine.

(2) It is an offence for a person without lawful authority or excuse –

a) to make; or

b) to have in his custody or under his control,

any thing which, to his knowledge, is or has been specially designed or adapted for the making of a counterfeit of a currency note.

(3) Subject to ss(4) below, it is an offence for a person to make, or to have in his custody or under his control, any implement which, to his knowledge, is capable of imparting to any thing a resemblance –

a) to the whole or part of either side of a protected coin; or

b) to the whole or part of the reverse of the image on either side of a protected coin.

(4) It shall be a defence for a person charged with an offence under subsection (3) above to show –

a) that he made the implement or, as the case may be, had it in his custody or under his control, with the written consent of the Treasury; or

b) that he had lawful authority otherwise than by virtue of paragraph (a) above, or a lawful excuse, for making it or having it in his custody or under his control.'

Section 17(1) is punishable as s15(1), and ss17(2) and 17(3) are punishable as s15(2); see further *R* v *Maltman* (1994) The Times 28 June.

Section 18 creates the offence of reproducing British currency notes. It states:

'18(1) It is an offence for any person, unless the relevant authority has previously consented in writing, to reproduce on any substance whatsoever, and whether or not on the correct scale, any British currency note or any part of a British currency note.

(2) In this section:

"British currency note" means any note which –

a) has been lawfully issued in England and Wales, Scotland or Northern Ireland; and

b) is or has been customarily used as money in the country where it was issued; and

c) is payable on demand; and

"the relevant authority", in relation to a British currency note of any particular description, means the authority empowered by law to issue notes of that description.'

The offence does not carry with it the possibility of imprisonment.

Section 19 creates two offences relating to the making and distribution of imitation British coins. It states:

'19(1) It is an offence for a person –

a) to make an imitation British coin in connection with a scheme intended to promote the sale of any product or the making of contracts for the supply of any service; or

b) to sell or distribute imitation British coins in connection with any such scheme, or to have imitation British coins in his custody or under his control with a view to such sale or distribution,

unless the Treasury have previously consented in writing to the sale or distribution of such imitation British coins in connection with that scheme.

(2) In this section –

"British coin" means any coin which is legal tender in any part of the United Kingdom; and

"imitation British coin" means any thing which resembles a British coin in shape, size and the substance of which it is made.'

Punishment as for s18.

Sections 20 and 21 create offences relating to the unlawful importation and exportation of counterfeit notes and coins, by providing:

'20 The importation, landing or unloading of a counterfeit of a currency note or of a protected coin without the consent of the Treasury is hereby prohibited.

21(1) The exportation of a counterfeit of a currency note or of a protected coin without the consent of the Treasury is hereby prohibited.

(2) A counterfeit of a currency note or of a protected coin which is removed to the Isle of Man from the United Kingdom shall be deemed to be exported from the United Kingdom –

a) for the purposes of this section; and

b) for the purposes of the customs and excise Acts, in their application to the prohibition imposed by this section.

(3) In s9(1) of the Isle of Man Act 1979 (which relates to the removal of goods from the United Kingdom to the Isle of Man) after the word "below" there shall be inserted the words "and s21(2) of the Forgery and Counterfeiting Act 1981".'

25

Strict, Vicarious, and Corporate Liability. Bigamy. Perjury

25.1 Strict liability

25.2 Vicarious liability

25.3 Corporate liability

25.4 Bigamy

25.5 Perjury

25.1 Strict liability

Strict liability is the term used to describe the imposition of criminal liability without proof of fault on the part of the defendant. As such it represents an exception to one of the basic principles of criminal liability, that actus reus and mens rea must be proved. It was suggested in Chapter 2 that it is the presence of the defendant's mens rea or 'fault' that can be said to justify the punishments imposed under the criminal law. If this is correct, then it would appear that to punish a defendant for the commission of a strict liability offence is, per se, unjust. Some reported cases do indeed give this impression, see *R* v *Larsonneur* (1933) 24 Cr App R 74 considered at 2.4 above, but as will be seen from what follows, the courts rarely interpret an offence as being one of truly absolute liability (ie requiring no mens rea whatsoever), and where liability without fault is imposed, it tends to be for quasi-criminal, or 'regulatory' offences, the punishment for which rarely involves loss of liberty.

The rationale of strict liability

The purpose of imposing strict liability is to place the onus upon those who engage in a particular activity to ensure that they do not transgress the prohibitions laid down by the law. In simple terms, the law is suggesting that those who are in any doubt as to whether their actions will fall foul of the law should avoid such activities. It was observed by Lord Hailsham in *Smedleys Ltd* v *Breed* [1974] AC 839, that if the imposition of strict liability caused injustice to the defendant, one way for

344

him to avoid it was to desist from the activity that involved him in the commission of offences, and that this might be the view taken by the courts where the activity was viewed as unnecessary or inefficient. Hence the person selling food to the public must accept that the onus is upon him to ensure that it is fit for consumption. If this increases the cost of his product, then that should be passed on to all his consumers. Should he not be able to comply with the law and operate as a commercially viable outfit, then he should cease trading. The man attracted to a young girl is taking the risk that, although she consents to sexual intercourse with him, she may be below the age of consent. He can avoid this risk, ultimately, by remaining celibate. Similarly, the individual asked to carry another's bag through customs without having the opportunity to ascertain its contents can avoid liability by refusing to act as a courier. One of the factors behind the court's decision in *Kirkland* v *Robinson* (considered below), was that there was no social utility in the defendant's possession of wild birds.

Statutory interpretation

Given that strict liability offences are almost invariably created by statute, the manner in which they will operate rests to a large extent on how the courts decide to interpret them.

One of the basic rules of statutory interpretation is the presumption in favour of mens rea. Where a statutory provision creates a criminal offence but no reference is made to the mens rea that must be established, the courts will nevertheless assume that Parliament intended the offence to involve the proof of some degree of mens rea, unless there is sufficient evidence to the contrary. Some of the factors considered by a court in deciding whether an offence is one of strict liability are considered below, but before turning to them it should be understood that a court's finding that an offence does require proof of some mens rea does not necessarily mean that mens rea will have to be proved in relation to every element of the actus reus.

A comparison of the decisions in *R* v *Prince* (1875) LR 2 CCR 154, and *R* v *Hibbert* (1869) LR 1 CCR 184, is illustrative of this point. The defendants in both cases were charged with offences under s55 of the Offences Against the Person Act 1861 (now repealed), namely the unlawful removal of a girl below the age of 16 from the custody of her father against his will. Hibbert had abducted a girl below the age of 16, but had been ignorant of the fact that she was living with her parents. Prince had similarly abducted a girl below the age of 16 who was living with her parents, but he had claimed that he honestly believed her to be older than 16. Hibbert was acquitted, but Prince convicted. An explanation for the contrasting results in these cases is that whereas the courts 'read in' a requirement of mens rea as regards certain elements of the actus reus, ie the defendant had to be aware that he was abducting a girl, and that she was in the custody of her parents, no mens rea was required as regards the girl's age. In other words, liability was absolute as regards this element, and Prince's defence of honest and reasonable mistake was of no avail.

The main purpose of the provision under which he was charged was to protect girls under the age of 16, not necessarily those roaming the streets.

The statute must be read as a whole
In determining whether the presumption in favour of mens rea is to be displaced, the courts are required to have reference to the whole statute in which the offence appears.

In *Cundy* v *Le Cocq* (1884) 13 QBD 207, the defendant was convicted of unlawfully selling alcohol to an intoxicated person, contrary to s13 of the Licensing Act 1872. On appeal, the defendant contended that he had been unaware of the customer's drunkenness and thus should have been acquitted. The Divisional Court interpreted s13 as creating an offence of strict liability since it was itself silent as to mens rea, whereas other offences under the same Act expressly required proof of knowledge on the part of the defendant. The conclusion was that where Parliament had intended mens rea to be proved under the Act it had stated such.

A similar approach may be taken by the courts when dealing with an offence which is silent as to mens rea, but in relation to which Parliament has enacted a specific statutory defence. In *Kirkland* v *Robinson* [1987] Crim LR 643, the defendant's conviction for unlawfully possessing four wild goshawks was upheld, despite his honest belief that they had been bred in captivity. Not only did the statute in question, the Wildlife and Countryside Act 1981, create other offences which expressly required proof of knowledge, but it provided a statutory defence to the offence with which the defendant had been charged, under s1(3). The Divisional Court concluded, therefore, that Parliament had intended there to be an absolute prohibition on the possession of such birds, subject only to the defendant bringing himself within the terms of the statutory defence.

Even the statutory defence may be construed in very narrow terms where the courts sense this is warranted by the context. Hence in *Smedleys Ltd* v *Breed* (above) the House of Lords upheld the defendant's conviction under s2(1) of the Food and Drugs Act 1955 ('selling food not of the substance demanded by the purchaser'), which had resulted from complaints that four tins of peas produced by the defendants had contained caterpillars. The 1955 Act had contained a statutory defence in s3(3), where it could be shown that the presence of the extraneous matter was an *unavoidable* consequence of the manufacturing process, but it was held, interpreting the provision literally, that the defence was of no avail to the defendants, as the presence of the caterpillars could have been detected by means of a visual check of every tin. Neither were their Lordships moved by the submission that there had been only four complaints in respect of approximately 3,500,000 tins. The paramount purpose of the legislation was seen as being the protection of the public, which would be respected even where it led to the imposition of impossibly high standards upon the defendants: see further *Alphacell Ltd* v *Woodward* [1972] AC 824 (imposition of strict liability for river pollution despite the taking of all reasonable precautions).

There is, arguably, a greater tendency on the part of the courts to regard a statute as imposing strict or absolute liability where the offence created is viewed as being 'regulatory' or 'quasi-criminal' in nature. As Lord Evershed observed in *Lim Chin Aik* v *R* [1963] AC 160:

> 'Where the subject-matter of the statute is the regulation for the public welfare of a particular activity – statutes regulating the sale of food and drink are to be found among the earliest examples – it can be and frequently has been inferred that the legislature intended that such activities should be carried out under conditions of strict liability. The presumption is that the statute or statutory instrument can be effectively enforced only if those in charge of the relevant activities are made responsible for seeing that they are complied with. When such a presumption is to be inferred, it displaces the ordinary presumptions of mens rea. Thus sellers of meat may be made responsible for seeing that the meat is fit for human consumption and it is no answer for them to say that they were not aware that it was polluted ... the distribution of bad meat (and its far-reaching consequences) would not be effectively prevented.'

Other areas where the courts have adopted this approach are offences created under building regulations: *Gammon Ltd* v *Attorney-General for Hong Kong* (1984) 80 Cr App R 194; supplying controlled medicines without a valid prescription: *Pharmaceutical Society of Great Britain* v *Storkwain* [1986] 1 WLR 903; carrying out unauthorised work on a listed building: *R* v *Wells Street Metropolitan Stipendiary Magistrate, ex parte Westminster City Council* (1986) The Times 22 May; and breach of an enforcement notice: *R* v *Collet* [1994] 1 WLR 475.

There must be some purpose in imposing strict liability

The courts will be reluctant to construe a statute as imposing strict liability upon a defendant, where there is evidence to suggest that despite his having taken all reasonable steps, he cannot avoid the commission of an offence.

In *Sherras* v *De Rutzen* [1895] 1 QB 918, the defendant was convicted of selling alcohol to a police officer whilst on duty, contrary to s16(2) of the Licensing Act 1872. The police officer had not been wearing the arm band that would have indicated that he was on duty. The Divisional Court held that the conviction should be quashed, despite the absence from s16(2) of any words importing proof of mens rea as an element of the offence. Wright J expressed the view that the presumption in favour of mens rea would only be displaced by the wording of the statute itself, or its subject matter. In this case the latter factor was significant, in that no amount of reasonable care by the defendant would have prevented the offence from being committed.

This approach was approved by the Privy Council in *Lim Chin Aik* v *R* [1963] AC 160, where the defendant had been convicted of contravening an order prohibiting, in absolute terms, his entry into Singapore, despite his ignorance of the order's existence. In allowing the defendant's appeal, Lord Evershed expressed the view that the imposition of strict liability could only really be justified where it would actually succeed in placing the onus to comply with the law on the defendant. As he explained:

'... it is not enough ... merely to label the statute as one dealing with a grave social evil and from that to infer that strict liability was intended. It is pertinent also to inquire whether putting the defendant under strict liability will assist in the enforcement of the regulations. That means that there must be something he can do, directly or indirectly, by supervision or inspection, by improvement of his business methods or by exhorting those whom he may be expected to influence or control, which will promote the observance of the regulations. Unless this is so, there is no reason in penalising him, and it cannot be inferred that the legislature imposed strict liability merely in order to find a luckless victim ... [w]here it can be shown that the imposition of strict liability would result in the prosecution and conviction of a class of persons whose conduct could not in any way affect the observance of the law, their Lordships consider that, even where the statute is dealing with a grave social evil, strict liability is not likely to be intended ... [i]t seems to their Lordships that, where a man is said to have contravened an order or an order of prohibition, the common sense of the language presumes that he was aware of the order before he can be said to have contravened it.'

Similar considerations motivated the House of Lords in *Sweet* v *Parsley* [1970] AC 132, to quash the conviction of a defendant who, following a police raid on a house which she had let out to students, had been prosecuted under s5(b) of the Dangerous Drugs Act 1965 of 'being concerned in the management of premises used for the smoking of cannabis'. The defendant had not known that drugs were being consumed there. As Lord Reid observed:

'If this section means what the Divisional Court have held that it means, then hundreds of thousands of people who sublet part of the premises or take in lodgers or are concerned in the management of residential premises or institutions are daily incurring a risk of being convicted of a serious offence in circumstances where they are in no way to blame. For the greatest vigilance cannot prevent tenants, lodgers or inmates or guests whom they bring in from smoking cannabis cigarettes in their own rooms. It was suggested in argument that this appellant brought this conviction on herself because it is found as a fact that when the police searched the premises there were people there of the "beatnik fraternity". But surely it would be going a very long way to say that persons managing premises of any kind ought to safeguard themselves by refusing accommodation to all who are of slovenly or exotic appearance, or who bring in guests of that kind. And unfortunately drug taking is by no means confined to those of unusual appearance.'

See also *Gammon Ltd* v *Attorney-General for Hong Kong* (above).

By contrast, in *R* v *Bezzina*; *R* v *Codling*; *R* v *Elvin* [1994] 1 WLR 1057, where the appellants were each convicted, at separate trials, of being the owner of a dog which, whilst dangerously out of control in a public place, had injured a person contrary to s3(1) of the Dangerous Dogs Act 1991, the court was persuaded that the imposition of absolute liability would serve a useful purpose. In dismissing the appeals against conviction, the court held that the presumption against strict liability was rebutted by the fact that: (a) the Dangerous Dogs Act 1991 addressed a matter of social concern and public safety; (b) the court was satisfied that the imposition of strict liability would encourage greater vigilance by owners in seeking to prevent the commission of prohibited acts, ie the court felt that it was proper to put the onus on the dog owner to prevent the occurrence of harm; and (c) the statute, when read as a whole indicated that s3(1) imposed absolute liability, since s3(2) afforded a defence where D left the dog in the charge of a fit and proper person, and s3(3) impliedly required mens rea where it referred to an owner 'allowing' a dog to be in a non-public place. Note that the court declined to deal with one of the more interesting points argued on appeal, ie what would the appellant's liability have been if a properly secured dog, released from the appellant's premises following a burglary, had caused injury to a member of the public whilst loose? Clearly such a question goes to the heart of the issue as to whether or not it was the intention of Parliament to incriminate 'blameless' dog owners.

Public danger posed by defendant's conduct: drugs and guns

As a general rule, the more serious the criminal offence created by statute, the less likely the courts are to view it as an offence of strict liability. However, the courts are sometimes persuaded to impose strict liability after concluding that the possible unfairness that this might involve for the defendant is outweighed by the potential harm to the public posed by his conduct. Hence in *R v Howells* [1977] 3 All ER 417, the defendant was convicted of possessing an unlicensed firearm, contrary to s58(2) Firearms Act 1968, despite his honest belief that it was an antique and thus exempt from the provisions of the Act. As Browne LJ observed :

'... the danger to the community resulting from the possession of lethal firearms is so obviously great that an absolute prohibition against their possession without proper authority must have been the intention of Parliament when considered in conjunction with the words of the section ... to allow a defence of honest and reasonable belief that the firearm was an antique and therefore excluded would be likely to defeat the clear intentions of the Act.'

The balancing of priorities that has to be carried out, in a sense, raises the same issue; what knowledge, if any, must a defendant have in order for the court to conclude that he was in possession of the drugs or guns?

In *Warner v MPC* [1969] 2 AC 256, an authority from which it is extremely difficult, if not impossible to extract a clear ratio, a majority of their Lordships appeared to hold that s1 of the Drugs (Prevention of Misuse) Act 1964, under which it was an offence to be in unlawful possession of a prohibited drug, did create an offence of strict liability as regards the nature of the substance in the defendant's possession, but it nevertheless had to be proved that he knew he was in possession of 'something'. Hence, if drugs were slipped into a defendant's pocket without his knowledge he could not be guilty under s1 because he would not have known he was in possession of anything. If, however, he was knowingly in possession of a package of some sort, but was ignorant of the fact that it contained cocaine powder, it became necessary to look at the defendant's knowledge as to the nature and quality of the package's contents. Where he was mistaken as to the nature of its contents, for example where he honestly believed it to contain boiled sweets, it would appear from the speeches of the majority that he was to be acquitted, although this may have been subject to such factors as the defendant's opportunity to check the contents, and the existence of any factors that should have made him suspect that it might contain drugs. Where, on the other hand, he knew the nature of the contents but was mistaken as to its quality, for example, where he believed the package to contain sherbet powder, it would appear that he could be convicted: see further *R* v *Fernandez* [1970] Crim LR 277.

If the controlled drug is not in a container of any sort, it is submitted that knowledge on the part of the defendant that he is in possession of 'something' will suffice. Applying these principles, the defendant in *R* v *Marriot* [1970] 1 All ER 595, was convicted of unlawful possession of a prohibited drug, when he was found to have 2 milligrams of cannabis smeared on the blade of a penknife in his possession. The conviction was upheld, on the ground that although he had not known the substance to be cannabis, he had known that there was something smeared on the blade of the knife.

With a view to removing some of the complexities introduced into this branch of the law by *Warner* v *MPC*, Parliament enacted the Misuse of Drugs Act 1971. Section 5 of the 1971 Act creates the offence of possessing a controlled drug, but s28(3)(b)(i) goes on to provide that a defendant should be acquitted if:

'... he proves that he neither believed nor suspected nor had reason to suspect that the substance ... in question was a controlled drug.'

The Court of Appeal in *R* v *McNamara* (1988) 87 Cr App R 246, held that as far as the 'container' cases were concerned, Parliament, in enacting s28, had not intended to relieve the Crown of the initial burden of proving that the defendant had known he was in possession of a container holding 'something', and that it in fact held a controlled drug. Once the prosecution had established these matters, however, the onus was then upon the defendant to bring himself within the terms of s28(3)(b)(i). With respect this is a helpful clarification of the law, but the point still appears to cause difficulty. In *R* v *Lewis* (1987) 87 Cr App R 270, the Court of Appeal held that a defendant could be in possession of drugs where they were found in his house, despite the fact that he had not known that they were there, because he had had an opportunity to find them. The difficulty with this ruling is that it is not analogous to the case of the defendant who has a box which he knows to contain *something*, but who fails to inquire as to what it is; Lewis did not discover the drugs because he did not know there was anything in the house to go searching for! See further *R* v *Conway and Burke* [1994] Crim LR 826.

In *R* v *Bradish* (1990) 90 Cr App R 271, the appellant was convicted of possessing a prohibited weapon (a CS gas canister) contrary to s5(1) of the Firearms Act 1968, despite his assertion that he had not known that the canister contained CS gas. Auld J, on behalf of the Court of Appeal, rejected the assertion that, unlike most of the authorities on possession of firearms, the appellant's was a 'container' case, and as such the authorities dealing with possession of dangerous drugs should be applied. The court noted the social dangers presented by offensive weapons; the absence of any mental element in the wording of the offence; the reference to the defendants state of mind in *other* sections of the Act; and the provision of specific defences in analogous legislation, but not in the 1968 Act. In particular the court refused to follow the 'half-way house' approach to mens rea and possession adopted by the majority in *Warner*, because it was decided before the enactment of the 1968, and it was thus significant that the legislature, when passing that Act, made no provision clarifying the position as to the need or not to prove mens rea in relation to possession.

As Auld J observed:

'... the possibilities and consequences of evasion would be too great for effective control, even if the burden of proving lack of guilty knowledge were to be on the accused. The difficulty of enforcement, when presented with such a defence, would be particularly difficult where there is a prosecution for possession of a component part of a firearm or prohibited weapon, as provided for by sections 1 and 5 when read with section 57(1) of the 1968 Act. It would be easy for an accused to maintain, lyingly but with conviction, that he did not recognise the object in his possession as part of a firearm or prohibited weapon. To the argument that the innocent possessor or carrier of firearms or prohibited weapons or parts of them is at risk of unfair conviction under these provisions there has to be balanced the important public policy behind the legislation of protecting the public from the misuse of such dangerous weapons. Just as the Chicago-style gangster might plausibly maintain that he believed his violin case to contain a violin, not a sub-machine gun, so it might be difficult to meet a London lout's assertion that he did not know an unmarked plastic bottle in his possession contained ammonia rather than something to drink.'

Reform

The difficulties in ascertaining whether a statutory provision creates liability without fault are adverted to in the commentary that accompanies the Code Report:

'An enactment creating an offence should ordinarily specify the fault required for the offence or expressly provide that the offence is one of strict liability in respect of one or more identified elements. It is necessary, however, to have a general rule for the interpretation of any offence the definition of which does not state, in respect of one or more elements, whether fault is required or what degree of fault is required. The absence of a consistent rule of interpretation has been a regrettable source of uncertainty in English law. Clause 20 [set out below] provides such a rule. It would implement a policy that we recommended in our Report on the Mental Element in Crime [(1978) Law Com No 89], though in a manner a good deal less complex than that suggested in the draft Bill appended to that Report. The proposal to include this provision was well supported on consultation.' [Vol II para 8.25]

The proposed clause states:

'(1) Every offence requires a fault element of recklessness with or respect to each of its elements other than fault elements, unless otherwise provided.
(2) Subsection 1 does not apply to pre-Code offences as defined in section 6 (to which section 2(3) applies).'

The clause would apply to offences in the draft code and to offences subsequently created; the interpretation of existing legislation would not be affected. The clause would create a presumption that mens rea, in at least the form of recklessness as defined elsewhere in the Code, would be required in relation to each element of an offence, unless otherwise provided. As the commentary states:

> 'We considered a suggestion that the clause should seek to make the presumption displaceable only by *express* provision requiring some fault other than recklessness, or stating that no fault is required, with respect to an element of an offence. We do not think that this would be appropriate. We are mindful of the "constitutional platitude" pointed out by Lord Ackner in *Hunt* [1987] AC 352 at 380 that the courts must give effect to what Parliament has provided not only "expressly" but also by "necessary implication". If the terms of a future enactment creating an offence plainly implied an intention to displace the presumption created by clause 20(1), the courts would no doubt feel obliged to give effect to that intention even if the present clause were to require express provision for the purpose.' [Vol II para 8.28]

The intended effect of the clause is illustrated in the examples provided in Appendix B to Volume 1:

> 'Under clause 147 a person commits burglary if he enters a building as a trespasser intending to steal in the building. Nothing is said as to any fault required in respect of the fact that the entrant is a trespasser. The offence is committed only if the entrant knows that, or is reckless whether, he is trespassing.' [example 20(i)]
>
> 'An offence of causing polluting matter to enter a watercourse is enacted after the Code comes into force. In the absence of provision to the contrary the offence requires (a) an intention to cause the matter to enter the watercourse or recklessness whether it will do so, and (b) knowledge that the matter is a pollutant or recklessness'. [example 20(ii)]

25.2 Vicarious liability

Vicarious liability involves holding A responsible in law for the actions of B. As a general principle the courts will not hold one defendant criminally liable for the actions of another, but this is subject to a number of exceptions. If D gives X a tablet to place in P's tea, telling him that it is an aspirin when in fact it is cyanide, with the result that P dies of poisoning, D will be held responsible in law for the death, and X will escape liability as an innocent agent. In a sense D is vicariously liable for the criminal acts of X, but it is perhaps better to view X as simply the means by which D achieves his ends.

As will have been seen from chapters 9 and 10, a defendant can be charged with an offence, despite the fact that he has only played out some accessorial role in its commission. One who counsels or procures the commission of an offence could be described as incurring a form of vicarious liability for the criminal acts committed by the principal offender, in the sense that his liability is derived from that of the person who commits the actus reus of the completed crime. What distinguishes such cases from the usual instances of vicarious liability, however, is that the counsellor or procurer will have some degree of mens rea: see further on this distinction *Ferguson* v *Weaving* [1951] 1 KB 814.

It is well known that employers can be held vicariously liable in civil law for torts committed by their employees in the course of employment. Where an employee commits criminal offences in the course of his employment, for example a solicitor's clerk defrauding a client of her property (see *Lloyd* v *Grace, Smith & Co* [1912] AC 716), there is no reason *per se* why the employer should also incur criminal liability, unless he can be shown to have actively participated in the commission of the offence, in which case the normal rules of accessorial liability will apply.

There are sound policy reasons, however, for recognising that in certain situations the law ought to impose vicarious criminal liability on an employer, particularly where a statute creates criminal liability of a regulatory or 'quasi-criminal nature'. Much depends on whether the court regards the imposition of vicarious liability as having being intended by Parliament as a necessary means of ensuring the effective operation of the law in question. Three situations in particular needs to be noted.

Statutory duty placed on an employer

Where a statute creates and imposes a legal duty upon a particular person, he will normally be liable for the failure of those acting on his behalf to ensure the performance of that duty. As Atkin J observed in *Mousell Brothers Ltd* v *London & North Western Railway Co* [1917] 2 KB 836:

> 'I think that the authorities cited ... make it plain that while prima facie a principal is not to be made criminally responsible for the acts of his servants, yet the legislature may prohibit an act or enforce a duty in such words as to make the prohibition or the duty absolute; in which case the principal is liable if the act is in fact done by his servants. To ascertain whether a particular Act of Parliament has that effect or not regard must be had to the object of the Statute, the words used, the nature of the duty laid down, the person upon whom it is imposed, the person by whom it would in ordinary circumstances be performed, and the person upon whom the penalty is imposed.'

The courts may, however, be willing to recognise a relaxation of this principle where the offence places D under a personal duty and goes on to provide for a 'due diligence' defence. For example in *Seabord Offshore* v *Secretary of State for Transport* [1994] 1 WLR 541, the House of Lords held that the owner of a vessel could be criminally liable for a failing to ensure that it was operated in a safe manner, contrary to s31 of the Merchant Shipping Act 1988, but could not be criminally liable if this circumstance arose through the acts or omissions of his employees, if he himself had taken all reasonable steps to prevent its occurrence. See chapter 26, section 26.11, for further details.

Act of the servant imputed to the employer

Cases such as *Griffiths* v *Studebakers Ltd* [1924] 1 KB 102, suggest that an employer can be vicariously liable in respect of strict liability offences committed by an employee during the course of his employment provided the wording of the offence is appropriate. In that case, an employee of the defendant company had taken a number of prospective purchasers for a trial run in one of the company's cars. The company was charged with using the vehicle contrary to the Road Vehicles (Trade Licences) Regulations 1922, on the ground that more than two passengers were carried on the trial run. In upholding the conviction, the Divisional Court held that the company could be said to be using the vehicle through its employee. As the offence was one of strict liability, there was no conceptual difficulty in holding the company liable as the principal offender, and the employee liable as an aider and abettor (although note that there can be no accessorial liability without fault). Similarly employers have been found guilty of 'selling' goods in contravention of what is now the trades descriptions legislation (see *Coppen* v *Moore (No 2)* [1898] 2 QB 306), and of 'keeping' a vehicle without a licence (see *Strutt* v *Cliff* [1911] 1 KB 1). *National Rivers Authority* v *Alfred McAlpine Homes East Ltd* [1994] 4 All ER 286, concerned pollution of the River Medway during the construction of a housing estate by the respondent company. The pollution had been caused by wet cement being discharged into a culvert running through the site into the river. The company, charged with contravention of s85 Water Resources Act 1991, conceded that its employees had caused this pollution whilst constructing a water feature on the site, but the justices dismissed the information as disclosing no case to answer on the basis that those responsible for the discharge, the site agent and manager, were not sufficiently senior to be identified with the 'controlling mind' of the company. On appeal the court held that the pollution had been caused by employees of the respondent company who were actively responsible for the operation of the site whilst acting in the course of their employment. Only if the pollution could be shown to have been caused by the intervention of some third party would the company be relieved of liability. Simon Brown LJ seemed to regard the case one involving vicarious corporate liability, thus falling within the same category as *Alphacell Ltd* v *Woodward* [1972] AC 824, in the sense that the company should be criminally liable for the pollution resulting from its authorised procedures. Morland J also approached the offence as one that imposed vicarious liability, despite the absence of any clear words to that effect in the statute, and his justification for adopting such an approach is instructive. He stated:

> 'In my judgment, to make the offence an effective weapon in the defence of environmental protection, a company must by necessary implication be criminally liable for the acts or omissions of its servants or agents during activities being done for the company. I do not find that this offends our concept of a just or fair criminal justice system, having regard to the magnitude of environmental pollution, even though no due diligence defence was provided for ... [I]t can be strongly argued that the respondents by their activities directly caused the flow of polluting matter into the stream. It is difficult to see in principle why it

should matter whether those activities are essentially mechanical by their plant or essentially manual by their servants or agents.'

Given that, in the cases considered above, it is the employer who is regarded in law as having committed the actus reus of the offence, not the employee, there are two situations where the application of this principle may prove difficult. First where the wording of the given offence requires proof of some physical activity, such as 'driving', that cannot be performed by an artificial legal entity such as a corporation: see further *Richmond upon Thames LBC* v *Pinn and Wheeler Ltd* [1989] Crim LR 510 The Times 14 February. Secondly, where the wording of the offence implies proof of knowledge that cannot be established on the part of the employer. Thus, in *James & Son Ltd* v *Smee* [1955] 1 QB 78, the defendant employers were charged with permitting a vehicle to be driven with defective brakes, contrary to vehicle use regulations. The Divisional Court quashed the conviction, holding that the use of the word 'permitting' in the statute implied some degree of mens rea, in that one could only permit something if one knew of it. There was no evidence to suggest that the defendants had known of the vehicle's defective brakes, and hence they had not had the mens rea necessary for a conviction. Similarly in *Readhead Freight Ltd* v *Shulman* [1988] Crim LR 696, the Divisional Court held that although the defendant company had, through its transport manager, caused an offence to be committed by the company's drivers not filling in their time sheets as required by law, there could be no liability in the absence of any evidence that the it had issued any instruction or mandate to this effect.

The delegation principle

In *Vane* v *Yiannopoullos* [1965] AC 486, Lord Morris expressed the view that:

'... the principle "respondeat superior" finds no place in our criminal law. If a master tells or authorises his servant to do some particular act any criminal liability in the master that might result, either as a principal or as an accessory, springs from the authorisation and not simply from the relationship of master and servant ... I am not prepared to accept that there are any canons of construction which are specially applicable to legislation dealing with licensing, or that in such legislation the principle "respondeat superior" commands some exceptional yet general acceptance.'

Despite the force of these comments, the evidence is that the courts will not necessarily permit an employer or licensee to escape liability, even for offences requiring proof of mens rea, by delegating the management of an establishment to his servants. Thus, in *Allen* v *Whitehead* [1930] 1 KB 211, D was convicted of permitting a cafe, which he owned but which was managed on his behalf by a servant, to be used as a place of resort by prostitutes, the knowledge of D's manager being imputed to the owner; see also *Linnet* v *MPC* [1946] KB 290. The rationale for the 'delegation' principle is to ensure that individuals cannot escape legal liability simply by placing the running of their businesses in the hands of others. If it were otherwise, a licensee could, for example, flout the licensing laws with impunity by installing a manager to operate his public house. The legislation stipulates that only the licensee can be punished as a principal offender, and the licensee would be able to deny any mens rea on account of his absence at the time the offence was committed.

In *R* v *Winson* [1969] 1 QB 371, the appellant, who held a justices' on-licence under the terms of which he was prohibited from selling alcohol to persons who had been members of the club for less than 48 hours, visited the bar infrequently, and had effectively delegated the running of the bar to a manager. Following evidence that alcohol had been sold at the club in breach of the terms of the licence, he was convicted under s161(1) of the Licensing Act 1964 of knowingly selling liquor to persons to whom he was not permitted to sell. Dismissing his appeal, Lord Parker CJ observed:

> 'The principle of delegation comes into play, and only comes into play, in cases where, although the statute uses words which import knowledge or intent such as in this case "knowingly" or in some other cases "permitting" or "suffering" and the like, cases to which knowledge is inherent, nevertheless it has been held that a man cannot get out of his responsibilities which have been put upon him by delegating those responsibilities to another ... If one licensee chooses to say to his co-licensee, although not his servant: "We are both licensees and both keepers of this house, but I am not going to take any part in the management of this house, I leave the management to you", he is putting his co-licensee into his own place to exercise his own powers and duties and he must, therefore, accept responsibility for what is done or known by his co-licensee in that exercise.'

It is possible that the doctrine can work to the defendant's advantage. In *DPP* v *Rogers* [1992] Crim LR 51, the licensee of a public house had been dismissed by the brewery and was on suspension pending an appeal against his dismissal. The respondent, the area manager for the brewery, appointed relief managers to run the business. The prosecution's claim that the respondent was aiding and abetting the unlicensed sale of alcohol by the relief managers was rejected by the Divisional Court on the basis that they were acting as delegates of the dismissed manager, and therefore had his authority to sell liquor. The problem with this interpretation, however, is that the dismissed manager had not consented to the appointment of relief managers, and would presumably have incurred vicarious liability for any breaches of the Licensing Act 1964 by the relief managers, unless the courts were willing to distinguish between wilful delegation, and enforced delegation.

The problem will often be one of degree; has there been delegation of management or not? In *Vane* v *Yiannopoullos* (above), the defendant licensee, who was licensed to sell alcohol to those of his patrons who ordered meals, was charged under s22(1) of the Licensing Act 1961, of knowingly selling alcohol to persons to whom he was not permitted to sell, after one of his waitresses had sold alcohol to two youths in contravention of the terms of the licence. The defendant had been on the premises at the time, but on another floor. The magistrates had dismissed the case against the defendant on the basis that he had not had any mens rea, and the prosecutor's appeal was dismissed by the House of Lords on the basis that there had not been complete delegation of management to the servants of the licensee, or alternatively because the licensee had not absented himself. Whether or not there has been any such delegation will often be a nice question of fact and law: see further *Howker v Robinson* [1973] 1 QB 178.

Reform

The draft Code contains the following restatement of vicarious criminal liability in clause 29:

'(1) Subject to subsection (3), an element of an offence (other than a fault element) may be attributed to a person by reason of an act done by another only if that other is –
(a) specified in the definition of the offence as a person whose act may be so attributed; or
(b) acting within the scope of his employment or authority and the definition of the offence specifies the element in terms which apply to both persons.
(2) Subject to subsection (3), a fault element of an offence may be attributed to a person by reason of the fault of another only if the terms of the enactment creating the offence so provide.
(3) This section does not affect the application in relation to any pre-Code offence (as defined in section 6) of any existing rule whereby a person who has delegated to another the management of premises or of a business or activity may, in consequence of the acts and fault of the other, have the elements of the offence attributed to him.'

The limits that clause 29 would impose upon the scope of vicarious liability are considered in the commentary:

'Subsection (l)(b) provides for two conditions to be satisfied before an offence may be interpreted as applying to a person who did not himself do the prohibited act. The relevant element of the offence must be expressed in terms which are apt for the defendant as well as for the person who in fact acted   Secondly, the person who in fact acted must have done so within the scope of his employment or authority (that is, as the defendant's agent). These conditions are in accordance with the results reached in the great majority of cases. In their absence there can be no justification for imposing vicarious liability (unless, of course, Parliament has expressly provided for it). Under existing law an employee may disobey an express instruction from his employer and yet still be held to be acting within the scope of his employment [see *Coppen v Moore (No 2)* [1898] 2 QB 306].
    The reference in paragraph (b) to a person's "acting within the scope of his authority" extends, of course, to a case in which the person who does the prohibited act is acting for the defendant not as an employee but as an independent contractor. It was proposed in Working Paper No 43 to exclude such persons from the range of agents whose acts may give rise to vicarious liability. As this proposal would change the law without a clear case being made for doing so, clause 29 does not adopt it. The clause does not distinguish between the person who "uses" the defendant's vehicle as his employee and the person who "uses" the defendant's vehicle on a single occasion because the defendant has asked him to do so, whether or not for payment. This does not mean that a person will necessarily be liable for the act of his independent contractor even where the offence employs a verb like "uses". The matter remains one for judicial interpretation. It is one thing to hold that a person carrying on a business of supplying milk or heavy building materials "uses" a vehicle if he employs an independent contractor to supply those things in the contractor's vehicle. It would be quite another thing to hold that a householder

"uses" the removal van owned by the firm of removers whom he engages to carry his furniture to a new residence. Paragraph (b) also leaves open the possibility that, where an independent contractor does an act incidental to the act he was engaged to do, he will be held not to have acted within the scope of his authority. The courts have interpreted some offences requiring knowledge (notably licensees' offences) so as to permit a person's conviction on the basis of the act and knowledge of one to whom he has delegated management of premises or of an activity. This "delegation principle" was regarded as anomalous by members of the House of Lords in *Vane* v *Yiannopoullos* and our Working Party proposed its abolition. Subsection (2) gives effect to this proposal so far as concerns offences created by the Code itself or by subsequent legislation. Parliament will have to provide clearly for the attribution to one person of the fault of another if it wishes this to occur. There can be no question, however, of proposing the abolition of the delegation principle as it has been held to apply to existing legislation. Some legislation is so drafted that abolition would seriously affect its enforceability. Subsection (3) therefore expressly preserves the application of the principle to pre-Code offences.' [Vol II paras 9.48–9.50]

The effect of the enacting clause 29 is illustrated in the examples contained in Appendix B to C Volume I:

'A statute provides that it is an offence for the holder of a justices' licence whether by himself, his servant or agent to supply intoxicating liquor on licensed premises outside permitted hours. No fault is required for this offence. D is the licensee of a public house. E, his barman, serves a drink to a friend outside the permitted hours. In the absence of any special defence D is guilty of the offence as a principal. Assuming fault on E s part, E is guilty as an accessory.' [example 29(i)]

'A statute provides that it is an offence for a person to sell goods to which a false trade description is applied. No fault is required for this offence. E, an assistant employed in D's shop, sells a ham as a "Scotch" ham. D has previously given instructions that such hams are not to be sold under any specific name of place of origin. The ham is in fact an American ham. Both D and E are guilty of the offence as principals.' [example 29(ii)]

25.3 Corporate liability

In cases of vicarious criminal liability the mens rea of an employee may be imputed to the employer, possibly a company. In cases of corporate liability, it is the company itself that is alleged to have committed the offence as the principal offender, the employee possibly being charged as an accessory, or more probably as a defendant in his own right.

It should be stated at the outset that the imposition of criminal liability on companies per se is so commonplace as to hardly merit comment, but this is because, in the vast majority of cases, it is strict (ie absolute) liability offences that are involved. Provided the company can be shown to have caused the commission of the offence through those acting on its behalf there should be no particular difficulty in upholding a conviction; see further *National Rivers Authority* v *Alfred McAlpine Homes East Ltd* (above). Clearly there are certain offences in respect of which an artificial legal person such as a corporation cannot incur liability: murder, because of the mandatory penalty; rape because of the nature of the actus reus. In *R* v *Coroner for East Kent, ex parte Spooner* (1989) 88 Cr App R 10, Bingham LJ was prepared to accept that a corporate body could be guilty of manslaughter where both the mens rea and actus reus could be established against those who were the 'embodiment of the corporate body itself'. On the facts, however, he was not satisfied that there was a sustainable case against the directors of Townsend Car Ferries Ltd in respect of the deaths resulting from the capsizing of the *Herald of Free Enterprise*. His doubts were realised when a prosecution for manslaughter was actually brought against the shipowners in *R v P & O European Ferries (Dover) Ltd* (1991) 93 Cr App R 72. At the trial at the Central Criminal Court, Turner J ultimately felt constrained to withdraw the case from the jury due to lack of evidence against the senior employees involved. The trial did involve at least a theoretical victory for the prosecution and proponents of corporate liability for manslaughter, in that in the course of argument the trial judge ruled that a company could incur liability for manslaughter. He stated (at p88):

> '... if it be accepted that manslaughter in English law is the unlawful killing of one human being by another human being (which must include both direct and indirect acts) and that a person who is the embodiment of a corporation and acting for the purposes of the corporation is doing the act or omission which caused the death, the corporation as well as the person may also be found guilty of manslaughter.'

How useful this ruling turns out to be in practice remains to be seen. Given the evidential difficulties of locating mens rea within a body corporate, the reluctance of the CPS to prosecute in the case of disasters may be understandable. The question of appropriate punishment also requires proper consideration. The obvious penalty in the form of a large fine may only serve to harm the shareholders, who will normally be innocent parties in the case. It may be that more imaginative forms of punishment need to be considered, such as the supervision of spending by the company on retraining employees, and product development.

Locating corporate mens rea

Where a corporation is charged with an offence requiring proof of fault the conventional wisdom is that the prosecution will have to show that those who can be regarded as the 'directing minds' of the company had the necessary mens rea. The decision that is often cited as the leading modern authority on this issue is that of the House of Lords in *Tesco Supermarkets Ltd v Natrass* [1972] AC 153. The defendant company was convicted, under s11 of the Trade Descriptions Act 1968, of displaying a misleading price notice. Posters had been placed in a store window advertising packets of washing powder for sale at 2s 11d, when in fact those in stock were being retailed at 3s 11d. The company sought to rely on the defence, provided by s24 of the Act, to the effect that it had taken all reasonable steps to prevent the commission of the offence, which had resulted from the act or default of another person, namely one of its store managers. In allowing the company's appeal, the

House of Lords held that the store manager, despite being an employee of the company, was in law to be regarded as 'another person' within s24 of the 1968 Act, ie he was not the embodiment of the company.

Regarding the task of locating mens rea within a company, Lord Diplock observed:

> '... what natural persons are to be treated in law as being the company for the purpose of acts done in the course of its business, including the taking of precautions and the exercise of due diligence to avoid the commission of a criminal offence, is to be found by identifying those natural persons who by the memorandum and articles of association or as a result of action taken by the directors, or by the company in general meeting pursuant to the articles, are entrusted with the exercise of the powers of the company ... [t]here has been in recent years a tendency to extract from Denning LJ's judgment in *H L Bolton (Engineering) Co Ltd* v *T J Graham & Sons Ltd* [1957] 1 QB 159 ... his vivid metaphor about the "brains and nerve centre" of a company as contrasted with its hands, and to treat this dichotomy, and not the articles of association, as laying down the test of whether or not a particular person is to be regarded in law as being the company itself when performing duties which a statute imposes on the company. In the case in which this metaphor was first used Denning LJ was dealing with acts and intentions of directors of the company in whom the powers of the company were vested under its articles of association. The decision in that case is not authority for extending the class of persons whose acts are to be regarded in law as the personal acts of the company itself, beyond those who by, or by action taken under, its articles of association are entitled to exercise the powers of the company.'

Lord Reid took a less legalistic approach, identifying those who could be the embodiment of the company in terms of constituting its directing mind as being the directors, and possibly other senior officers of the company carrying out functions of management. Viscount Dilhorne found it useful to talk in terms of those who were in actual control of the operations of the company, in the sense that they were not answerable to others in the company regarding the manner in which they discharged their duties. Presumably if those who constitute the directing will of the company delegate their functions to employees further down the chain of command, liability can still be imposed on the basis of a 'quasi-delegation' principle: see further *Moore* v *I Bressler Ltd* [1944] 2 All ER 515, and *R* v *ICR Haulage Ltd* [1944] KB 551.

Even if this issue is resolved, it may be that no one director or other responsible person has sufficient knowledge for the prosecution to prove that he had the necessary mens rea for the offence in question. It may be that the required degree of fault can only be proved by aggregating the knowledge of a number of directors or managers, and the decision of the court in *R* v *Coroner for East Kent, ex parte Spooner* (1989) 88 Cr App R 10 suggests that such aggregation is not permissible in a criminal trial.

Reform

As the Code Report commentary explains:

'The Code team, in considering how the criminal liability of corporations should be provided for in the Code, took as their point of departure a Working Paper on the subject prepared by our Working Party [Working Paper No 44 (1972)]. As that Working Paper was not followed by a Report, the team had no Law Commission recommendations to follow and were bound to attempt a restatement of the existing law as they understood it ... [Corporate liability] is a relatively recent judicial development and was not fully discussed in authoritative judgments before the House of Lords' decision in *Tesco Supermarkets Ltd* v *Nattrass* [above] ... We are conscious that we are here proposing the restatement of principles whose underlying theory and rationale remain strangely uncertain. It is comforting to note, however, that, although the Working Party did review other possible approaches to the subject (including that of abolishing corporate liability altogether), its discussion plainly tended towards the preservation of a slightly modified version of the status quo. Clause 30 incorporates some of those modifications ... the Code team expressed surprise at the number of points at which, in drafting their suggested clause, they had to fill in gaps in the law for want of authority. It has therefore been encouraging that the team's clause largely escaped criticism on consultation, and in particular that their proposals for the filling of gaps were not questioned. We have been able to adopt that clause with very minor amendments.' [Vol II paras 10.1–10.3]

Clause 30 provides:

'(1) A corporation may be guilty as a principal of an offence not involving a fault element by reason of –
(a) an act done by its employee or agent, as provided by section 29; or
(b) an omission, state of affairs or occurrence that is an element of the offence.
(2) A corporation may be guilty –
(a) as a principal, of an offence involving a fault element; or
(b) as an accessory, of any offence,
only if one of its controlling officers, acting within the scope of his office and with the fault required, is concerned in the offence.
(3)(a) "Controlling officer" of a corporation means a person participating in the control of the corporation in the capacity of a director, manager, secretary or other similar officer (whether or not he was, or was validly, appointed to any such office).
(b) In this subsection "director", in relation to a corporation established by or under any enactment for the purpose of carrying on under national ownership any industry or part of an industry or undertaking, being a corporation whose affairs are managed by the members thereof, means a member of the corporation .
(c) Whether a person acting in a particular capacity is a controlling officer is a question of law.
(4) A controlling officer is concerned in an offence if he does, procures, assists, encourages or fails to prevent the acts specified for the offence.
(5) For the purposes of subsection (4), a controlling officer fails to prevent an act when he fails to take steps that he might take –
(a) to ensure that the act is not done; or
(b) where the offence may be constituted by an omission to do an act or by a state of affairs or occurrence, to ensure that the omission is not made or to prevent or end the state of affairs or occurrence.

(6) A controlling officer does not act "within the scope of his office" if he acts with the intention of doing harm or of concealing harm done by him or another to the corporation.
(7) A corporation cannot be guilty of an offence that is not punishable with a fine or other pecuniary penalty.
(8) A corporation has a defence consisting of or including –
(a) a state of mind only if
(i) all controlling officers who are concerned in the offence; or
(ii) where no controlling officer is so concerned, all other employees or agents who are so concerned, have that state of mind;
(b) the absence of a state of mind only if no controlling officer with responsibility for the subject-matter of the offence has that state of mind;
(c) compliance with a standard of conduct required of the corporation itself only if it is complied with by the controlling officers with responsibility for the subject-matter of the offence.'

The possible accessorial liability of company officers is dealt with by Clause 31, which states:

'(1) Where a corporation is guilty of an offence, other than a pre-Code offence as defined in section 6 (to which section 2(3) applies), a controlling officer of the corporation who is not apart from this section guilty of the offence is guilty of it as an accessory if –
(a) knowing that or being reckless whether the offence is being or will be committed, he intentionally fails to take steps that he might take to prevent its commission; or
(b) the offence does not involve a fault element and its commission is attributable to any neglect on his part.
(2) Subsection (I) applies to a member of a corporation managed by its members as it applies to a controlling officer.'

As the commentary confirms, subsection (1) of Clause 30 is included for the avoidance of doubt. There is clear authority for the proposition that 'vicarious liability for offences of strict liability may attach to corporations as to other persons' (Vol II para 10.4). The difficulties surround the imposition of corporate criminal liability for offences requiring proof of fault. As the commentary explains:

'The attribution to a corporation of criminal liability for an offence involving fault is achieved by identifying the corporation with its "directing mind and will" – that is, with those of its human agents whose acts and states of mind are (in law) its acts and states of mind. This metaphysical notion of the common law has to be translated into legislative terms without resort to puzzling or misleading metaphor and with as much definition as the subject-matter will allow. The translation is made by subsections (2)–(5). The primary statement is in subsection (2): what is required to make a corporation liable, in any case in which fault is an element, is that "one of its controlling officers, acting within the scope of his office and with the fault required, is concerned in the offence". There are several phrases here which require elaboration.
    "Controlling officer". This key phrase is defined in subsection (3) ... This (subject to what is said in the following paragraph) is intended to capture the meaning of "directing mind and will" as explained in the opinions in the *Tesco* case. The phrase "director, manager, secretary or other similar officer" is taken from the common-form provision for the imposition of liability on company officers, which was recognised by members of the House of Lords as providing a useful indication of the persons concerned. Viscount Dilhorne referred to the person or persons "in actual control of the operations of the

company". Any of them "participates" in such control. He may do so as a member of the board of directors, as managing director, or perhaps as some other superior officer (to adapt the language of Lord Reid); or by virtue of a delegation of directors' powers ... The Code team followed a hint in Working Paper No 44 in not requiring the controlling officer to be validly appointed. They took the view, with which we agree, that an over-constitutional test for the identification of "controlling officers" would put a premium on disregard of the formalities of appointment and delegation. This aspect of their definition, and now of our own, rebels against some dicta in *Tesco* [at 199–200 per Lord Diplock]. The definition treats as a controlling officer any person who in fact participates in the control of a corporation by exercising the functions of a relevant office, whether as the result of appointment (valid or not) or *de facto*. It will, for example, include a kind of case about which the Northern Circuit Scrutiny Group was concerned: that of the bankrupt who runs a company of which members of his family are the nominal directors and shareholders.' [Vol II paras 10.5–10.7 Note that the Commission rejected the extension of liability to 'shadow directors' on the ground that this would involve too radical an extension of liability to undertake without wider consultation]

' *"One of its controlling officers acting... with the fault required ..."* This formula in subsection (2) gives effect to the provisional view of the Working Party that "a corporation should not be taken as having any required mental element unless at least one of its controlling officers has the whole mental element required for the offence".' [Vol II para 10.10]

' *"... is concerned in the offence"*. This shorthand expression in subsection (2) is explained in subsection (4), as elaborated in subsection (5). A controlling officer may render a corporation guilty of an offence by doing the acts specified for the offence; by being a party to the acts of others – procuring, assisting or encouraging those acts; or by failing to prevent relevant acts (of other controlling officers or of subordinates) or relevant events. Only the last of these possibilities needs elaboration ... *"Fails to prevent"*. It seems clear that a company must be guilty of a fraud offence if its managing director knows that company personnel are defrauding customers and turns a blind eye to what is going on. The perpetrators are not "encouraged" by his inactivity unless they know of his knowledge. An additional expression is needed. "Fails to prevent" will cover this kind of case and also some cases involving offences of omission or "situational offences". Some positive duty of a company may be entrusted to a subordinate; but he omits (and therefore the company omits) to do what is required; or a subordinate's actions give rise to a state of affairs capable of constituting an offence on the company's part. If in either case the offence requires fault, the company's liability depends upon some culpable failure on the part of a controlling officer. Subsection (5) explains that the failure required is a failure "to take steps that he might take" to ensure (in effect) that the offence is not committed. The subsection must of course be read together with the reference to "the fault required" in subsection (2).' [Vol II paras 10.11–10.12]

' *"Acting within the scope of his office"*. This phrase in subsection (2) embraces a number of limitations on corporate liability.

1. *The officer must be acting as such.* A corporation is not liable for what is done by any of its officers in a personal capacity.

2. *The officer must be acting within his sphere.* If only some of the functions of management are delegated to a controlling officer, the criminal liability of the corporation on the basis of identification with him should be limited to his activities in connection with those functions.

3. *Subsection (6). The officer must not be acting against the corporation.* Subsection (6) declares that an act done by an officer with the intention of harming the corporation is not done "within the scope of his office".' [Vol II para 10.13]

25.4 Bigamy

Section 57 of the Offences Against the Person Act 1861 provides:

'Whosoever, being married, shall marry any other person during the life of the former husband or wife, whether the second marriage shall have taken place in England ... or elsewhere, shall be guilty of (an offence) ... Provided that nothing in this section contained shall extend to any second marriage contracted elsewhere than in England ... by any other than a subject of Her Majesty, or to any person marrying a second time whose husband or wife shall have been continually absent from such person for the space of seven years then past, and shall not have been known by such person to be living within that time, or shall extend to any person who, at the time of such second marriage, shall have been divorced from the bond of the first marriage, or to any person whose former marriage shall have been declared void by the sentence of any court of competent jurisdiction.'

The wording of the offence, if given a literal interpretation, would lead to an absurdity. A person who is already married cannot marry. This was the problem faced in *R* v *Allen* (1872) LR 1 CCR 367. If a literal interpretation was applied the offence in s57 would be incapable of being committed. The court was of the opinion that Parliament could not have intended to legislate an absurdity. By application of the mischief rule of interpretation, the court substituted in the interpretation of the above phrase the wording 'whosoever being married, goes through another marriage ceremony ... shall be guilty'. In this way effect was given to the intention behind the section.

If the first marriage is void, then there is no legal effect from its 'celebration'; consequently D may go ahead with a second marriage without an order of the court. For present purposes, a marriage may be considered void if (1) the parties are within the prohibited relationships, (2) either party is under the age of 16, (3) the marriage was an invalid polygamous one and (4) the parties are not respectively male and female (see *Corbett* v *Corbett* [1970] 2 All ER 33). If the first marriage is only 'voidable' D is not free to marry again, until an order of the court has been obtained. A marriage may be voidable for a variety of reasons, for example, because it had not been consummated. Whilst the second 'marriage' will of necessity be void, the second ceremony must be of a form that would normally be capable of producing a valid marriage.

A person whose marriage is valid in the country in which it was celebrated but which was potentially polygamous would be incapable of committing bigamy (*R* v *Sarwan Singh* [1962] 3 All ER 612), however, in *R* v *Sagoo* [1975] 2 All ER 926 it was said that a potentially polygamous marriage could be converted into a monogamous marriage, and thereby become a basis for a bigamy charge here, by a change of domicile or enactment by the country of celebration.

D has a defence if he or she can show that he or she has not seen or heard of his or her spouse for seven years. The fact that the lack of contact is caused by D's own desertion seems not to matter (*R* v *Faulkes* (1903) 19 TLR 250). It is uncertain whether or not D must prove the absence. Certainly he or she has at least an evidential burden, ie he must adduce some evidence of the lack of knowledge.

Though it has been held in Commonwealth cases that D must prove the absence, probably since *Woolmington* v *DPP* [1935] AC 1, this is not the case here. The seven year rule is merely a defence, and is not a presumption of death.

The mens rea of the offence, according to Lord Fraser in *DPP* v *Morgan* [1976] AC 182, is the intention to go through a marriage ceremony. In the light of the leading case of *R* v *Tolson* (1889) 23 QBD 168 this may be too restrictive an interpretation: see Chapter 15. Tolson was followed in *R* v *King* [1964] 1 QB 285; and *R* v *Gould* [1968] 2 QB 65.

25.5 Perjury

The modern law relating to perjury is contained in the Perjury Act 1911 which provides in s1(1):

> 'If any person lawfully sworn as a witness or as an interpreter in a judicial proceeding wilfully makes a statement material in that proceeding which he knows to be false or does not believe to be true he shall be guilty of perjury ...'

The maximum penalty following conviction on indictment is seven years imprisonment.

Actus reus

Lawfully sworn as a witness
A defendant can only commit perjury where he has been lawfully sworn as a witness. In practice this means that the defendant has sworn an oath, a matter now governed by the Oaths Act 1978. Section 5 of the 1978 Act allows a witness to affirm instead of swearing a religious oath, the effect of which is to put the witness in the same position for the purposes of perjury as if he had sworn an oath. A child can only be sworn as a witness if he or she understands the importance of telling the truth.

Judicial proceedings
Section 1(2) of the 1911 Act provides that the expression 'judicial proceedings' includes proceedings before any court, tribunal, or person having by law power to hear, receive, and examine evidence on oath. Whether a body other than a court of law has the power to administer the oath will be determined by the relevant enabling Act. Where an inferior body acts outside its jurisdiction in determining a matter, a witness giving false evidence cannot be guilty of perjury.

Makes a statement
Despite older authorities to the contrary, the view expressed in *R* v *Schlesinger* (1867) 10 QB 670 that a statement of opinion which is not generally held can amount to perjury, is to be preferred.

Material in that proceedings

A material statement is not simply one that relates to disputed questions of fact; it can extend to other matters, such as the creditworthiness of a witness. Section 1(6) of the 1911 Act provides that 'the question whether a statement on which perjury is assigned was material is a question of law to be determined by the court of trial'. The effect of this provision was made clear by the Court of Appeal in *R* v *Millward* (1985) 80 Cr App R 280, where it was held that the defendant did not have to know his statement was material in order to be guilty of perjury; its materiality was a matter to be determined objectively by the trial judge, the test being: would it have affected the outcome of the trial?

Mens rea

Wilfully

The prosecution must prove no more than that the statement was made deliberately and not inadvertently or by mistake: see *R* v *Millward* (above).

Knowledge or belief

The defendant must be proved to have known that his statements were untrue, or to have had no honest belief in their truthfulness. This creates the interesting possibility that a defendant might commit the offence of perjury by telling the truth where he nevertheless believes himself to be lying.

26

Recent Cases

26.1 Actus reus and mens rea

R v *Coles* [1994] Crim LR 820 Court of Appeal (Hobhouse LJ, Tudor-Evans and Rix JJ)

Reckless criminal damage – whether characteristics of the accused relevant to the direction on recklessness

Facts

The appellant, aged 15 at the time of the alleged offence and of lower than average mental capacity, had been playing in a hay barn with other children. The evidence was that he had tried to set fire to the hay whilst other children were in the barn. The children escaped unhurt. The appellant was charged with arson, being reckless as to whether the lives of others would be endangered. During the trial it was submitted that the *Caldwell* direction should be amended so that the assessment of whether or not the appellant had, by his actions, created an obvious risk of harm,

367

should be made more subjective. The trial judge rejected this submission stating that the test was whether or not the risk would have been obvious to the reasonable prudent adult person. Following the trial judge's ruling the appellant changed his plea to one of guilty and appealed.

Held

The appeal was dismissed. The first limb of the *Caldwell* direction was objective and the state of mind of the accused was irrelevant to the question of whether or not he had, by his act or omission, created an obvious risk of harm to persons or property. On appeal, the argument put forward on behalf of the appellant had been broadened to encompass the proposition that the second limb of the *Caldwell* test should have some regard to the defendant's capacity to foresee risk. The appeal court took the view that such an argument had failed in *Elliot v C* [1983] 1 WLR 939 and that that decision had been confirmed by the Court of Appeal in *R v R (Stephen Malcolm)* (1984) 79 Cr App R 334. It was not predisposed to depart from its own previous decision.

26.2 Criminal damage

Johnson v *DPP* [1994] Crim LR 673 Queen's Bench Division (McCowan LJ and Curtis J)

Criminal damage – belief that property is in need of protection

Facts

The appellant, a squatter, broke the lock on the front door of a property and replaced it with one of his own, prior to moving his belongings into the property. In particular he asserted that he had had a lawful excuse under s5(2)(b) of the Criminal Damage Act 1971 in that he believed that his belongings were in need of immediate protection, and believed that his actions were reasonable having regard to the circumstances. The Crown Court concluded that, whilst the appellant had broken the lock so that he could move his belongings in, and thus protect them from others, his property had not been in need of immediate protection, and that the appellant had had no belief that they were. The question stated for the divisional court was whether or not the Crown Court was entitled to come to such a conclusion as to the appellant's state of mind.

Held

The appeal was dismissed. The first question, which had to be approached on an objective basis, was whether or not the act of damage had been committed in order to protect property. If the answer was in the affirmative, a subjective approach could be adopted to the question of whether or not the accused honestly believed that the property was in immediate need of protection, and whether or not the steps taken were reasonable in the circumstances. The Crown Court had been entitled, therefore, to conclude that the appellant, in damaging the lock, had not acted in the belief that his actions were necessary to protect property.

26.3 Non-fatal offences against the person

Kerr v *DPP* (1994) The Times 5 August Queen's Bench Division (Butler-Sloss LJ and MacPherson J)

Whether police officer acting in the execution of duty – mistake as to identity of person arrested

Facts
The appellant had been restrained by a police officer who had mistakenly thought that the appellant was under arrest. The appellant, who had remonstrated with the officer and committed an assault, sought to appeal against her conviction for assaulting a police constable in the execution of his duty, contrary to s51(1) of the Police Act 1964.

Held
The appeal was allowed. The police officer had clearly been exceeding his powers in using physical force on the appellant, and had therefore not been acting in the execution of his duty.

R v *Chan-Fook* [1994] 1 WLR 689 Court of Appeal (Hobhouse LJ, Judge and Bell JJ)

Assault occasioning actual bodily harm – nature of actual bodily harm – whether psychiatric harm sufficient

Facts
The appellant suspected that the victim had stolen a ring belonging to the appellant's girlfriend. The victim's evidence was that the appellant had physically assaulted him whilst interrogating him about the disappearance of the ring. It was not disputed that, following the interrogation, the appellant had dragged the victim upstairs to his room and locked him in. Fearing that the appellant would return to carry out a more serious assault, the victim had tried to escape from the room by tying knotted bed sheets to the curtain rail and climbing out of the window. The curtain rail, unable to take the victim's weight, came away from the wall and he suffered a broken wrist and a dislocated pelvis as a result of his fall to the ground. The trial judge left the charge of assault occasioning actual bodily harm, contrary to s47 of the Offences Against the Person Act 1861, to the jury on the basis that, even

if the appellant had not physically assaulted the victim, the nervous hysterical condition induced in the victim by the interrogation, as evidenced by his attempts to escape, could amount to actual bodily harm. The appellant was convicted and appealed.

Held

The appeal was allowed.

Hobhouse LJ:

'[Actual bodily harm] are three words of the English language which require no elaboration and in the ordinary course should not receive any. The word "harm" is a synonym for injury. The word "actual" indicates that the injury (although there is no need for it to be permanent) should not be so trivial as to be wholly insignificant. The purpose of the definition in s47 is to define an element of aggravation in the assault. It must be an assault which besides being an assault (or assault and battery) causes to the victim some injury.

The danger of any elaboration of the words of the statute is that it may have the effect, as was pointed out by the House of Lords, of altering, or at the least distracting the jury from, the ordinary meaning of the words. Further, as can be seen from the summing up in the present case, there may be an elision of the need to show some harm or injury. There will be a risk that language will be used which suggests to the jury that it is sufficient that the assault has interfered with the health or comfort of the victim, whether or not any injury or hurt has been caused. No doubt what is intended by those who have used these words in the past is to indicate that some injury which otherwise might be regarded as wholly trivial is not to be so regarded because it has caused the victim pain. Similarly, an injury can be caused to someone by injuring their health; an assault may have the consequence of infecting the victim with a disease or causing the victim to become ill. The injury may be internal and may not be accompanied by an external injury. A blow may leave no external mark but may cause the victim to lose consciousness.'

Having considered the definition of actual bodily harm provided by Lynskey J in *R v Miller* [1954] 2 QB 282, Hobhouse LJ continued:

'The first question on the present appeal is whether the inclusion of the word "bodily" in the phrase "actual bodily harm" limits harm to harm to the skin, flesh and bones of the victim. Lynskey J rejected this submission. In our judgment he was right to do so. The body of the victim includes all parts of his body, including his organs, his nervous system and his brain. Bodily injury therefore may include injury to any of those parts of his body responsible for his mental and other faculties ...

Accordingly, the phrase "actual bodily harm" is capable of including psychiatric injury. But it does not include mere emotions such as fear or distress nor panic, nor does it include, as such, states of mind that are not themselves evidence of some identifiable clinical condition. The phrase "state of mind" is not a scientific one and should be avoided in considering whether or not a psychiatric injury has been caused; its use is likely to create in the minds of the jury the impression that something which is not more than a strong emotion, such as extreme fear or panic, can amount to actual bodily harm. It cannot. Similarly, juries should not be directed that an assault which causes an hysterical and nervous condition is an assault occasioning actual bodily harm. Where there is evidence that the assault has caused some psychiatric injury, the jury should be directed that the injury is capable of amounting to actual bodily harm; otherwise there should be no reference to the mental state of the victim following the assault unless it be relevant to some other aspect of the case, as it was in *R* v *Roberts* (1971) 56 Cr App R 95. It is also relevant to have in mind the relationship between the offence of aggravated assault comprised in s47 and simple assault. The latter can include conduct which causes the victim to apprehend immediate and unlawful violence: *Fagan* v *Metropolitan Police Commissioner* [1969] 1 QB 439. To treat the victim's fear of such unlawful violence, without more, as amounting to actual bodily harm would be to risk rendering the definition of the aggravated offence academic in many cases.

In any case where psychiatric injury is relied upon as the basis for an allegation of bodily harm, and the matter has not been admitted by the defence, expert evidence should be called by the prosecution. It should not be left to be inferred by the jury from the general facts of the case. In the absence of appropriate expert evidence a question whether or not the assault occasioned psychiatric injury should not be left to the jury. Cases where it is necessary to allege that psychiatric injury has been caused by an assault will be very few and far between. It is to be observed that there has been no reported case on the point since 1953 and the present case was not, on a correct assessment, a case where such an allegation should have been made. But, if there should be such a case, the evidential difficulties will be no greater than juries often have to consider in other aspects of the criminal law, for example, an issue of diminished responsibility. There is no reason for refusing to have regard to psychiatric injury as the consequence of an assault if there is properly qualified evidence that it has occurred.'

R v *Mandair* [1994] 2 WLR 700 House of Lords (Lords Mackay, Templeman, Goff, Browne-Wilkinson and Mustill)

Causing grievous bodily harm – whether a lesser included offence available

Facts

The defendant's wife suffered severe facial burns caused by sulphuric acid. The prosecution case was that he had thrown the acid at her. The defendant contended that the burns had been caused accidentally. On a charge of causing grievous bodily harm with intent contrary to s18 of the Offences Against the Person Act 1861, the jury (following guidance from the trial judge) returned a verdict of guilty on an alternative count of '... causing grievous bodily harm contrary to s20 ...' The defendant appealed successfully on the basis that he had been convicted of an offence unknown to law. The Crown appealed.

Held (Lord Mustill dissenting)

The appeal would be allowed as regards the availability of an alternative verdict under s20. The case would be remitted to the Court of Appeal for consideration of the remaining grounds of appeal (which related to the proper direction on mens rea under s20).

Lord Mackay:

'In my view "cause" in section 18 is certainly sufficiently wide to embrace any method by which grievous bodily harm could be inflicted under section 20 and since causing grievous bodily harm in section 18 is an alternative to wounding I regard it as clear that the word "cause' in section 18 is wide enough to include any action that could amount to inflicting grievous bodily harm under section 20 where the word "inflict" appears as an alternative to "wound". For this reason, in my view, following the reasoning of this House in *R v Wilson (Clarence)* [1984] AC 242 an alternative verdict under section 20 was open on the terms of this indictment.

The Court of Appeal in this case, following an earlier decision in *R v Field* (1992) 97 Cr App R 357, held that the jury had found the defendant guilty of an offence unknown to the law.

In my opinion, as I have said, the word "cause" is wider or at least not narrower than the word "inflict". I consider that the verdict of causing grievous bodily harm contrary to section 20 must be construed as a whole ... Since, as I said, causing grievous bodily harm is used in a sense which distinguishes it from wounding, I can read the verdict as a whole only as meaning that the causing of grievous bodily harm was contrary to section 20 in that it consisted of inflicting grievous bodily harm upon another person. Obviously it is highly desirable in matters of this sort involving the liberty of the subject that the precise words of the statute, so far as relevant, should be used in the jury's verdict but where, as here, the jury has actually returned a verdict which to my mind read as a whole is capable of having a clear meaning it is a technicality to decline to give it meaning because the word "cause" is not used in the section and thereby it is said that the defendant was convicted of an offence unknown to the law. A contravention of section 20 is certainly not an offence unknown to the law and I consider that in the circumstances in which the phrase was used "causing grievous bodily harm contrary to section 20" is perfectly comprehensible as meaning that an infliction of grievous bodily harm in what the defendant did in causing grievous bodily harm was a contravention of section 20.'

Lord Mustill:

'The reappearance of section 20 before your Lordships' House barely two years after it was minutely examined in *R v Parmenter* [1992] 1 AC 699 demonstrates once again that this unsatisfactory statute is long overdue for repeal and replacement by legislation which is soundly based in logic and expressed in language which everyone can understand. Meanwhile we must make of sections 18 and 20, those staples of the Crown Court, the best that we can ... The point is very short and I cannot develop it beyond submitting that whereas in the case of both words there must be a causal connection between the defendant's act and the injury, in the case of the "cause" the nature of the connection is immaterial (provided the chain of events is short enough to satisfy the criminal law of causation), but the word "inflict" conveys the idea of a direct and immediate doing of harm. It is true that in *R v Martin* (1881) 8 QBD 54 and *R v Halliday* (1889) 61 LT 701 injuries suffered when the frightened victim was attempting to escape were assumed to bring the case within section 20; but the point was not raised. On the other hand *R v Clarence* (1888) 22 QBD 23, *R v McCready* [1978] 1 WLR 1376 (which on this point I believe to have survived *Wilson*) and *R v Salisbury* [1976] VR 452, an Australian decision which (if correctly read his speech) was approved by Lord Roskill in *Wilson*, support the narrow reading of "inflict". Opinions to the same effect are contained in the 14th Report of the Criminal Law Revision Committee, Offences against the Person (1980) (Cmnd 7844), pp69–70, para 153; the Report of the Law Commission on Offences against the Person (1993) (Law Com No 218), p18, para 12.15, fn 112; *Archbold, Criminal Pleading Evidence & Practice*, 45th ed, vol 2 (1994), p210, para 19–208, *Smith & Hogan, Criminal Law*, 7th ed (1992) pp425–426; and a case note by Professor JC Smith (as he then was) on *R v Snewing* [1972] Crim LR 267. In addition, this reading was taken for granted by the court in *Field*, in the passage already quoted. Thus, although the distinction is undoubtedly very narrow and often of no practical significance I believe that is none the less real, and therefore reject the submission that the words used by the clerk "causing grievous bodily harm" have exactly the same meaning as "inflicting grievous bodily harm", and that the hypothetical verdicts conveyed by the response of guilty to the two versions of the clerk's question will not have exactly the same meaning.'

R v *Notman* [1994] Crim LR 518 Court of Appeal (Rose LJ, Jowitt and Buxton JJ)

Assault occasioning actual bodily harm – direction on causation

Facts
The appellant had been involved in a fracas at a shop from which he had previously been barred. A police officer was called to the incident, and the appellant charged at him. The officer stuck out his leg to impede the appellant's progress and suffered injury to his ankle. The appellant was charged, inter alia, with assault occasioning actual bodily harm. The trial judge directed the jury that they could convict on the assault charge if they were satisfied that the appellant's actions had been the 'substantial cause' of the officer's injury. The appellant was convicted and appealed on the ground, inter alia, that the judge should have directed the jury in accordance with *R* v *Roberts* (1971) 56 Cr App R 95 on the issue of causation.

Held
The direction on causation had been adequate. Following *R* v *Hennigan* (1971) 55 Cr App R 262, it was sufficient that a trial judge made clear to the jury that the defendant's actions had to be more than a de minimis cause of the injury in question. The expression 'substantial cause' was suitable for these purposes, as it avoided the complexities of legal cause and the rules of remoteness.

26.4 Voluntary manslaughter

R v *Sanderson* (1994) 98 Cr App R 325 Court of Appeal (Criminal Division) (Roch LJ, McCullogh and Alliot JJ)

Diminished responsibility – nature of abnormality of the mind

Facts
The appellant had killed a woman, and at his trial for murder sought to raise the defence of diminished responsibility based on evidence of his long term use of heroin and cocaine. There was a conflict of expert medical evidence as to the relevance of the drug taking as regards diminished responsibility. For the appellant it was contended that he suffered from an abnormality of the mind, namely paranoid psychosis, that arose from inherent causes, such as the appellant's upbringing, and

had been exacerbated by his drug taking. For the Crown it was contended that the appellant did suffer from a form of paranoia that was related to drug use, and that he would not suffer from any paranoia if the drug taking ceased. The appellant was convicted of murder and appealed.

Held

The appeal would be allowed, and a conviction for manslaughter on the grounds of diminished responsibility substituted.

Roch LJ:

"In this case there could not have been any real issue that the appellant, at the time he killed Miss Glasgow, was suffering from an abnormality of mind. He had no reason to want her death apart from his deluded beliefs for weeks. The way in which he inflicted death upon her and his subsequent behaviour all indicated that at the time his judgment and control over his emotions were not those of a normal mind. The first issue which arose on the medical evidence was the nature of that abnormality of mind: was it a paranoid psychosis, that is to say a serious disorder of the mind in which the appellant was suffering from fixed delusions centering around some perverted idea which had some important bearing on his actions, or was he suffering from simple paranoia?

The second issue which arose out of the medical evidence was the cause of the abnormality of mind. Was the abnormality of mind due to inherent causes, the appellant's childhood and upbringing, possibly exacerbated by drug addiction, or simply a side effect or consequence of his drug-taking? It is now well established by authority that for abnormality of the mind to come within the subsection it must be caused by one of the matters listed in the subsection; that is to say it must arise from a condition of arrested or retarded development of mind – of which there is no suggestion in this case – or from inherent causes or be induced by disease or injury.

Dr Bowden's evidence was that the appellant did not have the mental illness of paranoid psychosis and that as far as he was aware medical science showed that the taking of heroin and cocaine could not injure the structures of the brain. Consequently, his evidence was to the effect that the appellant did not and had not had any injury or disease which could have induced the paranoia. Further, his evidence denied that the paranoia arose from inherent cause; it arose simply because the appellant used cocaine. There was no evidence that his use of cocaine was involuntary.

In those circumstances, in our judgment the Common Serjeant was quite correct to direct the jury that if they accepted the evidence of Dr Bowden and rejected that of Dr Coid the defence of diminished responsibility had to fail. In our judgment the jury could not have found that the appellant was suffering from an abnormality of mind within section 2(1) on the evidence of Dr Bowden. Consequently, the first ground of appeal fails.

The Court considers that there is substance in the second and third submissions made by the appellant's counsel, and that for the reasons which we shall give shortly, the jury's verdict in this case is unsafe and unsatisfactory.

Cases of diminished responsibility can become difficult and confusing for a jury, and it is important that the judge in directing the jury should tailor his directions to suit the facts of the particular case. We think it will rarely be helpful to the jury to read to them section 2(1) in its entirety. Further, we consider that Annex F would have been of greater assistance had the words in brackets been confined to "arising from any inherent cause or induced by disease", there being no evidence of arrested or retarded development or of injury.

The judge in his directions to the jury at p9G, which we have already cited, then summarising the defendant's medical evidence and comparing it with the Crown's medical evidence, referred to the abnormality of mind arising from any inherent cause or disease on three occasions. In his final direction to the jury on diminished responsibility at the end of the summing-up, the judge again referred to those two potential causes when he said:

"Has the defendant proved that he was suffering from an abnormality of mind through inherent cause or induced by disease, that is to say a paranoid psychosis which is a mental illness, whether exacerbated by drugs or not?"

Again the jury were being directed to consider whether the abnormality of mind arose either from inherent cause or was induced by disease. Further, that direction was so worded that the jury could understand the disease to be the mental illness of paranoid psychosis.

However, earlier in the summing up, the judge summarised Dr Coid's opinion in this way:

"Dr Coid's opinion was this: 'The defendant was at the time of the killing and is now suffering from paranoid psychosis, a mental illness, forming incorrect and abnormal beliefs about other people. This was there already, irrespective of drug abuse. Although paranoid psychosis can be exacerbated by the use of cocaine over the years and much worse, nonetheless, quite apart from the drugs, paranoid psychosis, the mental illness, was there and that amounted to an abnormality of mind,' which is, when you call it inherent or resulting from disease."

We take it the last part should read: "which it is, whether you call it inherent or resulting from disease."

Thus the jury were being told Dr Coid was saying that the abnormality of mind was paranoid psychosis. In our opinion it was those apparently contradictory directions which must have given rise to the jury's questions. Although their questions are not free from ambiguity the jury were probably asking:

"1. What is meant by induced by disease or injury, that is to say what does induced mean?
2. Is paranoid psychosis a disease or injury which can induce an abnormality of mind?"

The judge interpreted the second question as being: "Can a paranoid psychosis be induced by disease or injury?" and told the jury that he did not know; that "nobody speaks of paranoid psychosis arising from disease of injury." That was simply not correct.

The judge had summarised the appellant's doctor's evidence at p9H:

"It is said for the defence through Dr Coid that there was an underlying paranoid psychosis or mental illness which amounted to an abnormality of mind within the Act. It arose from an inherent cause or disease of long-standing."

Again, at p23E in summarising Dr Coid's evidence the judge told the jury that Dr Coid was saying that paranoid psychosis amounted to an abnormality of mind which it was whether one said it arose from inherent cause or was induced by disease.

The judge should have sought clarification of the jury's questions, and then, if the real difficulty was whether the mental illness or paranoid psychosis was a disease within the meaning of the subsection, he should have directed them that the medical evidence they had was that this abnormality of mind was the mental illness of paranoid psychosis, if Dr Coid was right, and if Dr Coid was correct as to the aetiology of that mental illness, then it came within the words: "arising from any inherent cause" and was therefore within the subsection. In our judgment the answers that the judge gave failed to answer the questions which we believe the jury were asking, and would, in any event have confused them rather than have helped them.

Mr Worsley for the Crown submits that the central issue was left to the jury. The judge finally left to the jury the substantive defence which the appellant was raising. The jury were being told, correctly, that if they accepted Dr Coid's evidence, then the defence, subject to their view on the second question set out in Annex F, would succeed, whereas if they preferred Dr Bowden's evidence, the defence failed. Thus, submits Mr Worsley, even if the questions had been clarified and direct answers given, the jury's verdict would have been the same. He invites us to apply the proviso.

To that submission, Mr Jones replied that the questions themselves showed that the jury were inclined to accept that there was a paranoid psychosis, ie Dr Coid's evidence, rather than Dr Bowden's simple paranoia resulting from the taking of cocaine. The jury's concern was whether the paranoid psychosis came within the subsection. The jury should have been directed that the paranoid psychosis described by Dr Coid could, as a matter of law, come within the subsection. Had that direction been given, the probable verdict would have been one of manslaughter.

We agree with that submission by Mr Jones.

Before concluding this judgment, the Court pays tribute to the arguments of both counsel, and especially to the submissions of Mr Jones, who took us to the legislation on mental deficiency preceding the 1957 Act and two lines of authorities. The first was cases such as *Seers* (1984) 79 Cr App R 261, 264, on the nature and degree of impairment of mental responsibility which is within the section, and the second, cases where the defendant had been abusing drugs or alcohol, such as *Fenton* (1975) 61 Cr App R 261 and *Tandy* (1988) 87 Cr App R 45.

Mr Jones submitted that "disease" in the phrase "disease or injury" in section 2(1) meant "disease of the mind" and was apt to cover mental illnesses which were functional as well as those which were organic. This interesting and difficult question does not, in our view, require an answer in this case. We content ourselves with observing that we did not find the pre-1957 Act authority particularly persuasive in deciding what is meant by "disease or injury" in section 2(1) of the 1957 Act because those authorities were concerned with the meaning of words used by judges to delimit the special defence of insanity which originally resulted in a verdict of guilty by reason of insanity and lead to the defendant being sent to a secure mental institution. We incline to the view that that phrase "induced by disease or injury" must refer to organic or physical injury or disease of the body including the brain, and that that is more probable because Parliament deliberately refrained from referring to the disease of, or injury to, the mind, but included as permissible causes of an abnormality of mind " any inherent cause" which would cover functional mental illness.

For those reasons we allow this appeal, quash the conviction of murder and substitute the conviction of manslaughter.'

26.5 Involuntary manslaughter

R v *Adomako* [1994] 3 WLR 288 House of Lords (Lords Mackay, Keith, Goff, Browne-Wilkinson and Woolf)

Killing by gross negligence – fault required

Facts
The defendant was a locum tenens anaesthetist employed at a hospital. He was assisting during an operation on a patient for a detached retina. During the operation the tube from the patient's ventilator became detached. By the time the defendant became aware that something had gone wrong, the damage caused to the patient had become irreversible and he died. The defendant was convicted of manslaughter following a direction from the trial judge, in terms of gross negligence as the basis for liability rather than recklessness. Lord Taylor CJ summarised the ingredients of the offence as follows: proof of the existence of the duty, breach of the duty causing death, and gross negligence. Gross negligence could be any of the following (i) indifference to an obvious risk of injury to health; (ii) foreseeing the risk and determining to run it; (iii) appreciating the risk, intending to avoid it, but displaying a high degree of negligence in the adoption of avoidance techniques; (iv) failure to advert to a serious risk that goes beyond 'mere inadvertence' and which D should have adverted to because of the duty he was under.

Following an unsuccessful appeal the Court of Appeal certified the following point of law of general public importance for consideration by the House of Lords: 'In cases of manslaughter by gross negligence not involving driving but involving a breach of duty is it a sufficient direction to the jury to adopt the gross negligence test set out by the Court of Appeal in the present case following *R* v *Bateman* (1925) 19 Cr App R 8 and *Andrews* v *DPP* [1937] AC 576 without reference to the test of recklessness as defined in *R* v *Lawrence* 1982 AC 510 or as adapted to the circumstances of the case?'

Held
The appeal would be dismissed, the certified question being answered in the affirmative.

Extracts from the judgment:

Lord Mackay (having referred to *R* v *Bateman* (1925) 19 Cr App R 8 and *Andrews* v *DPP* [1937] AC 576) observed at p295–298):

'In my opinion the law as stated in these two authorities is satisfactory as providing a proper basis for describing the crim of involuntary manslaughter. Since the decision in *Andrews* was a decision of your Lordships' House, it remains the most authoritative statement of the present law which I have been able to find and although its relationship to *R* v *Seymour (Edward)* [1983] 2 AC 493 is a matter to which I shall have to return, it is a decision which has not been departed from. On this basis in my opinion the ordinary principles of the law of negligence apply to ascertain whether or not the defendant has been in breach of a duty of care towards the victim who has died. If such breach of duty is established the next question is whether that breach of duty caused the death of the victim. If so, the jury must go on to consider whether that breach of duty should be characterised as gross negligence and therefore as a crime. This will depend on the seriousness of the breach of duty committed by the defendant in all the circumstances in which the defendant was placed when it occurred. The jury will have to consider whether the extent to which the defendant's conduct departed from the proper standard of care incumbent upon him, involving as it must have done a risk of death to the patient, was such that it should be judged criminal.

It is true that to a certain extent this involves an element of circularity, but in this branch of the law I do not believe that is fatal to its being correct as a test of how far conduct must depart from accepted standards to be characterised as criminal. This is necessarily a question of degree and an attempt to specify that degree more closely is I think likely to achieve only a spurious precision. The essence of the matter which is supremely a jury question is whether having regard to the risk of death involved, the conduct of the defendant was so bad in all the circumstances as to amount in their judgment to a criminal act or omission.

My Lords, the view which I have stated of the correct basis in law for the crime of involuntary manslaughter accords I consider with the criteria stated by counsel, although I have not reached the degree of precision in definition which he required, but in my opinion it has been reached so far as practicable and with a result which leaves the matter properly stated for a jury's determination.

My Lords in my view the law as stated in *R v Seymour (Edward)* [1983] 2 AC 493 should no longer apply since the underlying statutory provisions on which it rested have now been repealed by the Road Traffic Act 1991. It may be that cases of involuntary motor manslaughter will as a result become rare but I consider it unsatisfactory that there should be any exception to the generality of the statement which I have made, since such exception, in my view, gives rise to unnecessary complexity. For example in *Kong Cheuk Kwan v The Queen* (1985) 82 Cr App R 18 it would give rise to unnecessary differences between the law applicable to those navigating vessels and the lookouts on the vessels.

I consider it perfectly appropriate that the word "reckless" should be used in cases of involuntary manslaughter, but as Lord Atkin put it "in the ordinary connotation of that word". Examples in which this was done, to my mind, with complete accuracy are *R v Stone* [1977] QB 354 and *R v West London Coroner, ex parte Gray* [1988] QB 467.

In my opinion it is quite unnecessary in the context of gross negligence to give the detailed directions with regard to the meaning of the word "reckless" associated with *R v Lawrence (Stephen)* [1982] AC 510. The decision of the Court of Appeal Criminal Division in the other cases with which they were concerned at the same time as they heard the appeal in this case indicates that the circumstances in which involuntary manslaughter has to be considered may make the somewhat elaborate and rather rigid directions inappropriate. I entirely agree with the view that the circumstances to which a charge of involuntary manslaughter may apply are so various that it is unwise to attempt to categorise or detail specimen directions. For my part I would not wish to go beyond the description of the basis in law which I have already given.

In my view the summing up of the judge in the present case was a model of clarity in analysis of the facts and in setting out the law in a manner which was readily comprehensible by the jury. The summing up was criticised in respect of the inclusion of the following passage:

"Of course you will understand it is not for every humble man of the profession to have all that great skill of the great men in Harley Street but, on the other hand, they are not allowed to practise medicine in this country unless they have acquired a certain amount of skill. They are bound to show a reasonable amount of skill according to the circumstances of the case, and you have to judge them on the basis that they are skilled men, but not necessarily so skilled as more skilful men in the profession, and you can only convict them criminally if, in your judgment, they fall below the standard of skill which is the least qualification which any doctor should have. You should only convict a doctor of causing a death by negligence if you think he did something which no reasonably skilled doctor should have done."

The criticism was particularly of the latter part of this quotation in that it was open to the meaning that if the defendant did what no reasonably skilled doctor should have done it was open to the jury to convict him of causing death by negligence. Strictly speaking this passage is concerned with the statement of a necessary condition for a conviction by preventing a conviction unless that condition is satisfied. It is incorrect to treat it as stating a sufficient condition for conviction. In any event I consider that this passage in the context was making the point forcefully that the defendant in this case was not to be judged by the standard of more skilled doctors but by the standard of a reasonably competent doctor. There were many other passages in the summing up which emphasised the need for a high degree of negligence if the jury were to convict and read in that context I consider that the summing up cannot be faulted.

For these reasons I am of the opinion that this appeal should be dismissed and that the certified question should be answered by saying:

"In cases of manslaughter by criminal negligence involving a breach of duty, it is a sufficient direction to the jury to adopt the gross negligence test set out by the Court of Appeal in the present case following *R* v *Bateman* 19 Cr App R and *Andrews* v *Director of Public Prosecutions* [1937] AC 576 and that it is not necessary to refer to the definition of recklessness in *R* v *Lawrence* [1982] AC 510, although it is perfectly open to the trial judge to use the word 'reckless' in its ordinary meaning as part of his exposition of the law if he deems it appropriate in the circumstances of the particular case."

We have been referred to the Consultation Paper by the Law Commission on Criminal Law, Involuntary Manslaughter (1994) (Law Com No 135), and we have also been referred to a number of standard textbooks. I have also had the opportunity of considering the note on *R* v *Prentice* by Sir John Smith [1994] Crim LR 292 since the hearing was completed. Whilst I have not referred to these in detail I have derived considerable help in seeking to formulate my view as a result of studying them.

I have reached the same conclusion on the basic law to be applied in this case as did the Court of Appeal. Personally I would not wish to state the law more elaborately than I have done. In particular I think it is difficult to take expressions used in particular cases out of the context of the cases in which they were used and enunciate them as if applying generally. This can I think lead to ambiguity and perhaps unnecessary complexity. The task of trial judges in setting out for the jury the issues of fact and the relevant law in cases of this class is a difficult and demanding one. I believe that the supreme test that should be satisfied in such directions is that they are comprehensible to an ordinary member of the public who is called to sit on a jury and who has no particular prior acquaintance with the law. To make it obligatory on trial judges to give directions in law which are so elaborate that the ordinary member of the jury will have great difficulty in following them, and even greater difficulty in retaining them in his memory for the purpose of application in the jury room, is no service to the cause of justice. The experienced counsel who assisted your Lordships in this appeal indicated that as a practical matter there was a danger in over elaboration of definition of the word "reckless". While therefore I have said in my view it is perfectly open to a trial judge to use the word "reckless" if it appears appropriate in the circumstances of a particular case as indicating the extent to which a defendant's conduct must deviate from that of a proper standard of care, I do not think it right to require that this should be done and certainly not right that it should incorporate the full detail required in *Lawrence.*'

26.6 Inchoate offences

Attorney-General's Reference (No 3 of 1992) [1994] 1 WLR 409 Court of Appeal (Lord Taylor CJ, Schiemann and Wright JJ)

Attempted arson – whether recklessness as to life being endangered sufficient

Facts

The respondents had thrown a petrol bomb from a moving car towards a stationary car. The stationary car was occupied and there were persons nearby on the pavement. The petrol bomb missed the stationary car and hit a wall behind it. The respondents were charged with attempted aggravated arson, contrary to s1(2) of the Criminal Damage Act 1971, one count alleging recklessness as to whether life would be endangered. The trial judge directed that the respondents be acquitted on the ground that the endangering of life was a consequence of criminal damage under the aggravated offence, and thus recklessness was not sufficient mens rea where the charge was one of attempt.

The following question was referred to the Court of Appeal:

'Whether on a charge of attempted arson in the aggravated form contemplated by s1(2) of the Criminal Damage Act 1971, in addition to establishing a specific intent to cause damage by fire, it is sufficient to prove that the defendant was reckless as to whether life would thereby be endangered.'

Held

The certified question was answered in the affirmative.

Lord Taylor CJ:

'... In the present case, what was missing to prevent a conviction for the completed offence was damage to the property referred to in the opening lines of section 1(2) of the Act of 1981, what in the example of a crane, which we gave earlier in this judgment, we referred to as "the first named property". Such damage is essential for the completed offence. If a defendant does not intend to cause such damage he cannot intend to commit the completed offence. At worse he is reckless as to whether the offence is committed. The law of attempt is concerned with those who are intending to commit crimes. If that intent cannot be shown, then there can be no conviction.

However, the crime here consisted of doing certain acts in a certain state of mind in circumstances where the first named property and the second named property were the same, in short where the danger to life arose from the damage to the property which the defendant intended to damage. The substantive crime is committed if the defendant damaged property in a state of mind where he was reckless as to whether the life of another would thereby be endangered. We see no reason why there should not be a conviction for attempt if the prosecution can show that he, in that state of mind, intended to damage the property by throwing a bomb at it. One analysis of this situation is to say that although the defendant was in an appropriate state of mind to render him guilty of the completed offence the prosecution had not proved the physical element of the completed offence, and therefore he is not guilty of the completed offence. If, on a charge of attempting to commit the offence, the prosecution can show not only the state of mind required for the completed offence but also that the defendant intended to supply the missing physical element of the completed offence, that suffices for a conviction. That cannot be done merely by the prosecution showing him to be reckless. The defendant must intend to damage property, but there is no need for a graver mental state than is required for the full offence.

The trial judge in the present case, however, went further than this, and held that not merely must the defendant intend to supply all that was missing from the completed offence – namely, damage to the first named property – but also that recklessness as to the consequences of such damage for the lives of others was not enough to secure a conviction for attempt, although it was sufficient for the completed offence. She held that before a defendant could be convicted of attempting to commit the offence it had to be shown that he intended that the lives of others should be endangered by the damage which he intended.

She gave no policy reasons for so holding, and there is no case which bound her so to hold. The most nearly relevant case is *R v Khan (Mohammed Iqbal)* [1990] 1 WLR 813 ...

... An attempt was made in argument to suggest that *R v Khan (Mohammed Iqbal)* was wrongly decided. No policy reasons were advanced for that view, and we do not share it. The result is one which accords with common sense, and does no violence to the words of the statute.

What was missing in *R v Khan (Mohammed Iqbal)* was the act of sexual intercourse, without which the offence was not completed. What was missing in the present case was damage to the first named property, without which the offence was not complete. The mental state of the defendant in each case contained everything which was required to render him guilty of the full offence. In order to succeed in a prosecution for attempt, it must be shown that the defendant intended to achieve that which was missing from the full offence. Unless that is shown, the prosecution have not proved that the defendant intended to commit the offence. Thus in *R v Khan (Mohammed Iqbal)* [1990] 1 WLR 813 the prosecution had to show an intention to have sexual intercourse, and the remaining state of mind required for the offence of rape. In the present case, the prosecution had to show an intention to damage the first named property, and the remaining state of mind required for the offence of aggravated arson.

The judge in the instant case was faced, as we have been faced, not only with citations of views held by the Law Commission at one time on what should be the law of attempt (Law Commission Report on Criminal Law: Attempt and Impossibility (1980) (Law Com No 102)), but also with various articles in legal journals and books commenting on those views. It is right to say that at one time it was proposed that intention should be required as to all the elements of an offence, thus making it impossible to secure a conviction of attempt in circumstances such as the present. However, this proposal has not prevailed, and has been overtaken by *R v Khan (Mohammed Iqbal)*, and a formulation of the draft code which does not incorporate the proposal.

While the judge in the instant case opined that *R v Khan (Mohammed Iqbal)* was distinguishable she did not indicate any policy reasons for distinguishing it. We see none, and none has been submitted to us directly.'

Yip Chiu-Cheung v *R* [1994] 3 WLR 514 Privy Council (Lords Jauncey, Griffiths, Browne-Wilkinson, Mustill and Slynn)

Conspiracy – whether undercover agent has mens rea

Facts

The appellant had entered into an agreement with N, an undercover police officer, whereby N would fly from Australia to Hong Kong, collect a consignment of heroin from the appellant, and return with it to Australia. N kept the Australian and Hong Kong authorities fully informed of the agreement, and they undertook to allow him free passage from Hong Kong and into Australia. The purpose of N's mission was to identify not only the suppliers of the drug in Hong Kong, but also the dealers in Australia. N in fact missed his flight to Hong Kong and proceeded no further with the plan to meet the appellant.

In due course, however, the appellant was charged with, and convicted of, conspiring to traffic in dangerous drugs. He appealed on the ground that there could be no conspiracy given that his co-conspirator, N, had been acting to promote law enforcement, and that N's purpose had been to expose drug-trafficking. The appeal was dismissed by the Court of Appeal of Hong Kong and renewed before the Privy Council.

Held

The appeal would be dismissed.

Lord Griffiths:

'... it was submitted that the trial judge and the Court of Appeal were wrong to hold that Needham, the undercover agent, could be a conspirator because he lacked the necessary mens rea or guilty mind required for the offence of conspiracy. It was urged upon their Lordships that no moral guilt attached to the undercover agent who was at all times acting courageously and with the best of motives in attempting to infiltrate and bring to justice a gang of criminal drug dealers. In these circumstances it was argued that it would be wrong to treat the agent as having any criminal intent, and reliance was placed upon a passage in the speech of Lord Bridge of Harwich in *R v Anderson (William Ronald)* [1986] AC 27, 38–39; but in that case Lord Bridge was dealing with a different situation from that which exists in the present case. There may be many cases in which undercover police officers or other law enforcement agents pretend to join a conspiracy in order to gain information about the plans of the criminals, with no intention of taking any part in the planned crime but rather with the intention of providing information that will frustrate it. It was to this situation that Lord Bridge was referring in *R v Anderson*. The crime of conspiracy requires an agreement between two or more persons to commit an unlawful act with the intention of carrying it out. It is the intention to carry out the crime that constitutes the necessary mens rea for th offence. As Lord Bridge pointed out, an undercover agent who has no intention of committing the crime lacks the necessary mens rea to be a conspirator.

The facts of the present case are quite different. Nobody can doubt that Needham was acting courageously and with the best motives; he was trying to break a drug ring. But equally there can be no doubt that the method he chose and in which the police in Hong Kong acquiesced involved the commission of the criminal offence of trafficking in drugs by exporting heroin from Hong Kong without a licence. Needham intended to commit that offence by carrying the heroin through customs and on to the aeroplane bound for Australia.

Neither the police, nor customs, nor any other member of the executive have any power to alter the terms of the Ordinance forbidding the export of heroin, and the fact that they may turn a blind eye when the heroin is exported does not prevent it from being a criminal offence.

The High Court of Australia in *A v Hayden (No 2)* (1984) 156 CLR 532 declared emphatically that there was no place for a general defence of superior orders or of Crown or executive fiat in Australian criminal law. Gibbs CJ said, at p540:

> "It is fundamental to our legal system that the executive has no power to authorise a breach of the law and that it is no excuse for an offender to say that he acted under the orders of a superior officer."

This statement of the law applies with the same force in England and Hong Kong as it does in Australia.

Naturally, Needham never expected to be prosecuted if he carried out the plan as intended. But the fact that in such circumstances the authorities would not prosecute the undercover agent does not mean that he did not commit the crime albeit as part of a wider scheme to combat drug dealing.'

26.7 Defences

R v Horne [1994] Crim LR 584 Court of Appeal (Russell LJ, Smith and Dyson JJ)

Duress caused by threats – objective test – relevant characteristics of the accused

Facts
The appellant was charged with obtaining welfare benefits by deception. There was evidence that he had been pressurised into committing the offences, and although he had not been directly threatened with violence, one of his co-conspirators referred to a drug-dealer that he knew who was willing to 'sort people out'. The implication was that the appellant might be subjected to violence if he did not go through with the scheme. During the trial counsel for the appellant sought to admit expert psychiatric evidence relating to the likely effect of this pressure upon the appellant. The trial judge refused to admit the evidence, the appellant was convicted, and appealed to the Court of Appeal.

Held

The appeal was dismissed. The trial judge had correctly applied the law as laid down in *R* v *Graham* (1982) 74 Cr App R 235, to the effect that D was to be judged according to the standards of the person of reasonable firmness, ie an average member of the public, sharing the characteristics of D. The key question related to the scope of the term 'characteristics'. Given that the reasonable person was of average fortitude, it would have been a contradiction in terms to ask the jury to assess the expert evidence of the appellant's personal vulnerability or pliancy falling short of psychiatric illness.

R v *Kingston* [1994] 3 WLR 519 House of Lords (Lords Keith, Goff, Browne-Wilkinson, Mustill and Slynn)

Involuntary intoxication – whether a defence

Facts

The respondent, a homosexual paedophile who had committed an indecent assault on a 15-year-old boy, claimed that prior to these acts he had been drugged by his co-defendant, and could not recall the incident. There was a difference of medical opinion as to the extent to which the drugs, believed to have been consumed by the respondent, would have affected his ability to recall the incident. However, there was no evidence to suggest that the drugs would have made the respondent do anything he would not have done under normal circumstances. The trial judge ruled that whilst it was not open to the jury to acquit the respondent if they found that his intent to commit the indecent assault had been induced by the surreptitious administration of drugs by his co-defendant, it was open to them to find that secretly administered drugs could negative the respondent's mens rea. The respondent appealed successfully to the Court of Appeal.

The prosecution appealed to the House of Lords.

Held

The appeal would be allowed.

Lord Mustill (having reviewed the facts, his Lordship continued):

'On these facts there are three grounds on which the respondent might be held free from criminal responsibility. First, that his immunity flows from general principles of the criminal law. Secondly, that this immunity is already established by a solid line of authority. Finally, that the court should, when faced with a new problem acknowledge the justice of the case and boldly create a new common law defence.

It is clear from the passage already quoted that the Court of Appeal adopted the first approach. The decision was explicitly founded on general principle. There can be no doubt what principle the court relied upon, for at the outset the court [1994] QB 81, 87, recorded the submission of counsel for the respondent:

"the law recognises that, exceptionally, an accused person may be entitled to be acquitted if there is a possibility that although his act was intentional, the intent itself arose out of circumstances for which he bears no blame."

The same proposition is implicit in the assumption by the court that if blame is absent the necessary mens rea must also be absent.

My Lords, with every respect I must suggest that no such principle exists or, until the present case, had ever in modern times been thought to exist. Each offence consists of a prohibited act or omission coupled with whatever state of mind is called for by the statute or rule of the common law which creates the offence. In those offences which are not absolute the state of mind which the prosecution must prove to have underlain the act or omission – the "mental element" – will in the majority of cases be such as to attract disapproval. The mental element will then be the mark of what may properly be called a "guilty mind". The professional burglar is guilty in a moral as well as a legal sense; he intends to break into the house to steal, and most would confidently assert that this is wrong. But this will not always be so. In respect of some offences the mind of the defendant, and still less his moral judgment, may not be engaged at all. In others, although a mental activity must be the motive power for the prohibited act or omission the activity may be of such a kind or degree that society at large could not criticise the defendant's conduct severely or even criticise it at all. Such cases are not uncommon. Yet to assume that contemporary moral judgments affect the criminality of the act, as distinct from the punishment appropriate to the crime once proved, is to be misled by the expression "mens rea", the ambiguity of which has been the subject of complaint for more than a century. Certainly, the "mens" of the defendant must usually be involved in the offence; but the epithet "rea" refers to the criminality of the act in which the mind is engaged, not to its moral character.'

His Lordship referred to the Privy Council decision in *Yip Chiu-Cheung* v *R* [1994] 3 WLR 514, and concluded:

'I would therefore reject that part of the respondent's argument which treats the absence of moral fault on the part of the appellant as sufficient in itself to negative the necessary mental element of the offence.'

Having considered the respondent's arguments based on *Pearson's Case* 2 Lew 144, and *Hale's Historia Placiforum Coronae*, he continued:

'There is, however, another line of authority to be considered, for it is impossible to consider the exceptional case of involuntary intoxication without placing it in the context of intoxication as a whole. This area of the law is controversial, as regards the content of the rules, their intellectual foundations, and their capacity to furnish a practical and just solution. Since the law was not explored in depth during the arguments and since it is relevant only as part of the background it is better not to say any more about it than is strictly necessary. Some consideration of the law laid down in *R* v *Majewski* [1977] AC 443 is however inevitable. As I understand the position it is still the law that in the exceptional case where intoxication causes insanity the M'Naghten Rules (*M'Naghten's Case* (1843) 10 Cl & F 200) apply: see *Director of Public Prosecutions* v *Beard* [1920] AC 479, 501 and *Attorney-General for Northern Ireland* v *Gallagher* [1963] AC 349. Short of this, it is no answer for the defendant to say that he would not have done what he did had he been sober, provided always that whatever element of intent is required by the offence is proved to have been present. As was said in *R* v *Sheehan* [1975] 1 WLR 739, 744C, "a drunken intent is nevertheless an intent". As to proof of intent, it appears that at least in some instances self-induced intoxication can be taken into account as part of the evidence from which the jury draws its conclusions; but that in others it cannot. I express the matter in this guarded way because it has not yet been decisively established whether for this purpose there is a line to be drawn between offences of "specific" and of "basic" intent. That in at least some cases a defendant cannot say that he was so drunk that he could not form the required intent is however clear enough. Why is this so? The answer must I believe be the same as that given in other common law jurisdictions: namely that such evidence is excluded as a matter of policy ...

... There remains the question by what reasoning the House put this policy into effect. As I understand it two different rationalisations were adopted. First that the absence of the necessary consent is cured by treating the intentional drunkenness (or more accurately, since it is only in the minority of cases that the drinker sets out to make himself drunk, the intentional taking of drink without regard to its possible effects) as a substitute for the mental element ordinarily required by the offence. The intent is transferred from the taking of drink to the commission of the prohibited act. The second rationalisation is that the defendant cannot be heard to rely on the absence of the mental element when it is absent because of his own voluntary acts. Borrowing an expression from a far distant field it may be said that the defendant is estopped from relying on his self-induced incapacity.

Your Lordships are not required to decide how these two explanations stand up to attack, for they are not attacked here. The task is only to place them in the context of an intoxication which is not voluntary. Taking first the concept of transferred intent, if the intoxication was not the result of an act done with an informed will there is no intent which can be transferred to the prohibited act, so as to fill the gap in the offence. As regards the "estoppel" there is no reason why the law should preclude the defendant from relying on a mental condition which he had not deliberately brought about. Thus, once the involuntary nature of the intoxication is added the two theories of *Majewski* fall away, and the position reverts to what it would have been if *Majewski* [1977] AC 443 had not been decided, namely that the offence is not made out if the defendant was so intoxicated that he could not form an intent. Thus, where the intoxication is involuntary *Majewski* does not *subtract* the defence of absence of intent; but there is nothing in *Majewsjki* to suggest that where intent is proved involuntary intoxication *adds* a further defence.

My Lords, in the absence of guidance from English authorities it is useful to inquire how other common law jurisdictions have addressed the same problem.'

His Lordship reviewed the relevant Scottish authorities and continued:

'My Lords, I cannot find in this material any sufficient grounds for holding that the defence relied upon is already established by the common law, any more than it can be derived from general principles. Accordingly, I agree with the analysis of Professor Griew, Archbold News, 28 May 1993, pp4–5:

"What has happened is that the Court of Appeal has recognised a new *defence* to criminal charges in the nature of an exculpatory excuse. It is precisely because the defendant acted in the prohibited way with the intent (the mens rea) required by the definition of the offence that he needs this defence."

There is thus a crucial difference between the issue raised by the second line of argument and that now under scrutiny. As to the former, the Law Commission aptly said, in Consultation Paper No 127 (1993) on Intoxication and Criminal Liability, pp4–5, para 1.12:

"The person who commits criminal acts while he is intoxicated, at least when he is voluntarily so intoxicated, does not therefore appeal to excuse; but rather raises the prior question of whether, because of his intoxicated state, he can be proved to have been in the (subjective) state of mind for liability. Issues of intoxication are, thus, intimately bound up with the prosecution's task of proving the primary guilt of the defendant: that he did indeed do the act prohibited by the definition of the offence with the relevant state of mind."

By contrast, the excuse of involuntary intoxication, if it exists, is superimposed on the ordinary law of intent.

To recognise a new defence of this type would be a bold step. The common law defences of duress and necessity (if it exists) and the limited common law defence of provocation are all very old. Since counsel for the appellant was not disposed to emphasise this aspect of the appeal the subject was not explored in argument, but I suspect that the recognition of a new general defence at common law has not happened in modern times. Nevertheless, the criminal law must not stand still, and if it is both practical and just to take this step, and if judicial decision rather than legislation is the proper medium, then the courts should not be deterred simply by the novelty of it. So one must turn to consider just what defence is now to be created. The judgment under appeal implies five characteristics.

1. The defence applies to all offences, except perhaps to absolute offences. It therefore differs from other defences such as provocation and diminished responsibility.

2. The defence is a complete answer to a criminal charge. If not rebutted it leads to an outright acquittal, and unlike provocation and diminished responsibility leaves no room for conviction and punishment for a lesser offence. The underlying assumption must be that the defendant is entirely free from culpability.

3. It may be that the defence applies only where the intoxication is due to the wrongful act of another and therefore affords no excuse when, in circumstances of no greater culpability, the defendant has intoxicated himself by mistake (such as by shortsightedly taking the wrong drug). I say that this may be so, because it is not clear whether, since the doctrine was founded in part of the dictum of Park J in *Pearson's Case*, 2 Lew 144, the "fraud or stratagem of another" is an essential element, or whether this was taken as an example of a wider principle.

4. The burden of disproving the defence is on the prosecution.

5. The defence is subjective in nature. Whereas provocation and self-defence are judged by the reactions of the reasonable person in the situation of the defendant, here the only question is whether this particular defendant's inhibitions were overcome by the effect of the drug. The more susceptible the defendant to the kind of temptation presented, the easier the defence is to establish.

My Lords, since the existence or otherwise of the defence has been treated in argument at all stages as a matter of existing law the Court of Appeal had no occasion to consider the practical and theoretical implications of recognising this new defence at common law, and we do not have the benefit of its views. In their absence, I can only say that the defence appears to run into difficulties at every turn. In point of theory, it would be necessary to reconcile a defence of irresistible impulse derived from a combination of innate drives and external disinhibition with the rule that irresistible impulse of a solely internal origin (not necessarily any more the fault of the offender) does not in itself excuse although it may be a symptom of a disease of the mind: *Attorney-General for South Australia* v *Brown* [1960] AC 432. Equally, the state of mind which founds the defence superficially resembles a state of diminished responsibility, whereas the effect in law is quite different. It may well be that the resemblance is misleading, but these and similar problems must be solved before the bounds of a new defence can be set.

On the practical side there are serious problems. Before the jury could form an opinion on whether the drug might have turned the scale witnesses would have to give a picture of the defendant's personality and susceptibilities, for without it the crucial effect of the drug could not be assessed; pharmacologists would be required to describe the potentially disinhibiting effect of a range of drugs whose identity would, if the present case is anything to go by, be unknown; psychologists and psychiatrists would express opinions, not on the matters of psychopathology familiar to those working within the framework of the Mental Health Acts but on altogether more elusive concepts. No doubt as time passed those concerned could work out techniques to deal with these questions. Much more significant would be the opportunities for a spurious defence. Even in the field of road traffic the "spiked" drink as a special reason for not disqualifying from driving is a regular feature. Transferring this to the entire range of criminal offences is a disturbing prospect. The defendant would only have to assert, and support by the evidence of well-wishers, that he was not the sort of person to have done this kind of thing, and to suggest an occasion when by some means a drug might have been administered to him for the jury to be sent straight to the question of a possible disinhibition. The judge would direct the jurors that if they felt any legitimate doubt on the matter – and by its nature the defence would be one which the prosecution would often have no means to rebut – they must acquit outright, all questions of intent, mental capacity and the like being at this stage irrelevant.

My Lords, the fact that a new doctrine may require adjustment of existing principles to accommodate it, and may require those involved in criminal trials to learn new techniques, is not of course a ground for refusing to adopt it, if that is what the interests of justice require. Here, however, justice makes no such demands, for the interplay between the wrong done to the victim, the individual characteristics and frailties of the defendant, and the pharmacological effects of whatever drug may be potentially involved can be far better recognised by a tailored choice from the continuum of sentences available to the judge than by the application of a single yea-or-nay jury decision. To this, there is one exception. The mandatory life sentence for murder, at least as present administered, leaves no room for the trial judge to put into practice an informed and sympathetic assessment of the kind just described. It is for this reason alone that I have felt any hesitation about rejecting the argument for the respondent. In the end however I have concluded that this is not a sufficient reason to force on the theory and practice of the criminal law an exception which would otherwise be unjustified. For many years mandatory sentences have impelled juries to return merciful but false verdicts, and have stimulated the creation of partial defences such as provocation and diminished responsibility whose lack of a proper foundation has made them hard to apply in practice. I do not think it right that the law should be further distorted simply because of this anomalous relic of the history of the criminal law.

All this being said, I suggest to your Lordships that the existing work of the Law Commission in the field of intoxication could usefully be enlarged to comprise questions of the type raised by this appeal, and to see whether by statute a merciful, realistic and intellectually sustainable solution could be newly created. For the present, however, I consider that no such regime now exists, and that the common law is not a suitable vehicle for creating one.'

26.8 Property belonging to another

R v *Dubar* [1994] 1 WLR 1484 Courts-Martial Appeal Court (Farquharson LJ, McKinnon and Laws JJ)

Theft Act 1968 – s5(3) – proper direction

Facts

The appellant, a sailor on *HMS Battleaxe*, had been contacted by a fellow sailor, Spratt, who wanted to purchase a car. The appellant indicated that he had some useful contacts in the motor trade, and in due course stated that he could obtain a second-hand Ford car for Spratt for £1,800. Spratt handed the money to the appellant in cash. The appellant, who failed to provide the car and did not repay the £1,800, was convicted of theft following trial at a Naval Court-Martial. The appellant sought to challenge his conviction on two grounds:

1. That the judge-advocate had misdirected the court as to s5(3) of the Theft Act 1968 by stating that if the court was satisfied as to certain facts then, as a matter of law, the appellant was under a duty to deal with Spratt's money in a particular way. The appellant contended that, on the basis of *R* v *Hayes* (1976) 64 Cr App R 82 and *R* v *Hall* [1973] QB 126, the judge-advocate should have directed the court to determine the facts concerning the agreement between the appellant and Spratt regarding how the money should be dealt with and then invited the court to determine whether or not the agreement gave rise to a legal obligation within the terms of s5(3).

2. That the judge-advocate may have wrongly failed to direct the court as to when the alleged appropriation of Spratt's money occurred.

Held

The appeal was allowed. As regards the proper direction to be given in determining whether or not an obligation arose for the purposes of s5(3), there were irreconcilable differences between the approach of Lawton LJ in *R* v *Mainwaring* (1981) 74 Cr App R 99, and the approach of Edmund-Davies LJ in *Hall* (above), which had in turn been approved by Lord Widgery CJ in *Hayes* (above). The judge-advocate had correctly expressed the law by directing the court that if it found certain facts to be made out then, *as a matter of law*, an obligation arose to which s5(3) applied. Thus *Mainwaring* was to be followed in preference to the obiter dicta in *Hall* and *Hayes*.

Given, however, that the evidence contained in bank statements revealed that by 31 January 1992 the appellant had paid the £1,800 into his bank account and subsequently withdrawn sums that made the account overdrawn, the appropriation of the £1,800 must have occurred by 31 January. The judge-advocate's direction to the effect that the court had to be satisfied that the appropriation had occurred by 15 May (the date of the appellant's arrest) was therefore a misdirection that rendered the conviction unsafe and unsatisfactory, as the court may have been persuaded that the appellant's dishonesty after 31 January could have justified a conviction for theft.

26.9 Sections 15, 16, 17 and 20 Theft Act 1968

R v *Scott-Simmonds* [1994] Crim LR 933 Court of Appeal (Roch LJ, Potter and Smith JJ)

False accounting – whether document an 'account'

Facts

The appellant, an accountant, had provided E with false accounts to enable E to apply for a mortgage. Following an unsuccessful submission of no case the appellant pleaded guilty to two counts of false accounting contrary to s17(1)(a) of the Theft Act 1968. On appeal it was contended on behalf of the appellant, inter alia, that the trial judge had erred in not construing the word 'account' more narrowly, in particular in ruling that a document that had been false from its inception could still be an account.

26.10 Forgery and Counterfeiting Act 1981

R v *Jeraj* [1994] Crim LR 595 Court of Appeal (Lord Taylor CJ, Auld and Mitchell JJ)

Forgery – instrument purporting to be made in circumstances in which it has not

Facts

The appellant was employed as the manager of a branch of an Indian bank. He met two men at a London hotel and, following discussions, signed a document on bank notepaper. The prosecution alleged that the letter amounted to verification of his bank's endorsement of a letter of credit drawn by the Banco Unidyn de Bolivia. The prosecution case was that the letter of credit and the Banco Unidyn de Bolivia never existed and that the document signed by the appellant was part of a banking fraud that would be perpetrated in the United States. The appellant contended that he had been duped by the two men and had signed the document merely as confirmation that he had seen a letter of credit that had been drawn up in a form acceptable to his bank. Following conviction, the appellant appealed on the ground that the trial judge had wrongly ruled that the document could amount to a forgery within s9(1)(g) of the Forgery and Counterfeiting Act 1981.

Held

The appeal was dismissed. Under s(9)(1)(g) of the 1981 Act a document was to be regarded as false if, inter alia, it purported to have been made in circumstances in which it was not in fact made. The court regarded itself as bound by the earlier Court of Appeal ruling in *R* v *Donnelly* (1984) 79 Cr App R 76, where a jewellery valuation certificate was held to be false because it purported to have been made following the examination of certain jewellery which did not in fact exist; therefore it told a lie about itself, ie the circumstances in which it had been made. Had the jewellery in fact existed and the appellant simply overvalued it for insurance purposes, the document would not have been false, simply inaccurate.

26.11 Strict, vicarious and corporate liability

Seaboard Offshore v *Secretary of State for Transport* [1994] 1 WLR 541
House of Lords (Lords Keith, Bridge, Jauncey, Browne-Wilkinson and Nolan)

Merchant Shipping Act 1988 s31 – whether liability absolute – imposition of vicarious liability

Facts

The appellant company was convicted of failing to take all reasonable steps to ensure that one of its ships was operated in a safe manner as required by s31 of the Merchant Shipping Act 1988. The vessel in question had put out to sea within three hours of a new chief engineer joining the crew. Due to the lack of time given to familiarise himself with the vessel, he inadvertently flooded the engines, although the ship and its passengers were not put in danger. The magistrates' court held that the company could be guilty of the offence, provided that anyone within the company had given the order for the ship to leave port in these circumstances. The divisional court allowed the appeal because, even if s31 created an offence of absolute liability (given the need to ensure the safety of vessels and passengers at sea) it did not automatically follow that the offence imposed vicarious liability on the company for the acts of its employees. In the absence of evidence of how the company was managed, the court felt that it had not been open to the justices to conclude that the company could be liable no matter how junior the employee who had taken the decision that the ship should put to sea. On the basis of *Tesco Supermarkets* v *Natrass* [1972] AC 153, the court had to be satisfied as to whether an officer of the company empowered to make the relevant decision had done so. On appeal by the prosecutor, the Secretary of State for Transport, the following point of law of general public importance was considered;

'(1) Whether s31 of the Merchant Shipping Act 1988 creates an offence of strict liability.
(2) Whether a manager is or may be vicariously liable for a breach of duty under s31 of

the Act of 1988 which arises from any act or omission by any of the manager's servants or agents.'

Held

The appeal was dismissed. It was not helpful to discuss the offence in terms of strict liability. Liability arose from a failure to take reasonable steps to ensure that the vessel was operated in a safe manner. The duty placed on the owner, manager or charterer was a personal one. The owner could be criminally liable for a failure to discharge that duty, but could not be criminally liable for the acts or omissions of his employees if he himself had taken all such reasonable steps.

Index

HLT Publications

HLT books are specially planned and written to help you in every stage of your studies. Each of the wide range of textbooks is brought up-to-date annually, and the companion volumes of our Law Series are all designed to work together.

You can buy HLT books from your local bookshop, or in case of difficulty, order direct using this form.

The Law Series covers the following modules:

Administrative Law

Commercial Law

Company Law

Conflict of Laws

Constitutional Law

Contract Law

Criminal Law

Criminology

English Legal System

Equity and Trusts

European Union Law

Evidence

Family Law

Jurisprudence

Land Law

Law of International Trade

Legal Skills and System

Public International Law

Revenue Law

Succession

Tort

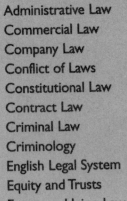

The HLT Law Series:
A comprehensive range of books for your law course, and the legal aspects of business and commercial studies.

Each module is covered by a comprehensive six-part set of books

● Textbook

● Casebook

● Revision Workbook

● Suggested Solutions, for:
  ● 1985-90
  ● 1991-94
  ● 1995

Module	Books required	Cost

To complete your order, please fill in the form overleaf

Postage	
TOTAL	

Prices (including postage and packing in the UK):
Textbooks £19.00; Casebooks £19.00; Revision Workbooks £10.00; Suggested Solutions (1985-90) £9.00, Suggested Solutions (1991-94) £6.00, Suggested Solutions (1995) £3.00.
For Europe, add 15% postage and packing (£20 maximum). For the rest of the world, add 40% for airmail (£35 maximum).

ORDERING

By telephone to 01892 724371, with your credit card to hand

By fax to 01892 724206 (giving your credit card details).

By post to:

HLT Publications,
The Gatehouse, Ruck Lane, Horsmonden, Tonbridge, Kent TN12 8EA

When ordering by post, please enclose full payment by cheque or banker's draft, or complete the credit card details below.

We aim to dispatch your books within 3 working days of receiving your order.

Name

Address

Postcode

Telephone

Total value of order, including postage: **£**

I enclose a cheque/banker's draft for the above sum, or

charge my   ☐ Access/Mastercard   ☐ Visa   ☐ American Express

Card number

Expiry date

Signature

Date

Publications from **The Old Bailey Press**

Cracknell's Statutes

A full understanding of statute law is vital for any student, and this series presents the original wording of legislation, together with any amendments and substitutions and the sources of these changes.

Cracknell's Companions

Recognised as invaluable study aids since their introduction in 1961, this series summarises all the most important court decisions and acts, and features a glossary of Latin words, as well as full indexing.

Please telephone our Order Hotline on 01892 724371, or write to our order department, for full details of these series.